By-elections in British politics

Also by Chris Cook and published by UCL Press

What happened where: a guide to places and events in twentieth-century history (with Diccon Bewes)

By-elections in British politics

Edited by
Chris Cook

and
John Ramsden

UCL
PRESS

First published in 1997 by UCL Press.

UCL Press Limited
1 Gunpowder Square
London EC4A 3DE
UK

and

1900 Frost Road, Suite 101
Bristol
Pennsylvania 19007-1598
USA

The name of University College London (UCL) is a registered
trade mark used by UCL Press with the consent of the owner.

British Library Cataloguing-in-Publication Data
A catalogue record for this book is available from the British Library

Library of Congress Cataloging-on-Publication Data are available

ISBNs: 1-85728-534-4 HB
　　　 1-85728-535-2 PB

Typeset in Garamond by Mathematical Composition Setters Ltd, Salisbury,
Wilts.
Printed and bound by TJ International Ltd, Padstow, UK.

To David Butler, Emeritus Fellow, Nuffield College, Oxford

Contents

List of tables   ix

Notes on contributors   xi

Introduction and acknowledgements   xiii

1 By-elections and their interpretation   1
David Butler

2 The Newport by-election and the fall of the Coalition   13
John Ramsden

3 By-elections of the first Labour Government   37
Chris Cook

    Note: 1924 to 1931   59
Chris Cook and John Ramsden

4 St George's and the Empire Crusade   65
Gillian Peele

    Note: 1931 to 1939   87
John Ramsden

5 Interpreting East Fulham   94
Martin Ceadel

6 Oxford and Bridgwater   112
Iain McLean

7 By-elections of the Second World War   130
Paul Addison

    Note: 1945 to 1960   151
Chris Cook

8 Orpington and the 'Liberal revival'   157
Ken Young

CONTENTS

9 By-elections of the Wilson Government   180
   David McKie

10 Lincoln and the Liberal surge, 1972–73   194
   Richard Jay

11 The Wilson–Callaghan Government of 1974–79: by-elections
   (eventually) bring down a Government   215
   Peter Rose

12 'Breaking the mould?' The Alliance by-election challenge,
   1981–82   228
   John Stevenson

13 By-elections since 1983: did they matter?   244
   Ivor Crewe

Appendix A: The results of contested by-elections   269

Appendix B: Summary tables   300

Appendix C: Bibliography   303

Appendix D: Index of outstanding results   306

Appendix E: Index of persons   315

List of tables

Table 1.1	Reasons for by-elections, 1918–70 and 1970–97	3
Table 1.2	By-elections, 1918–97	4
Table 1.3	Pro-government swing-back between by-election results and subsequent general election in the same constituencies	8
Table 1.4	Subsequent result in seats changing hands in by-elections	10
Table 2.1	News coverage during the campaign	22
Table 6.1	Oxford: Voting intention 1938 by reported vote 1935	122
Table 6.2	Oxford: Reported vote 1935 by voting intention 1938	123
Table 6.3	Oxford: Voting intention by newspaper taken	124
Table 6.4	By-elections 1938–39: mean swing (based on electorate) against National Government, and standard deviations	125
Table 6.5	Views on Czechoslovakia, 22 September 1938: Mass-Observation sample	126
Table 6.6	Popularity of Chamberlain, 29 September 1938: Mass-Observation sample	127
Table 7.1	Contests and unopposed returns in Conservative and Labour seats, May 1941–April 1945	131
Table 7.2	Swings to Labour substitutes 1943–45 and to Labour 1945	142
Table 8.1	The Liberal vote in post-war general elections	158
Table 8.2	Orpington UDC election results, 1956–61: votes cast	159
Table 8.3	Orpington division Parliamentary election results, 1950–59	160
Table 8.4	Some originally Conservative-held wards in Orpington	171
Table 8.5	Liberal party membership, finance and full-time agents	177
Table 8.6	Liberal performance in the 1959 and 1964 general elections	177
Table 9.1	By-elections, July 1966–November 1967	188
Table 9.2	By-elections, July 1966–November 1968	191
Table 13.1	Summary of by-election results, 1979–97	247

Table 13.2 Summary of by-election voting patterns, 1979–97   248
Table 13.3 Causes of by-elections, 1945–79 and 1979–96   250
Table 13.4 Correlations of decline in Conservative vote at   254
            Conservative-defended by-election seats, 1983–April
            1996
Table 13.5 Unusually 'good' and 'bad' Conservative by-election   255
            performances in Conservative-defended seats,
            1983–96

Notes on contributors

Paul Addison is Endowment Fellow at the University of Edinburgh. He is the author of *The road to 1945*.

David Butler is Emeritus Fellow, Nuffield College, Oxford. He has authored, or co-authored the Nuffield College general election studies since 1951. He is also co-editor of *British political facts, 1900–94*.

Martin Ceadel is Fellow and Tutor in Politics at New College, Oxford. His recent publications include *Thinking about peace and war* and *The origins of war prevention: The British peace movement and international relations, 1730–1854*.

Chris Cook is the former Director of the Modern Archives Unit at the London School of Economics and author of over 30 works on history and politics.

Ivor Crewe is Vice-Chancellor and Professor of Government at the University of Essex. His most recent publications include *SDP: the birth, life and death of the Social Democratic Party* (with Antony King) and *The British electorate, 1963–92* (with Neil Day and Anthony Fox).

Richard Jay is Senior Lecturer in Politics at Queen's University, Belfast. He is the author of *Joseph Chamberlain: a political study* and co-author of *Political ideologies*.

David McKie is a columnist for the *Guardian*, where he has been Parliamentary Correspondent, and Deputy Editor.

Iain McLean is Professor of Politics at the University of Oxford and Fellow of Nuffield College, Oxford. He is joint editor of *Electoral Studies*. Recent publications include *The concise Oxford dictionary of politics* (general editor).

Gillian Peele is Fellow and Tutor in Politics at Lady Margaret Hall, Oxford. She is co-editor of *Developments in British politics* (with Patrick Dunleavy and Andrew Gamble).

John Ramsden is Professor of Modern History at Queen Mary and Westfield College, London. He is the author of three twentieth century volumes of the Longman *History of the Conservative party* (1978, 1995 and 1996).

Peter Rose is a former political journalist. He has recently completed a doctoral thesis *The Labour Government's Northern Ireland policy, 1964–69.*

John Stevenson is Reader in Modern History at the University of Oxford and is Fellow and Tutor in History at Worcester College, Oxford. He has written widely on British history, including *British society, 1914–45* and *Third Party politics since 1945.*

Ken Young is Professor of Politics and Vice-Principal at Queen Mary and Westfield College, London. From 1987 to 1990 he was Director of the Institute of Local Government Studies at the University of Birmingham. His latest book is *Local government since 1945* (with Nirmala Rao).

Introduction and acknowledgements

By-Elections in British Politics has been planned as a major investigation into the diverse aspects of an important feature of British politics. By-elections, despite their real shortcomings as indicators of public opinion, continue to influence Governments more than either opinion polls or local government elections. They still arouse a relatively high level of participation among voters, and they provide excitement for newspapers and television, for politicians and historians.

In this new publication, the differing nature of by-elections has been explored through case studies, using the most appropriate avenue of approach for the analysis of each example chosen. Newport (1922) contributed to bringing down Lloyd George as Prime Minister; St. George's (1931) helped save Baldwin as Conservative Party leader; Oxford and Bridgwater (1938) provided a rare opportunity for the electorate to give their views on foreign policy at a crucial time; Orpington (1962) administered a severe jolt to Macmillan's Government. Each of these is thus examined as an individual campaign, allowing the author of these chapters to explore the relationship between national events and the way in which they were perceived locally. East Fulham (1933) has received so much comment that it became a historiographical problem, and it is treated as such. In contrast, the by-elections held during the Second World War, during the Labour Governments of 1924, 1964–70 and 1974–79, and the centre party upsurges of 1970–73 and 1981–82, require a different approach. Since in these cases the impact was cumulative rather than individual, these groups of contests have been looked at as a whole.

However, even the widest of perspectives cannot bring all of the diverse campaigns of the almost 80 years since 1918 within a uniform framework. It would be misleading to ignore the relatively unexciting and unimpressive results of the by-elections of the later 1920s or of the 1950s, but it would be inappropriate to regard them as either individually or cumulatively comparable to East Fulham, Orpington or Hillhead. We have therefore provided editorial passages to cover these periods not covered in detail in the case study chapters, and detailed appendices which cover *all* by-elections since the First World War introduced something akin to democracy in British elections.

We also include an introductory chapter by David Butler which looks at the general issues raised by the interpretation of by-elections, and a concluding chapter by Ivor Crewe which both reviews the most recent experience and concludes that while the nature of the impact of by-elections on British politics may have changed, yet the impact is still there. These chapters frame our more narrowly-focused case studies within broader perspectives.

A quarter of a century has elapsed since the original idea for this book was first developed in discussions between a number of Fellows and students of Nuffield College in 1973. Our original volume, published by Macmillan in 1974 and long both out of print and also increasingly out of date with the passing years, owed a considerable debt to the Warden and Fellows of Nuffield. It seems appropriate to us to acknowledge that debt again, since so many of our new as well as our continuing authors went through a career-shaping experience at Nuffield. It is particularly appropriate for us to express our thanks to David Butler, the creator of psephological studies in Britain and an important influence on the work of almost all the authors in this book. We dedicate this book with respect and affection to 'D.E.B.'

Chris Cook and John Ramsden
May 1997

CHAPTER 1

By-elections and their interpretation

David Butler

In the time of Charles II, when Parliaments had no limit to their duration, by-elections were the prime sources of MP recruitment. When John Wilkes was repeatedly returned by the electors of Middlesex in 1769–70, or when Foxite support was tested at Westminster in 1783, national attention was clearly focused on the verdict of by-elections.[1] However, in pre-Reform days there were few constituencies with a broad enough, or free enough, franchise for by-elections to be given much value as pointers to popular opinion. After 1832 the situation began to change (for example, a by-election at Walsall in 1842 seems to have had some significance in the development of the Corn Law struggle), but it was not until the coming of mass politics in the second half of the nineteenth century that by-elections became a frequent source of comment. It was thought, probably incorrectly, that the deceptively favourable outcome of contests at Southwark and Sheffield in February 1880 lured Disraeli into announcing the general election which ended his rule.

Certainly, with the advent of a popular press, by-elections attracted a new degree of interest, being treated almost as major sporting events. By the end of the century the letters and diaries of politicians contain increasingly frequent observations on their outcome. Perhaps 1904 and 1905 (with seven government defeats in each year) provide the period when by-elections had most significance for British politics. They did not then bring down a government (they never have except, indirectly, in 1979),[2] but they did much to destroy its morale, as well as to preserve the uncertain unity of the opposition. Mass politics were now conducted on a national scale. As long as there were no opinion polls and only a few local elections were fought on a party basis, there was nothing to compete with by-elections as indicators of how the political tide was flowing.

However, 1918 constitutes a turning-point in electoral history, marking the biggest leap towards a universal franchise and the arrival of the Labour Party as a nationwide political force. Because the style of politics changed so abruptly at that time, it offers an appropriate moment to begin a study of the role of by-elections in modern politics.

Incidence

The incidence of by-elections has been very uneven. Since 1918 the annual average number, 15, conceals a variation between 39 in 1940 and 2 in 1966 and 1987. In fact the number of by-elections has fallen sharply. From 1919 to 1939 the annual average was 18, while from mid-1945 to mid-1970 it was 11.[3] From 1970 to 1996 it was 6. Fewer elderly MPs have stayed on to die in harness – the two septuagenarians elected to the 1992 House of Commons constituted the smallest number on record; fewer MPs have resigned in mid-Parliament for business or personal reasons; and fewer have been appointed to government posts – partly because of the end of overseas governorships and of the use of the House as a path to judicial office and partly because, recently, the increased volatility of the electorate has made governments more chary of creating vacancies even in 'safe' seats. In 1957 Mr Macmillan refrained from the customary offering of the Lord Chief Justiceship to the Attorney-General because the Attorney's seat was thought marginal. Most of the really outstanding government defeats since 1960 – Orpington, Leyton, Dudley, Sutton and Cheam, Ashfield and Ribble Valley – were in by-elections that could have been avoided.

Other causes of by-elections have disappeared. Until the passage of the Re-election of Ministers Act in 1926 the holders of certain offices had to offer themselves for re-election upon appointment; between 1919 and 1926 this caused 20 by-elections – and in two of them the incumbent was defeated.

Members of Parliament seem also to have become less prone to seek re-endorsement from their constituents over an issue of policy or a change of party: there were nine such by-elections between 1900 and 1914 and four in the inter-war years. But since the defeat of the Duchess of Atholl at Kinross and West Perthshire in 1938 the only such tests in Britain have followed the resignations of Dick Taverne at Lincoln in 1973 and of Bruce Douglas-Mann in 1982 (although it was only the intervention of the 1955 general election that prevented Sir Richard Acland from fighting a by-election at Gravesend over nuclear weapons). However, in 1986 the device was collectively invoked by the 15 Unionists in Northern Ireland who resigned in protest at the Anglo-Irish Agreement and stood for re-election to provide a referendum on the issue.

Successful election petitions, which from 1900 to 1914 resulted in 13 by-elections, have also declined. The only unseatings for electoral offences in the last 50 years were in 1922 and 1923, although in the 1950s there were three by-elections in Northern Ireland when election victors were declared ineligible (one for being a clergyman, one for being a felon and one for being a government contractor).

Table 1.1 Reasons for by-elections, 1918–70 and 1970–97.

	1919–70		1970–97	
Death	380	(48%)	98	(64%)
Resignation	242	(30%)	25	(16%)
Elevation to Peerage	110	(14%)	12	(8%)
Succession to Peerage	29	(4%)	1	(1%)
Re-election of Ministers	20	(3%)	–	
Disqualification	4	(0.5%)	–	
Seeking re-election	4	(0.5%)	16	(10%)
Expulsion	3	(0.4%)	1	(1%)
Election petition	2	(0.3%)	–	
Bankruptcy	1	(0.1%)	–	
Voting before oath	1	(0.1%)	–	
Total	796	(100%)	153	(100%)

Note: Based in part upon F. W. S. Craig, *British parliamentary election statistics 1918–70*, p. 42. The percentages exceed 100 due to rounding.

Succession to the peerage is another cause of by-elections that has diminished. Fewer heirs to titles sit in the House (18 in 1924, 2 in 1995). Moreover, since Anthony Wedgwood Benn's struggle to repudiate his viscountcy (which produced by-elections in 1961 and 1963 as well as the 1963 Peerage Act), they have been able to stay in the House by renouncing their title, like Lord Lambton in 1970.[4]

Timing

When an MP's seat falls vacant there is no statutory obligation to fill the vacancy. By convention it is left to the Whips of the former Member's party to move for a writ to be issued instructing the local returning officer to proceed.

Over the years the Whips have changed their habits and, in conjunction with party headquarters, have given more importance to timing, and to national as opposed to local considerations. In the 1920s by-elections were called more promptly after the vacancy occurred; they were held at times (in August or in Christmas week) which would now be regarded as almost impossible; they were much less consciously grouped together. Throughout the period since 1918 there are examples of by-elections taking place as soon as the vacancy occurred. However, in the 1960s, although by-elections were called in every month of the year, there was much more of a tendency, whatever the delay involved, to group them together on dates in March (after the new register on 15 February), or in May–June (after the local elections), or in October–November (after the summer holidays and party conferences and before the Christmas rush). Sometimes the timing has been

Table 1.2 By-elections, 1918–97.

	Total		Con		Lab		Lib		Other		yearly	
	Seats	changes	+	−	+	−	+	−	+	−		
1918–22	108ᵃ	27	4	13	14	1	5ᵇ	1	4	2	27	25%
1922–23	16	6	1	4	2	−	3	1	−	1	16	38%
1923–24	10	3	2	1	1	1	−	1	−	−	10	30%
1924–29	63	20	1	16	13	1	6	3	−	−	14	32%
1929–31	36	7	4	1	2	4	−	1	1	1	15	19%
1931–35	62	10	−	9	10	−	−	1	−	−	15	16%
1935–45	219	30	−	29	13	1	−	−	17	−	23	14%
1945–50	52	4	3	−	−	−	−	−	−	3	11	6%
1950–51	16	−	−	−	−	−	−	−	−	−	10	−
1951–55	48	1	1	−	−	1	−	−	−	−	13	12%
1955–59	52	6	1	4	4	−	1	1	−	1	12	12%
1959–64	62	9	2	7	6	2	1	−	−	−	15	14%
1964–66	13	2	1	1	−	1	1	−	−	−	9	15%
1966–70	38	16	12	1	−	15	1	−	−	−	9	42%
1970–74	30	9	−	5	2	3	5	−	2	1	9	30%
1974	1	−	−	−	−	−	−	−	−	−	1	−
1974–79	30	7	6	−	−	7	1	−	−	−	6	23%
1979–83	20	7	1	4	1	1	4	−	1	2	5	35%
1983–87	31ᶜ	5	−	4	1	1	4	−	1	1	8	19%
1987–92	23	8	−	7	4	1	3	−	1	−	4	35%
1992–97	18	10	−	9	4	−	4	−	2	1	4	55%

ᵃ Up to 1918, and to a lesser extent to 1926, the number of by-elections is inflated by the necessity for Ministers to stand for re-election on appointment. In 53 such cases the returns were unopposed.

ᵇ In 1918–22 Opposition Liberals won 5 seats and lost 2, Coalition Liberals lost 9.

ᶜ This figure includes the Unionist MPs seeking re-election in January 1986.

affected by local difficulties in candidate selection and sometimes by the desire to wait for a more favourable political climate or to arrange things so that an awkward result may be masked by a better one.[5]

While the moving of a writ has normally been a routine matter, on occasions it has been moved by another party or has been opposed in protest about delays in holding the by-election or other matters. The war-time opposition used this tactic on several occasions and in the 1960s and 1970s the Liberals threatened it, notably over the six-month delays in calling the Orpington and Lincoln by-elections. The Speaker's Conference of 1973 (Cmnd. 5500) recommended that by-election writs should be moved within three months of the vacancy occurring; in 1987 this requirement may have accelerated by a day or two the announcement of the general election; since otherwise the writ for a vacancy in Cardiff North would have had to be moved. The pre-election politics of 1997 were affected by the need to call a by-election in Wirral South.

Function

By-elections are so much discussed as barometers of public opinion that it is easy to ignore their basic function – the replacement of a Member of Parliament. The replacement of Members is not trivial in scale. From 1918 to 1970, by the time each Parliament was dissolved it had on average 53 Members (8 per cent) who had come in at by-elections; the figure for 1970 to 1992 had fallen to only 20 per parliament (8 per cent). In most cases this was a routine matter: the former incumbent's party followed ordinary procedures to find a successor, usually much of the same ilk, and he was duly elected. Only 140 (18 per cent) of the 795 by-elections between 1919 and 1970 resulted in a change in party representation (see Table 1.2). But on occasion a by-election was designed to bring into the House a special person to strengthen the government – either defeated Ministers like the MacDonalds in 1936, Patrick Gordon Walker in 1965, or new talent, like Ernest Bevin and Oliver Lyttelton in 1940 or Frank Cousins in 1965. Oppositions, too, have eagerly used the first by-elections of a Parliament to bring back their more heavyweight casualties – Arthur Henderson in 1923 (and again in 1933), Arthur Greenwood in 1932, Harold Macmillan in 1945, and Anthony Barber in 1965.

By-elections serve other less noticed functions. They offer tryouts for party tactics: they have been used to test innovations in publicity, field organization and even private polling methods. They offer training-grounds for party agents: the statutory expense returns do not reveal the number of full-time officials who have come in from other constituencies to help in the campaign.[6] They provide a platform for speeches that might otherwise be less remarked, an extra opportunity for public education (as distinct from vote-gathering). They even, in the key period 1957–63, supplied an excuse for the broadcasting authorities to learn how to venture much more boldly into the field of political reporting; in the 1958 Rochdale contest Granada TV defied the government and broke the ban on television coverage while the campaign was going on. They have also provided the testing-ground for exit polls and other survey approaches.

None the less, the main interest in by-elections has undoubtedly lain in what they are thought to reveal about the state of public opinion, both in relation to specific issues and to the likely outcome of the next general election.

By-elections as indicators

The idea that a by-election in one corner of the country can reveal what voters in 658 other constituencies are thinking does, of course, imply some important assumptions about national uniformity. Furthermore, the idea that a by-election at one point gives a key to the result of a subsequent general election implies some equally significant assumptions about the consistency of voting behaviour over time and in different situations.

The assumption of national uniformity is, of course, challenged after every by-election. Special local circumstances can almost always be found to excuse an awkward result – something in the candidate or in the organization or in the impact of a particular issue. However, it is plain that in general elections, national behaviour is remarkably uniform; in elections since 1950 three constituencies out of four have shown a swing within 2 per cent of the national average. In by-elections the variation has been appreciably greater. Even simultaneous by-elections can yield sharply different swings – as Ashfield and Grimsby showed in April 1977 – and usually it is hard to explain why. The factor that seems most regularly in evidence is the fall in turnout which tends to be much greater in safe seats and in urban seats than in marginal or rural ones. But it is also clear that in by-elections voters are more affected by special factors such as a local grievance or by the personality of the candidate. However, although a graph of by-election swings showing the movement of government popularity can look decidedly jagged, clear trends still emerge. The anti-government swings in 1960 varied between −2 per cent and 3 per cent; in 1963 they varied between 4 per cent and 14 per cent, in 1977 between 7 per cent and 20 per cent and in 1991 between nothing and 29 per cent. But on balance the difference between the average swing in 1960 (−1.7 per cent) and in 1963 (8.1 per cent) offers a reasonable indication of the Conservative slump in that period.

The impact of a by-election depends on how it is interpreted. Undoubtedly now, as always, victory or defeat makes most impact. A government may be more damaged by losing a seat on a 5 per cent swing than by suffering a 15 per cent swing yet just holding on in some safer constituency. Before psephological sophistication began to creep in during the 1950s, the focus tended to be on absolute figures – the drop in the vote for a party or the change in the majority – even when a general fall in turnout made them very misleading. Now the focus is, perhaps to excess, on the percentage swing. Dependence on one single indicator is likely to be even more deceptive in by-elections than in general elections: turnout, retained vote and presence of third candidates must be taken into consideration before any verdict on the meaning of a by-election result is offered.

But the problem is psychological as much as statistical. Election results have to be set against expectations. The Conservatives in 1962 and the Labour Party in 1969 managed to present as triumphs the fact that they had actually held on to seats which, a few years previously, they would never have dreamed of considering vulnerable. The party managers face a pre-election dilemma. If they display optimism in order to encourage the faithful in the constituency, they court a severe verdict in the postmortem. If they discount the result in advance in order to induce pleasant surprise among observers, they may induce local defeatism and an unnecessarily bad outcome. The Conservative archives show how they faced this dilemma in South Hammersmith in 1949 and in North Hull in 1966. To some extent they are at the mercy of the press. By-elections do attract extensive, though seldom high-quality, newspaper coverage. The picture of the situation that is built up by reporters does much to condition the reaction to the final outcome. In the 1960s opinion polls also played a major role. If Gallup or a National Opinion Poll (NOP) chose to cover a by-election, the result was often discounted in advance. The fact that an NOP forecast gave no hint of the overturn in Leyton in January 1965 did much to heighten the shock of that result.

In recent years by-elections, by producing ever more extreme results, have lost much of their power to shock. Conservative and Labour governments each lost some very safe seats in the course of the 1960s and 1970s and by 1990 it seemed impossible for the party in power to hold on to any seat at all. After the 1987 election the Conservatives retained the first three seats they defended – but in each case it seemed due only to a split between Liberal and Social Democrat candidates. From then until 1997 the Government endured 15 successive by-election defeats, never indeed coming near to victory. All records were broken with the 35 per cent swing to the Liberal Democrats in Christchurch in July 1993 and with the 29 per cent swing to Labour in Dudley West in December 1994.

Whatever people may think at the time, and whatever their consequences for contemporary political strategy and morale, by-elections do offer historians (particularly those concerned with the pre-1945 pre-opinion poll era) guidance on mass reactions that is very difficult to get from any other source. In some cases a detailed look at by-election figures challenges established historical ideas. For example, the myth of Labour's forward march from 1900 onwards receives no support from an examination of the by-elections after 1910: the First World War was to transform the situation, but in July 1914 the Labour Party could look back to four by-election losses and no gains over the past four years; they came third in every seat they fought. The period before the Second World War offers another example. After the 1945 upheaval it was widely said that an anti-Conservative landslide had long been brewing and that a normal general election held in 1940 would have shown substantial Labour gains.

The by-election results run counter to this contention. Although, once the electorate had recovered from the shock of 1931, there appears to have been a very sharp swing in favour of Labour, from 1933 onwards their support seems, if anything, to have declined. The reason for the belief that Labour was gaining ground presumably lies in the fact that between 1935 and 1939 they won 13 seats from the government. But a study of the votes cast does not suggest any trend in their favour. They might be said to have won by-elections only because they fared so ill in the 1935 general election.[7]

By-elections and general elections

It is plain that by-elections give results that go against the party in power. Between 1922 and 1997 governments gained four seats in by-elections and lost 126. Only ten of the 316 by-elections between 1955 and 1997 could be construed as showing a pro-government swing. Only three government gains have been recorded since the war. It is never safe to regard by-elections as offering a direct mirror of how the voting would go in a general election. Although the situation in the 1920s was confused, general elections, with few exceptions, have shown a government recovery compared with the by-elections of the previous year. Especially in recent years, a large proportion of the seats which changed hands in by-elections have reverted to their former allegiance. Tables 1.3 and 1.4 offer some measure of this recovery.

Table 1.3 Pro-government swing-back between by-election results and subsequent general election in the same constituencies.*

Comparable seats			Comparable seats		
1929	5	+3.9%	1966	6	+4.8%
1935	6	+5.8%	1970	8	+4.7%
1950	3	(+3%)	1974	5	+4.0%
1951	5	+4.2%	1979	6	+1.2%
1955	6	−0.4%	1983	3	+1.6%
1959	5	+3.4%	1987	4	+5.9%
1964	12	+2.3%	1992	4	+5.9%

*The time period included varies from six to 12 months before the election. The 1950 figures involve major approximation owing to redistribution. Comparisons in 1922, 1923 and 1924 are very difficult. In four by-elections in 1922 the Labour opposition won 4.5 per cent more of the vote on average than in the November general election. In two by-elections in 1923 the Conservative Government fared decidedly better and in two decidedly worse than in the December general election. In each of five comparable by-elections in 1924 Labour fared better (in four of them decidedly better) than in the October general election. No by-election in 1931 was nearly as bad for Labour as the general election. In 1945 the Conservatives recovered ground in only one of the four seats they had defended in by-elections during the previous 12 months.

Although from 1923 to 1966 examples of the recovery at general elections of by-election losses were not numerous, they included some of the most famous by-election reverses:

1922	1935	1970	1987
Leyton W.	Fulham E.	Carmarthen	Portsmouth S.
Widnes	Wavertree	Hamilton	Fulham
Wrekin	Swindon	Pollok	Ryedale
Dartford		Ladywood	
Dover	1945	Dudley	1992
Woolwich E.	Newcastle N.	Acton	Govan
Dudley	Wallasey	Swindon	Vale of Glamorgan
Kirkcaldy	Skipton	Walthamstow W.	Mid-Staffs
Penistone	Eddisbury	Oldham W.	Monmouth
Heywood and	Motherwell		Eastbourne
Radcliffe		1974	Ribble Valley
Southwark S.E.	1959	Bromsgrove	Langbaurgh
Clayton	Lewisham N.	Sutton and Cheam	Kincardine and
Leicester E.	Torrington	Ripon	Deeside
	Kelvingrove	Govan	
1923			1997
Mitcham	1964	1979	Christchurch
	S.Dorset	Walsall N.	
1929	Brighouse and	Workington	
Lancaster	Spenborough	Stechford	
N.Midlothian		Ashfield	
Southwark N.	1966		
	Leyton	1983	
1931		Croydon N.W.	
Paddington N.		Crosby	
		Northfield	

It is easy to build on this pattern of slump and recovery some theory of how voters react to by-elections. They seldom feel very concerned. Usually there is very little national publicity about the contest and such as there is tends to be reserved to the last day or so, too late to build up interest on a general election scale. Even the exceptional concentration of volunteer and professional workers from outside the constituency can seldom prevent a large fall in turnout. In all but 23 of the 429 by-elections in 1945–1995, participation was below the level of the previous general election – and almost all the exceptions (for example, Torrington in 1958, Kinross and West Perthshire in 1963 or Hamilton in 1967) had special factors and had been built up by the national press. But in addition to the increase in freedom not to vote, there is also the freedom to vote differently. By-elections encourage the citizen to try his luck

Table 1.4 Subsequent result in seats changing hands in by-elections.*

	Number lost	Recovered	
1918–1922	27	13	48%
1922–1923	6	1	17%
1923–1924	3	0	
1924–1929	20	3	15%
1929–1931	7	1	14%
1931–1935	10	3	30%
1935–1945	52	5	10%
1945–1950	2	0	
1950–1951	0	0	
1951–1955	1	0	
1955–1959	5	3	60%
1959–1964	7	2	29%
1964–1966	2	1	50%
1966–1970	16	9	56%
1970–1974	9	4	44%
1974–1974	0	0	
1974–1979	7	4	57%
1979–1983	7	3	43%
1983–1987	6	3	50%
1987–1992	8	8	100%
1992–1997	9	1	11%
1918–1997	204	64	32%

*The University by-elections in 1946 and two by-elections in Bristol South-East in 1961 and 1963 are excluded from this table.

and vote for the other side although he would not dream of doing so in a general election when his vote might actually change the party in power. Leyton in 1919 and again in 1965, Dudley in 1921 and again in 1968 produced their sensational results not primarily through abstention but through a sizeable number of party loyalists voting for the other side. The same was true of the Empire Crusade and the Anti-Waste League successes of over 60 and 70 years ago and of the Nationalist and Liberal successes of recent years. In 1968, 43 per cent of Scotsmen told NOP interviewers that they would consider supporting the SNP in a by-election; when asked whether they would do so in a general election the figure fell to 20 per cent.

Such tendencies are probably sharper now than ever before. The growing volatility of the electorate makes it increasingly dangerous to apply rules of thumb learned from the past. The Conservatives, after losing Orpington in 1962 on a swing that would have cost them every other seat in Britain (save only South Kensington), came within a hair's breadth of returning to office in 1964; the Labour Government, which on a single day in 1968 lost three seats with swings of 15, 18 and 21 per cent, managed to go into the 1970 election as odds-on favourites. The Centre victories in more recent years (Crosby 1981 – 20 per cent swing; Ryedale 1986 – 19 per cent swing; Ribble Valley 1991 – 25 per cent swing) aroused expectations which, within 18 months, were sadly nullified by a general election. Politicians have learned to become increasingly blasé about by-elections, at least until the last year of a parliament. They may offer some guide to the public mood; but who now would dare to give a figure for the likely difference between a by-election result today and what would happen in an immediate general election? It is much more necessary to hesitate before extrapolating to a general election that is two or three years off.

Conclusion

This book concentrates in the main on by-elections as political events. Newport helped to bring about the fall of Lloyd George in 1922, Westminster St George's saved Baldwin in 1931, East Fulham conditioned the whole rearmament debate of the mid-1930s, Orpington heralded and stimulated the Conservative disarray of 1962–3, and Hamilton in 1967 gave impetus to the Scottish Nationalist upsurge. Although not many others among the 994 contests from 1918 to May 1997 can claim such importance, and governments have become increasingly hardened to defeat, the explosive potential of by-elections is always there. Sudden and solid evidence of the withdrawal or return of support to a government can transform the political mood – and the Prime Minister's strategy in timing the next general election. Independents and minor parties can test whether any groundswell of sympathy exists – although usually they find it is not there. The accident of by-elections undoubtedly shaped the pattern of successive Liberal and Nationalist revivals since the 1960s. The Anti-Waste League in 1921, the Empire Crusade in 1930 and the war-time dissidents in 1942–4 used by-elections, with some measure of success, to make themselves a force to be reckoned with. In the post-1945 period, if the special case of nationalism is excluded, no such challenges have been made. Edward Martell on a People's League platform at East Ham North in 1957, Sir Piers Debenham on an anti-Market platform at South Dorset in 1962, and John Creasey calling for an all-party government at Oldham West in 1968 all just saved their deposits (when deposits were set at 12.5 per cent), but, except for Dick Taverne's triumph at Lincoln in 1973, they were the only candidates to have done so since 1945 when fighting both the major parties in an English by-election. It must be much harder today for anyone to get as far as Randolph Churchill did in 1935 when, fighting his father's battle on the India question, he won 24 per cent of the vote at Wavertree. But, as Lincoln showed, the possibility is always there. By-elections continue to supply one of the safety-valves of the British political system.

Notes

1   But the actual term by-election did not come into use until the middle of the nineteenth century.

2   But the possibility remains. For example, the shadow of by-elections hung heavily over the Labour Governments of 1950–1, 1964–6 and 1974–9 (when the majorities ranged from 6 to minus 28), while the 15 losses Labour suffered in 1966–70 were only endurable by a government which had started the Parliament with a handsome majority.

3   Of course, many of the by-elections in 1918–22 and in 1940–5 produced unopposed returns. Since 1950 there have been only three uncontested by-elections, all in Northern Ireland. The victor at Armagh in 1954 was the last MP ever to be returned unopposed.

4   Apart from Lord Lambton, the only MPs to inherit a peerage since 1960 were Viscount Hinchingbrooke (now Victor Montagu), whose father died in 1962 before renunciation was possible, and the Earl of Dalkeith who succeeded to the Dukedom of Buccleuch in 1973. By contrast to the two successions in 1961–70, there were 13 in 1931–40.

5   The grouping of by-elections is now emphasized by the fact that they are all held on Thursdays. Although one has to go back to 1931 for a general election held on another day (Tuesday), parties continued to experiment with by-election days down to the 1960s. The result in Orpington on a Thursday, 14 March 1962, may have been affected by the near-success of the Liberals in Blackpool North where voting took place a day earlier, on Wednesday. When Roxburgh voted on Wednesday, 24 March 1965, it might have provided the last parliamentary contest to be held on anything but a Thursday, had not administrative errors led to the Manchester Exchange by-election being called for Wednesday, 27 June 1973, instead of Thursday, 28 June, and the Hamilton by-election for Wednesday 31 May 1978. It is worth noting that in 1991 the Hansard Society Commission on Election Campaigns *Agenda for change* recommended a general move of polling-days from Thursday to Saturday, citing opinion survey evidence in support of the change.

6   By-election expense returns, which are hard to come by, must be far more misleading than those for general elections. In a key contest the amount of effort put in by party headquarters, including on occasion expensive market research and large numbers of paid agents, could be costed at a substantially higher value than all the local activities duly recorded in the expense return. There were growing indications that expense returns, which (given the temptations to spend and the absence since 1929 of any petition challenging overspending) are normally so surprisingly accurate, are sometimes less conscientiously compiled after by-elections and this was recognized in the Representation of the People Act of 1989 which allowed for a fourfold increase in the permitted maximum for by-elections only.

7   See D. E. Butler, *The electoral system in Britain since 1918*, 2nd edn (Oxford, 1963) pp. 184–6, for a fuller discussion of this point.

CHAPTER 2

The Newport by-election and the fall of the Coalition

John Ramsden

General Election, 1918	(Electorate 40,146)	
Haslam (Coalition Liberal)	14,080	(56.4)
Bowen (Labour)	10,234	(41.0)
Thomas (Independent)	647	(2.6)
Coalition Liberal majority	3,846	Turnout 62.2%
By-election, 18 Oct 1922	(Electorate 42,645)	
Clarry (Conservative)	13,515	(40.0)
Bowen (Labour)	11,425	(33.8)
Moore (Liberal)	8,841	(26.2)
Conservative majority	2,090	Turnout 79.2%
General Election, 1922	(Electorate 42,645)	
Clarry (Conservative)	19,019	(54.3)
Bowen (Labour)	16,000	(45.7)
Conservative majority	3,019	Turnout 82.1%

Newport was the only British by-election which brought down a government – such has been claimed and widely accepted. Tom Jones noted in his diary:

> Chamberlain's effort to preserve the Coalition under the leadership of the Prime Minister defeated. Vote largely determined by Bonar Law's speech and by the victory of the Conservative candidate at the Newport by-election announced this morning, and partly by Chamberlain's clumsy, unsympathetic, and unhumorous handling of the meeting itself.[1]

Newport's influence was thus indirect: a Conservative won the by-election and this helped Conservative MPs to decide at the Carlton Club on the same day to withdraw their support from Lloyd George's Coalition. The *National Review* gave a less moderate account in its November 1922 issue:

> Newport caused a veritable stampede among the Coalitioners of the Carlton Club, who, until that moment, had been prepared to swear that black was white or that white was black, according as they were directed by the despot of Downing Street or his deputy in the leadership of the Unionist Party… It instantly transformed the political situation.

These immediate judgements, accepted almost universally at the time, have been followed by most later commentators. In the mythology of the 1920s, Newport is inextricably bound up with the fall of Lloyd George, who never set foot in the constituency during the campaign nor issued any official statement about it. For Liberals, Newport was the Tories' excuse for breaking up the Coalition and conveniently forgetting all that they owed to L. G. and his followers. For Conservatives, Newport was the moment when Conservatism re-established its touch with the grass roots, and received clear instructions to go it alone with Bonar Law and Baldwin.[2]

All such interpretations are the same basic idea when seen from different points in the political spectrum; they all agree that Newport was a vote against the Coalition Government. But all suffer from the flaw that they are unsure of the most basic facts of the campaign itself. It has never been established whether Lynden Moore was an Independent Liberal or Coalition Liberal candidate – a fact crucial to any interpretation. On the very day of declaration, Newport was attributed a false significance which has obscured its real importance ever since. Historians have recognized its influence on the fall of Lloyd George, but have not seen that this was due to a faulty interpretation of the facts. Nor has it been seen that Newport is more valuable for general implications than for any short-term influence. (In any case, the Carlton Club meeting would probably have voted against coalition even without Newport, and Bonar Law decided to go before knowing the Newport result. Newport did not decide the vote, but probably guaranteed an overwhelming majority.) But Newport was the first election in modern circumstances which was fought by the candidates of the three modern parties, all with an apparently equal chance; in some ways it was also the last, because after 19 October 1922 the Liberals were seen to be the third party, whose success – however insubstantial or temporary – would occasion surprise. The special circumstances of the by-election made it a good test of how voters would react to the existence of three parties, and the model of behaviour established at Newport held good for the rest of the inter-war years.

The national background

The background to Newport was the background to the Lloyd George Coalition and the problems of Newport were those of the Coalition. Coalition had first come in May 1915, after nine months of war and party truce. However, it was Lloyd George as Prime Minister (from December 1916) and the prolongation of Liberal–Conservative collaboration after the war that really created internal dissension. Many were opposed to further coalition: a section of the Liberal Party broke away and remained under Asquith, but Conservative opponents of coalition watched frustratedly as their party supported Lloyd George. Loyalty was probably maintained only because of the Conservatives' current fear of Labour. Joint action, it was said, was the only way to keep Labour out of power. However, the Party Leader Austen Chamberlain and others went further, in calling for the fusion of Conservatives and Coalition Liberals into one new party. In 1920 both sides unceremoniously rejected fusion, but Chamberlain continued to preach its virtues and believed it to be inevitable. The bitter division of opinion over coalition or independence did not prevent Chamberlain's unopposed succession to the Conservative leadership in March 1921 – nominated by the same man who moved the Carlton Club resolution against him 18 months later. However, a decision could not be much longer delayed, for the life of the 1918 Parliament was running out. Before another election could be held, the Conservative Party and its leader would have to decide whether to back the Lloyd George government for another five years – perhaps for ever – or to ditch it once and for all.

The Lloyd George Coalition had a very bad record in by-elections throughout its post-war term of office, but this has been exaggerated. Its performance must always be compared with the landslide victory which it had won in 1918, and the highly fortuitous nature of that result. In 1918 the electorate was in an unusually radical mood, and yet Lloyd George and his Conservative supporters, by exploiting the patriotic moment that followed the end of the war, persuaded them to fill the House of Commons with Conservatives and Coalition Liberals. It was only to be expected that by-elections would show a great deviation from the 1918 results, not least because the election had been fought with an electoral pact, a low turnout and an inadequate register. Furthermore, the very size of the victory increased discontent inside the government, as different groups struggled for influence and as backbenchers revolted against the Whips almost at will.

Conservative votes had created an overall Conservative majority in the House of Commons, but the Prime Minister and several of the Cabinet were Liberals and much of its legislation had a distinctly Liberal flavour. Conservative activists became increasingly hostile to a government for which they were responsible but with which they seemed to have little influence. Considering all these factors, the Coalition was not doing so badly. It had many bad results, but they were never consistently bad, indeed not consistent at all. Part of this was due to the fact that the 1918 election had produced a crop of unusual contests, unusual parties and unusual results. It would have been most surprising if by-election swings from the 1918 results had shown any regular pattern. For example, on the same day in 1920 the government lost Dartford with one of its worst results and held both seats at Stockport with one of its best. But these wild fluctuations were little comfort to a government which saw its fortunes apparently varying randomly from bad to catastrophic.

Maurice Cowling described Spen Valley (20 December 1919) as the government's worst result, and psychologically it certainly was.[3] But Spen Valley was a freak Labour win with under 40 per cent of the vote. Much worse for the government was Bromley (17 December) where Labour polled 47.5 per cent of the vote when standing for the first time, or St Albans (10 December) where Labour nearly won. Spen Valley made its impact because it was the third in this disastrous series, but particularly because Spen Valley actually changed hands. The government defeats which were the worst statistically were both defeats by Liberals in March 1919: Leyton West was lost on a swing of 24.8 per cent and Hull Central on a swing of 32.9 per cent. Labour gained Bothwell and Widnes during the summer of 1919, and government defeats at Louth (twice), Dartford, Dudley and Kirkcaldy continued into the spring of 1921. Thereafter the tide began to turn, and only in the winter of 1921–2 did Labour's fortunes temporarily revive. Government candidates were again doing quite well in the summer of 1922, holding Wolverhampton West and even gaining Hackney South, which they had failed to win in 1918.[4] A similar pattern of massive defeats in 1919 and 1920 followed by a revival in 1921 and 1922 can be detected in local government elections. It will be as well to suggest some explanations, since results over the last few years determined what contemporaries expected from Newport.

First, it might be pointed out that coalitions naturally attract bad results in elections which may influence their policy without threatening their survival. By bringing more than one group into government they create internal friction, but also push the opposition parties into temporary unity. The same thing happened to the National Government of the 1930s. Thus, in 1918–22, the Government faced one Liberal or Labour candidate in 44 by-elections and had the advantage of both Liberal and Labour candidates against them only 23 times. More important was the fact that the government could afford to lose many seats that it had won in 1918 without any serious risk of losing a general election. This view is borne out by an examination of the seats which actually changed hands. Labour gained 14 seats, only two of which were not to be regularly won by Labour in the inter-war years, and both of these (Spen Valley, and Heywood and Radcliffe) were won on a fortunate split of the vote. It is difficult to see how a government of the Right could have shed many tears over the loss of Pontypridd. When the Coalition could come close to winning Penistone against both Liberal and Labour (March 1921) they had no real reason to worry about their performance.

This touches on the vital point: contemporary observers had no effective tools for the measurement of opinion after the result was declared. 'Swing' was far in the future, and no serious attempt was made to distinguish between different types of constituency. The political organizer who used percentages was still a pioneer. If it seems clear to us that the government should not have worried because Labour won Pontypridd, it was certainly not clear at the time. The commonest measure of electoral performance was the tradition of the constituency. Unconscious of any change which had been brought about by the rise of the Labour Party, the war, or the redistribution of 1918, the comparisons were made not with the last general election but with 1895 and 1900 – the last occasions when the Conservatives had won in peace-time. This naturally failed to take account of the rise of Labour as a party bidding for working-class votes. It is because he knows of this that the Conservative can today reconcile himself with equanimity to the loss of Pontypridd.[5]

What the by-elections of 1918–22 should have shown observers was a gradual but definite transformation of British politics. The old politics of nineteenth-century Britain were passing away although still to be seen: middle-class Liberals optimistically trying to unite radicalism with local vested interests, and a demagogic Conservatism with substantial working-class support, playing the beer issue and banging the Imperial drum. This old model of politics had been long in decline as class and economic factors began to determine voting patterns, but it was only the hostility between Liberals and Labour after the First World War that made its final death possible. As long as the Coalition survived, Asquithian Liberals and Labour had enough in common in their hostility to it to postpone the death of the old politics a little longer. Liberals and Labour usually managed to avoid fighting each other in by-elections, and both of them gained seats from the government. Labour was steadily winning a solid base of working-class support, but that support was showing distinct regional, social and occupational variations. Contemporaries stressed the support rather than the limitations and variations, and this goes far towards explaining their mistaken hopes of Newport.

Labour leaders for the first time enjoyed the electoral support which ideology told them they should enjoy, and were in an understandably euphoric mood. However, as post-war boom was followed by inter-war slump in 1921, revolutionary fervour and the industrial militancy both began to evaporate. Labour therefore began a strategy of concentration on the by-elections which it believed it should win in a campaign for power and began to ignore those seats which might have seemed possible in 1919 but were seen to be hopeless by 1921. None of the seats left uncontested were marginal, and the seats which were contested could now be given additional assistance, funds and speakers.[6] This was the background to Labour's hopes for Newport. It needed only a small turnover of votes for Labour to capture the seat; it was in South Wales, where Labour had been doing particularly well, and it was undeniably a working-class stronghold. Thus, Labour had an explanation of recent electoral trends which led them to see Newport as an inevitable gain. It was, however, only a partial explanation which ignored the regional and local variations shown by the results. As Pontypridd, so Newport – or so they expected.

The government's losses alarmed both Conservatives and Coalition Liberals, and the net effect was a fatalism which led them to expect that Labour would win Newport too. However, Conservatives were not as obsessed with working-class seats as Labour understandably was. They did not like to see Labour winning industrial and mining seats, but most of these, especially in Wales, were lost by Coalition Liberals rather than Conservatives anyway. Dudley was the only traditionally Conservative seat won by Labour, and the shock that this defeat caused was as much due to the unexpected eclipse of a Minister (Sir Arthur Griffith Boscawen) seeking routine re-election as to the result itself. More serious to most Conservatives was the loss of safe middle-class seats to right-wing Independents, such as the Anti-Waste League. This threat too was receding by 1922, after the 'Geddes axe' had made a great point of cutting government expenditure. The Conservative gain in August 1922 was Hackney South, which had been won by Horatio Bottomley in 1918. At Newport the party was defending its first working-class seat for seven months, and was fighting only its second Welsh seat in the entire Parliament. The first had been Rhondda West, where on 21 December 1920 the Conservatives had intervened in a seat where Labour had been unopposed in 1918, and scored a highly respectable 41.5 per cent of the vote in a straight fight with Labour. If the moral was that a Conservative candidate would do better than a Coalition Liberal in a Welsh industrial seat, then it had been forgotten by October 1922. Conservative gloom at a by-election in Newport was thus matched by Labour's justifiable but exaggerated confidence.

The fall of the Coalition in Newport

In 1922 Newport was a moderately large industrial town, which had expanded rapidly in the later nineteenth century. Its economic character was chiefly as a port, serving the inland Monmouthshire industrial valleys, and so relying on the prosperity of the coal, steel and heavy engineering industries. Since 1536 Monmouthshire had occupied a strangely intermediate status between England and Wales: the administrative phrase was always 'Wales and Monmouthshire', but population censuses still listed it as an English county. Newport's industrial expansion had been largely achieved by attracting immigrants from England, and so it was far from typical of Welsh boroughs. Indeed, nationality had been a political issue, for Conservatives tended to regard Monmouthshire as English, while Liberals stressed its Welshness. For a port which looked across the Bristol Channel, and many of whose inhabitants derived from England, the Welsh culture which nourished Liberalism further west may have been more of a novelty than a source of inspiration.[7]

As in the country at large, the root cause of Newport Conservatives' hostility to the Coalition Government was not anything that it had done but the fact that it existed at all. It must be doubted whether any lasting coalition could ever work on the basis of a secret electoral pact like that of 1918, especially in a country like Britain where the effective control of local parties is in local hands. The Liberal–Labour pact of 1903 had run into similar troubles in 1911–14; perhaps only the weakness of every participating group but the Conservatives saved the National Government of the 1930s from a similar fate. Traditional local rivalries and entrenched personal hostilities can be much too strong to be abandoned at a word from Westminster.

In 1918 the sitting MP for Monmouth Boroughs was Lewis Haslam, a Liberal first elected in 1906. Since Monmouth Boroughs had been composed overwhelmingly of the town of Newport, which was given its own MP in the redistribution of 1918, Haslam wished to remain MP for Newport. Haslam was a moderate Liberal who had supported Lloyd George and the war, so he was able to get the 'coupon' and stand in 1918 as the official Coalition Government candidate. The Conservatives had little influence over the distribution of coupons in Wales, since most of the sitting MPs were Coalitionist Liberals, and herein lay the cause of the breach of 1922.[8] Welsh Conservatives had an even longer tradition of hating Lloyd George than had their English colleagues, and so they were very disappointed by an electoral pact which turned over almost every seat in Wales to Lloyd George Liberals. However, the allocation of coupons was accompanied by a good deal of moral pressure from Conservative Party managers and Central Office. More seriously, the pressure was only successful when it was promised that the electoral pact would run for one election only: this tactic restrained the diehards from breaking the united front in 1918, but only at the price of trouble later.

An Independent candidate emerged for the 1918 election in Newport, but the local Conservatives gave full support to Haslam, who was duly re-elected. However, when Conservatives went to him to press for Conservative policies, he naturally failed to give them satisfaction, and they – just as naturally – felt that they had been betrayed. Here too, Newport was typical of many places where Liberal MPs refused to act as Conservatives just

19

because Conservative votes had helped to elect them, or vice versa. A breach finally occurred in 1920 and 1921, with parliamentary discussion of the question of liquor licensing. This arose as a problem because of the restrictions which had been imposed during the war, but some Liberals certainly wished to continue restrictions, and even to extend them, in peacetime. The 1921 Licensing Bill was treated in Parliament as a subject which had a special local relevance to Newport, for it had to be decided whether Monmouthshire should be included with England or with Wales for licensing purposes; the Bill included it with Wales, and hence threatened Sunday closing. The Conservative MP for Monmouth, Leolin Forestier-Walker, told the Commons of mass protest meetings in Newport. The Marquess of Salisbury and the Earl of Plymouth both tried to amend it in the House of Lords, quoting similar evidence.[9] However, Haslam was a believer in temperance, whose views had never been disguised and had been frequently cited both for and against him at previous elections. Newport Conservatives felt that his partisan support for such a divisive measure justified their withdrawal of support.

It was therefore in the summer of 1921 that the Newport Conservatives began to look for a candidate, having decided to fight the next general election, irrespective of any national agreement or electoral pact. Efforts to find a candidate went on through the winter, and there were disputes both about the principle of breaking with the Coalition and about the choice of a candidate. However, unity was established when a meeting of over 300 members unanimously adopted Reginald Clarry on 26 July 1922. The political situation was such that Clarry began campaigning at once, expecting a general election in the autumn, and he even canvassed in the political clubs before his selection had been confirmed by the general meeting of the association.

Clarry was given official backing by the anti-Coalition right wing of the Conservative Party (officially called the 'Free Conservatives') through their leader, Lord Salisbury, and by their mouthpiece, the *Morning Post.* He was also supported by Lord Tredegar, an influential local figure, whose nephew, Leolin Forestier-Walker, sat for neighbouring Monmouth as the only Conservative MP in the county. But it must be stressed that although Clarry was a Conservative who was quite independent of the party's leadership, he was not an Independent Conservative. Duly selected by the local party, he was as much the official Conservative candidate for Newport as Austen Chamberlain was for Birmingham West. Clarry would have remained official candidate even if Chamberlain had disowned him in public – which he dare not do. Chamberlain's instruction that Central Office should not help Clarry was a private one, and while London political correspondents might hint that Chamberlain was not happy with Clarry's candidature, in Newport he still appeared as the official candidate. This was the more important because Clarry was posing as the apostolic heir of

Disraelian Conservatism and was preaching the party's established principles. A single word of support from Austen Chamberlain to the Liberal candidate in Newport – which Chamberlain would have dearly loved to give – would have wrecked Clarry's campaign completely. However, as both Chamberlain and Clarry well knew, it would also have wrecked Austen Chamberlain as party leader. In effect, Clarry had all the advantages of being independent; he had nothing to defend – and yet did not have to appear as a rebel. The rift between Clarry and Austen Chamberlain only appeared in the last week of the campaign, when Chamberlain came out finally for a continued coalition and Clarry denounced him as 'sadly out of touch with the industrial population'. Clarry remained official Conservative candidate, and after the Carlton Club it was Austen Chamberlain who became the Independent.

The campaign

Lewis Haslam died suddenly on 12 September, his illness having been reported only on the previous day, and the by-election campaign began at once. Clarry was already in the field and Bowen, the Labour candidate, had been officially in the field since 1918. Only the Liberals were caught unprepared.

For the next five weeks, until polling on 18 October, the national press carried regular reports on the progress of the campaign. However, news from Newport had to fight for its place on the main news pages, and it can only have been the expectation of the seat changing hands that kept it there. This was because the papers were simultaneously occupied with a series of severe national and international crises (see Table 2.1). Even papers printed in Newport rarely led with news of the by-election, and so the election campaign was conducted against a continuous backdrop of political crisis: headlines like 'War at Chanak?', 'Conservative Party Splits', 'Lloyd George to Resign?', or 'Cabinet to Call General Election' were typical.

With such a background of political speculation, it might be argued that Newport was not really a by-election at all, but was rather a general election fought in one constituency only. Such is the implication of all interpretations which see Newport as causing the fall of Lloyd George. And yet, in reality, the national and international crises were not live issues in the campaign at all. As J. H. Thomas noticed, the attitude of all the candidates practically amounted to the statement, 'For God's sake, don't connect me with the Coalition'.[10] In other words, on the most vital question of all, they simply had no grounds for disagreement. More surprisingly, none of the candidates was able to exploit the fact. Only the Liberal, Lynden Moore, took any stand on Chanak, which was to back up the government's firm action, but he seems to have been inspired more by traditional Liberal dislike of the Turks than by anything intrinsic to the crisis itself. Clarry and Bowen were content to talk about the weakness of the government in general terms, perhaps because the popular reaction was so unpredictable. It was even thought likely that Lloyd George would achieve a lightning victory over the Turks and then hold another 'khaki' election during the rejoicing which followed. This was the more serious for Newport, since it was possible right up to the last week of the campaign that Parliament would be dissolved, the by-election cancelled and another month of campaigning begun. Taking too firm a stand on the issues of the national crisis, which was developing and changing daily, might be giving dangerous hostages to fortune.

Whatever their motives, the Newport candidates hardly reacted to the political crisis at all. Paradoxically, it seems to have been just because there was a national political crisis that national policy issues were ignored throughout the campaign.

Table 2.1 News coverage during the campaign.

Date	National news	Newport news
12 Sep		Death of Haslam
15 Sep	Govt asked the Dominions for military assistance against Turkey	Readoption of Bowen as Labour candidate
17 Sep	Meeting of Ministers at Chequers discussed calling a general election	
19 Sep		Liberals searching for a candidate. Clarry already actively campaigning.
27 Sep		Moore adopted as Liberal candidate
30 Sep	Gen. Harington at Chanak agreed to a conference with the Turks	
7 Oct	Bonar Law's letter to *The Times* about Chanak	
10 Oct	Cabinet decided to call a general election, as a Coalition	Nomination day at Newport. Labour reported as being very confident
12 Oct		5 Conservative MPs campaigning for Clarry
14 Oct	Austen Chamberlain made a pro-Coalition speech at Birmingham	
15 Oct	L.G.'s Manchester speech. Carlton Club meeting called for 19 Oct	Clarry's first open attack on Austen Chamberlain
17 Oct		Henderson in Newport. Lord Salisbury supported Clarry
18 Oct	Bonar Law decided to oppose the Coalition	POLLING DAY AND COUNTING
19 Oct	CARLTON CLUB MEETING AND RESIGNATION OF THE GOVERNMENT	Newport result announced at 2 am.

All were against Lloyd George's Coalition, but none could be sure that it was about to fall and none could predict what form of partisan or bipartisan government would replace it. As long as the parties were in this state of flux, it was useless for their local spokesmen to campaign on detailed policy issues since these were more than likely to be abandoned or compromised in some new political grouping. Only Labour could fight with the national party and the local candidate in complete harmony; the Conservatives had no programme outside that of the Coalition which Clarry had rejected, and Moore refused to link his name to either the Coalition Liberal or the Asquithian Liberal programmes. In a very general sense, the campaign was fought over the same ground as every election – which party should govern? – but this could not be reduced to detailed programmes which won or lost votes. The Conservatives may have felt after Newport that they would win a general election, but they would have been hard pressed to explain why. The Newport campaign was thus a useless forum for the testing of party policy – as the Conservatives showed by fighting the following general election with no policy at all. However, it was just because the Newport electors were forced to choose between the parties rather than between their policies that it provided such a useful indicator for the future.

The candidates

The three candidates in the by-election were far from typical of either their parties or their supporters, but, in the absence of issues or policy discussion, much of the campaign was taken up with discussing each other's relative fitness to be MP for Newport.

J. W. Bowen was the most unremarkable of the three, and the most orthodox in his views and presentation. It was difficult for opponents to paint him as a dangerous revolutionary, but it was perhaps equally difficult for his supporters to raise any real enthusiasm for him. He was General Secretary of the Postal Workers' Union and therefore lived and worked in London. Although both he and his wife came from South Wales, and although he had already fought the Newport seat once, he was said to be something of an outsider. He was typical of the worthy but uninspiring trade unionists who filled the ranks of Labour candidates in the 1920s. His experience in trade unionism, friendly societies, health insurance and the Workers' Travel Association witnessed his own personal dedication to the Labour movement, but did not necessarily prove his popularity with the rank and file. There may have been some truth in Clarry's jibe that he was more in touch with the workers of Newport than was Bowen, since he alone visited them in their natural habitat – which to Clarry was the clubs and pubs.

Reginald Clarry was thus a very different sort of candidate, and his qualities and qualifications made a startling contrast with the local party's first and second choices for the candidature. W. R. Lysaght was the largest employer in Newport, and Sir Leonard Llewelyn was also a local worthy who was heavily involved in the coal and steel industries. Both were respected and very wealthy local men, but both were amateurs at the political game. Clarry, a self-made man who had become a successful civil engineer, was undoubtedly a player rather than a gentleman. He was brash, self-confident, forward and prepared to talk to anyone or anybody in order to win votes. Thus, on one day, he held a series of special meetings with local businessmen to discuss the town's industrial problems, spoke at dock and factory meetings, and made his daily round of the clubs and pubs. With a sympathetic press 'from the *Western Mail* and the *Monmouthshire Evening Post* (both dailies published in Newport) and an experienced agent, he could be sure that his campaign was well publicized. Despite the army of Labour frontbenchers who came down to Newport in support of Bowen and the impressive array of local notables who supported Moore, it was Clarry who made the running in the local campaign. Even the Liberal *South Wales News* used up much of its space attacking Clarry rather than giving positive support to Moore. Clarry made the best use of his style by campaigning on old (but suddenly topical) issues like Ireland and beer. Had the campaign required a sober and circumspect Conservative candidate, Clarry would have appeared much less attractive. When Moore described Clarry as typical of the Conservatives as 'the stupid party'; or when Bowen said that Clarry represented all that he hated in Conservatism, they were both paying grudging tributes to his success in selling himself. As the campaign descended more and more to personalities, it was Clarry's personality which was most talked about.

However, it was the Liberal candidate whose selection and whose character most affected the outcome. The background of Liberalism in Newport was not unlike the rest of South Wales, but the Newport Liberals' support of Lloyd George in 1918 makes it difficult to assess their real opinions. In constituencies where the Liberal Association supported Asquith, Lloyd George had by 1922 tried to set up his own local party, but where the local association supported Lloyd George, the Asquithians offered no opposition. The decision to back Lloyd George may have concealed the fact that many local Liberals preferred Asquith, and the events of 1922 suggest that this was the case. The Liberal Association was as usual dominated by middle-class and professional men, and their first choice to replace Haslam was Sir Garrod Thomas, their own president and the chairman of the Newport Property-Owners' Association. While negotiations with Thomas dragged on, there was speculation about the sort of campaign which the Liberals would fight. *The Times* reported that many local Liberals wanted to fight for a free Liberal rather than a

Coalitionist, but since they approached Reginald McKenna, Lady Bonham Carter, Lady Rhondda and Sir Harry Webb, as well as Thomas, there may well have been considerable internal dissension. The man eventually selected was a clear compromise choice, since he refused to tie himself to either wing of the Liberal Party. He was William Lynden Moore, the Newport coroner, and a well-known local solicitor with a family background of long service to the town. He was not an impressive speaker or an approachable candidate, and his worthy but ineffective efforts contrasted badly with Clarry's image as young, thrusting and aggressive. He was an old-world Liberal, who would probably have been happy enough to support the Coalition in 1922 if circumstances had permitted it. Dissension in his own local party was one reason for not doing so, but Clarry's appearance made it impracticable anyway. The very existence of a Conservative candidate made it pointless for Moore to run as a Coalition Liberal, since by doing so he might well have alienated some potential Liberal supporters, without winning Conservative votes to compensate. As Austen Chamberlain informed Sir Malcolm Fraser, of Conservative Central Office: 'Lynden Moore is, of course, a Coalition Liberal and he means to support the Coalition; but since he cannot obtain Conservative support, he is forced so to trim his sails as to get the largest amount of support from other quarters.'[11]

This ignored Moore's difficulties from within the local party, but was basically correct. However, Chamberlain's conclusions from this were not so sound, because he assumed that what he could see was equally visible in Newport. Moore refused to endorse either Lloyd George or Asquith as Liberal leader, and attacked the Coalition at least as often as he supported it. He fought under the slogan of 'reunited Liberalism' and defined his position in this somewhat unenlightening way: 'I am neither a "pro" nor an "anti". I am told that that is taking up an impossible position; I am not a "Mr Facing-both-ways". I am not a revolving tee-totum, nor a whirling dervish. I intend to keep my face in one direction, and that is the direction in which Liberal progress marches.' This concealed a very simple fact that the Coalition lost Newport not on polling day but on nomination day: 'Whoever gets to the top of the poll, the Government will have lost a supporter', noted *The Times*. The survival of the Coalition, insofar as it depended on Newport at all, depended now on neither Moore nor Clarry winning, but on a Labour victory which would teach Liberals and Conservatives the value of mutual co-operation. Chamberlain summed this up in his letter to Fraser:

> Newport is giving us a beautiful illustration of the results of a split...but...we must not allow Newport to land us in a general engagement all along the line. I should say, therefore, in reply to your enquiry: Do the least that you can without making a breach with our

Conservative friends. They are going to be beaten whatever you do or don't do, but I do not want them to attribute their defeat to you. I want you to be in a position to point the moral when the election is over and the seat is lost.

Only a Labour victory could give Chamberlain the evidence he needed, and after nomination day he put back the date of the Carlton Club meeting, so that it would meet after the Newport result was known rather than on polling day as originally planned. A Labour victory *was* widely expected, and Chamberlain's moral was widely drawn in advance of the result, so that a Carlton Club meeting on 18 October might well have taken a rather different decision. However, this negative argument for the Coalition was as irrelevant as the positive ones when considered from the viewpoint of Newport rather than London. It would make sense only if Clarry and Moore were both seen as rebels against the Coalition, but both simply ignored the Coalition. They were not fighting an election to decide the survival of the Coalition, but about which of the alternatives should succeed it. Chamberlain was unable even to make the Coalition an issue in Newport, and yet he continued to act as if it was the only issue.

Organization

The organization of the three parties in Newport provides an interesting contrast but was surely of less importance than was claimed afterwards. Such is always the case, for the real effect of organization is only slight or negative. It can be taken as an adequate explanation for none of the shock results with which this book deals, but probably contributed to all of them.[12]

Labour's campaign was described by the *Daily Express* as 'an endless procession of national figures', and this distinguished it from both the other parties. Margaret Bondfield, J. R. Clynes. John Hodge, Arthur Henderson, George Lansbury and J. H. Thomas all came to Newport to speak for Bowen, and Labour tried to use the presence of so many heavyweights to create a sense of irresistible impetus for their campaign. The organization was run by the party's National Agent, as was usual in marginal by-elections, and other outside assistance was drafted in. They were the only party which published canvass figures, which gave further justification for optimism. On 17 October the *Daily Chronicle* reported that Labour's 'complete' canvass had found 45 per cent favourable, 20 per cent doubtful and 35 per cent against. These were excellent findings in a three-party campaign, but they bore very little relation to the actual result. They undoubtedly believed the figures – on the eve of poll Arthur Henderson said privately that nothing under a 2,000 majority would satisfy him – but they were derived from a canvass that was far from complete. They surely published them in the hope of keeping their bandwagon rolling forwards, after its progress had slackened in the last week. 'Labour's stock has fallen', reported *The Times,* and more extravagant organizational claims were made in reply. In fact, the Labour organization was neither as good as they claimed when they expected to win nor as bad as they claimed when they lost.

Moore's organizational problems derived from his refusal to link himself to either wing of the old Liberal Party, since either could have given him the resources which he needed. He actually relied on Coalition Liberal help, but only on an undercover basis: the Coalition Liberals' Chief Welsh Agent was in charge of his campaign, and the *Morning Post* triumphantly reported that it had spotted Sir Alfred Mond's agent also working for Moore in Newport. Moore may have received money from Lloyd George, but the bedrock of his organization must have been the local Newport Liberals. It is hardly surprising that their electoral machine was rather rusty, for they had not fought against Conservative candidates even in local elections since 1913. They had never fought an independent campaign in the redistributed constituency or with the larger, post-1918 electorate. In seven of the nine wards, Liberal ward committees had to be set up during the campaign because no local organization existed. The lack of a professional local agent can only have compounded all these problems.

The Conservative campaign was thought to be the weakest, but was probably the best. As the official candidate of the local party, Clarry could call on Raymond Gibbs, the full-time local agent; Gibbs was a great asset for this sort of campaign since he was experienced both as an agent and as a local organizer: he had been Chief Recruiting Officer for Newport during the early years of the war. Austen Chamberlain had cut off some of the Central Office assistance which was usually given for by-elections: money, advice, literature and teams of trained organizers and speakers. It is not clear what was withheld, but certainly Clarry did not lack for any of these, because they were all available elsewhere. When forced to fight his second election campaign in two months, for the general election of 1922, Clarry was still able to spend right up to the legal maximum. If Central Office withheld money for the by-election, then Clarry had enough wealthy backers to provide it for him, but the rather ambiguous relations between Austen Chamberlain and Sir George Younger (party chairman) make it quite likely that Central Office ignored Chamberlain's instructions altogether. Lord Salisbury's Free Conservatives sent down staff from their London office, including Miss Goring Thomas who had been a Central Office Area agent. Other local agents came in to assist, and even Lord Curzon asked his friends if they could make their agents available to assist with the campaign; some at least did so. The Free Conservatives also provided some heavyweight speakers of their own, and Salisbury and

Colonel John Gretton MP, both sent telegrams of support which were read at Clarry's meetings. At one meeting five MPs spoke for Clarry, which at least helped him to show that he was not a rebel against his party as his opponents were claiming. Even the lack of front-bench support was not very serious, since convention would have prevented Cabinet Ministers intervening in a by-election anyway. Until this convention was dropped by Baldwin in 1927, only Labour used its sledgehammers to crack walnuts. Before 1927, party leaders sent letters of support to local candidates, but did not usually visit the constituencies to speak or canvass unless they were themselves candidates. Even here, the Labour advantage was more apparent than real, because Labour's national speakers were unacquainted with what was happening in the Newport election. They duly came down to address one mass meeting, delivered a tirade against the Coalition Government and then returned to London, without realizing that exactly similar sentiments could have been heard at a meeting addressed by either Clarry or Moore. They added nothing distinctive to the Labour campaign except their names.

At the grass roots, the Conservative machine, pepped up since they decided to look for a candidate the previous summer, and directed by experienced local men, was more than a match for Labour's 'national' approach to the campaign. One more interesting variation occurred which further invalidated Labour's stance: its 'procession' of national speakers all claimed that to vote Labour was the only way to put an end to the Lloyd George government. They were even more out of touch than Chamberlain, for he at least had seen that a Labour victory – and nothing else – could preserve the Coalition. Insofar as Newport voters were voting for or against Lloyd George and his government, they could not rationally vote Labour.

Issues

On 21 October, Bowen attributed his defeat 'to over-confidence, shortage of motor cars, and the fact that some districts were not canvassed, while national issues were lost in local problems'. In fact, the only issue worthy of the name was drink, which Bowen regarded as a local question which should not be allowed to obscure real, national problems. Indeed, that he felt this way goes far towards explaining his failure at Newport. Clarry had made himself known in the clubs before the by-election, and was backed not only by the six Conservative clubs in Newport but also by the non-political clubs. Nor was this support simply contrived by a clever Conservative campaign, for the Licensed Victuallers' Association organized independent support for Clarry after sending a questionnaire to all the candidates. Moreover, in South Wales both Liberals and Labour had traditional ties with the Nonconformist chapels and the temperance movement, which the Licensing Bill controversy of 1921 and the by-election merely re-established. During the campaign Labour and Liberals usually met in the Temperance Hall, while Conservatives used theatres or hotels. Many local politicians were also involved in the local campaign which was being run by the Temperance Council of the Christian Churches, and on several mornings the newspapers carried reports of local temperance meetings addressed by Philip Snowden. The embarrassment of Bowen and Moore was well shown by the way in which they reacted to the LVA questionnaire and to questions asked at their meetings. Hedging and refusing to commit themselves, they relied on counter-attacks to show that Clarry was irresponsible to raise the subject at all. So obvious did these tactics become that Clarry was backed by a local temperance leader, W. R. Williams of Cardiff, who had lost patience with Bowen and Moore. In a letter to the press, he characterized Clarry as 'honest' and dismissed the others as 'shifty and evasive'. More typical of Liberals was the reaction of the *South Wales News* to Clarry: 'He belongs to the most stupidly reactionary party in the state, the party which has in the past resisted every liberty won by the people except, perhaps, the liberty to drink as much beer as they could carry without being locked up.' Few genuine believers in temperance can have been converted by the honesty with which Clarry denounced the temperance movement, but there were probably very few genuine believers in temperance in Newport. There were fewer Noncon-formists in Monmouthshire than in any other Welsh county, and the demonstrations against the 1921 Licensing Bill were clear evidence of local feeling.

Several reports suggest that Clarry won a large number of working-class votes:

> The men in Lysaght's works voted Conservative practically to a man, and the local agent expressed the view afterwards that 'the working classes had never understood the Coalition. They had regarded it rightly or wrongly as a wangle and as an attempt to ally capitalist forces against the worker.'[13]

The appearance of a Conservative agent defending the working classes against a capitalist conspiracy only surprises a reader after generations of class politics. There was a long tradition of working-class Conservatism in Newport, and this had been part of the reason for the local party's hostility to the Coalition. Earlier in 1922, a report on the Association of Conserva-tive Clubs' rally at Swansea included this passage: 'Mr W. Stevens (Docks Conservative Club, Newport) is not one of those who would go to the stake to defend the Coalition – and in effect said so – and many present endorsed his views.'[14] It was also claimed locally that the government had lost Pontypridd to Labour in July only because the Coalition Liberal candidate was a temperance fanatic who could not get working-class support. Perhaps 'as Pontypridd, so Newport' was right after all.

But how much did the drink issue really affect the outcome of the Newport by-election? Only once before had the Conservatives held the seat (Monmouth Boroughs in 1900) and then they had exploited exactly the same issue. However, since the drink issue was just one of many reasons why they regularly polled well among working-class voters, its effect should be seen as continuous rather than sudden. It was this which delayed the polarization of Newport politics along class lines and made it possible for the Conservatives to come near to winning the seat. But they won the seat in 1923, 1931 and 1935 without the same advantage of beer as a topical issue. Drink undoubtedly contributed to the Newport result at every election before 1945, but can hardly be said to have been decisive in 1922. Its emergence during the campaign was the re-creation of old antagonisms rather than the creation of new ones, and the Liberals had only themselves to blame, for it was their Licensing Act which had revived them.

Another issue, which the Liberals tried to exploit and which Bowen regarded as equally irrelevant, was local identity. Moore made much of the fact that he alone was a local man, and this was especially turned to advantage against Clarry, who was not only not from Newport but was from Swansea. A local JP, T. H. Mardy, in a leaflet which the Liberals circulated, reminded voters of the services which Moore had given to the town as coroner and as legal adviser on its parliamentary business, especially in cases involving disputes with other Bristol Channel ports. Since Swansea was a direct rival to Newport, the lesson was obvious. Mardy's slighting references to 'a gentleman from Swansea' are also representative of something deeper: as Liberalism was driven in upon itself after the First World War, it relied more and more on local roots and its revivals were increasingly the manifestations of local protest movements, less and less related to national politics. As early as 1922 Liberals were proclaiming that only a Newport man was qualified to represent Newport. When we consider the galaxy of national figures who were approached before Moore became their desperation choice, this claim carries rather less conviction. In effect, the only thing to be said in favour of Moore was that he was a local man, so they said it as loudly and as often as possible.

Clarry's best defence – apart from giving all his pamphlets and messages to electors a letterhead which implied that he lived in Newport – was to stress his knowledge of industry and Newport's reliance on industry. Here again he was fortunate in the events which accompanied the campaign, for it was conducted alongside a major strike at Ebbw Vale which was bad for local trade and employment, and also did great damage to the Labour campaign because the strike caused inter-union disputes which spilled over into Newport. The continuing strike seemed to justify Clarry's demands for trade union reform to counter the threat of imminent industrial anarchy, and he received an unsolicited bonus when the South Wales miners chose the eve of poll to call a coal strike. Bowen could not be smeared personally – although the *Morning Post* had an excellent try by way of publicizing his involvement in the Council of Action - but political Labour always suffers for the actions of industrial militants and, by comparison with Clarry, Moore would once again appear as weak and ineffectual.

Yet the most important issue in the campaign was none of these; it was the simple question of who was going to win. This became an issue rather than just an interesting speculation because expectations were obviously going to determine the actual outcome. In a genuinely three-horse race, the voters must consider not only who they would like to win but also who they would not want to win, and then they must balance these conflicting aims. During the inter-war years many voters faced this situation, especially those who had a clear preference for Conservative or Liberal but whose first priority was the defeat of Labour. In these circumstances, all the Newport candidates had to show complete confidence in their own victory, for any slight acknowledgement of the possibility of defeat might cause a rush of votes away to other candidates. They each therefore spoke of their nearest rival as if he had already come third, in the hope of winning some of his votes. Analysis of this 'third-party squeeze' is unusually difficult when there is no obvious third party. Moreover, the newspapers from which most information on the campaign is derived were all aware that their predictions might affect the result. Thus, the headlines of the *South Wales News* and *South Wales Argus*, both Liberal, on 14 October were 'No hope for Mr R. Clarry' and 'Conservative out of the running'. The Conservative *Western Mail* replied on 18 October with 'Don't waste votes on Mr Lynden Moore.' The committed London newspapers also slanted their reports from Newport, with the *Daily Herald* backing Bowen, the *Morning Post* and *Daily Telegraph* backing Clarry, and the *Daily Chronicle* backing Moore; backing meant giving favourable predictions as well as editorial support. *The Times* provides the best example, for its ownership was changing during the campaign, and it became distinctly more favourable to Clarry in the last week.[15]

However, some points can be discerned through this fog of press distortion. On the one hand, most observers expected a Labour win in the early part of the campaign but were not so sure by the last week, and most of them realized that the Liberals were fading away at the end. By polling day it was expected that Bowen would win from Clarry with Moore a poor third: Robert Sanders, Deputy Chairman of the Conservative Party (and a strong supporter of breaking with Lloyd George) noted on 22 October that 'this morning the Newport election result came as a cheering surprise. I am told the liquor question had a good deal to do with it'.[16] The best evidence for this is in the reaction of the Liberals: they indignantly denied that Moore was merely a stopgap candidate who was showing the flag, and they even panicked to the extent of issuing a special leaflet which denied that they had no chance of winning. It quoted Moore as saying: 'My opponents, afraid of the result, are anxious to shake your belief in the solidity of my support, and weaken, as they hope, the chances of my success.' Candidates with solid support do not issue such leaflets: Moore was surely right in his analysis of the situation but incapable of arresting the trend. The most likely explanation of the result is that some middle-class Liberals, fearing a Labour win, voted for Clarry rather than Moore, because Clarry appeared to have a better chance of beating Bowen. Nor was this an unusual phenomenon in the inter-war years; describing a letter to the *Manchester Guardian,* in which Gilbert Murray explained his reasons for voting Conservative in 1931, Malcolm Muggeridge remarked: 'like all good Liberals, he only believed in supporting Conservatives when there was a possibility that they might otherwise be defeated'.[17] Such a joke could not have been made in 1922; the novelty of Newport was that the squeezing of the Liberals took place for the first time. If any one issue determined the outcome of the Newport by-election, it was surely the electors' expectations of the result itself.

The result

Immediate reaction to the result was overshadowed by the imminence of the Carlton Club meeting and the realisation that Newport could materially alter its decision. Clarry's victory was announced at 2 a.m., so most newspapers had no more than the figures in stop-press columns and some did not catch it at all. Only the *Morning Post* and *The Times,* in their London editions, gave it full prominence, and only *The Times* backed this up with a leader. Conservative MPs who attended the Carlton Club at 11 a.m. that morning had therefore heard the result only recently, and they were 'buzzing with the sensational news'.[18] It was therefore important that *The Times* – the only informed comment then available – chose to underline heavily what it saw as the significance of the result:

> The Country will see in it a most complete condemnation of the Coalition Government as such and a vindication of those Conservatives throughout the country who have been so determined to preserve their individuality in previous by-election contests. By these the Newport result will be hailed as the emancipation of the party.

The moral was clear, and it was very different from that which Austen Chamberlain had wished to draw. But 'the most exciting boomerang in the long history of British political strategy', as Beaverbrook called it, was entirely of Chamberlain's making.

It was therefore only after the Carlton Club meeting and the resignation of Lloyd George that most politicians and newspapers made their comments on Newport. The *Morning Post* saw it as a vindication of Lord Salisbury, and the *Morning Advertiser* as a victory for 'the trade', but the overwhelming consensus was that Newport had been a vote against the Coalition. It was now that Bowen and Moore brought out the drink issue and organization to explain their defeat, but they too accepted the anti-Coalition explanation. But this simply does not stand up to examination. The Coalition had no candidate at Newport and it was not even a topic of disagreement between the candidates who were there. And if the Conservative Party, which was part of the Coalition, could profit from its unpopularity, then why could not Labour which was wholly, and the Liberals who were partly, outside it? By Chamberlain's own argument, a voter could help the Coalition only by voting Labour, and that was nonsense. In effect, the voters who would have supported a Coalition candidate tested Moore and Clarry as anti-Labour candidates and found Clarry to be the most hopeful. Newport was less an anti-Coalition vote than an anti-Labour vote; *The Times* admitted that 'the significance of the Newport election lies in the heavy defeat of Labour expectations'; and Bowen complained that 'the campaign appeared to me to wind up in a determination to keep Labour out at any cost'.

It is therefore necessary to explain the consensus view that Newport was an anti-Coalition vote. If it is wholly wrong, why did it gain such wide credence? Labour's and Liberals' reasons are obvious enough: it gave them an alibi for a surprise defeat and also suggested that the Newport result might not be a guide for the coming general election for which the Coalition would not exist. (This self-delusion merely meant that they got the result of the general election wrong as well.) Conservative reasons are more difficult to find. Many of them felt a little guilty for the rebellion against Austen Chamberlain and for stabbing the Coalition Liberals in the back. What better defence than to interpret the Newport result to show that they had acted in accord with the wishes of the electorate? If Newport was an anti-Coalition vote, then it would justify the decision taken at the Carlton Club, although the evidence suggests that they would have taken the same decision without Newport (perhaps by a much smaller majority). It was thus in the interests of everyone except Austen Chamberlain to interpret Newport as an anti-Coalition vote, and he could scarcely now claim that he had been wrong throughout the last month. Newport therefore passed into mythology.

Local evidence was different, and ignored: 'It is a Conservative victory pure and simple; it is not an anti-Coalition victory', said the *Western Mail*. Moreover, this correct interpretation was implicitly accepted when the new Conservative government called an immediate general election. 'We should not be surprised to find in the end that the electorate is represented very much in the proportion in which their votes were cast at the recent Newport election', commented The *Economist*. Amazingly, this was almost an exactly correct prediction (though achieved by a curious pattern of two and three-cornered contests nationally): in the 1922 general election the Conservatives got 38 per cent of the vote (40 per cent in the Newport by-election), Labour got 31 per cent (34 per cent) and the Liberals came third with 30 per cent (26 per cent). As Newport, so the nation.

Surprisingly, the Newport constituency turned out to be a very good political indicator for the inter-war years, although nobody could have known it in 1922. It was a critical marginal which the Conservatives needed to win in order to win a parliamentary majority.[19] The 1922 general election in Newport confirmed the verdict of the by-election: Moore stood down and, on a higher poll, his votes split slightly in favour of Clarry. The Conservatives almost lost Newport in 1923, held it easily in 1924, lost in 1929 and won easily in 1931 and 1935. With all its peculiarities, Newport succeeded in representing the marginal political nation. Factors like drink and the squeezing of Liberal voters must all be seen as gradually changing elements which always distorted the relationship between local and national politics in the inter-war years. Before 1914 Newport had been a fairly safe Liberal seat, and after 1945 it was a safeish Labour seat which fell to the Tories only in the 1980s heyday of Thatcherism. 1922 showed that the transition from the old politics to the new – from church and club versus chapel and temperance society to class versus class – was under way but far from complete. As Newport, so the nation.

Note on sources

There is an extensive coverage of the national crises which form the background to Newport, but the following are the most useful:
Lord Beaverbrook, *The decline and fall of Lloyd George* (1963).
M. Cowling, *The impact of Labour, 1920–1924* (1971).
R. R. James, *Memoirs of a Conservative* (1969).
R. T. McKenzie, *British political parties*, 2nd edn (1963).
K. O. Morgan, 'Lloyd George's stage army'; in A. J. P. Taylor (ed.), *Lloyd George: twelve essays* (1971).
Sir C. Petrie, *The life and letters of Sir Austen Chamberlain* (1939).
D. Walder, *The Chanak affair* (1969).

Information on the local background is to be found in:
M. Kinnear, *The British voter* (1968).
K. O. Morgan, *Wales in British politics* (1963).
K. O. Morgan, 'Twilight of Welsh Liberalism'; *Bulletin of the board of Celtic studies*, xii (1968).

H. Pelling, *The social geography of British elections, 1885–1910* (1967).

Detailed information on the campaign and the local personalities has come from *The Newport year book* (1922 and 1923), *Who's who in Newport* (1922) and overwhelmingly from local and national newspapers, especially *The Times*, the *Morning Post*, the *Western Mail*, the *South Wales Argus* and the *South Wales News*. There is also a useful collection of leaflets and other contemporary documents in the Newport Central Reference Library. The drink issue can be explored through the *Morning Advertiser* and the *Conservative Clubs' Gazette*. No complete set of the *Monmouthshire Evening Post* seems to have survived. M. Kinnear's *The Fall of Lloyd George* (1973) gives the most detailed account of the political background, but has nothing about Newport itself.

Notes

1   T. Jones, *Whitehall diary*, I (1969) p. 210.
2   see D. Ogg, *Herbert Fisher* (1947) p. 113, and Sir C. Petrie, *The Carlton club* (1955) p. 179, for typical examples.
3   M. Cowling, *The impact of Labour, 1920–1924* (1971) p. 112.
4   The only by-election which was genuinely won by the Coalition was the gain of Woolwich East from Labour in March 1921, and was the more interesting in that the defeated Labour candidate was Ramsay MacDonald, the party's ex-leader. He was defeated by Captain R. Gee, VC, a war-hero, ex-miner and 20-year serving soldier, who managed to fight the campaign entirely on MacDonald's pacifist record. It should perhaps be seen as the last episode of the 1918 general election, and was certainly more 'khaki' than many contests then.
5   The syllogism, 'as goes Pontypridd, so go Portsmouth and Preston', he knows to be quite untrue. His predecessor in 1922 did not and indeed could not know it.
6   By-elections in single-Member seats:

1919 and 1920	1921 and 1922
Number of by-elections 38	51
Number in Coalition-held seats 31	44
Number in Coalition-held seats contested by Labour 23 (74%)	18 (41%)

7   The population of Newport County Borough in 1921 was 92,369; it had almost trebled since 1871, and half the inhabitants had been born outside the town. About seven-eighths of the employed population worked in the transport, engineering or iron and steel industries. However, as well as this concentration of heavy industrial workers, Newport also had the third highest proportion of 'middle-class' residents (unoccupied or in non-manual occupations) in Wales. (Information from various Census tables 1871, 1911 and 1921.)
     In 1921 only about 2 per cent of the inhabitants of Newport were able to speak Welsh, compared with an average in Welsh constituencies of 37 per cent. See M. Kinnear, *The British voter* (1968) p.136.
8   Twenty-two coupons were issued in the 36 Welsh seats: 19 to Liberals, 2 to Conservatives and 1 to the National Democratic Party. In areas like Cardiff, where the local Conservatives were relatively strong, there were no coupons, but where Liberalism was strong it also had the benefit of the coupon. See F. W. S. Craig, *British parliamentary election results, 1918–1949* (1969).

9   *Hansard*, House of Commons, 22 July, 2 Aug 1921; House of Lords, 15 Aug 1921. After his victory at Newport, Reginald Clarry tried to get the new Conservative Government to repeal the 1921 Act, but the then Home Secretary, W. C. Bridgeman, refused (House of Commons, 5 July 1923).

10 *Spectator*, 21 Oct 1922.

11 Austen Chamberlain Papers, Birmingham University Library, AC 33/2/32, Chamberlain to Fraser, 6 Oct 1922.

12 This is the modern view. See, for example, R. T. Holt and J. E. Turner, *Political parties in action* (1968) throughout. Although it was not so before 1914, the larger constituencies and expense limitations imposed in 1918 probably created the modern situation, with the limited role of local organization. Of course, hardly anyone in 1922 was aware of this.

13 J. Green, *Mr Baldwin* (1933) p.63. There is similar evidence in local newspapers.

14 *Conservative Clubs' Gazette* (June 1922).

15 See *History of the Times* (London: The Times, 1952) iv (2) pp. 722–67.

16 J. Ramsden (ed.) *Real old Tory politics: the political diaries of Sir Robert Sanders, Lord Bayford, 1910–35*, (1984), p. 191.

17 M. Muggeridge, *The thirties* (London: Fontana, 1971) p. 136.

18 F. Owen, *Tempestuous journey* (1954) p. 658.

19 This assumes a uniform national swing with few variations. Although many constituencies between the wars varied considerably from the national pattern, Newport did not.

CHAPTER 3

By-elections of the first Labour Government

Chris Cook

In the two years from the Newport by-election of October 1922 to the formation of Baldwin's second ministry following the general election of October 1924, British politics underwent a period of rapid transition. These two years saw three general elections and four Prime Ministers. They also saw a transformation of the political scene: Lloyd George fell from power, never to hold office again; the Labour Party formed its first ever administration, even though still a minority party. But of all the changes, the most lasting was perhaps the fate of the Liberal Party. Reunited and resuscitated, the party had fought the election of 1923 on its favourite fiscal battleground, with a vigour and a sense of purpose it had not known since pre-war days. Ten months later it emerged from the election of 1924 like the army of Napoleon which recrossed the Berezina in 1812, an exhausted, demoralized rabble that could never challenge successfully for supremacy again.

In the immediate wake of the 1922 general election, however, all these events were still in the future. Bonar Law had won on a programme proclaiming 'Tranquillity' and it seemed that the by-elections would not show any dramatic shifting of votes.

Indeed, until a series of by-election reverses for the government early in March 1923, only four fairly unexciting contests had taken place. At Portsmouth South (13 December 1922), in a by-election caused by the resignation of H. R. Cayzer, the sitting Member, the Conservative candidate was opposed only by an Independent. The Liberals, who had fought in 1922, failed to raise sufficient energy to field a candidate. The Conservatives easily retained the seat, with turnout falling from 73.7 per cent to 57.7 per cent. In the Newcastle East by-election, interest was added to the contest when Arthur Henderson was brought forward as Labour candidate (he had been defeated at Widnes in the 1922 general election).

The significance of the result in Newcastle East was the inability of the Liberal candidate to make headway against Labour in a traditionally Liberal industrial seat. Labour was, in fact, able to increase both its vote and its percentage of the poll. The succeeding by-election in Whitechapel produced a similar result. Despite the withdrawal of a Conservative candidate, Labour very substantially increased its hold on this East End seat, raising its share of the total poll from 40.2 per cent to 57.0 per cent. In the Darlington by-election on 28 February 1923 a straight fight took place, although the Liberals had contested the seat at the previous election. The by-election result again demonstrated the ability of Labour to capture a further portion of the former Liberal vote.

In none of these by-elections had seats actually changed hands. This position was rapidly altered by a batch of by-elections held early in March. Partly as a result of talk of government plans to decontrol rents, and partly as a result of an internal Conservative quarrel, the first of these by-elections, at Mitcham, produced a dramatic result. In a constituency in which in 1922 the Conservatives had taken 65 per cent of the poll in a straight fight with the Liberals, in the by-election the seat was sensationally won by Labour. Partly, this was explained because the official Conservative candidate, Sir Arthur Griffith-Boscawen, was faced by an Independent Conservative supported by Lord Rothermere.[1] The Independent took 12.7 per cent of the poll, a sufficient level of support to let Labour in, with the Liberals trailing a very poor third with 15.2 per cent of the poll.

In every sense, however, Labour's gain was nothing short of spectacular. Mitcham was hardly the seat to set Socialists dreaming of the promised land.[2] Chuter Ede, the Labour candidate, found on his arrival in the division that the local party consisted of a voluntary secretary and a few scattered trade union branches. This handicap was somewhat reduced by a campaign extremely well organized from headquarters – so well organized, in fact, that the local Conservatives were instructed to imitate it.[3] Particular use was made by Labour of the mass canvass; no doubt this was one factor that caused turnout to rise abruptly from 52.7 per cent to 66.2 per cent.

Labour's triumph in Mitcham was followed by two further Conservative losses. In a straight fight the Liberals gained the suburban Willesden East constituency while Labour captured their first-ever seat in Liverpool, the marginal Edge Hill division which was won largely on Conservative abstentions (turnout fell from 70.5 per cent to 58.1 per cent).

After this flurry of by-election reverses, the next by-elections evoked little excitement. The death of Sir O. Thomas, the sitting Independent Labour Member, enabled a fairly united Liberal Party in Anglesey to recapture a traditional Liberal stronghold; indeed, the co-operation of the two wings of the party in Anglesey and the recapture of the seat spurred moves towards reunion at national level, but very little materialized. The very safe Conservative seat of Ludlow produced no excitement. With no organization whatsoever, Labour's intervention was rewarded with only 7.8 per cent of the poll. As one leading Labour agent bemoaned after the election, virtually every working-class Labour man still continued to vote for the Liberal.[4]

In the Berwick-upon-Tweed by-election, where the sitting National Liberal had been unseated on petition and his wife subsequently stood as an official Conservative in his place, the voting revealed very little change. The intervention of a Labour candidate again hit the Liberal share of the poll, while the Conservative vote was almost exactly that polled by the National Liberal the previous November – a perfect example, if any were needed, of the extent to which nominal National Liberals were so often Conservatives in all but name. As in Ludlow, Labour intervention was probably the cause of the increase in turnout.

With very little comfort from previous by-elections, the Liberals were able to console themselves with a gain in the Tiverton by-election on 21 June 1923. In a very high poll (88.1 per cent), in which the Conservatives also increased their total vote, the Liberals gained victory by 403 votes. Little of significance can really be interpreted from the result, since whereas Labour had contested the division officially in 1922, the same candidate in 1923 was not officially endorsed and polled only 495 votes.

Much more significant of the standing of the Liberals were the by-elections in Morpeth and Leeds Central. In the mining division of Morpeth, which Labour won in 1922 on a minority vote, the Conservatives stood down to give the Liberals a clear run.[5] The result was a Labour triumph, with 60.5 per cent of the vote on an increased turnout. It was yet further evidence that the miners had finally deserted the Liberals. Similarly, in Leeds Central, in a three-cornered contest the Liberal share of the vote in this Conservative-held seat slumped from 22.2 per cent to 11.0 per cent.

The final three contested by-elections (four by-elections were pending at the Dissolution on 16 November 1923) all occurred in safe Conservative territory. A second by-election in Portsmouth South was caused by the appointment of the Rt Hon. L. O. Wilson, the sitting Conservative, as Governor of Bombay. On a very low poll (54.9 per cent), the Conservatives retained the seat against Liberal opposition. The Yeovil by-election, on 30 October 1923, was perhaps most significant as an example of Liberal difficulties in recapturing votes that had been lost to Labour. Not having fought the seat in 1922, the Liberals were unable to dislodge Labour from second place at the by-election.

Whereas at least the Yeovil Liberals were attempting to regain lost ground, no such animation stirred what remained of the ranks of the Rutland and Stamford Liberals. No Liberal had contested the division in 1922 and none appeared at the by-election, despite warnings by senior officers of the Eastern Counties Liberal Federation that such lack of action would cause irreparable damage to the future prospects of the party.[6] In a straight fight with Labour, the Conservatives easily retained the seat.

In all, despite the losses suffered by the Conservatives in March, the more recent by-elections had not shown any signs of a major shift of votes against the government. Rather, the significance of the by-elections had been Labour's ability to consolidate and extend its gains in industrial areas – mainly at the expense of the Liberals – and Labour's slow but definite advance in rural areas – again hitting hardest at the Liberals. Certainly, the by-elections gave little indication of the electoral earthquake that was to come with Baldwin's disastrous Tariff Election on 6 December 1923, but they had not, in any case, been fought on the tariff question.

The place of the general election of 1923 in the chronology of the rise of the Labour Party and the downfall of the Liberals lies outside this essay.[7] However, the fact that very few observers expected the Ramsay MacDonald government to survive more than a few months, together with the extreme interest and excitement engendered by the advent of a Labour Government, meant that the by-elections of 1924 were followed with considerable interest.

Labour wanted to see in the by-elections confirmation of its new place in the political order. The Conservatives looked eagerly for signs that the débâcle of 1923 was behind them and that frightened, moderate opinion was rallying to the natural party of stability.

Of all the parties, however, the by-elections were perhaps of most significance for the Liberals. Each by-election in fact constituted a problem for the party. Indeed, the by-elections were a microcosm of a larger dilemma. What attitude should the party adopt to the Labour Government that the Liberals had themselves voted into office? What should be the role of the party, vis-à-vis Labour, in Parliament? What should be party policy in the constituencies, in, for example, adopting candidates against sitting Labour Members? And what should be the policy of the party in by-election vacancies?

The Liberals failed to adopt a consistent, or indeed at times *any*, policy towards these three pressing questions. The party, with two leaders but little leadership, drifted from thoughts of co-operation and liaison with Labour towards a sullen, uncoordinated and unthought out policy of opposition to the government. It was a policy which led to the vote against MacDonald over the Campbell case and on to the electoral débâcle of October 1924.

It was hardly surprising that the Liberals in 1924 found themselves faced with a dilemma that was to prove insuperable. To begin with, having just fought an election on the essentially negative policy of defending the status quo (i.e. free trade), the Liberals had then turned the Conservatives out to install Labour. Even this decision, welcomed though it was by the bulk of Liberal workers in the constituencies and the federations, seems to have been taken only after Asquith had been tempted to do a deal with the Conservatives in order to install a minority Liberal Government. Certainly, the Liberal decision to install Ramsay MacDonald – without so much as a prolonged meeting of the two leaders, much less any terms or agreed areas of *modus vivendi* – was a heavy blow to Liberalism. This decision in itself, though damaging, would not have been disastrous had the Liberals pursued a constructive policy in 1924. This the Liberals never did – although certain Liberals knew what they wanted. Lloyd George was eager for co-operation with Labour to put radical measures on the statute book – at least until the Labour Party adopted a candidate against him in Caernarvon and until the Abbey by-election seemed to show the strength of the anti-Socialist forces. Meanwhile, Churchill, F. E. Guest and the other right-wingers wanted no truck at all with Ramsay MacDonald. Asquith, not for the first time in his life, wanted to wait and see.

'Wait and see', however, was hardly a policy. Just as, at Westminster, Liberals had to decide their policy as issues came before the House (and usually finished by voting in all three possible ways), so by-elections fell vacant in the constituencies. It was, perhaps, something of a lucky chance for the Liberals that two of the ten by-elections of the first Labour Government fell vacant in seats that posed no problem of policy – Dover and the City of London, both Tory citadels, and both uncontested even in December 1923.

In fact, the Dover by-election (of 12 March 1924) was something of a non-event, having been caused when the sitting Conservative Member (the Hon. J. J. Astor) inadvertently voted in the House before he had taken the Oath. Although there was some inclination among the Labour ranks to bring forward a candidate (the seat had been unopposed in 1923), party headquarters dissuaded them. Of the dormant Liberal Association, nothing was heard.[8]

The first contested by-election, on 1 February 1924, in the double-member City of London division, could hardly have occurred in a less interesting seat. Unopposed in 1923 (and indeed at every general election between the wars except 1929), the seat was the sort of Conservative citadel in which even a Liberal candidature produced no ruffling on the waters of the moat. In the event, a straight fight ensued between Conservative and Liberal (there was no Labour organization in the constituency). A touch of comedy was added to the contest by the fact that the Liberal candidate had himself made efforts to secure the Conservative nomination.[9] The result, not indeed unexpected, was a Conservative victory with 70.1 per cent of the poll on a 41.9 per cent turnout.

The first significant by-election, and the first real policy dilemma for the Liberals, occurred with the vacancy at Burnley, caused by the death of the sitting Labour Member. Here, polling took place on 28 February. The contest soon assumed a national interest when Arthur Henderson, who in the previous general election had lost his seat at Newcastle East through a tacit Conservative–Liberal pact, was put forward as Labour candidate.

The seat was only moderately safe for Labour. In the 1923 general election, Labour had polled 16,848 votes, the Conservatives 14,197 and the Liberals a quite strong 13,543. The local Liberals were keen to contest the by-election and indeed had a candidate ready. The issue, however, was hardly this simple. The appearance of a Labour Cabinet Minister as candidate placed the Liberals in a difficult dilemma. At a time when the Parliamentary Liberal Party had only just voted Labour into power, and when Lloyd George in particular had visions of a lasting Labour–Liberal co-operation towards putting radical measures on the statute book, a vigorous Liberal by-election attack on Henderson, in a seat which Labour held only on a minority vote, was hardly good tactics.

Thus, after correspondence with headquarters, the Burnley Liberals were dissuaded from fielding a candidate. This decision only led to further complications, for while the bulk of the Liberal voters in Burnley could probably be expected to support Labour, the Liberal Executive was much more pro-Conservative (indeed, in municipal elections in the town a fair degree of tacit Conservative–Liberal agreement went on). Thus, somewhat petulantly, the Liberal Executive proclaimed a position of neutrality, and it was left to the Labour and Conservative candidates to woo the 13,500 Liberal votes.

To this extent, Henderson started at an advantage. From the beginning his campaign was almost a model of an orthodox, Nonconformist Liberal candidature. Indeed, in a Lancashire town where Nonconformity was as much a social-cum-political as a purely religious power, Henderson's election address was studded with quotations from the *Methodist Recorder* and the *Wesleyan Recorder*. (Henderson himself was, of course, a Nonconformist.) Not surprisingly, even *The Times* correspondent covering the by-election found that Henderson's campaign speeches could be endorsed by the average Asquithian and that the Labour candidature was 'the next best thing to a regulation Liberal'.[10]

The Conservative campaign, by contrast, was largely an emotional anti-Socialist attack centred on the dangers of a Labour Government. The editorials of the *Burnley Express* tried hard to depict Henderson as a harbinger of the Red Peril. The Labour Party was denounced as anti-Christian and in 'international alliance' with Soviet Russia, while Henderson was linked by association with the *Socialist Arbeiter Internationale*. It was hardly realistic tactics, considering the studied moderation of Henderson.

A minor sensation during the campaign, again causing consternation in the Liberal ranks, was a letter of support made public by Churchill to Camps, the Conservative candidate. Urging the Liberals in Burnley to support Camps, Churchill argued that 'no difference of principle' now separated Liberalism and Conservatism. Churchill's letter continued; 'All the great issues on which they quarrelled before the war have been settled by agreement... Differences exist, no doubt, of mood, of temperament, of degree. But they are not differences of fundamental principle.' It was a strange argument from a politician who two months earlier had been fighting a rival Conservative in the Leicester West constituency. In fact, Churchill's letter was more significant in indicating his own impatience to range himself under the Conservative banner, than in persuading the Liberal vote in Burnley to move right.

The outcome of the polls was a complete vindication of Henderson's tactics. Labour won with 24,571 votes to the 17,534 of the Conservative, a 7,037 majority and a swing to Labour of 5.4 per cent.

The significance of the result was seen by the *Westminster Gazette*. In an editorial headed 'Burnley and the Average Voter', the paper observed that the result indicated in no uncertain terms 'a clear indication of the willingness of the average Liberal to give the Labour Government a square deal'.

Equally, the lesson of the by-election was not lost on Labour organizers. The increased majority in the absence of a Liberal gave added support to the view that not only was the bulk of moderate Liberal opinion willing to give the new Labour Government a chance, but that it was the Liberal Party which had finally to be broken before Labour could really achieve power. Thus, at a time when Lloyd George was contemplating Liberal–Labour co-operation, the Labour hierarchy and organizers were thinking more and more of the destruction of the Liberal Party.

The rash of adoptions of Labour candidates in rural constituencies and in safe middle-class seats after Burnley was a reflection of this new determination. Among the unlikely constituencies in which Labour candidates were adopted within a few weeks of Burnley were Henley, St Marylebone and Bedford.[11]

Nor was the lesson of the by-election lost on, of all people, Lord Beaverbrook. Writing in the *Sunday Express* on 9 March 1924, under an article headed 'The Necessity for Liberalism', Beaverbrook warned that, if the Liberal Party went under, its voters, as in Burnley, would vote Labour. How many Burnleys, asked Beaverbrook, are there in England today? Clearly, there were too many for the Beaver who, despairing of his rather bizarre attempts to restore Liberalism in mid-1924, went off to Canada.

Beaverbrook, however, was not to leave for his native Canada before the outcome of the by-election which excited most interest and emotion of any in 1924 – the by-election in the Abbey division of Westminster.

Perhaps the most surprising aspect of the by-election in Abbey was that it surprised anyone. The constituency, like the adjacent St George's division which it rather resembled, was a rock-solid Tory stronghold whose main electoral interest in previous contests had taken the form of rival Conservative candidates.

After an unopposed election in Abbey in 1918, a by-election in August 1921 had produced both a strong Anti-Waste League candidate (R. V. K. Applin) and a Liberal to oppose J. S. Nicholson. Nicholson won, but Applin came an easy second with 34.9 per cent of the poll. In the 1922 general election, Nicholson found himself opposed by a token Labour candidature (the Liberals having abandoned the struggle) and yet another Independent Conservative. On this occasion Nicholson won easily, with over 75 per cent of the total poll.

Meanwhile St George's was also producing electoral fun and games. In a by-election in June 1921 in the division, an Anti-Waste League candidate (J. M. M. Erskine) had beaten a strong Conservative opponent in Sir Herbert Jessel. In the 1922 general election, Erskine went on to win against an official Conservative.

When considering the significance of the Abbey by-election, it is particularly important to remember the somewhat maverick electoral behaviour of both Westminster constituencies and their highly untypical electorates.

It was, perhaps, surprising that the Abbey constituency was so much a Tory playground, for the seat contained a considerable working-class element and much bad housing. Indeed, the *Daily Herald* had been running articles highlighting 'Wealthy Westminster's Housing Scandal'. *The Times* correspondent spoke quite rightly of 'a considerable working-class population' in such areas as the Vauxhall Bridge Road and Soho, together with the Covent Garden Market area and theatreland. The fact that Labour had only once put up a token fight in the constituency, taking 13.6 per cent of the poll in the 1922 general election, was due much more to the difficulties of maintaining any form of permanent organization in the seat than in getting support during a spirited by-election campaign. Certainly, in 1922 Labour had made only a token canvass.

In such a safe Conservative seat, it remained to be seen who would succeed in obtaining this plum nomination. Even before Churchill's announced intention to seek the nomination, there were indications that yet another internal Tory feud would mark the by-election. An independent Conservative–Democratic candidate, Lieutenant-Colonel George Parkinson, had already announced that he would stand and had opened up committee rooms in Shaftesbury Avenue. His candidature was certainly not entirely frivolous, having the support of such people as J. C. Gould MP together with some local backing.

From the start, rumours abounded that Churchill wanted to stand, indeed, that he had set his sights on the Abbey division as the official Conservative candidate. From this time on, considerable intrigue surrounded the selection of the candidate by the Westminster Abbey Constitutional Association. The possibility that Churchill would seek to stand in Abbey threw the Conservative leadership into something of turmoil. Baldwin himself was prepared to support Churchill's return to the Conservative fold, but, having talked it over with Austen Chamberlain, agreed that it was too early for Winston to come out as a Conservative with credit to himself. Baldwin's intention was to explain this to Churchill and offer to find him a safe Conservative seat later on – as Chamberlain observed 'when he will have been able to develop naturally his new line and make his entry into our ranks much easier than it would be today'.

Austen Chamberlain's fear, that Winston would try and rush his fences, was fulfilled completely. The exact dealings which Churchill had with the Abbey Constitutional Association are still difficult to determine. It seems the party chairman lobbied the officials of the association intensely on Churchill's behalf, with the result that Churchill was invited to address them on condition that he accepted their decision on a candidate as final. Churchill refused. The final decision by the association on their candidate was taken on Monday 3 March, at a private meeting in Caxton Hall. The meeting was far from unanimous. Eventually the association adopted Otho Nicholson, son of Colonel W. G. Nicholson, the MP for Petersfield, and nephew of the late Member. The only other candidate, John Gatti, received 70 votes to Nicholson's 353.[12]

This decision, which caused considerable acrimony in the association, ended Churchill's hopes of the nomination; but it did not end his interest. There were, to Churchill, considerable attractions in standing as an Independent. However, such colleagues as Edward Grigg, Viscount Grey and Sir Hamar Greenwood all attempted to persuade Churchill against this course, arguing that it was a premature action which might spell disaster.[13] Birkenhead, however, urged him on, as did Lords Wargrave and Burnham. The actual decision, by Churchill, to run as an Independent was partly brought on by Parkinson, the other Conservative rival. It would seem that Parkinson offered to withdraw only if Churchill would definitely stand. Parkinson offered Churchill 15 minutes to make up his mind. According to the *Daily Herald*: 'Mr Churchill then called up two of his friends on the telephone. One was Lord Birkenhead. He returned, struck his chest, and said "I stand. And now let's have a smoke."'

Meanwhile the likelihood of Churchill as a candidate had prompted the Labour Party on 5 March to decide to enter the field. The party chose Fenner Brockway, who in fact entered the contest with few illusions. As he confessed after the declaration of the poll: 'When I was invited to contest this seat, I asked what was the chance of success. I was told none. My purpose was not to gain the seat, but to take up Mr Churchill's challenge to Socialism.'[14]

The story of Liberal intervention in Abbey proved a typical example of indecision and uncertainty. At a meeting of the Abbey Liberal Executive, on 26 February, the Liberals chose Scott Duckers as their prospective candidate, but declared that they would contest the division only if

Churchill stood – a fairly illogical position, which did nothing to enhance their subsequent campaign.

The result of all this was that, when nominations closed on 11 March, the by-election had produced four contenders: Nicholson, Churchill, Brockway and Scott Duckers. During the campaign the main centre of attention was Churchill. Indeed, *The Times* correspondent referred to Churchill's campaign as 'a daily variety show'.

From the start of the campaign Churchill, vociferously assisted by Beaverbrook and Rothermere, appeared intent on exploiting internal party differences within the Conservative Party. Indeed, the amount of Liberal support Churchill received was negligible. The bulk of the Parliamentary Liberal Party opposed his candidature. His supporters included only a few Liberal MPs who formed a right-wing coterie within the party – such figures as Colonel England, J. S. Rankin and Austen Hopkinson – all of whom were to range themselves under the Constitutionalist banner in the 1924 general election.

On the Conservative side, however, Churchill's supporters were many. Balfour supported Churchill; the press lords were behind him; Birkenhead and the old Coalitionists were there. Neville Chamberlain noted in his diary the welcome of many backbenchers for Churchill's move.[15] Among leading backbenchers prominent in support of Churchill were Sir Philip Sassoon, Sir Arthur Bull, Rear-Admiral Sueter and Commander Burney. Lord Wargrave, in a supporting letter, flattered Churchill as 'the most brilliant recruit since Chamberlain'. It was all rather like the return of an exceptionally prodigal son.

Indeed, far too little emphasis has been given in accounts of Abbey to Churchill's local support. Churchill, at his adoption meeting, was proposed by John Gatti, the defeated candidate for the official Conservative nomination, and was seconded by Captain Lyon Thomson, a member of the Executive Committee of the Abbey Constitutional Association. Another influential local supporter was R. W. Granville Smith, the chairman of the Westminster Constitutional Association. Perhaps more significantly, Churchill had the enthusiastic support of Erskine, MP for St George's.

Against these, however, were those Conservatives who would have no truck with Churchill or any of his works. Leo Amery was among the front-runners here. As he bitterly observed of Churchill's candidature, it was a case of 'true to type'. Amery noted in his diary: 'Winston will desert his Liberal colleagues with the same swift decision that led him to climb over the railings and escape without Haldane and Le Mesurier 25 years ago.'[16]

During the campaign there were effectively only three candidates, for Scott Duckers proved to be a contender in name only. His was a ghost campaign, lacking organization, helpers, enthusiasm and certainly policy. It even lacked speakers. With Asquith ill, Duckers wrote on 12 March to Lloyd George asking him to speak during the campaign. Sylvester replied that Lloyd George had very heavy commitments and could not come.

Certainly, Lloyd George proved to be a man of few words during the by-election. Having refused to speak on Ducker's behalf, Lloyd George played no part in the by-election. As Grigg wrote to Bailey, Lloyd George was watching events, closely and suspiciously, to see if the by-election might lead to a revival of Coalitionism.[17]

Indeed, even apart from Lloyd George, nothing went right for Duckers. His manifesto declared that he was not a Socialist but was in agreement with the aspirations of Labour – hardly a winning battle-cry in Westminster. At the same time, Duckers attacked the 'military opportunism' of the Labour Government – again, not an effective weapon against Fenner Brockway. It was, perhaps, most galling of all that during the campaign no one took any notice of Duckers; Churchill claimed the fight was between himself and Fenner Brockway. Brockway claimed it was between himself and Nicholson. As Lloyd George appropriately remarked in his article on the inquest on Abbey, Scott Duckers had 'contributed nothing to the national need' – forgetting that, during the by-election, Lloyd George himself had contributed nothing to the Liberal need.

With passions in the Conservative ranks running so high, it needed only one spark to set alight a major conflagration. As Baldwin wrote to J. C. C. Davidson: '... this incursion of Churchill into Westminster has been a great worry. It is causing trouble in the Party, just as I thought we were pulling together again. Leading the Party is like driving pigs to market.'[18] On 14 March it seemed as if, perhaps, none of the pigs would ever arrive. Baldwin later recounted to Davidson his version of events:

Last Saturday I had a really worrying day. I got back tired and longing for bed soon after eleven on Friday night ... I found a letter which, mercifully, I opened. It contained a letter from Balfour to Winston wishing him success and a note saying he wouldn't send it if I objected. To leap into the car again and drive off to Carlton Gardens was the work of a moment. I stayed with him till after midnight. He was leaving for Cannes in the morning. We had a long and intimate talk and he consented without demur not to send the letter which I kept in my pocket.

Baldwin then slept peacefully, only to be rudely awakened in the morning:

Next morning I opened my *Times* in bed as is my custom and to my horror set eyes on a letter from Amery to Nicholson. I saw in a moment what that meant. By ten o'clock a letter came round from A. J. B. saying that Amery's letter had altered everything and that it wasn't fair, etc., and his letter ought to go to Winston but he was leaving at once and left me to do as I thought right.

About eleven, first communication from Austen: of course he was all over the place and if Balfour's letter was bottled up he would let fly! I found by lunch time that it was common knowledge that Balfour had written the letter and that I had it. I released it, as I was in honour bound to, after Amery's letter for which I was responsible technically, though I never dreamed he would be such a fool.

All this chaos in the Conservative hierarchy was, of course, music for Beaverbrook's ears. Even before these latest developments, Beaverbrook wrote a long letter to a friend giving his account of the Abbey election and of Baldwin in particular:

The Abbey Division of Westminster, which Churchill is contesting against an official Tory, has been another terrible hash-up on the part of the Conservatives. Most of the leaders of Conservatism wanted him back, but they had not the nerve, or the power, to thrust him on the local Conservative Association, which is supposed to choose the candidate. Now, whatever happens, there will be bad trouble. If Churchill gets in, he will return 'savaged' against the Conservatives. If he is beaten there will be all kinds of accusations of 'betrayal' against the Tory leaders.[19]

Beaverbrook continued:

The third possibility is, that the Socialist will slip in between the Official and the Independent Conservative Candidates. In that event the blame for the disaster will be placed upon Baldwin – and justly too. The Ex-Prime Minister is a very well-meaning man, but utterly unfit mentally for high command.

Meanwhile, Beaverbrook gave his friend his own version of Baldwin's conversation with Austen Chamberlain about Churchill's candidature:

The funny side of the position is, that after Baldwin had privately endorsed Churchill's candidature, he went down into the country to secure Austen Chamberlain's help and approval. Chamberlain has, of course, been 'coalescing' with Winston Churchill and Birkenhead for years – so Baldwin naturally counted on his warm approval. Instead of which Chamberlain was very frigid and said he would not support Churchill for Westminster until he repented in sackcloth and ashes for his Liberal past, and joined the Tories openly as a penitent convert. The Tory right was, of course, delighted with Austen Chamberlain's attitude and have reinstated him in favour – and *they* count most for the moment.

Beaverbrook's scorn at Baldwin and the course of Abbey was not confined to a private letter. In the *Sunday Express* on 16 March, Beaverbrook delivered a blistering attack. In an article entitled 'The Abbey Division – And Mr Baldwin', Beaverbrook attacked Baldwin's leadership as a 'terrible failure' and Nicholson as 'an unknown individual whose main qualification is that he is the late member's nephew'.

Thus, as the short campaign in Abbey drew to a close, the political temperature had risen to boiling-point. Even the normally fairly subdued *Times* correspondent, having observed Churchill being assailed by turnips in Covent Garden, referred to 'the most remarkable election known in Westminster since the Ballot Act did away with the hustings'. Nor did the Labour campaign lack its highlights, with Fenner Brockway canvassing St James's Palace and York House in search of Socialist votes, and with Oswald Mosley supporting his campaign.

The climax of the by-election in fact turned out to be the result itself. Even the announcement was dramatic. After a very close count, it appeared that Churchill had won: Beaverbrook's early edition of the *Evening Standard* on 20 March proclaimed 'Churchill Wins'. The announcement was premature. Nicholson was home, by the shortest of short heads 43 votes. The full result was:

Nicholson	8,187	*(35.9)*
Churchill	8,144	*(35.8)*
Brockway	6,156	*(27.0)*
Scott Duckers	291	*(1.3)*

Turnout, at 61.6 per cent, was easily the highest in the division at an inter-war election, comparing with 38.5 per cent in the 1921 by-election, 49.0 per cent in 1922 and 58.4 per cent in 1929.

Not surprisingly, the dramatic result in Abbey produced a welter of comment. Lloyd George, who had said nothing during the campaign, formed his own conclusions on the significance of the Abbey poll. In an article headed 'The Lessons of the Abbey Election' which appeared on 22 March in the *Daily Chronicle*, Lloyd George declared that, not only was the Liberal Party now impotent, but its power had been 'shattered and distributed in bits among the other parties'. Lloyd George went on to attack Scott Duckers as 'just the type of candidate who tars Liberalism with the Little England brush'. The next day Duckers rightly retorted that neither Lloyd George nor any other Liberal leader had made the slightest intimation on these lines during the campaign, and accused Lloyd George of starting 'a new campaign of jingo Imperialism'.

Aside from this personal argument, the real impact of Abbey on Lloyd George was to set him thinking again on the possibilities of a revived Coalition. To Lloyd George, Churchill's vote demonstrated the strength of anti-Socialist Liberalism. The bulk of the press agreed with this interpretation. As the *Observer* commented on 23 March, Liberalism had cut an abject figure, with the party 'going the way to be smashed to pieces at the next election'. All agreed the result was a particularly impressive advance for Labour.

Historians have, by and large, not disagreed with this interpretation. A right-wing verdict on the Abbey by-election has been given by Maurice Cowling. According to Cowling, 'the Abbey by-election demonstrated the strength of anti-Socialist Liberalism and the weakness of the Liberal Party'.[20] Though stated by contemporaries, and repeated by historians, this verdict is hardly justifiable. It is based on two quite erroneous assumptions: 1) that the size of Churchill's vote was due to Liberals voting for Churchill to demonstrate their anti-Socialist tendencies; 2) that the vote obtained by Scott Duckers was in any sense a meaningful Liberal poll.

Neither of these two factors stands up to examination. To begin with, if *every* Liberal who had cast a vote in the Abbey by-election of 1921 had voted for Churchill in March 1924, Churchill would have polled 2,500 votes. The great bulk of Churchill's votes must have been *Conservative* votes; to this extent, like Abbey in 1921 or St George's that same year, the by-election of 1924 was a demonstration of the unorthodox Toryism of the two constituencies, not a demonstration of the strength of anti-Socialist Liberalism.

Nor was Scott Duckers's vote a meaningful yardstick to gauge Liberal strength. As we have seen earlier, he only entered the contest to spite Churchill (which he did, since 291 Liberal votes would have seen Churchill home) and he hardly campaigned. This fact was recognised after the result. As J. A. Spender wrote in the *Westminster Gazette*: '... no one can suppose that an organised Liberal Party throwing its back into the fight as the other parties did would not have polled a very much larger number of votes than was recorded for Mr Scott Duckers.'[21] Nor was this merely pique on the part of the *Westminster Gazette*; as the paper had written earlier in the campaign, in many ways the only party that could be indifferent to the result was the Liberals.

This, in fact, leads on to the great paradox of Abbey. The by-election which had least to do with the fortunes of the Liberal Party produced most debate and despair about the party. The other by-elections, with very much more evidence of the state of the party, were almost ignored, their lessons not heeded.

The Abbey by-election also produced additional dissatisfaction at Asquith's leadership of the party. Even though, for part of the time, he had been incapacitated by illness, none the less, criticism by rank-and-file Liberals was mounting.[22] After Abbey, no by-election occurred until towards the end of May. Nothing happened in these weeks to revive the dreary fortunes of the Liberals. Meanwhile, Labour's considerable cause for optimism at the result in Abbey was reinforced by their good performance in the next by-election in the West Toxteth division of Liverpool. This city, like Birmingham, had been stony ground for Labour for many years. Until the Edge Hill by-election of 6 March 1923, Labour had not won a single parliamentary seat within the city. The old religious cleavage still tied the Protestant working class fairly solidly to Alderman Salvidge's well organized Tory machine.

Edge Hill, in 1923, had indicated a slight shifting in the position; now the West Toxteth by-election provided Labour with a second opportunity. For the Liberals – who had won two seats in Liverpool quite unexpectedly in December 1923 (in Wavertree and West Derby, the latter in the absence of a Labour candidate) – Edge Hill might also have seemed a useful testing-ground. Indeed, the Princess ward within the constituency had something of a Liberal vote.

However, the local Liberal Association viewed the by-election rather differently. No candidate was put forward and indeed the association actually recommended its supporters to vote Labour. This action enraged Salvidge, and was partly a factor in ensuring that there was no Conservative–Liberal co-operation in the 1924 general election in Liverpool.

Meanwhile a possible candidate for the Conservative nomination was again Churchill. Indeed, Churchill had addressed a meeting of the Liverpool Conservative Workingman's Association on 7 May at the instigation of Salvidge, the first Conservative meeting addressed by Churchill for 20 years. However, Churchill's Irish record virtually excluded him from consideration for West Toxteth, especially in view of the critical situation over the Ulster boundary. In the event, Tom White, a leading Orangeman and city councillor, was chosen.[23] The Conservative campaign was fought largely on religion and Ulster: Salvidge tried hard to keep the issue to the safeguarding of Ulster's boundaries. Supporting the Conservative candidate, the Liverpool Grand Master of the Orange Order pledged the support of his Orangemen if Ulster had to fight to resist any transfer of its territories in the boundary adjustment. Every effort was made to pull a full Orange vote for the Conservative. The Provincial Grand Secretary of the Liverpool Province of the Loyal Orange Lodges declared that it was 'the bounden duty' of all members to return 'their tried and trusted friend'.

Labour, as in Burnley, carefully wooed the Liberal vote, and Snowden's free-trade budget helped in this direction. In the event, Labour won the seat by 2,471 votes on a swing of 4.6 per cent. It proved another useful boost for Labour morale, with Labour organizers claiming to have finally captured the old Liberal vote.[24]

The following day, on 23 May, Labour's morale received a further strong boost from the result of the by-election in the Kelvingrove division of Glasgow. Kelvingrove, indeed, proved to be one of the most significant of the by-elections of 1924. Both the nature of the campaign, and indeed the result itself, foreshadowed the 1924 general election. The by-election was caused by the death of the sitting Conservative Member. In the elections of 1918 and 1922 the seat had been safely Conservative. Indeed, in 1922 Labour had not intervened, leaving a straight fight between Conservative and Liberal. However, Labour's sweeping successes in Glasgow in 1922 led Labour to contest the division in 1923. Labour's standard-bearer was Aitken Ferguson, a founder-member of the Clyde Workers' Committee, a prominent local Communist and a highly popular candidate within the ranks of the local party. However, the National Executive of the Labour Party refused to endorse his candidature, with the net result that he fought the election as an Independent Labour man.

The result was something of a sensation. The Conservative polled 11,025, Ferguson 10,021 and Grieve, the Liberal, 4,662. Labour, only 1,000 votes behind the Conservatives, welcomed the by-election as a chance to secure victory in a highly promising marginal seat. Ferguson was again nominated by his union, the boilermakers, but the Glasgow ILP strongly favoured Patrick Dollan, the leader of the Labour group on the city council. With strong support in the local party for Ferguson, Dollan withdrew to avoid an embarrassing split.[25]

The Liberal nominee was Sir John Pratt, whose campaign was financed adequately by Lloyd George. The decision to fight Kelvingrove was about the only decision the local Liberals did take during the course of the by-election. The campaign by the Liberals, whose range of policy resembled the stocks of Mother Hubbard's cupboard, was a disaster. As the Liberal admitted sadly after the result, the campaign had been virtually a plebiscite for or against Communism, in which his party had been on the sidelines.[26]

If, as in Abbey, the Liberal candidature was an also-ran, Labour also encountered difficulties caused by the Communist affiliations of their candidate. After Ben Shaw, the Secretary of the Scottish National Executive, had written to Egerton Wake, National Agent of the Labour Party, on 9 May urging that Ferguson be officially endorsed, the National Executive Committee had voted 14–5 in favour of endorsement on 16 May. However, events during the campaign caused second thoughts. An advertisement by the Communist Party appeared in the *Workers Weekly* (16 May) asking for money to finance Ferguson's campaign, and setting out a policy that was markedly more advanced than anything the Labour Government could approve. The result was that Arthur Henderson wrote to Wake urging the National Executive Committee to reconsider its attitude. In the event a peculiar compromise was reached in which endorsement was not withdrawn but no official support was given.

All this had little moderating effect on Ferguson. The *Times* correspondent wrote of 'the astounding boldness of his Communistic, revolutionary and confiscatory avowals'. Certainly, the tone of the campaign was heated and highly emotional. Ferguson happily called for the appointment of a trade unionist nominated by the TUC as Ambassador to Soviet Russia, while the Conservative, having no need of a Zinoviev letter, launched a full assault on the Red Threat and danger of revolution.

In the event the Conservatives retained the seat with an increased vote and an increased majority. The figures were: Conservative, 15,488; Labour, 11,167; Liberals, 1,372. The result was a Liberal disaster: as the *Glasgow Herald* remarked, the outcome was 'amazing evidence of the slump of Liberal stock'. And, as Grigg wrote to Bailey, the result was nothing less than a catastrophe for Sir John Pratt.[27]

Perhaps the result should have come as little surprise to Scottish Liberalism, for there had been persistent dreary accounts of the low morale of the party north of the Border during the spring of 1924.[28] Kelvingrove confirmed the worst of these forebodings. The by-election also fore-shadowed the outcome of the 1924 general election in Scotland, where, in an emotional campaign, the bulk of the Liberal vote which still remained in 1923 went over to the Conservatives in 1924. Or, expressed differently, by 1923 the rump of the former Scottish Liberal vote was already of a much more right-wing calibre than was general south of the Border.

After the disastrous performance at Kelvingrove, a further blow fell to the Liberals in the Oxford by-election, where a vacancy arose when the election of the sitting Liberal, Frank Gray, was declared null and void after a petition. Oxford, from 1918 onwards, presented a rather sensational electoral history. In the 'coupon' election the historian J. A. R. Marriott had romped home on the Coalition Conservative ticket with 70.7 per cent of the poll in a straight fight with a Liberal. In 1922 the tables had been completely overturned. The Liberal, Frank Gray, won in another straight fight with 59 per cent of the poll and a turnout of 83.8 per cent.

It was a sensational result. Partly, no doubt, it owed something to the dynamic, if eccentric, actions of Frank Gray, whose campaign tactics included blocking the exit from Oxford Station to prevent late (and predominantly Conservative) commuters from reaching the polls in time. Such other items as an individual birthday card to each elector eventually led to Gray's downfall on petition. Nonetheless, Liberal politics in Oxford were nothing if not colourful.[29]

There was much more, however, to Liberal strength in Oxford than Frank Gray's personal vivacity. Oxford was one of the few centres in the 1920s where the Liberals were entrenched at municipal elections. Of Oxford's four wards, the South ward was a Liberal monopoly, while the East was virtually so. Of the 108 councillors elected in Oxford during the years 1919–27, 60 were Liberal (55.6 per cent), 46 Conservative (42.6 per cent) and 2 Labour (1.8 per cent). It would, as can be seen, be quite wrong to attribute Gray's startling electoral victory to purely personal factors.

Certainly, Gray's 1922 victory left the Conservatives in the town demoralised. When the 1923 election campaign was announced, the party was without a candidate. Captain R. C. Bourne was hastily adopted, but Gray easily retained the seat.[30]

The unseating of Gray on petition upset this position rather radically. This time the Conservatives had readopted Bourne early in January; Labour, also, had decided to contest the division for the first time. It was now the Liberals who were on the defensive. Much of the subsequent campaign was occupied with debate over the abolition of the McKenna duties, with its local interest for Oxford.[31] The Liberal campaign rested almost entirely on trying to arouse a sympathy vote for the departed sitting Member. The Conservative machine, on a thorough canvass, estimated the result as Conservative, 12,400, with 12,000 against and 3,000 uncanvassed. It proved a fairly accurate forecast.

In the event, the Liberals lost the seat by 1,842 votes. The Conservatives took 10,079 votes (47.8 per cent), the Liberals 8,237 (39.1 per cent) and Labour 2,769 (13.1 per cent). The real significance of the result lay, not in the Conservative triumph, but in Labour's ability to take sufficient Liberal votes to deny them victory. Oxford proved to be the only Liberal by-election loss during the first Labour Government, but the lessons of the final three by-elections gave little encouragement to the Liberals.

A vacancy occurred in the safe Conservative seat of Lewes when the sitting Member, W. R. Campion, was appointed Governor of Western Australia. Here was a constituency, predominantly rural and with very little trade union working-class electorate, that would have seemed fertile Liberal territory. The very opposite was the case; no Liberal had contested the division since January 1910. At the three post-war elections, straight fights had ensued between Conservative and Labour, with the exception of 1918 when an Independent also took the field, polling 3.6 per cent of the vote.

With Liberal organization moribund, Labour had profited considerably, raising their share of the poll to 32 per cent in 1922 and 40.4 per cent in 1923. For the by-election on 9 July, Labour fielded the same candidate as in 1923, B. W. R. Hall. On this occasion the Liberals entered the battle. The result was little less than an insult to the party. Thirteen years without a candidate had its effect. The party came in a weak third, well behind Labour. The full result, compared to 1923, was:

1923			*By-Election*		
Conservative	9,474	*(59.6)*	Conservative	9,584	*(52.0)*
Labour	6,422	*(40.4)*	Labour	6,112	*(33.2)*
			Liberal	2,718	*(14.8)*

It was, as Cowling has written, a quite irrelevant Liberal vote.[32] Perhaps more significant for the political climate in the country was the success of the Conservative in actually increasing his vote, despite Liberal intervention

– as indeed had happened in Oxford despite Labour intervention. In line with the general trend, turnout at Lewes increased from 58.1 per cent in 1923 to 67.3 per cent in the by-election.

The penultimate by-election of the first Labour Government, in the Holland-with-Boston constituency, rather defies analysis. A Labour-held seat in a highly rural Nonconformist constituency was itself highly unusual; in the 1923 election, Labour won only five seats in which the proportion of the electorate engaged in agriculture exceeded 35 per cent. To add to the complication, the sitting Labour Member, W. S. Royce, had in pre-war days been a leading Conservative in the same division. It was Royce's death that occasioned the by-election. The results in Holland-with-Boston since 1918 had been as follows:

	1918			*1922*	
Labour	8,788	*(39.8)*	Labour	12,489	*(39.1)*
Conservative	7,718	*(35.0)*	Conservative	11,898	*(37.3)*
Liberal	5,557	*(25.2)*	Liberal	7,535	*(23.6)*

	1923	
Labour	15,697	*(54.1)*
Conservative	13,331	*(45.9)*

The Liberals, having polled almost a quarter of the votes in 1922, had somewhat surprisingly abandoned the contest in 1923. The fact that Royce received a letter of support from Mrs Margaret Wintringham, the Liberal MP in adjacent Louth, and that Labour stayed out of contesting Louth, was probably more than a coincidence. It is certainly reasonable to assume that Labour attracted a fair degree of Liberal support in 1923.

At the by-election on 31 July the Liberals intervened, with a strong candidate in R. P. Winfrey. Labour's standard-bearer was Hugh Dalton. After a very short time, considerable bitterness developed between the Liberals and Labour, with the Liberals indulging in an extremely emotional tirade against the evils of Communism and atheism with which they, like the Tories in Burnley and Kelvingrove, sought to identify Labour.[33] The result of the Holland by-election, producing the only Labour by-election loss of the Parliament, did nothing to improve Liberal–Labour relations. The full result was:

Conservative	12,907	*(39.6)*
Labour	12,101	*(37.1)*
Liberal	7,596	*(23.3)*

The result had little consolation for the Liberals, whose share of the vote was lower than in 1918 or 1922. With a new candidate who did not have Royce's special connection with the division, Labour had no cause to be too dejected.

Having had no joy from any other by-election, it seemed that the Liberals might at last enjoy a change of luck at Carmarthen, where a safe Liberal seat fell vacant owing to the resignation of the Rt Hon. E. J. Ellis-Griffith. After the various complications of rival Liberal candidates in 1922, together with an Agricultural candidate, the result in 1923 had been more of a return to the traditional order of things:

Liberal	12,988	*(45.1)*
Conservative	8,677	*(30.1)*
Labour	7,139	*(24.8)*

Probably the most interesting feature of the 1923 result was the strength of the Labour vote. It was an impressive first attempt with an unknown candidate imported at the eleventh hour from North Wales. For the by-election, the Liberals adopted Sir Alfred Mond who had lost his seat in Swansea West the previous December – not that this had dissuaded him from writing to Asquith suggesting he become Chancellor in the event of a Liberal Government being formed.

Mond, who was eventually to join the Conservative Party, effectively fought a conservative campaign in the Carmarthen by-election. His tactics consisted of a trenchant attack on the insidious dangers of Socialism – Lady Mond declaring that Socialism and Communism would be the downfall of the country – together with insistence on Liberalism as the 'safe middle course'.

For a radical Welsh rural constituency, the by-election was a witness to a changing world. Times had indeed changed when a Conservative candidate could speak to a packed meeting in the Nonconformist chapel at Pencader, and when Liberalism would fight as the 'safe party'. In the event, aided by some 225 cars on polling day (compared with 6 Labour cars and a motor-bike with sidecar), the Liberals retained the seat fairly easily.

Even so, the party had little comfort in the result. The Liberal majority, and the party share of the poll, were both down, if only marginally. Labour had most cause again for comfort, moving into second place and increasing its share of the poll from 24.8 per cent to 28.8 per cent. Carmarthen proved to be the last by-election before the advent of the Russian Treaty and the Campbell case brought the first MacDonald ministry to an end.

Diverse though these by-elections had been, in the political situation of 1924 these contests lend themselves to a very definite interpretation. The lesson of the by-elections for the Liberal Party should have been clear. In every contest the party had polled a worse vote than in 1923; this was true from such Liberal-held seats as Oxford and Carmarthen through to Kelvingrove. Where the party had intervened (as in Lewes) there had been little impact. Equally disturbing was the ability of Labour to deny the Liberals victory in Oxford and to advance in areas as diverse as Carmarthen or Abbey.

The by-elections had also revealed the Liberals as a party bereft of policy and leadership. The party had come very near to ridicule, with a local Liberal Association in one area urging supporters to vote Labour, while others campaigned on a Red Scare anti-Labour ticket. To cap it all, with Asquith almost impossibly supine, Lloyd George, irritated by a Labour adoption at Caernarvon and fascinated by Churchill's antics in Abbey, could think only of intrigue towards a new Coalition.

Beyond the poor – at times disastrous – showing of the Liberals goes a more fundamental meaning of these by-elections. Three factors combine to demonstrate that these by-elections in many ways foreshadowed the general election of 1924: the ability of Labour to increase its vote even in strongly entrenched Liberal areas (e.g. Carmarthen and Oxford); the ability of the Conservatives to rouse the electorate against the Socialist threat (as at Kelvingrove and Lewes); thirdly, and finally, the extent to which, long before the Russian Treaty and the Zinoviev letter, turnout was increasing and the campaigns becoming increasingly centred on the 'Bolshevist' nature of the Labour Party, even in such areas as Holland-with-Boston. It was significant that turnout *increased* in every by-election except for Burnley and Oxford. Even here, turnout was very high, at 82.4 per cent and 80.3 per cent respectively. Even though, no doubt, the course of events during the 1924 election campaign accentuated the difficulties facing a sorely tried Liberal Party, long before Campbell or Zinoviev, the writing was already on the wall.

Notes

1 For Rothermere's part in this campaign, see entry dated 2 March 1923 in Lord Bayford's diary, quoted in M. Cowling, *The impact of Labour, 1920–24* (1971) p. 257.
2 For the reluctance of the local Labour Party to contest the seat at all, see R. McKibbin, 'Labour: the evolution of a national party', unpublished DPhil thesis (Oxford, 1971) p. 410.
3 *Manchester Guardian*, 28 Feb, 1 Mar 1923.
4 McKibbin, 'Labour: the evolution of a national party', p. 273.
5 For examples of subsequent Conservative–Liberal co-operation in this and adjacent divisions, see *Yorkshire Post*, 13 Oct 1924.
6 Eastern Counties Liberal Federation, Minutes, Exec. Comm., 1 Oct 1923.
7 For two discussions on the significance of the 1923 general election, see M. Cowling, *The impact of Labour, 1920–24* (1971), and C. Cook, 'A stranger death of liberal England', in A. J. P. Taylor (ed.), *Lloyd George: Twelve essays* (1971).
8 *Dover and County Chronicle*, 8, 15 Mar 1924.
9 Gladstone Papers, BM Add. MSS 46,474/74, Donald Maclean to Herbert Gladstone.
10 *The Times*, 9, 14 Feb 1924.
11 *Daily Herald*, 4, 7, 8 Mar 1924.
12 *Westminster Gazette*, 4 Mar 1924.

13 See M. Cowling, *The impact of Labour, 1920–24*, p. 396. Others advising caution included Clementine Churchill. For support for Churchill, and the flavour of the campaign see M. Gilbert: *Winston S. Churchill, Vol 5, 1922–1939*, pp. 28–38 (1976).

14 *Daily Herald*, 21 Mar 1924.

15 Entry dated 17 Mar 1924 in Neville Chamberlain diary, quoted in M. Cowling, *The impact of Labour, 1920–24*, p. 396.

16 Entry dated 27 Feb 1924 in Leo Amery diary, quoted ibid., p. 398.

17 Altrincham Papers, Grigg to Bailey, 20 Mar 1924.

18 Quoted in K. Middlemas and J. Barnes, *Baldwin: a biography* (1969).

19 Beaverbrook Papers, Beaverbrook to Brisbane, Mar 1924.

20 M. Cowling, *The impact of Labour, 1920–24*, p. 396.

21 *Westminster Gazette*, 22 Mar 1924.

22 For examples of press criticism of Asquith's leadership at this time, see *Birmingham Post*, 24 Mar 1924, and *Newcastle Chronicle*, 24 Mar 1924.

23 For a useful account of this by-election, and of Liverpool politics during this period, see D. A. Roberts, 'Religion and Politics in Liverpool since 1900', unpublished MSc thesis (London, 1965) pp. 96–8.

24 *New Leader*, 30 May 1924; *Liverpool Post*, 23 May 1924.

25 For a detailed discussion of the campaign, see McKibbin, 'Labour: the evolution of a national party', pp. 333–5.

26 *Glasgow Herald*, 7 June 1924.

27 Altrincham Papers, Grigg to Bailey, 27 Mar 1924.

28 For the morale of Scottish Liberalism, see the letter from James Wood to Donald Maclean, 26 Apr 1924, in Gladstone Papers, BM Add. MSS 46, 474/87.

29 Much the most useful account of Oxford politics in this period is C. Fenby, *The Other Oxford* (1970). See also F. Gray, *Confessions of a Candidate* (1925).

30 Oxford Conservative Association, Minutes, Exec. Comm., 14 Nov 1923, 9 Jan 1924.

31 For an alarmist forecast of the increase in unemployment that the abolition of the McKenna duties would entail, see *Daily Telegraph*, 31 May 1924. For other aspects of the campaign, see 'Report on Oxford by-election', *Conservative Agents' Journal* (July 1924).

32 M. Cowling, *The impact of Labour, 1920–24*, p. 355.

33 See H. Dalton, *Call back yesterday* (1953) pp. 149–50.

Note: 1924 to 1931

Chris Cook and John Ramsden

The general election of 1924 returned Baldwin to power with an overwhelming majority. The Labour ranks could muster only 151 MPs; the Liberals managed a mere rump of 40. Against these, the Conservatives numbered 412, with an additional 7 Constitutionalists who voted consistently with the government in the lobbies.

Considering the massive realignment of seats and votes that had taken place in 1924, the by-elections in the first years of the new government displayed a fair degree of stability. It was not until the Stockport by-election of 17 September 1925 that Labour made its first gain from the Conservatives since the general election. During 1926 seats began to change hands more rapidly. Labour took Darlington from the Conservatives on 17 February 1926, East Ham North on 29 April and Hammersmith North a month later. Meanwhile the unhappy Liberal Party lost a by-election in the Combined English Universities seat to the Conservatives in March. The Liberals suffered additional humiliation when Commander J. M. Kenworthy, the sitting radical Liberal MP for Hull Central, joined the Labour Party. In the ensuing by-election Kenworthy was re-elected with 52.9 per cent of the poll, the Liberals taking a mere 9.5 per cent.

Two events in 1926 rather changed the political scene in Britain. The first was the defeat of the General Strike. The second was Asquith's retirement, in October, as leader of the Liberal Party. The accession of Lloyd George as leader of the Liberal Party brought a final attempt at the revival of the party. As so often when Lloyd George was involved, his old dynamism and energy brought a new sense of purpose. Within six months of his return, it seemed that at long last a real recovery was at hand. On 28 March 1927 the Liberals gained Southwark North from Labour. A series of by-election victories followed: Bosworth was won on 31 May 1927, Lancaster fell on 9 February 1928 and St Ives a month later. On 20 March 1929 Eddisbury fell to the Liberals, and the following day Holland-with-Boston was also gained. All these gains were from Conservatives and, with the partial exception of Bosworth, were in rural, agricultural areas. Had the

Liberals been able to follow up their initial victories in Southwark North and Bosworth with a gain in the Westbury by-election of June 1927 (which the Conservatives retained by a mere 149 votes), the revival might have gathered even further momentum.

As it was in the spring of 1928 optimism ran very high. Lord Rothermere wrote to Lloyd George on 10 April 1928: 'You are back to where the Liberal Party was at the election of 1923 ... In my opinion, an election today would give you just about the same number of followers.'[1] Rothermere continued: 'Continue as you are doing and I think you and I will agree ... that there is almost a certainty that the Liberals will be the second party in the next House. This would give you the Premiership beyond any question.' While Rothermere's political judgement does not have to be taken too seriously, nonetheless the Liberals were doing undeniably well, as the following figures indicate:[2]

*By-election Contests**

	No.	Average Conservative %	Labour %	Liberal %
May 1926–end 1927	10	37.9	33.6	28.5
Jan–Dec 1928	15	39.8	30.5	29.7
1929–General Election	5	33.6	44.6	21.8

* Three-party contests only

However, even at the height of Liberal success in 1928, Lloyd George himself realised that Liberal by-election victories would not necessarily mean gains at a general election. He wrote to Garvin of the *Observer* in October 1928: 'I have followed your analysis of the by-election figures. I am convinced that 'the triangle' will enable Labour to sweep the industrial constituencies next time.'[3] Lloyd George had written in similar vein to Philip Snowden: '... owing to the fact that Liberal and Labour candidates are fighting each other, there are 170 seats which will go to the Conservatives which in straight fights would have been either Labour or Liberal.'[4] Lloyd George's judgement was nearer the mark. Even armed with his sweeping land and unemployment policies, reinforced by Samuel's reorganization of the party, the Liberals could win only 59 seats in the 1929 general election.

As Lloyd George had foreseen, three-cornered contests had let Labour take no fewer than 287 seats. Indeed, even at the height of the Liberal resurgence, Labour was still gaining by-election victories. In February 1927 Labour gained Stourbridge from the Conservatives; in January 1927 Labour won Northampton, followed by Linlithgowshire in April, Halifax in July (a Liberal seat unopposed in 1924) and Ashton-under-Lyne in October. This last by-election attracted tremendous local interest and turnout reached

89.1 per cent, a record for any by-election. The result was announced to the waiting crowds by the firing of yellow rockets (Labour's colour in Ashton) from the roof of the Town Hall.[5]

Labour completed their successes prior to the 1929 general election by gaining three more seats early in 1929: Midlothian and North Peeblesshire (29 January), Battersea South (7 February) and North Lanarkshire (21 March), all from Conservatives. In all, the record of the parties at all by-elections between 1924 and 1929 was as follows:

Total by-elections: 63 (2 of these uncontested)
Candidates: 182 (Conservative 60; Labour 56; Liberal 59; Others 7)

Gains and losses (net):

Conservative   −15 (1 gain from Liberal, 11 losses to Labour, 5 losses
                          to Liberal)
Labour   +12 (11 gains from Conservative, 2 from Liberal, 1
                          loss to Liberal)
Liberal   +3 (2 losses to Labour, 1 to Conservative, 5 gains
                          from Conservative and 1 from Labour)

After the 1929 general election, Labour was again in office but not in power, for although it was the largest party in the House of Commons, it had no overall majority. As in 1923–4, the indecisive result of the general election meant that throughout Labour's time in office, great attention was paid to the results of by-elections (see above, pp. 37–57). If Labour could gain 20 seats over the life of the Parliament, they would reach an overall majority; if the Conservatives could gain 15 seats from Labour, they would be the largest party once again. Much more likely than either of these, the by-elections would show anxious politicians of all parties what the public were thinking. MacDonald's minority government, like the Labour Governments with unsafe majorities in 1924, 1950 and 1964, was looking keenly for the right moment to call another general election which would break the parliamentary deadlock. In the meantime there was a temptation to flirt with the Liberals in order to strengthen Labour's position at Westminster and at by-elections.

Early results, up to the end of 1929, appeared to give Labour grounds for hope: Labour candidates improved their position in every contest, and the parliamentary party ended the year with two more MPs than it had had immediately after the general election. But both these gains were technical rather than real. At Preston, W. A. Jowitt was re-elected after he had crossed over from the Liberals to Labour, but he had been elected originally on Labour votes as well as Liberal, and no Liberal opposed him at the by-election. At Liverpool Scotland the rarest of events occurred, when Labour actually gained the seat unopposed. T. P. O'Connor had held the seat as an Irish Nationalist since 1885, and after his death in 1929 he was succeeded by D. W. Logan, an official Labour candidate with strong Nationalist connections. Both Preston and Liverpool Scotland were seats where Labour was entering into its inheritance on becoming the major party of the Left – Irish and radical votes. Most such gains had already been made and there was small prospect of progress in this direction. Moreover, both Jowitt and O'Connor had already given regular support to Labour in the division lobbies, so neither gain made much parliamentary difference.

Labour's other early success was at Twickenham, and this too was complicated by special problems of interpretation. The Conservative candidate, Sir John Ferguson, was the herald of all the difficulties which the party was to suffer through its divisions over tariffs and the Empire. When he announced his conversion to Empire Free Trade, he was abandoned by Central Office and denounced by the party leaders. In the resulting confusion he almost lost a safe Conservative seat to Labour. Since the Liberal vote collapsed, it seems likely that many Liberals voted Labour to vote against tariffs. Twickenham was the forerunner of Bromley, Islington East, Paddington South and Westminster St George's, the by-elections which were to plague Baldwin well into 1931. This aspect is fully considered in Chapter 4. However, up to the end of 1929 Labour's record was good. In a more typical contest, at Tamworth, it had reduced the Conservative majority with a swing to Labour since the general election.

Baldwin's severe difficulties in 1930 and 1931 seem to have diverted attention away from Labour's increasingly serious plight. As the slump deepened and unemployment rose, Labour's performance at by-elections began to deteriorate; by 1931 it was doing as badly as any government since 1918. During 1930 and 1931 only one by-election registered a swing to Labour (Pontypridd, 0.5 per cent) while 20 showed a swing to the Conservatives. Many of these swings to the Conservatives were very large, and were more serious for MacDonald than for most Prime Ministers: as leader of a minority government, he had to regard *any* swing away as disastrous, for only a substantial swing to Labour would have justified him in calling a general election. Without a general election to provide a stable parliamentary majority, Labour could not take effective action to combat the economic crisis. Thus, the deterioration of the economy was both a cause of by-election results and was directly affected by them.[6] Different types of contest all showed Labour's poor performance. Where Scottish Nationalists or Communists intervened, Labour seemed to be affected more than proportionately. Even in straight fights with the Conservatives, Labour was suffering swings which, in a general election, would have put Baldwin securely back in Downing Street. The number of straight fights was in fact very small, and the pattern of interventions and withdrawals complicates any comparison with 1929. However, six of the constituencies which had by-elections in 1931 had had identical contests in the 1924 general election, and these six were a good cross-section of the electorate.[7] In 1924 the

Conservatives had polled 52.7 per cent of the Conservative–Labour vote in these constituencies; in the 1931 by-elections the Conservatives polled 53.7 per cent. Making allowances for interventions and withdrawals, the other by-elections of 1931 also show a pattern which is strikingly similar to that of 1924. It is clear that if Labour had been foolish enough to hold a general election in the summer of 1931, even as a united party, they would merely have returned the Conservatives to power with a large majority. This point is worth stressing because of the natural tendency to explain away the result of the 1931 general election as caused entirely by the events of the late summer, the economic crisis and the Labour split. It is undoubtedly true that Labour did much worse in November than it would have done in June, but only the scale of its defeat would have been different. Of course, without a Labour split and a National Government, there would have been no 1931 general election anyway.[8]

Perhaps because of the setbacks which the government was suffering in by-elections and in economic policy, there were negotiations for a Liberal–Labour pact. Labour would enact electoral reform, which could help only the Liberals, in return for a by-election pact and Liberal support at Westminster. Dark rumours of such a secret pact were certainly current in Conservative newspapers, and these were partly responsible for the Liberal splits in early 1931.[9] However, as an article in the *Conservative Agents' Journal* pointed out, such a 'squalid deal' might work at Westminster, but would never work in the constituencies,[10] Labour withdrew from the Scarborough and Whitby by-election in May 1931, and the Liberals almost gained the seat from the Conservatives. But when Liberals withdrew in favour of Labour candidates, they were unable to deliver the votes. Just as the Parliamentary Liberal Party was deeply split over the prospect of supporting Labour, so the Liberal voters were at least as likely to vote Conservative as Labour, if they were deprived of the chance to vote Liberal.[11] The last five contests of the 1929 Parliament illustrate the point:

Stroud:	Liberal at both elections, swing to Conservative 0.6%
Rutherglen:	Liberal and Communist withdrawal, swing to Conservative 6.5%
Gateshead:	Liberal withdrawal, swing to Conservative 13.9%
Manchester Ardwick:	no Liberal 1929 or 1931, swing to Conservative 9.8%
Liverpool Wavertree:	Liberal withdrawal, swing to Conservative 11.1%

If anything, then, the withdrawal of Liberal candidates actually harmed Labour; that is what had happened in the general election of 1924 and that was what was to happen in the general election of 1931. This effectively ruled out any real radical alliance for electoral purposes.

The freak results of the 1929–31 Parliament distort the total picture considerably: technically, Labour had lost four seats but had gained two and the Conservatives had gained four but lost one – an indecisive overall result. However, it does not require much analysis to show that this was misleading, and looking only at the seats which Labour lost to the Conservatives should have been enough. Fulham West and Sunderland would be won by the Conservatives only if they were doing better than Labour nationally, and Shipley had never been won by a Conservative before. Finally, Ashton-under-Lyne had actually been won by Labour in the run-up to the 1929 general election, but was regained by the Conservatives in April 1931. If gains and losses were to be the measurement of performance, then the message should have been clear.

Notes

1 Lloyd George MSS, Rothermere to Lloyd George, 10 Apr 1928.
2 D. E. Butler, *The electoral system in Britain since 1918*, 2nd edn (Oxford, 1963) p.181.
3 Lloyd George MSS, Lloyd George to Garvin, 31 Oct 1928.
4 Lloyd George MSS, Lloyd George to Snowden, 3 Oct 1928. Lloyd George estimated that, of these 170 seats, 108 would have been gained by Labour, 62 by Liberals.
5 F. W. S. Craig, *British parliamentary election statistics, 1918–1970*, 2nd edn (1971) p. 108.
6 This point is discussed on p. 182, in relation to 1964–6.
7 The six constituencies were: Woolwich East, Rutherglen and Manchester Ardwick (Labour-held), Salisbury and Stroud (Conservative-held) and Sunderland (Conservative gain). Doing as well as in 1924, or better, would suggest that the Conservatives were doing very well indeed.
8 Things were so bad by the summer of 1931 that it was recognized that an alliance with the Liberals was necessary if the government was to survive; see R. Skidelsky, *Politicians and the slump* (1967) p. 333. Skidelsky believes that the alliance with Lloyd George gave Labour cause for 'cautious optimism'. For an alternative view, see E. Shinwell, *Conflict without malice* (1955) p. 109.
9 The Liberal split is described in R. Douglas, *The history of the Liberal party, 1895–1970* (1971) pp. 208–32.
10 *Conservative Agents' Journal* (July 1931).
11 This refers to hard-core Liberal voters who could not be 'squeezed' in a three-party contest (see above, p. 31). If the Liberal candidate withdrew, they were faced with the same decision as marginal Liberal voters and seem to have reacted in the same way.

CHAPTER 4

St George's and the Empire Crusade

Gillian Peele

General Election, 1929	*(Electorate 53,914)*	
Worthington-Evans (Conservative)	22,448	*(78.1)*
Butler (Labour)	6,294	*(21.9)*
Conservative majority	16,154	Turnout 53.3%

By-Election, 19 March 1931	*(Electorate 54,156)*	
Cooper (Conservative)	17,242	*(59.9)*
Petter (Independent Conservative)	11,532	*(40.1)*
Conservative majority	5,710	Turnout 53.1%

General Election, 1931
Cooper (Conservative) Unopposed

General Election, 1935	*(Electorate 54,442)*	
Cooper (Conservative)	25,424	*(84.6)*
Freemantle (Labour)	4,643	*(15.4)*
Conservative majority	20,781	Turnout 55.2%

The St George's division of Westminster does not, at first sight, appear a likely setting for one of the most eagerly awaited by-elections of the inter-war years. Sedate and very prosperous, the constituency included within its boundaries many of London's most fashionable residential districts as well as Hyde Park and Buckingham Palace. Yet here, in March 1931 watched by the inhabitants of Mayfair and Knightsbridge, was conducted a bitter and abusive election campaign which commentators of the time believed would have an enormous impact on the course of political events. On the outcome of this by-election hung the future of Baldwin, the future of Indian constitutional advance and the future of the Empire Crusade. Today, when by-election results are generally interpreted as a verdict on the performance of the government, it may seem curious that the central issue of a by-election could have been the adequacy of the Leader of the Opposition. But that was clearly the case at St George's; in the absence of a government candidate (the Labour Party had contested the seat in 1929 for the first time and did not put up a candidate at the by-election), the electors had to choose between Alfred Duff Cooper, the nominee of the local Conservative Association, and Sir Ernest Petter, an Independent Conservative who was backed by the rudimentary Empire Crusade and United Empire Party organisations together with the Beaverbrook and Rothermere press.

It was evident from the beginning that the St George's contest would not be an ordinary by-election, and certainly by the time Petter entered the field everyone thought that this by-election would determine Baldwin's personal fate. In his first press statement the Independent Conservative put the issue thus:'My candidature is intended to be a definite challenge to Mr Baldwin's leadership of the Conservative Party.' Baldwin at one stage even considered taking up the Empire Free Traders' challenge directly by offering himself as a candidate in Westminster and, although he was dissuaded from such a course, this suggestion is some indication of how seriously the by-election was regarded at the time. Lord Beaverbrook had also staked a lot on the outcome of the confrontation. He threw himself into the fight in the belief that a victory in St George's would finally show Central Office that London was solidly in favour of a policy of Empire Free Trade and that Baldwin, with his equivocal position on this issue, would have to go. Opinions about the significance of the result when it was actually announced were somewhat less categorical than these prior speculations might lead us to believe. There is, however, a notable absence of any detailed treatment of the by-election either in terms of its immediate impact on the actors in the drama or in terms of its long-term significance for national politics. Admittedly, St George's did not pass into the political mythology of the 1930s in quite the same way as did East Fulham or Oxford; but it deserves a fuller account than it has hitherto received both because of its intrinsic interest and because of its place in the history of the Empire Free Trade movement.

It is, of course, possible to dismiss the whole Empire Crusade (to say nothing of Rothermere's United Empire Party) as an inherently mis-conceived venture, and it is perhaps a pity that a major contributor to our knowledge of the movement should take this view. [1] Empire Free Trade as expounded by Lord Beaverbrook demanded the creation of a single economic unit from the variety of territories within the British Empire. The argument was that the Dominions should provide all Britain's food while British industry could provide the rest of the Empire with the manufac-tured goods it required. All that was needed to put this plan into operation was a single protective tariff; but here the scheme ran into the old difficulties associated with food taxes as well as those associated with the new centrifu-gal forces which threatened the whole Imperial edifice. But such problems did not deter Beaverbrook. In 1930 he created a somewhat populist movement to convert the Conservative Party to his ideas, and he did not deny that, if the Conservatives proved recalcitrant, he was willing to split their party and possibly supersede it.

The contradictions discernible in the policy of the movement and the Empire Crusade's almost farcical electoral machine may thus lead one to conclude that this was nothing more than a frivolous interlude in Beaverbrook's career and in the pattern of British politics which, as for most of the twentieth century has been dominated by major parties. But if one's primary interest in the Empire Crusade is not because of its role in Beaverbrook's life, then it is possible to make a slightly different assessment. The structure of the country's politics was by no means fixed in the 1920s and 1930s. It was precisely at this time that a new party – especially one of the populist type – might have emerged as a major force on the barren scene of unemployment and economic distress.[2] Beaverbrook was very well placed to spearhead such a development – although to be successful it would obviously have had to construct a very much broader base than the Empire Crusade ever actually achieved; but it is by no means certain that it could not have done so. For what now seems remarkable about the Empire Crusade – and to a lesser extent about its uneasy ally the UEP – is the degree of electoral exposure and success which it obtained during its short life. This success cannot simply be attributed to Lord Beaverbrook's dynamic personality, nor be explained away as a perverse reaction by the electorate to a wholly freakish set of political factors. It will not, unfortunately, be possible to expand all these points at length in relation to St George's; nevertheless, the account of this by-election must be read not against the background of a political movement 'which seems in retrospect a trivial episode hardly worthy of record' but against the background of an embryonic attempt to refashion some elements of the Conservative Party into a new political alliance.[3]

The national background

The years 1929 to 1931 present a picture of mounting dissatisfaction with Baldwin's leadership of the Conservative Party. His inability to take a firm line on the issue of protection, his endorsement of the Labour Government's Indian policy and his general complacency all combined to fan the flames of dissatisfaction within the party. On the sidelines, Beaverbrook, Rothermere and, to some extent, Lloyd George were waiting to exploit the opportunity provided by Tory disarray to their own advantage. At Westminster the Labour Party rejoiced at the disunity which reigned on the opposition benches. Whether the promotion of Empire Free Trade – a slogan which touched a chord in Tory hearts both within and outside Parliament – or the pro-coalition manoeuvrings of some Conservatives was more dangerous to Baldwin's position than Churchill's marshalling of the diehard forces on the Indian issue is a matter for debate; together these rumblings threatened to destroy the Conservative Party and Baldwin with it.

The Tories had taken the defeat of 1929 very badly indeed. Criticisms of Baldwin's own role in the débâcle were to some extent deflected by the initiation of an investigation into the relationship between Central Office, the National Union and the leader of the party.[4] Investigations were also conducted at a local level, but here the constituency officials were determined that the blame for the events of May should not be laid upon the shoulders of the extra-parliamentary organization. Thus the Rochester and Chatham Constitutional Association, whose Member, Lieutenant-Colonel John Moore-Brabazon, had lost his seat at the general election, while admitting a 'certain want of cohesion and teamwork' at the local level, also mentioned 'the want of a couragous live Conservative policy and a lead from Conservative Headquarters, the delay in the issuing of the Prime Minister's Appeal to the Electors and the general apathy in the Party'.[5] The first few months in opposition are usually difficult for Conservative leaders, but the second half of 1929 was particularly troublesome for Baldwin. Beaverbrook's own campaign opened with an article in the *Sunday Express* in June, while the espousal of the doctrine of Empire Free Trade by the candidate at the Twickenham by-election set a pattern which was to be repeated in the following two years. Central Office withdrew its support from the heretic; he nevertheless held the seat - albeit with a much-reduced majority – after several prominent Conservative MPs added their encouragement to that given by Beaverbrook. Then, in October, Baldwin was hurled into another crisis by the Irwin declaration which promised India Dominion status.[6] The year culminated with the conversion of Beaverbrook's personal adherence to a policy of protective tariffs into a mass appeal for funds for a new political movement.

Baldwin's stock had thus been steadily falling throughout the latter half of 1929, but in 1930 it plunged to perhaps its lowest level ever. By March, J. C. C. Davidson (who remained the chairman of the party until the middle of the year) was already seriously worried by the Empire Crusade – as Beaverbrook's new movement had christened itself. Although he attested to the stability of the Conservative machine at the top, he thought that this was very like a pie-crust, for, as he said, 'the rank and file were seething with uncertainty and unrest underneath'.[7] The protracted negotiations of the Round Table Conference enabled Baldwin to keep the Indian problem at arm's length for much of 1930, despite the formation of a new back-bench committee to keep a watch on the situation and of an Indian Empire Society strongly opposed to any constitutional advance for India beyond the proposals of the Simon Commission. But twice in 1930 Baldwin had to submit himself to what amounted to votes of confidence in his leadership of the party. The second of these party meetings coincided with the first independent electoral success of the Empire Crusade; in a by-election in Paddington South in October, Admiral Taylor beat the official Conservative nominee Sir Herbert Lidiard, after a good deal of wrangling between Central Office and the local association.

This victory gave the Empire Crusade movement further electoral impetus, and at the beginning of 1931 Beaverbrook confessed to Rothermere that their tactics for 1931 should be to fight all possible by-elections. Rothermere agreed with this strategy although he differed from Beaverbrook in believing that India was 'far more vital to the British Empire than Empire Trade'.[8] The diehard camp in fact received a boost to their morale when Churchill finally resigned from the Opposition Business Committee over the tenor of Indian policy, but Beaverbrook, who had originally refused Churchill's plea for them to join forces,[9] only allowed the Empire Crusade to exploit this issue at Rothermere's insistence.[10] Beaverbrook was later to regret this submission to Rothermere's wishes.

An Empire Crusade and United Empire Party candidate entered the contest at Islington East – which was due to poll in mid-February 1931 – while Beaverbrook and Rothermere began to plan intervention in other by-elections and to choose suitable candidates to carry their banner in the event of a general election. On 8 January 1931 F. W. Doidge, the former financial director of the *Daily Express* and the chief organizer of the Empire Crusade, reported that it was unquestionably the intention of the local branch of the United Empire Party to put up a candidate against the former Secretary of State for War, Sir Laming Worthington-Evans, in the St George's division of Westminster. Beaverbrook thought that Keith Erskine, the son of the constituency's former Member, would make the best candidate in that situation. These speculations were given vital significance when, early in the morning of 14 February 1931, Sir Laming Worthington-Evans suddenly died. The Crusaders and the United Empire Party had another London seat to contest.

The constituency

The constituency of St George's covered an area of 1479 acres bounded by the Bayswater Road and Oxford Street to the north and by the Thames to the south. The constituency was divided into five wards which differed in both size and social composition. Victoria – the most populous of the five – was by far the poorest ward; the other wards Conduit, Hamlet of Knightsbridge, Knightsbridge St George's and Grosvenor – were nearer to each other in their socio-economic characteristics, but they too revealed differences in terms of wealth and political organization. The outstanding feature of the St George's electorate, however, was the high proportion of women it possessed. 61.4 per cent of the total of 54,156 voters were women – a number rivalled only in five other London constituencies: St Marylebone (61.1 per cent), Paddington South (61.7 per cent), Peckham (62.2 per cent), Hampstead (62.4 per cent) and Kensington South with the astonishingly high total of 69.0 per cent. Many of these women would, of course, be domestic servants 'working below stairs' in the homes of the upper-middle classes, and some of them would only have received the vote in 1928. This factor – together with the safeness of the seat – may go a long way to explain the relatively low turnout which St George's experienced even at general elections.

The local Conservative Association benefited from the opulence of the constituency, and its annual income of £2000 made it self-supporting. It was therefore able to make a relatively generous grant towards the poorer London constituencies – a fact which pleased Central Office but which was not altogether to Worthington-Evans's liking when he was asked to make an annual donation of £300 to the constituency coffers. In the end Worthington-Evans was allowed to give only £100 a year because, as he argued, the tendency to rely on the Member for money was not only 'vicious and pernicious' in itself but also had the effect of encouraging sloth in the local party.'[11] Yet although the organization was healthy and although the character of the constituency was overwhelmingly Conservative, this did not mean that there was always unanimity in St George's. Indeed, its electoral record reveals a surprising pattern of independent behaviour. James Erskine, the division's Member from 1921 to 1929, had been elected at a by-election with the support of the Hanover Square Conservative Association and the Anti-Waste League, despite the fact that the official Conservative candidate was Sir Herbert Jessel. Anti-Semitism was thought to have lost the election for Jessel, but when the former Chief Whip, Leslie Wilson, contested the seat at the general election of 1922, he too was defeated by Erskine. Eventually Erskine's position was accepted and he was returned unopposed in 1923 and 1924, while the two rival Conservative associations which were survivals of the 1918 redistribution were amalgamated in 1924. The fact that Erskine was returned unopposed in 1923 and 1924, and the proximity of the constituency to Whitehall and Westminster, made the seat an ideal one for a busy Cabinet Minister, especially given the failing health of Sir Laming Worthington-Evans. Erskine was induced to retire, was knighted in 1929 and was replaced by the Secretary of State for War. The latter's death after representing St George's for less than 20 months meant that a new official Conservative representative would have to be found.

Preparing the ground: the candidates emerge – and recede

When Worthington-Evans died, the campaign in Islington East was still going on. Beaverbrook was naturally anxious to announce the Crusaders' intention of fighting the St George's vacancy before Islington East polled in order to make as much electoral capital as possible from the development. He accordingly telegraphed to Rothermere to ask for authority to make a statement on St George's, and Rothermere replied on 16 February that the decision should be made public on Wednesday (18 February) if Worthington-Evans's funeral had by then taken place. Rothermere also told Beaverbrook that a deputation of the United Empire Party and the Empire Crusade was approaching Esmond Harmsworth to see if he would stand as a candidate at St George's. Beaverbrook still thought that Keith Erskine might be the best man for his purposes, but felt that the Empire Crusade could announce its intention to fight the seat without committing itself to any particular candidate. Thus, when a member of the audience at an election meeting in Islington East on Wednesday asked whether Lord Beaverbrook intended to fight in St George's, Beaverbrook was able to reply that he would.

On the same day that Lord Beaverbrook was addressing the Empire Crusade meeting in Islington East, the St George's Conservative Association convened a special meeting of the executive committee to convey its sympathy to Lady Worthington-Evans and to set in motion the machinery for selecting a new candidate. Although the committee could not have known it at the time, the selection process was to be one of the most sensational aspects of the by-election and its difficulties alone were almost to oust Baldwin from the leadership. A selection committee was appointed in the normal way and its members – the officers of the association together with five other powerful figures on the committee, including Lord Howe and Lord Jessel (the former contender for the seat) – began their task of sifting through the list of aspirants for one of the safest constituencies in the country.

Five days later the selection committee met again and Brigadier-General Cooper, the chairman of the association, related the rather surprising details of a meeting he had had with Erskine, the ex-Member. Erskine had apparently intimated that he was willing to be considered for the vacancy, but this was not an offer which the selection committee was likely to welcome without qualification. It was agreed, however, that Erskine should be interviewed again and the committee decided in principle to recommend three names to the executive committee for the final process of selection. Among the list of possible candidates at this stage were Geoffrey Ellis, Sir Edward Grigg (a former Liberal who had served as Lloyd George's secretary), Sir William Ray (a prominent member of the LCC) and Lieutenant-Colonel Moore-Brabazon (a former junior Minister and a distinguished pilot).[12]

Islington East had polled on 19 February and the result had been a disaster for Central Office and something of a triumph for the Rothermere–Beaverbrook axis. Although Brigadier-General Critchley, the

Press Lords' candidate, had not actually captured the seat, he had pushed the official Conservative into third place. The Labour winner, as *The Times* was quick to point out, owed her seat to the fact that the Tory vote had been split. This added a certain edge to the selection proceedings in St George's because it was vital to find a first-rate candidate who could rally loyal Conservatives in the constituency against the Empire Crusade. On Wednesday 25 February the selection committee interviewed the potential runners with great care. As a result of the ballot taken after the interviews, it was decided to submit the names of Moore-Brabazon, Grigg and Ray to the executive committee. Sir James Erskine's name was then added despite the fact that his bid for his old seat seemed likely to put the association in an embarrassing position.

No news of the events in St George's was at this stage given to the press, but two other developments on that Wednesday brought St George's close to the centre of the political stage. In the evening the local branch of the UEP resolved to put forward its own candidate at the by-election (there was no local Empire Crusade organization in the constituency until after the by-election) and, although there were rumours that Brigadier-General Critchley would be asked to stand, Ward Price, an associate of Rother-mere's, was chosen.[13] More important, however, from the national viewpoint was the memorandum which Robert Topping, the Principal Agent of the Conservative Party, was preparing to send to Neville Chamberlain.[14] This document was a strongly worded condemnation of Baldwin's handling of Conservative policy and expressed the view that a broad section of opinion in the party now felt sure that it was time for Baldwin to go. Neville Chamberlain was placed in a difficult situation by the memorandum because his position as Baldwin's heir-apparent seriously curtailed his room for manoeuvre as party chairman. The loyalty which the chairman always owes to a leader, together with this delicate personal factor, meant that Neville Chamberlain could not precipitate Baldwin's departure. Baldwin himself knew nothing of the memorandum and Chamberlain resolved to keep its contents from him at least until the Newton Abbot speech – scheduled for 6 March – had been delivered. But Chamberlain's hand was to be forced by the news from St George's.

Until almost the end of February the only candidate to have emerged was Ward Price. On 27 February the scene was radically transformed when Lord Beaverbrook and Lord Rothermere managed to persuade Sir Ernest Petter, the chairman of an engineering firm and a former candidate in Bristol North for both Sir Henry Page Croft's National Party and for the Conservative Party, to stand as an Independent Conservative. In his election address Sir Ernest Petter threw down an explicit challenge to Baldwin's leadership, to the Conservative Party for its mishandling of the tariff issue, and to the moderate consensus on Indian affairs. The message on Baldwin was clear: 'I believe the continuance of Mr Baldwin as leader of the Conservative Party is fraught with great mischief to the party and to the nation.' Baldwin, according to Sir Ernest Petter, had failed to take any action to avert the ruin of British agriculture when what was needed was an extension of protection to agriculture and the restoration of British arable farming. As far as India was concerned, it was the duty of the Conservative Party to be 'the jealous guardian' of the 'splendid and beneficent rule' which the British had exercised in India for over 150 years. Suggestions that the Beaverbrook–Rothermere alliance intended to break up the Conservative Party had abounded in the press in recent months. But, said Sir Ernest Petter: 'It is not my aim or desire to disrupt the Conservative Party, which I believe to be the only agency which, under God, can avert disaster to our country. It is only my profound conviction that under its present leadership that mission will not be fulfilled which induces me to come forward at this time.'

In his press statement, which reached the morning papers on Saturday 28 February, Sir Ernest Petter claimed that he was standing as the candidate of neither the Empire Crusade nor the United Empire Party but simply as an Independent Conservative. He had, according to a number of newspapers, decided to come forward at the request of a number of electors. This explanation of Sir Ernest Petter's candidature and the ostensible independence which was claimed from the Press Lords was certainly a twisted version of the truth. Although the Beaverbrook and Rothermere press announced the decision to support Sir Ernest Petter after he had published his election address, the address itself had been scrutinized by Beaverbrook and some minor amendments made before publication. Moreover, Beaverbrook had planned the 'request' from the electors (who included such friends as Viscountess Chaplin and G. H. Pinckard, the owner of the *Saturday Review*) partly as a means of bringing pressure on Sir Ernest Petter himself and partly perhaps to create the impression of a spontaneous anti-Baldwin movement arising in the constituency.

It had been necessary to bring some pressure to bear on Sir Ernest Petter because he was not at all convinced that he wanted to become involved in a campaign run by what he, like Baldwin, called the 'gutter press'.[15] Yet he had been a lifelong supporter of protection and was seriously worried by the policy which the Labour Government, with Baldwin's support, was pursuing with regard to India. He delayed a decision by reserving the right to withdraw his offer to stand right up until six o'clock on the evening of 27 February. Beaverbrook, who made a secret arrangement with Sir Ernest Petter to pay all his election expenses, put the position to Rothermere thus: 'Petter has reserved the right to decline at 6 o'clock this evening. I think his brother will urge him not to stand. I am told Petter is meeting his brother this afternoon. Even if he decides on his brother's advice not to stand, I think he can be persuaded to come in, with a little assistance.'[16] Eventually Beaverbrook's view prevailed over that of Sir Ernest

Petter's twin brother, and the election agent (who had been Admiral Taylor's agent in Paddington South) rushed the election address to the Press Association.

In many ways, Beaverbrook regretted that Baldwin's personality and India rather than Empire Free Trade had become the dominant issues involved in the St George's challenge. But the news of Sir Ernest Petter's intervention was made all the more sensational by the immediate effect which it had on the aspirants for the official Conservative nomination. By this stage Moore-Brabazon was the favourite in the St. George's election stakes, but when he heard that Petter was going to stand on a platform which made it inevitable that any officially backed Tory would have to defend Baldwin's record, he withdrew his name from the list. Moore-Brabazon had been informed of the possibility that Petter would stand and he frantically tried to get in touch with Beaverbrook on 27 February. Three telephone calls to Stornoway House were unsuccessful and it is not clear whether Moore-Brabazon finally made his decision after an interview with Beaverbrook early on the morning of 28 February or whether he had relied simply on his own judgement and the information in the morning newspapers.

Moore-Brabazon's decision was made public in time for it to reach the Saturday evening newspapers and came as a bombshell to Central Office and to Baldwin. It was particularly embarrassing for the Tory leader because Moore-Brabazon had served in Baldwin's government and was no back-woodsman. The reasons for the sudden withdrawal could not be kept secret, and indeed the letter which Moore-Brabazon had sent to the chairman of the St George's Conservative Association made them plain:

> Since I came before you as a potential candidate to fight the cause of Conservatism in the division, there has appeared an independent with similar views to our own, but who questions openly the wisdom of continuing the present leadership of Mr Baldwin. I expressed at the time my misgivings on this matter but hoped that these differences might have been kept within the party to be arranged by ourselves. It is to be otherwise and these questions are now to be matters of public controversy. It will therefore come as no surprise to you to hear from me that I must withdraw my name from the list of candidates, as I cannot allow myself to be manoeuvred into pleading a cause I have not wholly at heart.[17]

Chamberlain realized that he could delay the confrontation with Baldwin no longer; he accordingly made some slight amendments to the Topping memorandum and sent it to Baldwin by hand on Sunday morning. Baldwin was initially prepared to accept retirement, but after consultation with his closest political allies he decided to stay and fight –

although the suggestion that he might contest St George's himself was quickly scotched.[18]

On Monday 2 March the St George's Conservative Association – unaware of the weekend manoeuvrings at Central Office – met to discuss the new situation created by Moore-Brabazon's action. The selection proceedings had been thrown into chaos, for not only had the favourite disappeared from the race but the second favourite – Sir William Ray – also looked as though he might withdraw from the list. Although Ray had in fact denied that he was about to follow Moore-Brabazon's example, he had expressed the opinion that the association should examine the position afresh and that, if necessary, he was willing to stand aside. It was clear that Ray did not particularly relish the idea of a fight on the issue of the leadership, and Beaverbrook later undertook to pay £250 towards his election expenses if he secured the nomination in the Wirral.[19] Sir Edward Grigg and Sir James Erskine, the other contenders for the St George's nomination, were no more comforting to the association than Sir William Ray. Sir Edward Grigg's political record would hardly have made him popular in St George's and he was in any case much more concerned at the time with the cause of 'Liberal–Unionist' unity.[20] It therefore came as no surprise when he made a statement to the effect that he would be unlikely to respond to an invitation to stand as the official Conservative candidate in the by-election. Thus the St George's Conservatives were in danger of being left with Sir James Erskine as the only available candidate. Central Office could not, of course, allow this to happen – for Sir James Erskine shared many of the views expressed by Sir Ernest Petter. Indeed, the former Member for St George's had been approached at an earlier stage with a request that he should contest the seat for the Empire Crusade. The suggestion had, however, been vetoed by Sir James Parr, one of Beaverbrook's collaborators in the Crusade organization, who commented on it thus:

> Yesterday some of my Crusader friends in the George electorate (late Worthington-Evans) came to see me and asked me to use my influence with you in favour of Sir James Erskine as a suitable crusade candidate. But I confess I am not impressed a bit with Erskine. He looks rather too elderly and 'moth-eaten'. Why not a younger and more striking personality with some 'ginger'![21]

The St George's Conservative Association could really do nothing but postpone the recommendation of any names at all, and the selection committee duly agreed to do this. Sir James Erskine was intensely irritated by the delay because the time would be used for consultations with Central Office on the choice of a candidate able to fight on the leadership issue; such was the tension in St George's that it did not seem at all strange when

Erskine communicated his anger to the press as well as to the chairman of the association.

Speculation about possible surprise candidates was rampant during the early part of that week and, although Beaverbrook did his best to find out who had taken up the challenge to Baldwin, he was unable to do so. Finally, the St George's Conservative Association learned on Thursday that Alfred Duff Cooper had volunteered to give up the safe seat which he was nursing to try his luck in London.[22] Naturally Sir James Erskine was furious at the news; his hopes of regaining his old seat faded with the appearance of a much younger man who had the advantage both of a distinguished war record and of having been Financial Secretary under Worthington-Evans in the late Baldwin administration. (Nor could Beaverbrook have been pleased by the choice: he was a close friend of Duff Cooper's wife – a daughter of the Duke of Rutland – and the godfather of the candidate's small son.) Nevertheless, Erskine insisted that he was still a candidate for the nomination and both he and Duff Cooper came to meet the executive committee of the St George's Association.

By this time some of the committee had become exasperated by the proceedings in the constituency. At the meeting which had been called to interview the two candidates for the nomination, one member withdrew before the ballot because he favoured 'an altogether different course of action'; while another resigned from the committee after Duff Cooper had received an overwhelming majority of the votes because he felt 'a little out of harmony with the decision of the committee'.[23] Perhaps some members resented the interference from Central Office; indeed, the resolution passed by the Association may have protested too much, for it described the selection thus: 'The Executive Committee most emphatically repudiates the suggestion in some sections of the press that any pressure had been brought to bear upon the Executive Committee, or any names suggested in order to influence its choice.' This did not convince the dissenters within the association and it did not convince Sir James Erskine. He had already made a strong attack on Baldwin's leadership before the committee which interviewed him, but at a general meeting of the association held on Friday 6 March to adopt Duff Cooper formally, he claimed that if the association had chosen him as its candidate there would have been no opposition at the by-election. Even if Erskine believed this himself, however, it was clearly not believed by the association, which gave a warm reception to Duff Cooper. Thereafter Erskine's support went to Petter.

In his address to the association, Duff Cooper commended Baldwin's handling of the Indian problem but skilfully identified neither India nor Empire Free Trade as the main issue to be decided by the election. Instead he focused attention on the Conservative Party's right to change its leader in its own way and its own time and on the attempt by the Press Lords to dictate to the party's members. This move was a very shrewd one because a campaign based on the actual efficacy of Baldwin's leadership might have been somewhat shaky. By turning the question into one of principle, Cooper had cast Beaverbrook and Rothermere in the role of evil and insolent conspirators whose presence on the political stage was a threat to the integrity of British public life.

As the constituency prepared itself for a campaign in what, as Lady Diana Cooper put it, was to be 'no baby- or butcherkissing election', Baldwin's personal fortunes began to look up a little.[24] News of the Irwin–Gandhi agreement reached England on the morning of 4 March and this had proved an 'absolute godsend' for the Tory leader. Several senior members of the party scented a change in the mood of the rank and file, and Baldwin's Newton Abbot speech of 6 March was both an attempt to build on the foundation of the good news from India and a vigorous assertion of his determination to retain the leadership. This strategy was not altogether successful and Baldwin's enemies interpreted a part of the speech to mean that future sessions of the Round Table Conference would be held in India. The party's India Committee held a tense, angry meeting and Baldwin mishandled the situation by allowing its hostile resolution to be given to the press. The resolution (which welcomed Baldwin's decision not to allow the Conservative Party to be represented at any future conference in India) was seen as a triumph for the diehards; the only reason why this mistake did not injure Baldwin more seriously was that by 11 March the campaign had opened in St George's, and press and public alike became absorbed with the affairs of the constituency.

The campaign: 'Mayfair goes mad'

In her autobiography, Lady Diana Cooper said that the St George's by-election was more reminiscent of an election in one of Disraeli's novels than of any of the contests she had experienced in the twentieth century.[25] The novelty of a contested election and the extent of the coverage given to the event in the national press added to the excitement. Open-air meetings proved ill-suited to the constituency and it soon became clear that the messages of the rival candidates would have to be spread by the traditional house-to-house canvass. This had its amusing side in an area inhabited by large numbers of the aristocracy as well as by some fifty Conservative MPs. Lady Diana recorded that 'after the hurly-burly' of an evening's canvassing, the following would occur: '... some greater or lesser house, the London-derry's or Juliet Duffs or Portia Stanley's would spread an open supper table with hot soup and restoratives for the fighting men and women.' Beaverbrook's office memoranda, on the other hand, are filled with notes such as: 'Please note Sir Harry McGowan will vote for Petter.' The fact that Beaverbrook was a friend of Lady Diana's (she recorded that she was in touch with 'the enemy' throughout the campaign) meant that the pro-Petter press did not spend all its time trying to vilify Duff Cooper, although the *Daily Mail* insisted on referring to the Tory candidate as 'Mickey Mouse'. Nevertheless, there were plenty of opportunities for both sides to fling verbal mud. Rothermere and Beaverbrook were described as an 'insolent plutocracy' by Baldwin, who excelled himself in eloquence during the campaign. The unfortunate Petter was labelled by Duff Cooper as 'the marionette and puppet of the Press'. The Rothermere press tried hard to make capital out of Cooper's attendance at an Independent Labour Party summer school in 1927 and constantly accused him of being a 'political softy' with no Imperial sentiment. The most ludicrous of these assertions had come before the opening of the campaign proper, when Lord Rothermere – apparently ill-versed in the English language – had charged Cooper with a lack of patriotism because he had delivered a lecture in Germany entitled 'An Apology for the British Empire'.

Petter's speeches in the campaign were generally rather weak and his presence at election meetings was usually overshadowed by that of Lord Beaverbrook, who addressed audiences in the constituency every evening before polling day. Sometimes Petter and Beaverbrook would conduct their meetings in separate halls at different ends of St George's and then – at a prearranged time – would jump quickly into cars and cross to the other's meeting. The unfortunate chairman who was expected to maintain order while the transfer of speakers was effected would frequently be besieged by Cooper supporters so that Petter or Beaverbrook – when they eventually arrived – would have to retake the platform by force.[26] But where Sir Ernest Petter emphasized India and the need to remove Baldwin, Beaverbrook hammered home his own theme of Empire Free Trade. Even India he managed to present as an economic issue:

> Mr Baldwin announcing his policy at Newton Abbot the other day said that his object is the prohibition of unfair discrimination against British trade. That is not the policy of the Empire Crusader. No, the policy of the Empire Crusader is an advantage in the Indian market for English trade. For India is an economic issue in any case. Give prosperity to India and at once you give a desire for ordered government. With desire for ordered government all this agitation comes to an end. Empire Free Trade will bring prosperity to India as well as to every other part of the British Empire.

It was difficult to tell whether this was really Beaverbrook's considered opinion of the Indian problem or whether it was simply a way of exploiting the maximum personal advantage from a topic which his allies had raised but which rather bored him. The approach, however, cleverly raised the spectre of further economic distress in Britain and may have been seen as a means of attracting not only the votes of those concerned with the question of unemployment but also of those Westminster electors who had voted Labour in 1929; certainly, Beaverbrook was anxious to catch whatever protest votes were going in 1931 and he made an explicit appeal to non-Conservative voters thus:

> I want to make an appeal to the other parties to support Sir Ernest Petter, too, and he is advocating the only policy before the country that attempts to deal with the evils from which we suffer. The policy of Mosley in many respects resembles the policy of Empire Free Trade. So far as he supports the policy of Empire Free Trade, I say, God bless Mosley.

There was an obviously populist note in Beaverbrook's orations, and this – combined with his hammering of the unemployment issue and his call for a democratization of the Conservative Party – may have impressed working-class voters. His denial of Baldwin's taunt that he was an 'insolent plutocrat' was hardly designed to appeal to the traditional Tory voters in St George's:

> Mr Baldwin says that I am an insolent plutocrat. I wasn't born a plutocrat anyway. I wasn't born with any silver spoon in my mouth, I was born in humble circumstances, the son of a humble preacher of the Word and the grandson of an agricultural labourer... I have known what it is to work with my hands and I have known what it is to want food...

This was good demagogic stuff; it perhaps did not strike quite the right note in Hanover Square.

By comparison with the colour of Beaverbrook's campaign, the meetings held by Duff Cooper were somewhat dull. Yet his political machine was brought into operation effectively and his agent, L. A. Coombs, was vastly more competent than Clinton, who was organising Petter's campaign. The most memorable words uttered on Duff Cooper's behalf were undoubtedly contained in Baldwin's famous speech at the Queen's Hall two days before the constituency was due to poll. The words were not coined by Baldwin but by his cousin Rudyard Kipling and were hailed by the editor of *The Times* as a triumph.[27] Lord Rothermere had sneered that the Conservative leader could hardly be a fit person to restore the fortunes of the country when he had lost his own personal fortune; infuriated, Baldwin replied:

> The paragraph itself could only have been written by a cad. I have consulted a very high legal authority and I am advised that an action

for libel would lie. I shall not move in the matter and for this reason: I should get an apology and heavy damages. The first is of no value, and the second I would not touch with a barge-pole... What the proprietorship of these newspapers is aiming at is power, and power without responsibility – the prerogative of the harlot throughout the ages...

In vain did Beaverbrook protest that Rothermere had stolen the limelight from Petter and from himself; Baldwin had come off best in the oratorical battle, although it was by no means clear that this victory would be reflected in the votes.

The last days of the campaign were thus marked by a great deal of tension and excitement which spread far beyond the boundaries of the constituency. It certainly touched Parliament and, although the Conservative Members were obviously affected most, the by-election had an impact on Labour and Liberal Members too. Tory Members who lived in the division of St George's became directly involved when 45 of them composed a letter of encouragement to Duff Cooper which was duly published in all the newspapers on 16 March. The only problem about this letter was that not all the Tory Members who were voters in St George's had signed it. Some were conveniently out of London,[28] but one – Sir William Wayland – actually went so far as to send a letter of support to Petter. The letter ran thus: '...We are in urgent need of men such as yourself in the House, men with independence of thought, will-power and moral courage, as an antidote to the sloppy sentimentalism and turn-the-other-cheek spirit which is all too prevalent today.' This caused a storm in Wayland's constituency of Canterbury, and both the president (Lord Cushendun) and the chairman of the local Conservative Association (Lord Fitzwalter) publicly condemned its Member's action. But the real surprise came from the Labour benches when the Member for South Derbyshire, Major Graham Pole, wrote to Duff Cooper thus: 'I intend to vote for you as will three others in my household. No one who respects the decencies of public life can approve of the scurrilous Press propaganda against Mr Baldwin, and the return of your opponent would be a calamity from the point of view of clean fighting in politics.' The standards of public decency which Harold Laski had invoked in a personal message to Baldwin before the Tory leader faced the party meeting of October 1930 had thus prompted a Labour Member to vote for the official Conservative, although the *Daily Herald* and the majority of Labour Members maintained the disdainful neutrality which they had shown throughout the campaign. Two Liberals followed Major Pole's example: H. J. Tennant, a former MP and the brother of Lady Oxford and Asquith, announced his support for Duff Cooper, as did Geoffrey Mander, the MP for Wolverhampton East. It seemed to the majority of onlookers that the campaign based on personality assassination had been counter-productive - insofar as the assassinated personality had been Baldwin.

Perhaps Sir Ernest Petter's allies realized this – although they could have argued that Baldwin and Duff Cooper had been hurling as much abuse as anyone else – and the last days before polling saw a shift of emphasis to the Indian issue. The *Daily Mail* and *Evening News* had been featuring this issue by printing the slogans 'Gandhi is watching St George's' and 'Put Petter in and you put Gandhi out' in boxes throughout the papers during the election campaign. Beaverbrook was not too happy with this tactic for, although he knew that it was good propaganda and that the majority of the St George's electors read the Beaverbrook-Rothermere press, he felt that it broke the spirit, if not the letter, of the law governing election expenses.[29]

Yet when polling day actually arrived, *The Times's* prediction that canvassing efficiency would be crucial was largely borne out; and Duff Cooper's organization was superior to Petter's both in the efficiency of the original canvass and in getting the voters out on the day. Baldwin and his wife voted early in the morning and some 20 per cent of the voters had cast their preferences by midday. Although the rate fell off as the day wore on, the initial mood of excitement was sustained and then at six o'clock there was a great rush to the polls by residents on their way home from work. Odd spectacles could be seen throughout the day and the *Westminster and Pimlico News* waxed truly lyrical at the sight of 'master and man' going into the polls together – because the master had arrived in a chauffeur-driven car.

The Petter machine could only be described as erratic. At one point Ward Price became furious because he had just made a tour of the Pimlico area without seeing a single Petter car and had then come upon ten Petter cars standing idle in Chester Square. This was doubly irritating because Duff Cooper's cars had been making house-to-house calls all over the constituency while as yet Clinton had only managed to send for people who had definitely promised to vote for Petter. Ward Price telephoned Beaverbrook thus: 'Send a peremptory order to Clinton to send his cars to Pimlico making house-to-house calls...' It was also imperative that the final canvassing and collecting of the Petter supporters should be done during the middle of the day because otherwise it might be impossible for them to leave their homes and workplaces – especially if they were domestic servants.

An hour before the poll closed, Lord Beaverbrook telephoned Lady Diana Cooper to tell her that on his reckoning Cooper had won. He then gave her a breakdown of how the polling had gone by polling district, and this estimate – as she later admitted – turned out to be remarkably accurate.[30] It is difficult to say how Beaverbrook managed to predict the result so perceptively, but when the result was declared it was found that Duff Cooper had won by almost 6,000 votes.

It is impossible to establish where the Petter votes came from with any certainty, but the Beaverbrook document prompts a number of speculations about the basis of the Empire Crusade's support. The constituency, although very wealthy, had a large pocket of poverty in the Pimlico area. In the period 1885–1910, before the Westminster St George's constituency was formed from St George's Hanover Square and Westminster, it was recognised that Pimlico with its prostitutes and immigrants was becoming 'increasingly disreputable', while the area between Victoria Street and the river was distinctly poor.[31] Sir Ernest Petter's son who helped his father with the canvassing in 1931, records the fact that the 1929 Labour vote came largely from the Pimlico district with its predominantly Italian population of small shopkeepers, barrowmen and labourers.[32] The housing statistics provide evidence that the Victoria ward of the constituency was comparatively overcrowded. It is interesting to note that a measurement of housing pressure in London as a whole reveals that it was worst in three LCC boroughs – St Pancras, Islington and Paddington. Whether or not the poor housing conditions had anything to do with the Empire Crusade's success in Islington East and Paddington South is a debatable point; but Beaverbrook's breakdown of the voting suggests that it is probable that Petter's supporters were of a slightly lower social and economic origin than Cooper's. There is difficulty in analysing information which, in addition to the normal difficulties associated with aggregate data, is impaired by the very low turnout registered at the by-election. Nevertheless, the figures do seem to reveal a distinct pattern. Petter received the overwhelming support of the voters in the poorest districts of the constituency which were towards the river and the Vauxhall Bridge Road. The only significant exception to the trend in this area is the St Barnabas polling district which was on the doorsteps of Chelsea barracks. Apart from the obvious appeal of Cooper with his war record and his experience in the War Office, the Conservative organization was sufficiently well organized to bring many service voters and their wives back to London for the poll. Petter – who had difficulty in transporting electors who lived within the constituency – was unlikely to be able to convey them from Aldershot. Belgravia appears to be a transition area with the vote fairly evenly divided. The districts to the north around Mayfair were overwhelmingly pro-Cooper in character. It is important to note that this is the area which gave Erskine his support when, as an Independent with the backing of the Hanover Square Conservative Association and the Anti-Waste League, he successfully challenged the official Conservative candidate in 1921 and 1922. Petter, who had after all been a member of the equally right-wing National Party, might have been expected to enjoy some support from this area if the Empire Crusade appeal had been orthodox and right-wing. But its appeal was populist and Petter accordingly gathered in only some lower-middle- and working-class support together with a proportion of the protest vote which was unlikely to go to Cooper. The upper-middle classes and the aristocracy closed ranks in defence of the established order.

The impact of St George's

Duff Cooper's victory was widely interpreted as Baldwin's triumph. The Tory leader acknowledged his debt to the new Member for St George's by acting as one of his sponsors when he took his seat in the House of Commons. Those standards of public life so dear to all parties had, it seemed, been preserved from the attack mounted by impertinent outsiders who would not play the political game decently; the organ of the Establishment celebrated the result thus: 'St George's has done a good day's work for democracy and for the Press. Democracy must founder without newspapers to give it the facts along with the arguments...' The *News Chronicle* declared in its leader that the influence of Rothermere and Beaverbrook was destroyed: '... the St George's election has ended in the decisive defeat of the Wicked Uncles and their unfortunate candidate.'

Those people mainly concerned with the election's implications for Indian policy were even more relieved by the result than those who disliked the growing power of the press barons. Undoubtedly, the use to which the problem of Indian constitutional advance had been put in the campaign was deleterious to British relations with India and could have had far-reaching repercussions, as a letter to the Indian politician Sir Tej Bahadur Sapru shows: 'Thank God the St George's scandal is over! It was a miserable business. India was wantonly dragged in by the reptile press in order to injure Baldwin. Fortunately the attempt did not succeed.'[33]

Beaverbrook was bitterly disappointed by the result in St George's but he thought that he had been forced to fight on the wrong issues. He was sure that the Empire Crusade ought to concentrate on the economic advantages of the policy of Empire Free Trade and ignore problems such as India which would only attract the elderly diehard vote. What Beaverbrook wanted was a programme which would attract votes from all parties. As he wrote shortly afterwards: 'The defeat is due to my own stupidity. It was wrong to fight on India and the leadership of the Conservative Party. The issue might have been the cause and cure of unemployment. On that platform we can turn and win Socialist and Liberal votes.'[34] A. J. P. Taylor implicitly rejects this thesis, but the somewhat fragmentary evidence that exists at least invites an open mind on this issue. Beaverbrook never really got another chance to test the truth of his opinion before the formation of a National Government in August 1931 altered the whole basis of British political life – at least until 1945. Beaverbrook took what he could from the Stornoway Pact and continued to encourage the formation of local Empire Crusade groups in the Home Counties, but his enthusiasm had waned. Although St George's formed its own Empire Crusade group shortly after the by-election, the constituency had declared that the movement would never again be of national significance.

What, then, can be said of St George's in retrospect? Clearly, it was soon forgotten despite the tremendous build-up it had received in the press prior to polling day. Indeed, the claims made for it at the time look somewhat ludicrous now. To be sure, it had killed the Empire Crusade, but whether the voters of St George's ever really grasped the policies at issue is open to doubt; it is much more likely that those who supported Petter in St George's – like those who voted for the Empire Free Trade candidate in Islington and Paddington – were expressing a vague feeling of dissatisfaction with the state of parliamentary politics at the time. An analysis of this protest vote suggests that Beaverbrook might well have improved his position had he carried on his campaign on the lines which he envisaged rather than on those dictated by Rothermere. St George's certainly saved Baldwin from immediate disaster, but it hardly ensured him a tranquil future. India loomed on the horizon as an issue which would have to be handled with as much care as the tariff question; but it is probably fair to say that if Baldwin had been defeated at St George's, there would probably have been no revolt over India simply because it is unlikely that any other leader would have felt so personally committed to a liberal policy as to risk splitting his party over it. As for saving Britain from press dictatorship, the impact of St George's was more apparent than real; all it decided in that respect was that such influence as existed would be exerted from Printing House Square. That perhaps, in a curious way, points to the real significance of St George's. For above all it was a victory for the Establishment and a victory for the status quo. It was incidentally also a victory for the forces of moderation in British public life. British politics might have been totally shattered by the slump and a new kind of party might have emerged from the flux; St George's proved that the conventional party machines and the Establishment were still strong enough to resist attack and crushed one of the figures who might have made such an attack successfully. Baldwin was able to take a reasonably united party with him into a Coalition Government just five months after the by-election. It is conceivable that if St George's had voted differently, there might have been no National Government, no Government of India Act and no Conservative Party as we know it today.

Bibliographical note

The material contained in the Beaverbrook Papers in the House of Lords Record Office, London, is a rich source of information about the Empire Crusade and about its founder. The Baldwin Papers in the University Library, Cambridge, provide details about the effect which the Crusade and its supporters had on the Conservative Party at the time as well as giving an insight into Baldwin's personal view of these events.

Material about the constituency itself is to be found in the Worthington-Evans Papers and in the very full records of the St George's Westminster Constituency Association. The Worthington-Evans Papers have been given to the Bodleian Library, Oxford, while the St George's records are now deposited in the Westminster Central Library, London.

For the press account of the by-election and its prelude, I have relied heavily upon the *Westminster and Pimlico Gazette, The Times,* the *Daily Express,* the *Daily Mail* and the *Daily Herald.* All newspapers and periodicals dealing with current affairs and British political developments naturally commented upon Baldwin's difficulties and the Empire Free Trade movement; similarly it is possible to find reference to these events in the records of a number of other public figures of the period. The Salisbury Papers at Hatfield House, the Sapru Papers on microfilm in the Centre for South Asian Studies, Cambridge, and the Halifax Papers in the India Office Library are particularly valuable in this respect and for the background material which they contain.

Notes

1   A. J. P. Taylor, *Beaverbrook* (1972).
2   I am aware that the term 'populist' can cause confusion. I think, however, that it is justified both in relation to the style of the Empire Crusade and to its specific policies. For a general discussion of the phenomenon of populism, see E. Gellner and G. Ionescu, *Populism* (1970) esp. pp. 9–27, 153–250 and the more recent study by M. Canovan, *Populism* (1984).
3.   Taylor, *Beaverbrook* p. 273.
4.   See R. McKenzie, *British political parties* (1970) for a full account of this episode.
5.   *Report of the Special Committee of the Rochester and Chatham Constitutional Association* (copy in the Salisbury Papers). See also the correspondence between Frederick Stigant and the Marquess of Salisbury, in the Salisbury Papers.
6.   See K. Middlemas and J. Barnes, *Baldwin: a biography* (1969) pp. 530–44. For a full discussion of Baldwin's problems at this time, see Stuart Ball, *Baldwin and the Conservative Party: the crisis of 1929–31* (1988).
7.   See R. R. James, *Memoirs of a Conservative* (1969) p. 324.
8.   Beaverbrook Papers, Rothermere to Beaverbrook, 14 Jan 1931.
9.   See Beaverbrook Papers, Churchill to Beaverbrook, 23 Sep 1930.
10. The Beaverbrook Papers contain a number of telegrams from Rothermere to Beaverbrook urging him to concentrate on the Indian issue during the Islington campaign.
11. Worthington-Evans Papers, Worthington-Evans to Brigadier-General Cooper, 11 July 1929.
12. Moore-Brabazon was one of the Members defeated in 1929. Central Office was anxious for his return to Parliament. See Baldwin Papers, memorandum from Sir George Bowyer, 1 Dec 1930.
13. Ward Price withdrew from the contest as soon as Petter came forward and helped with the Petter campaign. See *The Times,* 4 Mar 1931.
14. The memorandum is reprinted in I. Macleod, *Neville Chamberlain* (1961) pp. 139–41.

15. I owe this information to Professor E. G. Petter's unpublished essay on the by-election.
16. Beaverbrook Papers, Beaverbrook to Rothermere, 27 Feb 1931.
17. See *Daily Mail,* 2 Mar 1931.
18. See James, *Memoirs of a Conservative,* pp. 357–8.
19. Beaverbrook Papers, memorandum, 2 Oct 1931.
20. See *The Times,* 3 Mar 1931.
21. Beaverbrook Papers, Parr to Beaverbrook, 7 Feb 1931.
22. See A. D. Cooper, *Old men forget* (1953) for an account of this move; also *The Times,* 9 Mar 1931, for Baldwin's letter to the chairman of Winchester Conservative Association.
23. Minutes of the St George's Conservative Association, 5 Mar 1931.
24. Lady D. Cooper, *The light of common day* (1959).
25. Lady D. Cooper, *The light of common day* (1959).
26. Petter's son recalled the fact that Lord Beaverbrook frequently brought in bodyguards from the East End to 'take care' of hecklers, and he remembers that these 'rough-necks' would regularly return after the meetings to 'collect' for their services (letter to the author, 27 Sep 1972).
27. Baldwin Papers, Dawson to Baldwin, 17 Mar 1931.
28. See Baldwin Papers, memorandum from Sir Patrick Gower to Sir Geoffrey Fry, 17 Mar 1931. It lists the MPs in St George's who definitely refused to sign a message of support to Duff Cooper. They were Commander Bellairs, N. Colman, Colonel Gretton, Sir Alfred Knox, Sir Basil Peto and R. Purbrick.
29. Newspaper circulation in St George's broke down as follows: *Daily Express,* 11,200; *Daily Mail,* 9,200; *Daily Chronicle,* 6,150; *Daily Herald,* 3,900; *Daily Telegraph,* 2,400; *The Times,* 2,100; *Morning Post,* 1,650 (Beaverbrook Papers).
30. Lady D. Cooper, *The light of common day.*
31. See H. Pelling, *The social geography of British elections,* 1885–1910 (1967).
32. Gordon Petter was, however, of the opinion that his father had alienated the Catholic vote in Pimlico by his refusal to support separate schools for the Catholic minority in Westminster (letter to the author, 27 Sep 1972).
33. Sapru Papers, Polak to Sapru, 23 Mar 1931.
34. Quoted in Taylor, *Beaverbrook,* p. 305.

Note: 1931 to 1939

John Ramsden

In the 1931 general election the new National Government was given a more overwhelming vote of confidence and Labour suffered a more comprehensive defeat than either had thought possible. Labour lost 215 seats and the National Government was returned to power with the support of 521 MPs out of 615. But the result was much less clear than the figures suggest, mainly because the composition of the government itself was to change. During the 1931 general election it included all prominent Liberals except Lloyd George, all prominent Conservatives except Churchill, and a number of ex-Labour leaders. After Snowden retired and MacDonald and Thomas were seen to represent little but themselves, the National Labour element in the government was less impressive than it had been in 1931.[1]

However, the major problem of interpretation is provided by the Liberals; the National Government was originally supported by almost all Liberal MPs and seems to have been supported by most Liberal voters in 1931. Only in about a quarter of the constituencies was there a Liberal candidate in 1931, and these fought the election as three teams rather than as one. Subsequently, the Liberal Nationals ('Simonites') remained in the government, while the other Liberals ('Samuelites' and Lloyd George's personal following) gradually disconnected themselves. It was therefore to be expected that Liberal support for the National Government would be less consistent in by-elections than it had been in 1931, but that it would fall away at different rates in different places. If leading local Liberals were 'Samuelites', then support might fall away rapidly, but if they were 'Simonites', local Liberals would remain loyal to the government. This sporadic pattern would also reflect the concerns of Liberals with the topical issues of the day, especially where they related directly to Liberal priorities, such as free trade or international co-operation. In 1931 Liberal voters had had to make a second-best choice in order to save the country from economic disaster; it was to be expected that their Liberalism would reassert itself as the determinant of their vote, but as long as the party was in confusion, their reaction would also be confused. The pattern would not be regular, in any geographical or chronological sense, but would reflect the real confusion that traditionally Liberal voters felt in a post-Liberal world. This would not of course preclude the Liberal voters in an individual constituency from moving overwhelmingly against the government if they were convinced that a real Liberal principle was at stake.[2] However, there appears to have been a general tendency for Liberals to move into opposition to the National Government, just as Liberal MPs were doing at Westminster. This can be shown by looking at seats which had had Liberal candidates in the 1929 general election. If 1929 is taken as the base, then the by-elections of 1932–4 can be measured to show whether the withdrawal of Liberal candidates helped either government or opposition. There were 24 such elections in 1932–4, and these show an interesting variation: in contests from which the Liberal withdrew, there was a mean swing to Labour of just 0.1 per cent, but when Liberals put forward a candidate for the by-election, there was a swing to the Conservatives of 1.8 per cent. There was thus an apparent tendency for the withdrawal of Liberal candidates to help Labour in these years. The point can be pressed further by looking at the last six months of 1933, during which the Liberal Party actually moved into opposition at Westminster. The mean swings during that time were: when Liberals withdrew, 5.4 per cent to Labour, and when Liberals stood again, 1.8 per cent to the Conservatives. The defection of Liberal supporters who had voted solidly for the National Government in 1931 may therefore be the major explanation for the government's decreasing votes in 1933 and 1934.

Not only had the government done outstandingly well in 1931, but Labour had also done very badly. Most of the 1931 gains can be explained by the maximization of Conservative and Liberal votes in favour of the government, but it is also clear that many Labour voters abstained, for the total Labour vote dropped by 1.75 million. The shock of Labour's sudden disappearance from power and the appearance of Snowden and MacDonald on the hustings attacking their late colleagues provide an adequate explanation for this. But it meant that, unlike the National Government, which had surely polled its maximum possible vote in 1931, Labour had some ground to make up. Time would cool fears that Labour had betrayed the nation in 1931, and time would therefore bring at least some Labour resurgence.

Indeed, some contemporaries expected that the extreme nature of the 1931 result would make government losses inevitable. This in itself suggests an equilibrium view of the party system, whereby any violent lurch would be followed by a compensating reaction. Thus, barely a week after the biggest general election win on record, Baldwin was warning the Conservative Party that great efforts would be needed if they were to retain some of the unlikely gains that they had made. The tone of his address suggested that the size of his victory was more an embarrassment than a cause for rejoicing; he warned his party not to be surprised if seats were lost, and clearly expected that they would be.[3] There was no particular reason why a government with a large majority should lose a large number of by-elections, but this had happened in 1900, 1906, 1918 and 1924.[4] Nor was it only the actual size of the government's majority which gave cause for alarm, but also the way in which the majority had been achieved. By going to the country as a combination of parties which was asking for a 'doctor's mandate', they were hoping to place the National Government securely above the old party battle-cries. On that platform, they had succeeded completely, but their very success made them more than usually vulnerable to the charge that by-elections lost would indicate the loss of popular support. As a National Government, their credibility depended much more on popular backing than a normal party government requires: if it was everyone's government, it was also no one's government, for the normal constraints of party loyalty would not apply. It is against this yardstick that East Fulham and Baldwin's desperate search for a rearmament mandate should be measured.

East Fulham was in fact the fourth seat which Labour gained from the National Government, but the first which could not have been anticipated in the aftermath of 1931. A. L. Rowse later described it as the loss by the government of just one of the 500 seats which they had won in 1931, and therefore a result of no significance at all.[5] But East Fulham was also the loss – by a large margin – of a seat which no Conservative had ever lost before, and in a straight fight with Labour. It was not important for itself, but because of the view that it had been caused by pacifism, and because of the implications which it suggested for other seats. This is an interesting comment on the changed expectations of governments since 1922: the Lloyd George government had regarded any loss as a serious blow, but the National Government woke up to its real unpopularity only when it lost a seat which it regarded as rightfully its own. It was a sign that the 'new politics' was establishing itself that the Conservatives could regard some seats as hopeless and others as almost invulnerable. It was when an apparently invulnerable seat was lost at East Fulham that the panic set in. The spectre of 1931-scale rout, in reverse, was raised.[6]

Throughout 1933 and 1934 the National Government lost more seats to Labour and suffered large adverse swings. Plenty of explanations have been suggested: economic troubles and unemployment, housing, the means test, and increasing concern about foreign affairs. Labour's optimism and the Conservatives' despair both grew as Hammersmith North, Upton, Lambeth North, Swindon and West Toxteth all changed hands. Only in mid-1935 did the government begin to recover; at last they justified their existence by producing an economic recovery and at last foreign affairs became an advantage rather than a hindrance to them. Lord Bayford noted on 21 April 1935:

> Till quite lately things have been going badly for the Govt. The peace propaganda undoubtedly did them harm... But the greatest point in the Govt's favour has been Hitler's declaration as to German rearmament. Bobby Monsell told me Hitler made his increased estimates for the Navy quite easy to obtain. I never knew our Central Office people so rattled as they were in February. They looked on no seat as safe.[7]

East Fulham was the only justification for such panic; it was the only traditionally Conservative seat which was lost to Labour in a representative contest throughout the 1930s. Thus, although they had approached the 1931 Parliament with a realistic view of the situation and a belief that losses were likely, the Conservatives ended in a blind panic when their expectations were realized. The Government really did no worse than might have been expected; it lost only 9 of the 48 government seats which fell vacant. However, an additional cause for concern was the small margins by which the other 39 were held. Here too the results were distorted by the government's victory in 1931; for no period of any length did they suffer swings which would have put Labour into power at a general election. Only East Fulham and Liverpool Wavertree of Labour's gains had not been won by Labour in 1929 (when Labour had *not* won a parliamentary majority), and these were both wildly untypical. In some constituencies the Conservatives did worse than in 1929, but in others, such as Skipton, they did better.

What, then, is the explanation for the government's performance? The most likely hypothesis again concerns the votes of Liberals and others who were not committed to Labour or Conservative. Most of these had voted for the National Government in 1931 or had at least withheld their votes from Labour, but a by-election presented them with a different kind of choice. In 1931 the only issue was whether in principle there should be a National Government; at by-elections after 1931 voters could express their dissatisfaction with government policies, without worrying about alternatives. Nor was this attitude confined only to Liberal and uncommitted voters, but was shared equally by Conservatives. Over the issue of India, the right wing of the Conservative Party kept up an unceasing barrage of criticism of the National Government. When they had failed to reverse government policy through the House of Commons or through the party, they somewhat belatedly appealed to the electorate. In February 1935 Randolph Churchill contested Liverpool Wavertree as an Independent Conservative opposed to the government's India policy. By splitting the Conservative vote he let Labour in, and a month later he supported another Independent Conservative at Lambeth Norwood. In November 1935 though Churchill was an official Conservative and National Government candidate at the general election, in Liverpool West Toxteth –

right next door to the seat which he had handed over to Labour in February. By February 1936 he was a rebel again, standing against Malcolm Mac-Donald at Ross and Cromarty. It is not entirely fanciful to see Randolph Churchill's antics as symbolic; he was prepared to intervene at by-elections to influence government policy so long as the fate of his party or of the government was not at stake. When a general election was called, he came back into line, and surely many voters must have acted similarly. The losses of East Fulham and Wavertree were keenly felt, but it was less widely reported that the government had won both seats back without difficulty in the 1935 general election. Of the other seats which it had lost to Labour, only Swindon was regained (by 975 votes). It can thus be argued that two distinct trends had emerged: on the one hand, Labour was winning back support which it had lost in 1931, and which it would now expect to retain; on the other hand, the National Government was generating protest votes which would disappear as soon as its survival was in doubt.

The ease with which the government retained power in 1935 seems to have devalued by-elections as political indicators. The government's worst fears had proved to be groundless in 1934–5, so perhaps they were determined not to be led astray again. The National Government lost more seats during 1935–9 than during its first term of office, but these losses never made the same impact and the mean swing did not reach the same level as in 1934. Once again, the gradual recovery of the economy and the reduction of unemployment provides the best single explanation. However, the same factors applied as before 1935: the government had been re-elected with a quite unspecific programme and so individual by-elections could be treated as referenda on particular aspects of government policy. In the context of the late 1930s this inevitably meant that foreign affairs became a major issue. Oxford and Bridgwater were not just by-elections which happened to take place soon after the Munich settlement: they were the 'Munich by-elections'.

This period, for the first time, did not consider by-elections in complete isolation. The first opinion polls were being taken and the British Institute of Public Opinion was founded in 1937. Gallup began a regular series of surveys on Britain and Tom Harrisson founded Mass-Observation.[8] These were all different in style and in reliability – Gallup was self-consciously scientific, while Mass-Observation was basically impressionistic but they all shared the same concern, which was to find out reliably and in detail what the public were thinking. They may have seen by-elections, the traditional indicator of public mood, as more suspect than before, but they were certainly influenced by the increasing use of public opinion as a political force. The League of Nations Union had organized the 'Peace Ballot' in 1934–5 in order to mobilize opinion against rearmament; the public outcry had driven Sir Samuel Hoare from office in 1935 after the Hoare–Laval Pact, and Baldwin had made a masterly use of public feeling during the Abdication crisis.[9] If the public and its views were to be so directly consulted, then it was at least desirable that those views should be reported accurately. The crude medium of by-election results therefore became merely a secondary political pointer instead of the only one. Instead of by-elections being used to interpret public opinion, public opinion – as measured in opinion polls – would henceforth be used to interpret by-election results, and soon to predict results in advance. It was to be several years and several general elections before opinion polls became predominant, but the trend began in the late 1930s.[10]

Overall, the pattern of results in 1935–9 was not unlike that of 1931–5; Labour gained 13 seats from the government, but only one of these (Greenock) had not been held by Labour before. There were some big swings to Labour, but never big enough to suggest an overall Labour majority.[11] In only 3 of their 13 gains did Labour win by a margin which implied a parliamentary majority, and in no year did the mean swing reach that level. Once again, the government was caused discomfort by the intervention of Independent Conservatives. This time there were no such interventions in seats which could be lost to Labour, but the public was treated to the rare spectacle of unpredictable and possibly close contests in Kinross and West Perthshire, and in Cheltenham. However, foreshadowing the disasters of 1943 or 1944 and recalling the dark days of 1934 were the interventions from Independents of the Left. These were at Combined English Universities in 1937 and then at Oxford City and at Bridgwater in 1938, described in Chapter 6.[12]

The common theme of all by-elections in the 1930s is the fact that many electors did not much like what the National Government was doing, although they did not of course all dislike the same things. Conversely, there was never during the inter-war years a majority of electors who favoured a Labour Government, and since that was the only alternative to a National Government in the 1930s, by-elections and general elections showed considerable differences. However, it was only when there were extreme circumstances (East Fulham) or a split Conservative vote (Liverpool Wavertree) that the National Government was in any real danger from Labour. It was only when an official or unofficial man of the Left was able to win more votes than a normal Labour candidate could do (Oxford or Bridgwater) that real difficulties arose, but then only at by-elections and not at general elections. That is the background to the by-elections of 1943–5, in which the basic political equilibrium of the 1930s was shattered.

Notes

1. In the 1931 general election MacDonald spoke of Labour 'betraying' the national interest and Snowden attacked his late colleagues with great bitterness. There is little doubt that this was a great electoral asset to the National Government, as described below.

2. See p. 98, for a consideration of how Liberal voters reacted at East Fulham. The concept of a block of ex-Liberal voters in the 1930s is discussed in D. E. Butler and D. Stokes, *Political change in Britain* (1969) pp. 249–74.
3. Conservative Party National Union Minutes at the Bodleian Library, Oxford, meeting of Executive Committee, 4 Nov 1931.
4. It also occurred to governments with large majorities in 1931, 1935, 1959, 1966, 1983 and 1987. The apparent exception is 1945, which is discussed on pp. 151–2.
5. A. L. Rowse, 'Reflections on Lord Baldwin', in *The end of an epoch* (1947) p. 86.
6. The concept of the 'new politics' is described on p. 17.
7. J. A. Ramsden (ed.), *The diaries of Sir Robert Sanders, Lord Bayford* (1984). Bayford had been Deputy Chairman of the Conservative Party during the Coalition Government and had a long-standing involvement in Central Office; Sir Bolton Eyres-Monsell was First Lord of the Admiralty and had previously been Chief Whip. Both of them therefore knew the mood of the party over several years.
8. See T. Harrisson and C. Madge (eds), *Britain, by Mass-Observation* (1939), and H. Cantril, *Public Opinion, 1935–1946* (Princeton, 1951).
9. During the Abdication crisis the mood of MPs changed dramatically over one crucial weekend. Baldwin said: 'I have always believed in the weekend. But how they do it I don't know. I suppose they talk to the stationmaster.' G. M. Young, *Stanley Baldwin* (1952) p. 242.
10. Gallup began regular surveys in Britain in 1938, but were not the first in the field. A poll conducted by Harrods among its customers in 1924 was surprisingly successful, and magazines had also tried to predict general elections. However, it was only after the failure of the *Literary Digest* in the 1936 US presidential election that the need for proper sampling methods was recognized.
11. D. E. Butler, *The electoral system in Britain* (1953 ed.) p. 184.
12. The Universities had a tradition of electing Independents, so it was not until Oxford that much attention was paid to this. The comparison with 1934 and 1943–5 is because it was only at those times that the government was threatened by candidates who could poll more than the maximum Labour vote, as in 1938.

CHAPTER 5

Interpreting East Fulham

Martin Ceadel

General Election, 1929	(Electorate 51,066)	
Vaughan-Morgan (Conservative)	15,130	*(44.4)*
Palmer (Labour)	13,425	*(39.4)*
Greenwood (Liberal)	5,551	*(16.3)*
Conservative majority	1,705	Turnout 66.8%
General Election, 1931	(Electorate 51,688)	
Vaughan-Morgan (Conservative)	23,438	*(68.7)*
Maynard (Labour)	8,917	*(26.1)*
Greenwood (Liberal)	1,788	*(5.2)*
Conservative majority	14,521	Turnout 66.1%
By-Election, 25 Oct 1933	(Electorate 51,642)	
Wilmot (Labour)	17,790	*(57.9)*
Waldron (Conservative)	12,950	*(42.1)*
Labour majority	4,840	Turnout 59.5%
General Election, 1935	(Electorate 50,682)	
Astor (Conservative)	18,743	*(51.4)*
Wilmot (Labour)	17,689	*(48.6)*
Conservative majority	1,054	Turnout 71.9%

The East Fulham by-election of 25 October 1933 has aroused more controversy than any other.[1] Caused by the death in August 1933 of Sir Kenyon Vaughan-Morgan, the Conservative who had held the seat since 1922, it was won dramatically two months later by Labour on a turnover of over 19,000 votes and a swing of 29.1 per cent. But it was not merely as a spectacular electoral upset that the result at East Fulham became controversial. It was cited as an indicator of the popular pacifism which delayed the National Government's rearmament programme, and it therefore became notorious as a political symbol of the locust years – the vital early years of the Hitler regime – during which Baldwin and MacDonald failed to build up adequate national defences. More recently, the by-election has become a matter of dispute among historians who have disagreed over the issues which the result reflected, despite subjecting the campaign at East Fulham to the minutest scrutiny.[2] This account will therefore seek not to retell the details of the campaign, but to answer three questions of interpretation which lie at the heart of the East Fulham controversy. Why did East Fulham become a political myth? What was the decisive issue or issues which determined the result? And what was the contemporary impact of the result?

The political myth

That East Fulham achieved political notoriety was a demonstration of the speed with which conditions in the 1930s changed, rendering obsolete and ludicrous attitudes and positions which had seemed sensible in the previous context. East Fulham, on 25 October 1933, was the first, most dramatic and the only actual government loss among six bad by-election results within five weeks. It occurred at a time when the National Government faced major problems both domestically and internationally. The domestic problems were the social effects of the economic crisis: unemployment and cuts in the social services. The international problems arose from the growing threat posed by the nine-month-old Nazi regime to the peace of Europe, for which the success of the World Disarmament Conference that had been sitting at Geneva since February of the previous year was seen to be crucial.

During the three years it took for East Fulham to become the centre of political controversy, the situation changed. There was a measure of economic recovery, but all prospects of disarmament faded and an arms race had begun. The most vocal criticisms of government defence and foreign policy were no longer those of militaristic warmongering but of inadequate vigilance and determination. It was while defending the government's rearmament programme in the Commons on 12 November 1936 that Stanley Baldwin invoked East Fulham and thereby ensured it political immortality. In reply to Winston Churchill's criticisms, he explained: 'We started late, and I want to say a word about the years the locusts have eaten.' These were the years 1933-4 when Baldwin, not yet (until June 1935) Prime Minister, had nevertheless been the most powerful man in the government. He went on, in what was to become one of the most notorious speeches of the decade:

I put before the whole House my own views with an appalling frankness. From 1933, I and my friends were all very worried about what was happening in Europe. You will remember at that time the

Disarmament Conference was sitting in Geneva. You will remember at that time there was probably a stronger pacifist feeling running through this country than at any time since the War. I am speaking of 1933 and 1934. You will remember the election at Fulham in the autumn of 1933, when a seat which the National Government was lost by about 7,000 [sic] votes on no issue but the pacifist. You will remember perhaps that the National Government candidate who made a most guarded reference to the question of defence was mobbed for it.

The accuracy or otherwise of Baldwin's interpretation of the issues at East Fulham, which now interests historians, received less attention than did the implications of what Baldwin went on to say:

That was the feeling in the country in 1933. My position as the leader of a great party was not altogether a comfortable one. I asked myself what chance was there – when that feeling that was given expression to in Fulham was common thoughout the country – what chance was there within the next year or two of that feeling being so changed that the country would give a mandate for rearmament? Supposing I had gone to the country and said that Germany was rearming and that we must rearm, does anybody think that this pacific democracy would have rallied to that cry at that moment? I cannot think of anything that would have made the loss of the election from my point of view more certain.

Four years later, in war-time when circumstances had once more dramatically altered, this unfortunately worded admission came to be quoted as part of the mounting indictment of Baldwin's inadequate leadership. With Churchill as Prime Minister of a Coalition Government unable to prevent the British Expeditionary Force being driven into the sea or the fall of France, ex-appeasers, Conservative anti-appeasers and the Labour Party found unity in a time of national crisis by agreeing to condemn Baldwin for the country's unpreparedness.

The fact of Baldwin's negligence was not discussed, merely the degree of his culpability. In his influential indictment of the National Government written in the immediate aftermath of Dunkirk, 'Cato' (Michael Foot) misdated the East Fulham by-election into 1935 and interpreted Baldwin's remarks about the loss of an election to refer to the 1935 general election.[3] Baldwin therefore stood accused of failing to alert the British people to the need for rearmament as late as November 1935. This error was compounded by Hamilton Fyfe in an article in 1941 which bowdlerized (and misdated) the 12 November 1936 speech so as to put into Baldwin's mouth an admission of having failed to inform the country of German rearmament explicitly in the 1935 election. Fyfe's article had been on 'Leadership and Democracy'[4] and the mistaken reference to 1935 crept even into constitutional textbooks as a stock illustration of when representative government should not defer to the general will.[5]

It was not until 1948 that R. Bassett put the record straight by pointing out that Baldwin was referring to a hypothetical election in the years 1933–4.[6] On the outcome of such an election Baldwin's judgement had been anticipated less than three weeks previously by Hugh Dalton, who wrote in the *New Statesman:* 'When early in the life of the last Parliament John Wilmot won East Fulham, though his outstanding personal qualities swelled his majority, he proved that a tide was running which, had a General Election come soon after, might easily have carried us to victory.'[7] Yet Baldwin had so phrased his speech as to invite the charge of putting party before country. In the words of his official biographer, G. M. Young: 'Never I suppose in our history has a statesman used a phrase so fatal to his own good name, and at the same time so wholly unnecessary, so incomprehensible. One can think of half a dozen ways of ending that passage, all convincing and all true.'[8] Young's lack of sympathy with his subject has become notorious, but his impressionistic style evoked not a 'guilty' man but an inadequate one. The 'appalling frankness' speech was an incompetent admission rather than an admission of incompetence. Baldwin's cloudy and equivocal phraseology has made it hard to estimate the degree to which he sought a mandate for rearmament in the 1935 general election campaign itself.

Although the more recent biography by Middlemas and Barnes has argued that he did explicitly seek such a mandate, earlier critics had argued that the notion of a mandate was irrelevant in a representative democracy. In the debate of 12 November 1936, Winston Churchill had argued that 'The responsibility of Ministers for the public safety is absolute and requires no mandate'. This remark was quoted approvingly in 1941 in A. L. Rowse's essay, 'Reflections on Lord Baldwin', which criticized Baldwin for failing to give public opinion the political leadership which the situation required and the apparently impregnable electoral position of the National Government facilitated. Churchill's remark was also quoted by C. L. Mowat in an article prompted by Young's biography which added very little to Rowse's arguments.[9] Baldwin having died in 1947, East Fulham had exhausted itself as a source of political controversy by the middle of the affluent 1950s.

The campaign issues

The facts
The explosion of historical research in the 1960s meant that East Fulham was rediscovered as a source of problems to resolve, in particular the central

problem of whether or not East Fulham had been 'lost in a wild flood of pacifism'.[10] Baldwin's view in 1936 that the election had been decided 'on no issue but the pacifist' had been accepted by his supporters and critics alike, but more recently it has been investigated by several historians, and in 1971 two detailed articles devoted entirely to the by-election appeared simultaneously. This historical activity has produced a fundamental division of opinion between those who regard the international situation as decisive, and those who believe that the domestic situation provides the explanation.

On many aspects of the election, however, all accounts are in agreement. For an indication of the political complexion of the constituency, which dated from 1918, the 1929 result was a better guide than the panic election of 1931.[11] Though the Conservatives had always held the seat, they were by 1929 closely challenged by Labour, with the Liberal vote holding the balance of power. Three factors contributed to the by-election result: Conservative abstention, a high turnout of Labour supporters, and a significant number of Liberals voting Labour.

This analysis is supported by the literary evidence, which is surprisingly clear-cut. All accounts agree that East Fulham is an extreme case of a disastrous candidate with a weak organization being defeated by an outstanding one with strong support. To start with the Conservatives, their adoption of Alderman W. J. Waldron as candidate had occasioned considerable infighting among a local party organization of acknowledged weakness, and his diehard views on India meant he had only half-hearted support from Central Office. Lacking the personal popularity of his predecessor who had held the seat for the five previous contests, Waldron had nevertheless been Mayor of Fulham six times in the 1920s, but, far from being a source of political strength, it identified him as responsible for imposing wage cuts on the borough council staff in 1931. As a local property-owner he was on the defensive over the housing problem. His campaign fared badly, culminating in the tactical blunder of a 'smear' leaflet about his opponent which completely rebounded.

The Labour candidate, John Wilmot, was, at the age of 38, nineteen years younger than his opponent but of equal political experience. His organization was helped by nearby constituencies, including Kennington where he lived. The organizer of the London Labour Party acted as his agent, and the party's national organization, untroubled by any policy divisions, sent their leader, George Lansbury, plus J. R. Clynes, Hugh Dalton, Herbert Morrison, A. V. Alexander, Arthur Greenwood and others to speak for Wilmot. It was Wilmot who took the initiative in the campaign, branding his opponent as a warmonger, and making a personal investigation of the housing situation in the borough, contrasting his findings with the plans of the Tory council. Waldron's attempt to wrest the initiative from Wilmot had been to 'smear' him with his involvement with a local Shareholders Provident Association, which Waldron claimed was inconsistent with his professed Socialism. But since the association was known to protect the small investor against fraudulent company promoters, it was a source of political strength – not least among middle-class voters – for Wilmot, who made his career in banking and later in business.

This raises the question of the Liberal vote. The Liberal Association had maintained its organization and contested every previous election except 1924. Although its 5,551 votes in 1929 had slumped to 1,788 in the crisis election of 1931, Wilmot believed Liberalism to be a force worth courting. He advocated free trade and electoral reform, and over the question of India he claimed his opposition to Waldron's diehard stance to be in the best Liberal tradition of Campbell-Bannerman. Waldron's chances of winning Liberal support were slender, since the tide of Liberal opinion was moving away from the National Government. In 1931 the Liberals had 'agreed to differ' on the question of protection, but after the Ottawa Conference the Liberal Ministers had resigned in September 1932, although they continued to sit on the government benches. In response to pressure in the National Liberal Federation they were to cross over, in November 1933, on to the opposition benches, leaving only the Simonite Liberal Nationals in the administration. There was no Simonite organiz-ation in East Fulham, and indeed throughout the campaign Sir John Simon was playing an unhappy role in the international crisis which broke during the campaign. Since the Great War, foreign affairs, and in particular support for the League of Nations, had become one of the two major areas of Liberal interest, and as the economic depression made free trade seem an unrealistic ideal, internationalism became the predominant Liberal preoccupation. Waldron actually attacked the League of Nations, to which most Conservatives were careful to pay lip-service. Therefore it was scarcely a surprise when, having sent a questionnaire to both candidates about their attitudes to matters of interest to Liberals, the Liberal Association announced a week before polling day that 'The replies of the two candidates having been received and considered, the Association, regarding the question of disarmament as of vital importance, recommends all Liberal voters to give Mr Wilmot their support'. The former Liberal candidate, J. H. Greenwood, joined Wilmot on his platforms to speak on disarmament, leaving Wilmot to deal with food prices and housing. The *Times* reporter, basing his calculations on the assumption that the Liberals would divide evenly, underestimated Wilmot's vote which was over 4,000 higher than the best previous Labour vote. A case can thus be made for hypothesizing that Liberalism was still a recognisable political entity in Fulham, and that in 1933 it largely supported Wilmot, mostly because of the disarmament question.

Where no opinion polls exist to provide additional evidence, all descriptions and explanations of electoral behaviour must necessarily be hypothetical and approximate. It is here argued that the most plausible such explanation of East Fulham was that Waldron failed to turn out all the Conservative voters, whereas Wilmot succeeded in mobilizing the maximum Labour vote. Waldron was a poor candidate in a difficult political situation, whereas Wilmot possessed all the qualities necessary to exploit grievances against the National Government. In addition, Wilmot was able to mobilize a significant majority of Liberals on the disarmament question. In this sense it can be argued that the disarmament issue was decisive.

But when looking for the 'decisive' factor, most historians have sought, not an explanation in terms of influence on a marginal group of floating voters, in this case ex-Liberals, but for an issue which predominantly influenced all voters. In seeking this their methodology has approached that of a literary content analysis of the manifestos and local press reports, on the implicit assumption that the significance of an issue is related to the number of references to it, with some weighting given to statements made near polling day. In the case of East Fulham this method has produced basic disagreement, and social and foreign policy questions were much discussed in a campaign which took place at a time of economic depression and international crisis. The evidence for each of these two schools of thought must be examined in turn.

Domestic issues
Three days after the election, Neville Chamberlain wrote to his sister Ida:

> Fulham made the PM very miserable but I confess I did not lose a minute's sleep over it. The press put it all down to Housing and lies about War. Both no doubt were factors but I heard yesterday from a friend who had been talking to a speaker (street corner) from Fulham what I had all along suspected, that the real attack was on the means test. [12]

This view is quoted by A. J. P. Taylor, who notes in his volume of the Oxford History that 'later investigation has confirmed this judgement'. [13] But if there was a major social issue articulated during the campaign, it was undoubtedly the overcrowded housing conditions, which Wilmot muckraked with great effect. Waldron, who was tactically routed on this question, might have pointed out that 17 of London's 28 boroughs were more overcrowded than Fulham, although of course to argue that things were worse elsewhere did not mean that housing could not be an important factor at Fulham, since simultaneous by-elections in other London constituencies might have produced even greater anti-government votes.

Inadequate housing plans were a consequence of the government's policy of deflation, and by October 1933 the economic tide had turned, so that rising food prices were becoming a source of discontent. The other important domestic grievance was unemployment, and Waldron was able to point out that the number out of work in Fulham had been reduced since the start of the year from 6,086 to 4,487. London was less troubled than other areas and, within London, Fulham had a good employment record. Thus, although an atmosphere of economic gloom persisted, conditions had improved steadily throughout the year, and it is hard to see that social conditions were as dominant in Fulham as they had been at Rotherham in February 1933, where the National Government had lost the seat on a 19.9 per cent swing. Social discontents were too deeply ingrained by the depression years for a Labour candidate to omit to exploit them, and they provided an appropriate stick with which to beat a local alderman and landlord. Nevertheless, by themselves they do not obviously explain why such a dramatic result should have occurred where and when it did.

Foreign issues

The argument that foreign affairs were the decisive issue provides an explanation not only for the National Government's poor by-election performance over the winter of 1933–4, but also for the fact that East Fulham was markedly the worst of those results. The World Disarmament Conference, which had been sitting at Geneva since February 1932 and on which hopes for European peace were seen increasingly to hang, was throughout 1933 in a state of continuous crisis. On 14 October 1933, just eleven days before polling at East Fulham, the crisis broke and Germany withdrew from the Conference and from the League of Nations. This walk-out was timed to follow a speech at Geneva by Sir John Simon, the British Foreign Secretary, in which he outlined a new plan for progressive general disarmament down to the level already imposed on Germany by the Treaty of Versailles. Since Germany was already rearming illegally, this plan, agreed by Britain, France, the United States and Italy, was less favourable to Germany than a previous Draft Convention put forward by Britain in March 1933. Germany had already studied the plan before it was formally presented to the Disarmament Conference by Simon, and had decided in advance to withdraw. However, the timing of the German withdrawal looked as if it had been precipitated by the British Foreign Secretary going back on an earlier offer to Germany. This impression was confirmed by a talk by the popular radio commentator on international affairs, Vernon Bartlett, which was broadcast by the BBC on the evening of 14 October. Though Bartlett was five years later the anti-appeasement victor of the Bridgwater by-election, he was initially sympathetic to the international aspirations of the Nazi regime. His talk, which he later admitted was 'a very strong, if indirect, criticism' of the British Foreign Secretary, ended his career as a regular BBC staff broadcaster, though 90 per cent of the thousands of letters he received supported his views. His broadcast had been an early plea for appeasement, implying that Britain and France were the potential threats to peace: 'our behaviour during the next few weeks is going to decide the issue between a real peace and another war ... We can swallow a little of our pride and meet the German point of view. It is worth swallowing any amount of pride if peace is at stake; civilisation is more valuable than prestige.'[14] According to this analysis, any rearmament by Britain would be an unhelpful and provocative act.

Germany never returned either to the Disarmament Conference or to the League of Nations. John Wheeler-Bennett's judgement, made the following summer, has stood the test of time: 'October 14th, 1933, may well go down as one of the outstanding dates in European history, for on that day the second or Locarno period of post-war history came to an end; what may come forth from the period which then began is still thought of with fear and horror.[15]

Interpretation

Where the quantity of discussion on any particular issue is not obviously preponderant, mere immersion in the terms of that discussion will not provide the answer as to which issue was decisive. Certain interpretative judgements must be made.

The first such point is methodological. How meaningful is it to expect a by-election result to be explicable in terms of a single issue? Modern work on electoral behaviour has undermined the nineteenth century's rationalist view of elections in terms of the voters listening to the evidence like a jury and delivering a verdict on the merits of the case. Voters vote in accordance with an overall image, compounded of habitual class and party loyalties as well as the issues of the moment. Yet historical by-elections are often still analyzed as if they necessarily reflect a single predominant issue. At East Fulham the dichotomy of 'social' and 'foreign' issues, around which the historiography of the by-election has revolved, is a false one. Rather than being alternatives, they were often linked together. Thus, in the 1920s and the depression of the 1930s the 'Clydeside' group of MPs argued that in conditions of social deprivation the worker had nothing to lose by foreign invasion. That money spent on armaments should be reallocated to the social services was a popular justification for disarmament, but an East Fulham heckler asked Waldron: 'What's the use of putting up houses if they are going to be knocked down by bombs?' Marxist analysis, to which the depression years gave an opportunity for unprecedented influence and relevance, provided a common critique of social and international questions. But the predominant linking theme was hostility to the National Government which had betrayed the trust which the nation had placed in it in 1931. Action and reaction being equal and opposite, disillusion was extreme. Wilmot talked of the need to check Fascism in Britain, a line of thought which implied that militarism was the necessary concomitant of the National Government's defence of the social and economic status quo, and illustrated the extent to which political trust had declined.

The context

In arguing that social and foreign policy questions were not mutually exclusive but different aspects of a widespread distrust of the National Government, the discussion has been widened from the election campaign itself to the general context of ideas and opinion. The importance of looking to the context of ideas to break the interpretative deadlock about the election is the second point that must be emphasized. This will, in a way that mere listing of references cannot, allow one to judge the relative emotional leverage of the various issues. It will be argued here that the impact of the peace question has been underestimated by historians impressed with the quantity of references to social issues. For example, in his article Heller describes as 'colourless' a message from Arthur Henderson urging the electors to vote Labour and avert another arms race. But Henderson, who had the previous month returned to Parliament at the Clay Cross by-election, was, as the President of the Disarmament Conference, at the peak of personal popularity, and Wilmot had commented on the importance of his message in an interview in the *Daily Herald* on 27 October 1933. Heller quotes two other messages, one by Wilmot and one by his wife, on the peace issue, describing the first as 'a studied piece of emotional ambiguity, a repeated invocation of the magic words Peace, League and Covenant', and the second as 'blatantly emotive'. But he fails to draw any conclusions as to why an intelligent, hard-headed and ultimately successful candidate should have resorted to such propaganda unless he believed it to be electorally efficacious. At East Fulham one candidate was branded as a warmonger, and a local paper, the *West London and Fulham Gazette*, wrote on 27 October that 'the masses were scared of the prospect of another European war, or the possibility – however remote – of Hitlerism gaining ground in this country'. A knowledge of the background of ideas on war is necessary to explain this fear. In his speech to the House on 12 November 1936, Baldwin claimed that Waldron had 'made a most guarded reference to the question of defence'. But in 1933 the whole question of defence was a confused and highly emotive issue. Matters were poised on a knife-edge: if disarmament were not achieved then an arms race would result, for Nazi Germany was bent on securing equality with the victors of the Great War, so that if they did not at once disarm to her level, she would rearm to theirs. It was an orthodoxy of the inter-war period that arms races led inevitably to war, the horrors of which had been painstakingly emphasized in order to gain support for the Disarmament Conference. On 29 November 1933 John Wilmot told the Commons that Lord Rothermere's *Daily Mail,* which was calling for massive and immediate air rearmament, was 'the principal organ, which represents – so nearly, as a rule – the opinions of the Government'. In such an atmosphere a 'guarded reference' to defence was impossible. Foreign affairs rarely interest voters simply because they rarely impinge on their daily existence. An air war was one drastic way in which foreign affairs could be brought home with a vengeance. The fear of war manifested at East Fulham was an unusual feature for an election campaign. It may therefore go far towards explaining an unusual result.

But how unusual was the East Fulham result when seen in the context of the other by-elections of 1933, and in particular of the 'little general election' of November 1933? 1933 produced several heavy swings against the government, but this was inevitable after the landslide of 1931, and in fact the little general election took place in seats which had swung more than average to the National Government in 1931. This is shown by comparing the 1933 by-election performances with both the 1931 and the 1929 general elections.[16] East Fulham stands out from contemporary by-election results which show a reasonably uniform reaction against 1931, and especially against 1929. It must be pointed out, however, that in an age that was innocent of the concept of 'swing' for comparing electoral performances, it was above all when a seat changed hands that contemporaries were impressed. This helps to explain why a 26.9 per cent swing at Putney in November 1934, which the National Government survived, attracted little attention.

The 1933 by-elections showed that, although the slump was still a cause for concern, the peace issue replaced it as the Labour Party's trump card. The peace question was a less objective or predictable determinant of electoral behaviour than were economic conditions, since a crisis atmosphere depended on the vagaries of the international situation and on the ability of the candidate to exploit them. The first peace by-election had been at Clay Cross on 1 September 1933, when, however, Arthur Henderson's official position as President of the Disarmament Conference prevented him from attacking the government. There were no such inhibitions at East Fulham, where the German withdrawal from the Conference and from the League, and the contrasting talents and views of the candidates, provided additional emotional fuel. The peace question continued to play a considerable role in the five by-elections of November 1933, as Dr Kyba has shown. John Wilmot visited Kilmarnock to speak for the Revd James Barr, who as MP for Motherwell from 1924 to 1931 had supported unilateral disarmament motions in Parliament and was later to be a sponsor of the Peace Pledge Union. At Skipton the Labour candidate claimed to be a pacifist. At Rusholme, Rutland and Harborough the Labour candidates all talked emotively of the horror of the next war, and claimed that Labour was the only peace party.

But even if it is conceded that the interesting factor about East Fulham was the crisis atmosphere about the peace question, was it therefore, as Baldwin claimed, a 'pacifist by-election? Both Heller and Stannage agree that, however important were the questions of disarmament, the future of the League of Nations, the foreign policy of the National Government and fear of war, these did not amount to pacifism. But although we can now see a distinction between these questions and a statement of pacifism, this distinction was hard to recognize in 1933. The problem is partly semantic. The word *pacifism* changed its meaning during the inter-war period. When first coined in the first decade of the century it meant simply being in favour of peace and arbitration rather than of militarism. With the development of anti-war feeling in the late 1920s to the point where almost no one would admit to being a militarist, the word became too vague to be helpful since we were 'all pacifists now'. The peace movement no longer needed to change people's attitude to war; what was required was to harness anti-war feeling into an effective method of war prevention. There were several alternative methods advocated by different sections of the peace movement. One of these, the technique of non-resistance and personal refusal to bear arms, which was historically associated with the Quakers, was described as pacifism. This particular meaning has taken over from the general meaning as the primary one, but in 1933 there was no primary sense. Instead there was linguistic confusion which reflected intellectual confusion.

The peace movement tended to view non-resistance, support for the League of Nations and revolutionary pacifism as complementary rather than conflicting alternatives, since all could be reconciled with support for the Disarmament Conference. But in January 1933 Hitler came to power, and the spectacular deterioration in the international situation in 1933 threatened the Disarmament Conference and brought the first European war scare since 1918. This produced two effects on the public mind. The first was an emotional reflex whereby the idea of expressing total opposition to militarism was confused with that of adopting a totally opposite position, pacifism. The most famous expression of this reaction was the Oxford Union's resolution 'That this House will in no circumstances fight for its King and Country', passed on 9 February 1933. But if this emotional response added to the confusion surrounding pacifism, it served also to stimulate discussion of war prevention at which the differences within the peace movement began to be clarified. This process can be seen at the National Peace Congress held at Oxford in July 1933.

But clarification itself produced confusing divisions. Although the Labour Party exploited the peace question, it was more seriously divided than the Conservative Party by the dispute between isolationists and those believing in the need for British commitments. On the Right, isolationism is well known for Lord Beaverbrook's campaign against the Locarno treaties, for which he claimed East Fulham to be a triumph. On the Left, Sir Stafford Cripps opposed Henderson's policy of support for the League of Nations by advocating a general strike against any attempt by the British Government to go to war, even in support of the League of Nations Covenant. This split dominated both the League of Nations Union's annual meeting at Edinburgh in June 1933 and the Labour Party Conference at Hastings in October 1933. At Edinburgh a compromise was adopted, but at Hastings confusion triumphed. A resolution was passed 'to take no part in war'; as well as a composite resolution calling, among other things, for the creation of an International Police Force, which was the most extreme demand of the League's supporters.

Linguistic confusion persisted even after the intellectual problem had been resolved. Thus Lord Allen of Hurtwood (formerly Clifford Allen, who had been imprisoned as a conscientious objector in the Great War) and Sir Norman Angell both insisted they were still pacifists even after they had abandoned their absolutist aversion to military sanctions. Baldwin also still used the word in its wider sense. Speaking in the Commons on 29 November 1933 on air defence, he reminded the opposition speakers, who had included John Wilmot, that 'the most ardent pacificists, using the word in its best sense, are among the soldiers and sailors and airmen of our country who took part in the last war and who know what the next war will be like'. ('Pacificist' was an early – and technically more correct – variant of 'pacifist'; which became less common during the 1930s.) Wilmot himself had served in the Great War, and soon developed into an orthodox supporter of collective security. Yet as late as 14 March 1935 he could tell the Commons: 'I do not quite know what is meant by a pacifist, but if it means a person who desires more than anything else to keep his country-men from the horrors of war, then I plead guilty to being a pacifist.' Confusion about the word was such that in 1933 few contemporaries would have made a distinction between the 'peace' question and the 'pacifist' question.

The contemporary impact

The contemporary impact of a by-election depends of course not on what actually happened, but on what was believed to have happened, and on what lessons it was believed could be learned from what happened.

For the national press the peace issue was the most noteworthy feature of East Fulham and the by-elections which followed. *The Times* had predicted a good Labour result on the basis of Wilmot's peace propaganda. The *New Statesman* concluded that 'Mr Wilmot's campaign was very largely fought on the peace issue', which thereafter became the basis of the Kilmarnock and Skipton elections.[17] The *Spectator* stated a similar view more judiciously: 'At Fulham, as everywhere, local and particular issues no doubt had their place, as well as general issues like housing, but it is clear that the question on which beyond all others votes turned was disarmament. It was on that, certainly, that the Liberal vote, such as it was, went to the Labour candidate.'[18]

But it was for the National Government to decide whether the election offered any lessons for governmental policy. Beyond Neville Chamberlain's letter to his sister, which has already been quoted, there appears to be no contemporary evidence for East Fulham being more than an understandable political disappointment for Baldwin. Indeed, the assertion that it was a traumatic shock rests largely on a personal anecdote related by G. M. Young: 'And it seemed to me that the shock had broken Baldwin's nerve. "It was a nightmare," he once said, speaking, for the only time, of the past with passion.'[19] A. L. Rowse has quoted an admission made to him by Baldwin during the Second World War that 'of course, at that time I was holding down a job which I was physically incapable of'.[20] It may therefore be that Baldwin's state of health rendered him peculiarly vulnerable to upsets. An alternative explanation is that in his declining years the reputation for honesty which Baldwin cultivated as part of his political style developed into a 'frankness' even more 'appalling' than that of 1936.

There is no evidence for East Fulham directly affecting the rearmament programme, since at the time there was no programme to be affected. The Hankey Committee did not report until February 1934, and there was no agreement about defence priorities. But nevertheless, discussions of defence all took place in the clear knowledge that rearmament was politically unpopular, especially if it meant building bombers and equipping an Expeditionary Force. However, the conclusion that rearmament should be kept to a minimum was dictated equally by diplomatic and economic considerations.

The effect of East Fulham and the by-elections which followed was to make the government conscious of the need to explain its foreign policy to the public as skilfully as possible. Stannage has shown that the government believed it had been misrepresented over the German walk-out from the Disarmament Conference. Simon wanted a White Paper to be published, and when Gilbert Murray expressed sympathy Simon telegraphed back that he would welcome a letter to *The Times* showing the government to have the support of the Chairman of the League of Nations Union.[21] The Conservative Party commissioned a report on East Fulham from Arthur Baker of *The Times*, who believed Wilmot's peace propaganda to have been decisive. Whether or not Baldwin saw this report, his speeches attempted to expose the opposition's tactics:

What an unedifying spectacle we have been witnessing during the last two or three weeks. What an outburst of scaremongering, largely because of Germany's withdrawal and largely because there were half-a-dozen by-elections taking place … I am the last person to mind attacks, but attacks on the Government to try to make people believe that the Government is not in earnest in its desire for peace have no other effect than to weaken our counsels in the world …[22]

After the announcement of the rearmament programme in July 1934, the government once again found it was being branded as a warmonger, most successfully by Dr Edith Summerskill at Putney in November 1934, where the swing against the government nearly equalled that of East Fulham, although the seat did not change hands. Since the strategic situation changed more quickly than did the entrenched hostility to armaments, defence remained a politically delicate issue. Only in the Abyssinian crisis of 1935, when the Labour Party committed itself to military force in support of collective security, did Baldwin manage to find the recipe that sugared the pill of rearmament. But he still made the distinction between a programme of repairing gaps in national defence and the still unthinkable policy of 'great armaments'. This distinction accounts for the ambiguity over whether Baldwin obtained a mandate for rearmament in the 1935 general election.

Baldwin did not believe public opinion could be hurried in a demo-cracy, and accepted, somewhat fatalistically, a two-year time-lag behind the dictatorships. But his reluctance to guide public opinion more energetically was also due to the fact that his own mind was not made up. In particular, he seems to have simultaneously accepted and shied away from the need to build an air force strong enough to deter Germany. His famous speech of 10 November 1932, which had warned that 'the bomber will always get through', was ceaselessly quoted both by pacifists and rearmers as vindi-cation of their viewpoints. By November 1936 the rearmers were in the ascendancy. When Baldwin referred to East Fulham he was citing it, not as a specific event, but as an example of the prevailing attitude which, it was implied, acted as an external constraint on government action. It was ironic that, in playing down his own doubts about rearmament, Baldwin laid himself open to the far graver charges of political cowardice and lack of statesmanship.

Conclusion

The historiography of East Fulham is a case study in the limitations of historical explanation. Since in the last analysis the mind of no one voter will ever be known, all explanations of collective behaviour can at best be simplistic hypotheses. With this in mind, certain statements must be offered tentatively about East Fulham. It became a political myth because events moved so rapidly in the 1930s as to make former attitudes and policies soon seem disastrously misconceived, a factor which was exacer-bated by Baldwin's injudicious phraseology in his speech of 12 November 1936. As for the campaign, it can be argued that a poor Tory candidate failed to mobilize the full support of a divided party, whereas an outstand-ing Labour candidate brought out his own support and attracted a considerable amount of Liberal support, explicitly on the issue of disarmament. To believe necessarily in the decisiveness of a single factor can lead to over-simplification, and to expect to find one among campaign literature, which tries to spread the vote-catching net as widely as possible, is unlikely to succeed except in unusually simple cases. East Fulham was not such a simple case, and can only be interpreted in its context. On that basis, it is here argued that although social questions were widely discussed, it was the peace question which had the greatest emotional impact. The peace question covers all fears of war and discussion of the international situation, and was dominated by the suspicion that the National Government had prejudiced the peace of Europe by provoking a German withdrawal from Geneva. The contemporary impact of East Fulham depended on what the result was believed to show. Most contemporary comment agreed with John Wilmot's description of the by-election in his maiden speech to the Commons on 13 November 1933 'as a symptom of what is a general feeling, a passionate and insistent desire for peace, not merely a nebulous desire for peace, but a demand that that desire should be translated into some practical disarmament accomplishment'. Baldwin quoted East Fulham not as an event with immediate consequences but as a symbol of a widespread popular attitude to armaments, which he himself shared. His successor as Prime Minister, Neville Chamberlain, provides another example of the consequences of sharing the peace-loving aspirations of public opinion.

Bibliographical note

The view that the peace question was an important factor is put forward in detail in C. T. Stannage, 'The East Fulham by-election, 25 October 1933', *Historical Journal* XIV (1971), pp. 165–200. The same interpretation can be found in A. J. P. Taylor: *The trouble makers* (1957) p. 186; J. P. Kyba, 'British attitudes toward disarmament and rearmament, 1932–35', PhD thesis, University of London, 1967, pp. 318–19 [subsequently published as P. Kyba: *Covenants without the sword: public opinion and British defence policy, 1931–35* (Waterloo, Ontario, 1983); K. Middlemas and J. Barnes: *Baldwin* (1969), pp. 744–6; and M. Beloff: *Wars and Welfare: Britain, 1914–45* (1984), p. 206.

The view that social issues were important is argued in detail in R. Heller, 'East Fulham revisited', *Journal of Contemporary History* VI (1971), 172–96. The same interpretation can be found in A. J. P. Taylor: *English history, 1914–45* (1965), pp. 367, 387; A. Marwick: *Britain in the century of total war* (1968) p. 251; and M. Pugh: *The making of modern British politics, 1867–1939* (1982), pp. 287-8 (which however places the by-election in the wrong year).

All quotations from parliamentary speeches are taken from Hansard. The Baldwin Papers contain nothing on East Fulham. No political papers survive for John Wilmot (created Baron Wilmot of Selmeston in 1960; died 1964); I am indebted to his widow, Lady Wilmot, for discussing with me the by-election and her husband's career. The context of ideas and opinion on the peace question is explored further in M. Ceadel, 'The "King and Country" debate, 1933: student politics, pacifism, and the dictators'; *Historical Journal* 22 (1979) pp. 161–84; M. Ceadel, *Pacifism in Britain, 1914–45: the defining of a faith* (1980); and M. Ceadel, 'Between the wars: problems of definition', in R. Taylor and N. Young (eds): *Campaigns for peace* (1987), pp. 73–99.

Notes

1. This controversy peaked in the early 1970s when the desire to find a scapegoat for Britain's failure to deter Hitler was still strong and the first thorough research into the 1930s was producing the inevitable attempts at revisionism. My essay dates from that period, and (except for some updating of the bibliographical note) is here reprinted unchanged. This is because no detailed attempt has been made to challenge its contention that, although a definitive explanation of the by-election is impossible, and although there are so many reasons why the Conservative candidate fared badly (including the National Government's general unpopularity at a time of economic recession, social problems in the constituency, and poor campaigning) that they are hard to disentangle, the distinctive feature of the East Fulham campaign was that it took place in the immediate aftermath of arguably the most critical international event of the interwar period, the collapse of the Disarmament Conference – a collapse for which the British government was at first widely blamed, and which can be assumed to have particularly upset the Liberals who, without a candidate of their own, were key floating voters. It thus seems plausible to conclude that, even if only as a marginal factor, the belief that National Government had shown insufficient commitment to disarmament and peace was crucial to the defeat of its candidate. Baldwin undoubtedly so concluded, though he muddied the waters by calling this factor 'pacifism' and implying not only that it was the sole electoral issue at East Fulham but also that its influence on the public mind remained equally strong throughout the next 15 months.

2. For the historiography of East Fulham, see the Bibliographical Note at the end of the chapter, but I should like here to acknowledge my particular debt to the work of Mr C. T. Stannage and Mr R. Heller.

3. 'Cato', *Guilty Men* (1940) pp. 31, 37. By the end of 1940 the book had run through 27 impressions in which the misdating of East Fulham was corrected but not the implication about the 1935 general election. Foot's co-authors were F. Owen and P. Howard, and the publisher was Victor Gollancz.

4. H. Fyfe, 'Leadership and Democracy'; *Nineteenth Century* (May 1941) p. 470.

5. See W. I. Jennings, *The British Constitution* (1941) pp. 216–7.

6. R. Bassett, 'Telling the truth to the people', *Cambridge Journal* (Nov 1948) pp. 84–95.

7. *New Statesman*, 24 Oct 1936, p. 617.

8. G. M. Young, *Stanley Baldwin* (1952) p. 229.

110

9   Rowse's article was reprinted in his *The end of an epoch* (1947) pp. 77–89; C. L. Mowat, 'Baldwin Restored', *Journal of Modern History* (1955) pp. 169–74.
10 Young, *Stanley Baldwin*, p. 177.
11 The figures for 1929, 1931 and 1933 are printed at the beginning of the chapter. Comparing 1933 with 1929, the Conservative vote fell by 2,180 (a 2.3 per cent fall in their share of the vote); the Labour vote increased by 4,365 (18.5 per cent); the Liberals, who in 1929 had polled 5,551 votes (16.3 per cent), failed to put up a candidate in 1933. Numbers voting fell by 3,366, but the electorate had increased by only 576 (1.1 per cent) over the four years.
12 I. Macleod, *Neville Chamberlain* (1961) p. 77.
13 A. J. P. Taylor, *English history, 1914–1945* (1965) p. 367.
14 Vernon Bartlett, *This is my Life* (1937) pp. 188–92; *Listener*, 18 Oct 1933, p. 570.
15 John W. Wheeler-Bennett, *The disarmament deadlock* (1934) p. 181.
16 Average government (i.e. Conservative) share of vote in 1933 compared with 1929 and 1931:

	1929	1931
By-elections, Jan–Sep 1933	+6.2	−15.5*
East Fulham, 25 Oct 1933	−2.3	−26.6
By-elections, Nov 1933	+6.2	−22.9

*Excluding East Fife and Altrincham, where there were no contests in 1931

17 *New Statesman*, 11 Nov 1933, p. 575.
18 *Spectator*, 27 Oct 1933, p. 562.
19 Young, *Stanley Baldwin*, p. 177. J. C. C. Davidson has written that East Fulham 'stunned' Baldwin, but his draft memoirs, written 30 years later, were probably influenced by subsequent accounts. R. R. James, *Memoirs of a Conservative* (1969) pp. 397–8.
20 A. L. Rowse, *All Souls and appeasement* (1961) p. 55.
21 Murray Papers, Sir John Simon to Gilbert Murray, telegram, 9 Nov 1933.
22 Speech to the annual conference of the Scottish Unionist Association, Edinburgh, 17 Nov 1933; see *The Times*, 18 Nov 1933.

CHAPTER 6

Oxford and Bridgwater

Iain McLean

Oxford

General Election, 1935		(Electorate 38,557)	
Bourne (Conservative)	16,306		*(62.8)*
Gordon Walker (Labour)	9,661		*(37.2)*
Conservative majority	6,645	Turnout 67.3%	

By-Election, 27 Oct. 1938		(Electorate 36,929)	
Hogg (Conservative)	15,797		*(56.1)*
Lindsay (Independent Progressive)	12,363		*(43.9)*
Conservative majority	3,434	Turnout 76.3%	

General Election, 1945		(Electorate 45,775)	
Hogg (Conservative)	14,314		*(45.3)*
Pakenham (Labour)	11,451		*(36.2)*
Norman (Liberal)	5,860		*(18.5)*
Conservative majority	2,863	Turnout 69.1%	

Bridgwater

General Election, 1935		(Electorate 43,367)	
Croom-Johnson (Conservative)	17,939		*(56.9)*
Blake (Liberal)	7,370		*(23.4)*
Loveys (Labour)	6,240		*(19.8)*
Conservative majority	10,569	Turnout 72.7%	

By-Election, 17 Nov. 1938		(Electorate 44,653)	
Bartlett (Independent Progressive)	19,540		*(53.2)*
Heathcoat Amory (Conservative)	17,208		*(46.8)*
Independent Progressive majority	2,332	Turnout 82.3%	

General Election, 1945		(Electorate 53,896)	
Bartlett (Independent Progressive)	17,937		*(45.8)*
Wills (Conservative)	15,625		*(39.9)*
Corkhill (Labour)	5,613		*(14.3)*
Independent Progressive majority	2,312	Turnout 72.7%	

The Oxford and Bridgwater by-elections pose problems of interpretation similar to those at East Fulham five years earlier. The British electorate is notoriously uninterested in, and uninformed about, foreign policy issues; yet these three by-elections, in the eyes of the candidates and of most commentators, were won and lost on foreign policy. Politicians and journalists regarded the results as the voters' verdicts on the foreign policy issues of the day. Stanley Baldwin thought that East Fulham had been fought and lost 'on no issue but the pacifist'; and that the voters' verdict made it impossible to present the country with a rearmament programme. In October and November 1938 Oxford and Bridgwater were taken to be the voters' commentary on Munich, though there was some dispute as to what the voters were saying.

When Neville Chamberlain returned to Britain with the Munich proposals, on 30 September 1938, an unusually large number of by-elections were imminent. Of the eight contests between Munich and the end of 1938, Oxford (27 October) and Bridgwater (17 November) have attracted special attention as tests of Chamberlain's popularity, because in each case the conventional opposition parties withdrew in favour of a non-party, anti-Munich candidate.

The main problem in interpreting Oxford and Bridgwater is the same as for East Fulham: can we confirm or rebut the hypotheses about public opinion offered by contemporary politicians and journalists and quarrelled over by historians? As this chapter will largely be about public opinion, it seems fitting to mention at the outset some of the traps for the unwary involved in the study of opinion, especially when this involves election results and swing.

Swing is not simply a matter of the net transfer of votes from one party to another between two elections. It involves all manner of other movements, for example: to and from abstention; into and out of the constituency; on to and off the electoral roll by comings of age and deaths. In a typical constituency between general elections nowadays, about half of the electorate in each of the elections are not electors in the same constituency at the other. So it is not possible to infer anything about individuals, or even groups of individuals such as the Liberal vote, from aggregate election statistics. Indeed, it only makes matters worse to speak, as commentators often do, about the behaviour of the Liberal vote, the women's vote and so on, as revealed in aggregate election statistics. Not only can we not tell whether blocks of voters moved in a certain way, but we have no right to assume that such blocks exist in any size. To pursue the example of the Liberal vote: by the late 1930s the social bases of the traditional Liberal vote were rapidly crumbling. If 10 per cent of the electorate voted Liberal in each of two successive elections, we cannot infer from these aggregate statistics that even one individual voted Liberal both times. There is a danger of ascribing to the electorate more coherent patterns of partisanship than it displays.

113

It is both the strength and the weakness of the measure swing that it attempts to collapse all the movements of electoral opinion into one. It is the only yardstick yet devised for comparing different elections, and it will be used in this way in this chapter. But its effectiveness diminishes rapidly as the number of parties rises above two. Unfortunately, even in a straight fight there is a third alternative, or party, available, namely abstention. Therefore we cannot assume that swing tells us anything about the proportion of the electorate which has switched from one party to the other. To avoid being hoist with my own petard, I treat swing as simply a measure of the change in party A's share of the electorate relative to party B's (and therefore I have related it, in this chapter, to the total electorate, not only to those who voted). It makes no assumptions as to how this change has come about. All the figures of swing used in this chapter assume that there are only two parties: the National Government and the opposition. Seats where both Liberals and Labour were strong in 1938 have been omitted from all comparisons.

Another problem of interpretation arises from the common assumption by the political elite that it knows how ordinary electors think. This view is still prevalent today; it was almost universal in the 1930s. It strongly coloured the relationship between press and politicians. Around the time of Munich, Chamberlain regarded Geoffrey Dawson, editor of *The Times*, as a guide to the state of public opinion. Dawson wrote on 28 September 1938 that his leader the previous day had,

> produced a good deal of attention and approval. One sentence in it suggesting that public opinion was ahead of the Government in seeing the urgency and importance of a settlement with Berlin caused the PM to ask me to come and see him ... so that he might tell me what he at any rate had been trying to do.[1]

Duff Cooper, who resigned as First Lord of the Admiralty over Munich, noted that 'Many would have expected that women would have been more ready than men to accept the spurious peace at its face value ... But it was not so.'[2] He explained that he knew 12 married couples who were divided over Munich, and in each case the husband was pro-Chamberlain and the wife was against. Life would be much simpler if we could accept that the views of Duff Cooper's friends accurately mirrored those of the mass electorate; but a generation of survey evidence shows that elite and mass opinion often differ widely. They appear to have done in this case, as Mass-Observation data discussed later showed women as being more pro-Munich than men.

These remarks may appear negative. But there are immense difficulties in the way of anyone who tries to assess public opinion in the 1930s, and we should suspect the credentials of anyone who professes to do so. It is better to come to cautious conclusions that can be justified than to bold ones that cannot. Some statements can be made from aggregate election statistics, and the by-elections of 1938 and 1939 as a whole provide a series about which some useful observations can be made. Oxford in 1938 saw the first constituency opinion poll ever taken in Britain. And Mass-Observation, which had recently been founded by an anthropologist, Tom Harrisson, was taking a keen interest in political affairs and accumulating reams of information about public opinion. None of this was based on reliable sampling methods, but it gives a better picture of public opinion than that handed down by politicians and journalists. Before looking at the figures, however, we ought to study the history of the two campaigns.

In August 1938 Captain R. C. Bourne, the Conservative MP for Oxford, died. In 1935 he had had a majority of 25.6 per cent of the votes cast in a straight fight with Labour. The pre-war Oxford constituency did not include the Cowley motor works and their attendant working-class housing, so that it was a less hopeful prospect for Labour than might be thought from a look at the city today. The Conservatives' chances at the by-election appeared to be enhanced by the likelihood of a three-cornered fight. The Liberals' prospective candidate had withdrawn in June, but in September they invited a recent graduate, Ivor Davies, to take his place. Davies was already prospective candidate for Aberdeenshire Central, and his only connection with Oxford was that he had presided at a Liberal students' conference there earlier that year. The Labour Party readopted Patrick Gordon Walker, who had fought in 1935. The Conservatives chose Quintin Hogg, a young Fellow of All Souls whose father, Lord Hailsham, was Lord President of the Council and an ex-Lord Chancellor. On 13 September, long before the Munich crisis had reached its peak, Davies offered to stand down on condition that the Labour candidate did likewise and a non-party anti-Conservative should be put up. This was, by Davies's own subsequent admission, a gimmick, but it set in motion a chain of unexpected consequences. It produced turmoil in the Labour camp because of its suggestion of a Popular Front. The heat which the question of candidatures was to arouse in the following month can be understood only in the light of Labour feelings about Popular Fronts in 1938. The Popular Front was a Communist doctrine, so to the orthodox it was heresy, and any prominent Labour supporter who favoured it was liable to expulsion. The most famous victim was Stafford Cripps, who was expelled from the party in January 1939.

There were some bona fide reasons for suspecting the Communists' enthusiasm for Popular Fronts. It was the result of a violent lurch in Comintern policy in 1934, which had been obediently followed by the leaders of all the surviving western Communist parties. The operation of Popular Fronts in France and Spain had been unhappy. In France the

Popular Front administration of 1936 had quickly disintegrated, and in Spain the Communists spent more energy in annihilating the rest of the Left than in fighting Franco. Nevertheless, the British Labour Party was probably too insular to pay much attention to these events; and in any case the truth of what was happening in Spain was not widely known in the UK. Native anti-Communism is enough to explain the Pavlovian reaction of Labour's National Executive Committee (NEC) to any Popular Front talk.

The Oxford Constituency Labour Party was already deeply suspect. In June the National Agent warned it: 'It has been reported to us that the Oxford CLP is associated with a movement in the city consisting of Communists and Liberals, and we shall be glad if you will let us know if this is accurate or not.' On hearing the party confess that the rumour was true, Transport House gave it 14 days to leave the Oxford Co-ordinating Committee for Peace and Democracy, on pain of disaffiliation. The party did so unwillingly: 'at the same time the Secretary was asked to inform Transport House of the discouraging effect on workers in the party of the attitude of the NEC'.[3] Not all of the local Labour Party were opposed to the line Transport House was taking. One of those who strongly supported it was the prospective candidate, Patrick Gordon Walker. Although himself a left-winger at this time, his unwillingness to give up a chance of winning the seat drove him into the arms of Transport House and the local right-wing, anti-Communist faction.

As the foreign affairs situation worsened during September, Davies's gimmick – by this time backed by the willingness of the quintessential member of the Great and Good, Gilbert Murray, to run as an Independent anti-Government candidate – was taken up in separate initiatives by two left-wing academics and Labour councillors, R. H. S. Crossman and Frank Pakenham (later Lord Longford). Their favoured candidate was A. D. Lindsay, the Master of Balliol College. Lindsay was a Scottish philosopher, whose recent term as Vice-Chancellor of the University had strengthened his reputation for combining high moral principles with consummate skill in political infighting. In the by-election, however, the former quality predominated. Lindsay weighed his passionate opposition to Munich against his desire for a quiet life after his term of office, and decided to stand if Liberals and Labour would both withdraw. A new appeal for them to do so was made on 10 October by Roy Harrod, the economist. ('Oxford ... is the home of compromise and sweet reasonableness', he wrote, ignoring a more famous reputation.) This initiative was welcomed by most of the Liberals and a large part of the Labour Party, but it stiffened the attitude of Gordon Walker and Transport House. On 11 October a meeting of the elections sub-committee of the NEC forbade Gordon Walker from standing down, a decision he accepted with gratitude.

The dominant, pro-withdrawal faction of the local party, however, was not prepared to accept this as final, and appealed to Transport House on the grounds that the circumstances were unique and quite different from the usual Popular Front situation; and that Lindsay, if elected, would not fight the seat again at a subsequent general election. After three days' hard bargaining, Transport House relented and announced that it would 'leave a definite decision in the hands of the local Labour Party', which decided by a large majority to withdraw Gordon Walker's candidature.

The Liberals were less well disposed to Lindsay, who was a long-standing Labour Party member – especially when he threatened to stand even if only Labour and not the Liberals withdrew. The party had spent some £200 or £300 on their campaign, and when they met on 17 October to consider whether to withdraw, this expenditure seemed to be a fatal obstacle. Only when a Labour councillor of substantial private means offered to pay this bill[4] was the way cleared for Lindsay's candidature, as an Independent Progressive. It was greeted enthusiastically by Davies, and extremely coolly by Gordon Walker, whose offer of help to Lindsay was prefaced: 'I am convinced that Labour has a policy wide, popular, and constructive enough to rally the country behind it. The Oxford City party has decided otherwise. I am not standing down. The local Labour Party is withdrawing the Labour candidate.'

The campaign was short but highly unusual. The *Oxford Mail* thought that 'All the spirit of old-time electioneering campaigns was recalled and spectators began to recall the scenes in 1922 when Frank Gray won the constituency for Liberalism'.[5] The University was passionately stirred by the issues, the city somewhat less so. *Picture Post* noted that:

> An interesting feature of the by-election was the intense interest taken by undergraduates, who had no votes, and the comparative apathy of the townsmen, who had. University men crowded to Dr Lindsay's meetings, although many of the older dons disapproved of his candidature ... Although Proctors, and even candidates, opposed too much activity by them, Oxford undergraduettes (sic) took a lively part on both sides.[6]

'A vote for Hogg is a vote for Hitler' proclaimed loudspeaker vans on Lindsay's behalf, though without his authority. (This slogan was reputedly devised by the linguistic philosopher J. L. Austin – 'the only proposition of Austin's I ever managed to understand', A. J. P. Taylor once confessed.) This, *The Times* noted, 'caused resentment on the Conservative side'. Letters, manifestos and counter-manifestos from dons and public figures proliferated in the *Oxford Mail* and spread into *The Times*. A pro-Hogg group of dons was worried that 'Mr Lindsay's nomination may contrive to obscure the central issue. For it is almost inevitable that a part of the votes he secures will have been cast as a tribute to his Vice-Chancellorship'.[7] Lord Nuffield wrote in to deny a rumour that he was supporting Lindsay: '... my political opinions favour no individual party, as I am convinced that a continuation of a National Government is our best assurance of the furtherance of the successful legislation and statesmanship which we have enjoyed since its inception.' Sir William Beveridge, Master of University College, wrote to Lindsay stressing his scholarly neutrality as an economist, but adding: 'what you said in your election address was jolly good'.

The candidates spoke of almost nothing except foreign affairs. Hogg observed: 'I believe that Mr Chamberlain has shown himself a greater expert on foreign policy, by what he did at Munich, than anyone in the last twenty years.' Hogg's public support came basically from National Government supporters, including National Labour men such as Kenneth Lindsay, the Labour candidate for Oxford in 1924, and Lord Sanderson, a former principal of Ruskin College. There was some sign of support for appeasement by organized Nonconformity – what A. L. Rowse once rudely called 'political Nonconformity in its deliquescence, without its conscience' – in that one pro-Hogg manifesto was signed by H. A. L. Fisher, Dr A. E. W. Hazell (Principal of Jesus College) and Dr L. P. Jacks (of Manchester College).

Lindsay's support was very diverse. On the Conservative side it included Churchill, Anthony Eden, Duff Cooper, Harold Macmillan and Edward Heath. Macmillan was the only Conservative MP actually to go to Oxford to speak for Lindsay, although, according to Oliver Harvey, Eden felt 'tempted' to intervene. Some Labour leaders, including Hugh Dalton, were hoping for a massive anti-Munich revolt among the Conservatives, which might have led the NEC to reconsider its attitude towards Popular Fronts.[8] But the Munich rebels were too diverse to form a homogeneous group. Many of them were liberals who were sharply divided from Churchill by his views on India.

The bulk of Lindsay's public supporters were Liberal, Labour or non-party figures. Within the Labour camp those most keen on Lindsay's candidature were not those closest to his own views but those most remote: the Communists and fellow-travellers. Because of the Popular Front imbroglio, there was a gap in Lindsay's support on the Labour right. Gordon Walker also continued to sulk, appearing on Lindsay's platforms only at the very end of the campaign. The chairman of the City Labour Party, one of the leading local Popular Fronters, told a public meeting that Lindsay understood the working class, 'and that the reason the working class is in the position it is today is because of the rotten system under which we live. We know there are many Conservatives in Oxford, like Mr Churchill and Mr Duff Cooper, who are not at all satisfied with the way things are going on.' Winston Churchill and the international proletariat were called in one sentence to Lindsay's aid. The result was declared on the night of 27 October; the figures appear in the table at the head of this chapter. In the three weeks following the Oxford by-election, four others took place. Three were more or less conventional party contests, at Dartford, Walsall and Doncaster, where the swings against the National Government were respectively 2.9, 0.4 and 2.6 per cent. The fourth was in the predominantly rural Bridgwater division of Somerset. Once again the Labour and Liberal parties supported an anti-Munich Independent.

On 10 October 1938 it was announced that the Conservative MP for Bridgwater had been appointed a High Court judge. This came as a complete surprise to local politicians of all parties, so that no party had any opportunity to make preparations for the necessary by-election. Within ten days, however, the local Conservative Executive had drawn up a short-list of two potential candidates, which was presented to the party's Central Council at a meeting in Bridgwater. That body adopted, almost unanimously, Patrick Heathcoat Amory, a member of a well-known Devon landed family, who expressed his pleased surprise at having been offered 'such a good constituency as this' at only 26. Choosing an opposition candidate was less straightforward. Sir Richard Acland, Liberal MP for Barnstaple (later to be a founder of the wartime Common Wealth Party and later again a Labour MP), had for some time been campaigning on behalf of a Popular Front. One of his supporters, a local vicar, suggested approaching a wartime colleague of his, Vernon Bartlett. Bartlett had been a foreign correspondent for *The Times* and the *News Chronicle*, was well known as a writer and broadcaster, and had been Secretary of the League of Nations Union. On being asked to stand, he complained that he knew nothing about party politics and less about agriculture. The complaints were swept aside: the fact that his grandfather had been a parson in the constituency for 57 years, his supporters assured him, would be enough to secure for him the affections of Bridgwater.

The Labour Party was split in the same way as at Oxford, but the prospects seemed better for the Popular Fronters. Relatively, Labour was much less important at Bridgwater (the Liberals had come second in 1935 and Labour had got only 19.8 per cent of the vote) and the local party was much poorer, not having well-connected Socialist dons to fall back upon. Accordingly, Transport House voted 'not to encourage a contest' at the by-election. A Labour candidate would receive no support from the party's by-election fund, to which the Bridgwater party had not paid its due contribution.

Besides, Oxford had driven a wedge into Transport House's anti-Popular Front campaign. If there were valid reasons for letting the Oxford Labour Party support Lindsay, then they should operate to let the Bridgwater party support Bartlett, who was evidently no more a Communist dupe than Lindsay. So when, on 18 October, the Secretary of the Labour Party told Bartlett that Transport House would 'strongly oppose' an Independent Progressive in Bridgwater, the threat was empty. By refusing for financial reasons to support a Labour candidate, the party had lost its only means of leverage on Bartlett and his supporters. Having been already endorsed by the Liberals, Bartlett received the official endorsement of the local Labour Party on 5 November.

The fame of the Bridgwater election has been mostly posthumous. While in progress it excited no especial attention – certainly much less than Oxford. A galaxy of anti-Munich speakers came down to help Bartlett, but their presence went unrecorded in the local press – in contrast with both Oxford, and Kinross and West Perthshire, which polled in December.[9] The absence of this information makes it even more difficult than elsewhere to assess the impact made on the constituency by foreign affairs. After the election Bartlett told acquaintances that he was surprised how much interest there was in foreign affairs. But he also said on occasion that he owed his victory to Tom Harrisson, of Mass-Observation, who insisted that he should speak about agriculture to his audiences, however ignorant he felt about it. At the annual dinner of the Bridgwater Chrysanthemum Society, 'Mr Vernon Bartlett said chrysanthemums were yet another subject about which he did not know as much as he ought to do (laughter).'

The confusion in popular attitudes to Munich was the same in Bridgwater as elsewhere. Immediately after Munich, the Vicar of Bridgwater said in a thanksgiving service: 'We owe a debt of gratitude to our Prime Minister which can never be repaid ... Death was robbed of its spoil by his faith, his perseverance, his prayers. The news was too good to be true.' When the campaign was under way, a Mrs Daisy Pryce-Michell entreated the women of Bridgwater: 'So, my friends ... we must send Mr Amory to Parliament to help Mr Chamberlain in his great effort for peace. If only I was not too delicate, I would gladly come and see some of you to help dispel any doubts you may have in your minds. God bless you all, and give His blessing of peace.' Unquestionably, however, many electors were beginning to have doubts. At one of Bartlett's meetings, an Amory supporter claimed that Chamberlain 'went to Munich like a British bulldog'. To which a voice from the back retorted: 'Next time why doan't 'ee send a retriever, so'er bring us back summat?' Pro- and anti-Munich letters were equally numerous in the local press.

Bartlett's own attitudes were characteristic of the liberal intellectual of the time. In the early 1930s he had been one of those who condemned the Versailles Treaty, and explained (if not excused) Nazi Germany by reference to its iniquity. Indeed, one of his broadcast talks, attacking the British Foreign Secretary for being unduly harsh on Germany at the Disarmament Conference in 1933, had led to the end of his regular contract with the BBC around the time of East Fulham. In a book on Nazi Germany published in 1933 he made several statements which have worn rather badly:

The Government now propose to get rid of the concentration camps without much delay. This drilling of youth, these provocative

speeches near the frontiers, these boring brass bands on the radio –
they are obviously all political blunders, but they are not made
because Germany wants war![10]

Remnants of the liberal 'let's be fair to Germany' attitude still persisted in
1938. The candidates were often asked at meetings about their attitudes to
German colonial claims, and Bartlett replied: 'Remembering that these
colonies up to twenty years ago belonged to Germany we should be
prepared to make sacrifices ourselves ... [but] in any concessions granted to
Germany there must be safeguards that she did not treat her colonies as she
had treated the Jews.' Nonetheless, the bulk of his campaign was devoted to
attacking Chamberlain's 'weak and vacillating foreign policy', while Amory
announced that he stood 'entirely behind the Prime Minister's policy of
rearmament on the one hand and conciliation on the other hand'. Polling
was on 17 November; the result was announced the following afternoon. As
at Oxford, turnout had risen sharply – this time by 9.6 per cent – and
there was a greater swing (7.6 per cent) than at Oxford (3.9 per cent)
against the government. Bartlett was to retain his seat against opposition
from both main parties in 1945, but in 1950, when he resigned, his
successor as Independent candidate came last.

What can the Munich by-elections tell us about public opinion at the
time? Contemporaries were agreed in seeing Bridgwater as a triumph for
the opponents of Munich. Feelings about Oxford were more mixed.
Conservatives naturally saw the result as a vindication of Chamberlain: 'It
is not my victory. It is Mr Chamberlain's', as Quintin Hogg said after the
announcement of the result. Those on the other side have tended to take
the view expressed by Lindsay and endorsed by his daughter and biographer:[11] namely that Oxford started the anti-Chamberlain bandwagon,
Bridgwater gave it a push and the Norway debate of May 1940 saw it
home. This has been contrasted with the view that public opinion stayed
with Chamberlain until Hitler occupied Prague in March 1939, and then
deserted him.[12] I shall attempt to examine these views in the light of what
evidence we have.

As mentioned earlier, Oxford in 1938 was the scene of a pioneer
opinion poll. Its methods were crude and its main defect was a serious
under-representation of prosperous electors – 'not because of an intentional
boycott, but usually because the maidservants answering the canvasser's ring
could not supply the information for the members of the household'.[13] But
with all its faults it is the only systematic evidence from any of the Munich
by-elections of what electors thought, as opposed to what journalists and
politicians thought they thought. Respondents' voting intentions in 1938
were compared with their reported votes in 1935, with the results shown in
Table 6.1.

Table 6.1 Oxford: Voting intention 1938 by reported vote 1935.

		Hogg 1938 %	*Lindsay 1938* %
Bourne	1935	70	16
Gordon Walker	1935	5	50
Didn't vote	1935	25	34
		100 ($n = 96^*$)	100 ($n = 88^*$)

*Note that these figures are close to the actual proportions voting for the two candidates – which increases confidence in the survey.
Source: Rae (1939).

Unfortunately, the reports of the poll give no information about those who said they would abstain at the by-election. The information in Table 6.1 is therefore incomplete, as is that in Table 6.2, which inverts the above results to show how those who reported voting for each candidate in 1935 said they would vote in the by-election. These figures suggest that the Hogg vote was substantially the traditional Conservative vote, and that the largest component of the Lindsay vote was the traditional Labour vote. It was thought at the time that Lindsay might not capture it, for several reasons. There was the reluctance of Gordon Walker and one section of the Labour Party to help him, or do any canvassing for him. There was the fear that working-class women might (*pace* Duff Cooper) be drawn into approving of Chamberlain as the man of peace. (In the survey, working-class women split 27:23 in favour of Lindsay and working-class men 28:16 – but we do not know whether the women were proportionately less 'conservative' in 1935.) It was also thought that Lindsay might suffer because of his remoteness from the working-class electorate, his hasty campaign and his diffidence as a candidate. As Tom Harrisson observed, '... his donnish advisers took it for granted that everyone in the town knew him as well as they did. They were wrong. Over half the Oxford electorate didn't know Lindsay from Adam'.[14] The chairman of the Liberal Association described Lindsay as 'magnificent but inaudible'. One of his students observed that he found it a 'harrowing experience' to have to go shaking hands with shop girls at a department store. (Since Lindsay was an active WEA organiser, it was presumably embarrassment, not dislike of the lower classes, that induced this feeling.) Ivor Davies described him as 'the worst Parliamentary candidate I have ever encountered'. As the pollsters in 1938 did not report the previous vote of potential abstainers, the proportion of 1935 Labour voters who abstained is unknown. Given the sharp rise in turnout, however, it is unlikely that it was very great.

The organiser of the survey thought that the high proportion of the Lindsay vote which came from previous non-voters indicated 'a considerable body of Liberal support for Lindsay, which was withheld in the case of the Labour candidate in 1935'. It is difficult to be sure. A large proportion

Table 6.2 Oxford: Reported vote 1935 by voting intention 1938. *Source*: Rae (1939).

		Bourne 1935 %	Gordon Walker 1935 %	Didn't Vote 1935 %
Hogg	1938	83	10	38
Lindsay	1938	17	90	62
		100 ($n = 81$)	100 ($n = 49$)	100 ($n = 64$)

of the 1935 non-voters tuned up by the survey must be not abstainers, but those either too young to vote in 1935 or not then living in the constituency. In the absence of a Liberal candidate in Oxford since 1929 one cannot tell how large the Liberal vote would have been, given the continued decline of the party throughout the 1930s.

The survey's most interesting finding is in the comparison of voting intention with newspaper taken (Table 6.3). These figures show a correlation between the political opinions of a paper and the voting intentions of its readers, and also between social class, as measured by paper taken, and voting intention. Because the original records have not survived, we cannot construct the multivariate model that would test the strength of these two effects. But one column demands close attention. The readers of *The Times* split two to one in favour of Lindsay. Not only was part of the social elite deserting the candidate favoured by most of the upper classes, but it was a part which read the paper more than any other identified with appeasement – the paper which told Chamberlain on 27 September that public opinion was in favour of a settlement with Berlin. This finding seems to confirm that the Lindsay vote was basically a working-class Labour vote, plus a tiny group (probably consisting mostly of dons) who supported Lindsay either because of his University reputation or because they shared his concern over Munich. People of this sort had made most of the running in the Lindsay campaign. Indeed, they (together with the working-class Popular Fronters in the Labour Party) had been responsible for Lindsay's candidature in the first place. Their assumptions about public opinion were shared by some of their opponents – for instance, the dons already quoted who wrote to *The Times* to complain that Lindsay might get an unfairly high share of the vote because of his reputation as Vice-Chancellor. But in fact the working-class electorate from which came most of Lindsay's support was quite unaffected by his standing in the University. Academics who spoke at meetings in east Oxford about 'The Master' in reverent tones were met with total bewilderment.

Bridgwater seems to be more clear-cut, but we do not have a contemporary opinion poll to hand. The swing of 7.6 per cent against the National Government was one of the highest – though not the highest – between Munich and the outbreak of war. Soon after the election Oliver Harvey

Table 6.3 Oxford: Voting intention by newspaper taken. *Source*: Rae (1939).

	Daily Mail %	Daily Telegraph %	Daily Express %	Oxford Mail %
Hogg	80	80	60	50
Lindsay	20	20	40	50
	100	100	100	100
	Daily Mirror %	The Times %	News Chronicle %	Daily Herald %
Hogg	38	33	25	16
Lindsay	62	67	75	84
	100	100	100	100

recorded: 'Vernon Bartlett told me about his election and how all the country people are passionately interested in foreign affairs and frankly bored by the agricultural part of his speeches.[15] On this point the evidence is conflicting; but there are certainly grounds for saying that Bridgwater is a rare case in British electoral history of a by-election whose result can be ascribed to a foreign policy issue.

But Oxford and Bridgwater were not the only by-elections of their period. In all, 19 by-elections were held in 1938 and 17 between January and August 1939. A meaningful figure for the swing against the government can be derived from 31 of these 36.[16] The by-elections may be divided into four periods, with one gap during which there were no contests.

1. January to July 1938: pre-Munich, 8 elections.
2. October to December 1938: in the shadow of Munich, 7 elections.
3. January to March 1939: post-Munich, pre-occupation of the rump of Czechoslovakia, 4 elections.
4. March to August 1939: from the occupation of Czechoslovakia to the outbreak of war: 12 elections.

Two main interpretations of the results of this group of elections have been offered. One is that of, for instance, Robert Rhodes James:

[Oxford] ... may be seen as evidence that revulsion against Munich had not yet assumed substantial proportions. Bridgwater ... was an encouragement, but it was soon checked when the Duchess of Atholl was defeated. These indications of popular feeling ... demonstrated that the post-Munich situation was still on balance to the Government's advantage ... The real turning point did not come until the occupation of the rest of Czechoslovakia in March 1939.[17]

The other, already mentioned, is that of D. Scott and R. Eatwell: namely that Oxford began a trend against the government which grew steadily, or at least continuously, until the fall of Chamberlain in May 1940. The by-election record does not support either hypothesis. The swings against the government in the four group elections are as shown in Table 6.4.

Table 6.4 By-elections 1938–39: mean swing (based on electorate) against National Government, and standard deviations.

	Swing %	Standard deviation %
1 Pre-Munich	2.6	2.8
2 Munich	4.1	4.6
3 Post-Munich	3.8	4.4
4 Post-Prague	3.3	4.9

There is little comfort for either school of thought in these figures. The elections which took place after March 1939 – when appeasement was finally pronounced dead – actually show a lower swing than those which occurred in the Oxford and Bridgwater period. Certainly, there was a consistent trend against the government. The notion that it would have won an overwhelming victory in an October 1939 general election, which Rhodes James seems to endorse, receives no support from these figures. Thirty out of the 31 seats swung in the same direction, against the National Government, and the only pro-Government swing was in a safe Labour seat. But there is no observable pattern, and the high standard deviations show that there was little consistency within the four groups corresponding to the changing pattern of foreign affairs. Few ways of categorizing the elections can impose any pattern on the results. Take, for instance, the five highest swings:

Bridgwater	17 Nov 1938	7.6%
Lewisham West	24 Nov 1938	5.2%
Ripon	23 Feb 1939	7.5%
Westminster Abbey	17 May 1939	8.2%
Hythe	20 July 1939	6.9%

These are all safe Conservative seats, but they have nothing else in common. Except for Bridgwater, they are not the seats most affected by foreign policy discussions.

The series of elections shows no association between changes of turnout and swing. However, one observation distinguishes Oxford and Bridgwater from other elections. At 27 of the 31, turnout dropped by amounts ranging from 0.6 per cent to 22.7 per cent. At two it rose by under 1 per cent. But at Oxford it went up by 9 per cent, and at Bridgwater by 9.6 per cent.

This is the best confirmation of the traditional view that popular concern about foreign policy led to increased interest in these elections. But this did not on its own produce unusually large swings. Probably, therefore, heightened interest in foreign affairs brought out marginal supporters of *both* sides – pro- as well as anti-Chamberlain. A vivid picture of the state of public opinion during the crisis is provided by Mass-Observation, some of whose early reports were collected in a Penguin Special called simply *Britain*, published in January 1939. This shows up the intensity, the confusion and the sheer changeability of opinion during the crisis. The percentage figures given are not based on reliable samples, but they were taken in working-class areas and certainly give a better measure of public opinion than do elite perceptions of it. Mass-Observation reported a succession of remarkable shifts in public opinion. Chamberlain's stock stood high on 15 September, after he had announced his first visit to Hitler over Czechoslovakia: 70 per cent of those asked thought his visit would help peace. Revelation of the Godesberg terms, however, provoked a sharp reaction against him on 21 and 22 September, with a striking difference between men and women (see Table 6.5). 350 answers to the question 'What do you think about Czechoslovakia?' were divided into four categories: Indignant (Czechs unfairly treated), No War (maybe unfair, but it avoids war), 'Pro-Chamberlain', and 'Don't Know'. The slump in pro-Chamberlain opinion was followed by a second peak after his announcement on 28 September of his proposed Munich visit. On the 29th a London sample produced the results shown in Table 6.6. The volume from which these figures are taken went to press before any post-Munich opinion figures became available, but there is no reason to doubt its assertion that 'at the moment of writing [November], antis are tending rapidly to build up again, while among men ... this build-up is more than among women'.

These figures confirm that women were more pro-Chamberlain than

Table 6.5 Views on Czechoslovakia, 22 September 1938: Mass-Observation sample.

	Men %	Women %	All %
Indignant	67	22	40
No War	2	16	10
Pro-Chamberlain	14	27	22
Don't Know	17	35	28

126

Table 6.6 Popularity of Chamberlain, 29 September 1938: Mass-Observation sample.

	Men %	Women %	All %
Pro	46	59	54
Anti	20	4	10
Mixed feelings	16	7	10
Don't know	16	30	26

men. They also show very wide fluctuations of opinion over a very short time, engendered by the contrary pressures of fairness to the Czechs and desire for peace. Chamberlain was overwhelmingly popular on 30 September. But the Munich terms were no better for the Czechs than the Godesberg ones which had made such an unfavourable impression on the public only a week earlier. So the relief of 30 September lasted days rather than weeks, and by the time of Oxford and Bridgwater confusion had set in again. People were still stirred by foreign affairs. But it was difficult for the ordinary elector to assess claim and counter-claim: 'Chamberlain got us peace'; 'Chamberlain gave Hitler all he wanted'. At Oxford and Bridgwater, with their Independent Progressive candidates, the confusion produced a rise in turnout.

Many commentators have assumed, without examining the evidence, that popular discontent with Chamberlain's foreign policy rose steadily from October 1938 onwards. This is not borne out by the by-election results. But, arguably, public opinion was neither for nor against Chamberlain except when dramatic events were in the offing. Most people, most of the time, had no views at all about foreign policy; foreign affairs played little or no part in their assessment of leading politicians. To look for a relationship between international events and the government's popularity may be to overestimate not only the electors' interest in foreign affairs but also the sophistication of their attitudes. Mass-Observation data, this time unpublished, provides a useful corrective. The surveys of attitudes conducted at Oxford and Bridgwater have unfortunately been lost; but one survives for Kinross and West Perthshire (21 December 1938), the other by-election to have been fought – by the candidates – specifically on foreign affairs. But the electors thought otherwise. Sixty-five per cent of those asked thought home affairs more important than foreign, 15 per cent thought foreign affairs more important, and the remaining 20 per cent did not know. Pro- and anti-Chamberlain views were related to personalities, not abstractions:

Woman, 50: 'Oh, the Duchess [of Atholl] is a fine woman – she is an' all. Ye know she will get in easily. I dinna know much about politics but I do know that if the Duchess says Mr Chamberlain is wrong he canna be right.'

Woman, 55: 'I've always been for the Duchess, but you can't do better than what Mr Chamberlain did, an old man – he went to Germany – why they might have killed him.'[18]

The Mass-Observation organizers had concluded about an earlier election (Fulham West in April 1938): 'No wide understanding about what is happening abroad. When concerned with foreign affairs it is almost always from a personal point of view: it will affect the family, take away a son, send up prices, let in foreigners, etc. Remarkable absence of clear-cut attitudes to the foreign position.' This impression of the nature of the 'belief-systems' of the electorate has been confirmed by modern studies.[19] For this reason alone, stereotypes of public opinion around the time of Munich would need to be queried. We have already discussed two hypotheses about public opinion: that a groundswell of anti-Chamberlain feeling built up from Oxford to May 1940, and that the nation supported its Premier until, but not beyond, March 1939. Neither is supported by the evidence presented in this chapter, any more than the contemporary press view, that Chamberlain would have won an October general election with a massive majority.[20] For the most part electors were uninterested in foreign affairs, but when they were interested they were confused and bewildered with no idea where to turn. Commentators would be wise to take heed of a warning written within two months of Munich:

> The month of September, 1938, will provide the historian of the future...with a supremely illuminating insight into sense and statesmanship and the status quo. But if, as has been the custom in the past, the historian accepts as statements of fact the numerous published assertions as to what the public of England are thinking about it all, he will, as so often before, be a typically lousy historian.[21]

Notes

1   Dawson's diary, as quoted in F. R. Gannon, *The British press and Germany, 1936–39* (Oxford: Clarendon Press, 1971) p. 73.
2   A. Duff Cooper, *Old men forget* (London: Hart-Davis, 1953) p. 251.
3   Minutes of Oxford Constituency Labour Party. Seen by courtesy of the late Harry Cole. Other quotations from the section on Oxford not otherwise identified are from the *Oxford Mail*, various dates in October 1938. See also I. Davies, 'How Hogg Won Oxford', *New Outlook*, October 1963. Other information on the

Oxford by-election was obtained in interviews with the late Ivor Davies and the late R. H. S. Crossman.

4 Richard Crossman – for it was he – made this claim in an interview in 1972.

5 For the rumbustious electioneering of Frank Gray, Liberal MP for Oxford from 1922 until his unseating on petition in 1924, see C. Fenby, *The other Oxford* (London: Lund Humphries, 1970).

6 *Picture Post*, 5 Nov. 1938; reproduced in T. Hopkinson (ed.), *Picture Post, 1938–50* (Harmondsworth: Penguin. 1970) pp. 24–30.

7 *The Times*, 20 Oct. 1938.

8 B. Pimlott, *Hugh Dalton* (London: Jonathan Cape 1985), pp. 258–260

9 Bridgwater was principally served by a Conservative weekly (so described in the contemporary press guides), the *Bridgwater Mercury*; Oxford by an independent daily evening paper, the *Oxford Mail*. There are few reports from Bridgwater in other papers circulating in the area or in the national press. Bridgwater got much less coverage than Oxford - perhaps because it was further from London and no leading communicators of the day had spent three years of their youth there. Quotations in the section on Bridgwater not otherwise identified are from the *Bridgwater Mercury*, various issues in October and November 1938. See also Vernon Bartlett, *And now, tomorrow* (London: Chatto & Windus, 1960).

10 V. Bartlett, *Nazi Germany explained* (London: Gollancz, 1933) pp. 243, 267.

11 D. Scott, *A. D. Lindsay* (Oxford: Basil Blackwell, 1971) p. 254.

12 R. Eatwell, 'Munich, Public opinion and the Popular Front', *Journal of Contemporary History*, **6** (4), pp. 122–39, 1971.

13 S. F. Rae, 'The Oxford by-election: a study in the straw-vote method', *Political Quarterly*, **10** (2) pp. 268–79. (1939) The quotation is from p. 277. The tables are derived from this source and from Rae's doctoral thesis: S. F. Rae, *The concept of public opinion and its measurement.* (Ph.D. thesis, University of London, 1939).

14 In *Picture Post*, 5 Nov. 1938.

15 J. Harvey (ed.), *The diplomatic diaries of Oliver Harvey* (London: Collins, 1970) p. 234.

16 The five exceptions are: Pontypridd and West Derbyshire (no contest in 1935), Combined Scottish Universities (no contest at the by-election), Colne Valley (where the strength of three parties, Conservative, Labour and Liberal, makes swing worthless), and Kinross and West Perthshire. In this seat the Duchess of Atholl, elected as a Conservative in 1935, resigned in 1938 as a protest against the government's foreign policy and stood again as an Independent. In a straight fight with a Conservative, which took place on a day of heavy snow, 21 December 1938, she lost by 1,313 (3.8 per cent) – We cannot derive a useful swing figure from a pair of contests when the same person is the government candidate in the first and the anti-government candidate in the second; so it has had to be omitted.

17 R. R. James, *Churchill: A study in failure* 2nd ed. (London: Weidenfeld & Nicolson, 1990) p. 340.

18 Mass Observation records, University of Sussex: file on Kinross by-election.

19 Ibid., file on West Fulham. See especially G. A. Almond and S. Verba, *The Civic Culture* 2nd ed (London: Sage, 1989); P. Converse, 'The Nature of Belief Systems in Mass Publics', in *Ideology and Discontent*, D. Apter (ed.), (Glencoe, NY: The Free Press, 1964), pp. 206–61.

20 The Gallup Poll figures for voting intention in February 1939 were: Government, 50%; Opposition, 44%; Don't Know, 6%.

21 T. Harrisson and C. Madge (eds), *Britain, by Mass-Observation* (Harmondsworth: Penguin, 1939) p. 103.

CHAPTER 7

By-elections of the Second World War

Paul Addison

The by-elections of 1939–45 were so unlike normal by-elections that at first it is hard to make sense of them. There were no contests between the three main parties. At the outbreak of the war, under the Chamberlain government, the Chief Whips of the Liberal, Labour and Conservative parties concluded an electoral truce whereby, when a seat fell vacant, the party which had held it previously would nominate a candidate, while the other two parties agreed not to do so. The agreement was to last for the duration of the war, or until one of the signatories withdrew. The purpose of the arrangement was to preserve a measure of national unity by confining party differences to the House of Commons. When all three parties joined the Churchill Coalition in May 1940, the truce acquired a deeper significance, as an essential precondition of unity within the government. Hence, although the rank and file of the Labour Party at times grew very restless with an arrangement which protected a Conservative majority of over 200, the truce was never seriously in question. Of the 141 seats which fell vacant during the war, 66 were filled unopposed, by the nominee of the incumbent party. In the remaining 75 seats a contest was forced by Independents and minor party candidates. A new party, Common Wealth, was formed in 1942 as a direct result of the vacuum created by the truce, and won three by-elections against government candidates.

The 104 citizens who came forward to fight by-elections were, naturally, a mixed bunch. Most have their interest as individuals, but too much concentration upon particular personalities can obscure their general significance. Broadly speaking, three types of candidate were dominant during three different phases of the war. Of the 22 who stood between September 1939 and the King's Norton by-election of May 1941, 15 were anti-war candidates of one kind or another, defying prevailing opinion. The arrival of the colourful carpetbagger, Noel Pemberton Billing, at the Hornsey by-election, marked a new departure. He was the first of a series of candidates who tried to tap the mainstream of underlying discontent with war-time conditions, and the growing record of military failure. Four such

130

Independents defeated government candidates in the first six months of 1942. The candidates of this phase were very much the products of a particularly frustrating phase of the war, and yet they have a broad relevance. War brought about a radical social climate at home, and this entailed for many a disillusion with pre-war Conservatism. Apart from this factor, it was inevitable that the grumbles engendered by wartime conditions should be directed first and foremost against the Conservatives, since they were the dominant power in the House and the government. The candidates of 1941-2 therefore displayed a vague radical anti-Toryism, preparing the way for the more positively opposed candidates of 1943-5.

The publication of the Beveridge Report in December 1942, with its promise of a New Deal for all, coinciding with the turn of the military tide towards victory, marked the beginning of a new phase. There was a strong trend back towards normal party strife, and the majority of challengers to the electoral truce in 1943-5 stood for recognizably Liberal or Socialist programmes. There was, then, an underlying logic to the long procession of candidates who followed in the footsteps of Pemberton Billing. After allowing for several exceptions, they can be described as harbingers of the Labour assault on the Conservative Party in the general election of 1945. The whole weight of their offensive, as Table 7.1 below indicates, was borne by the Conservative-held seats. This was partly because the majority of seats falling vacant were Conservative; primarily because the home front was characterized by a growing anti-Tory movement, while Conservatives themselves, enjoying their great majority in the House, and confident that Churchill would bring them a sweeping victory at the post-war general election, had no incentive for rocking the boat. Even when Labour seats were contested, later in the war, it was never by spokesmen for unofficial Conservatism.

In analysing the behaviour of voters, we are again faced with the extreme abnormalities of wartime. Until the Motherwell by-election of April 1945, all by-elections were conducted according to the electoral

Table 7.1 Contests and unopposed returns in Conservative and Labour seats, May 1941 – April 1945.

	Labour		Conservative	
	Vacant	Contested	Vacant	Contested
1941	6	0	16	8
1942	13	2	12	11
1943	2	1	21	18
1944	4	3	7	6
1945	2	2	3	3

register of March 1939, thus ignoring the rising crop of young voters, and the great movements of population necessitated by the war. A constituency in a great industrial area would be denuded not only of conscripts to the services, but of women and old people evacuated away from the risk of bombing and key workers directed to different parts of the country. An electorate might, therefore, be considerably distorted in its social composition. The victor of the Wallasey by-election, George Reakes, thought that one reason for his success was that, of the original population of 100,000 in 1939, 40,000, most of them from among the more well-to-do, had left in order to escape from an area of very high bombing.[1] Such shifts in population also make it difficult to estimate the level of turnout in most by-elections, and hence the level of interest aroused by the campaigns. Estimates were sometimes made of the live register, as opposed to the theoretical register of 1939. If we can rely upon such estimates for half a dozen of the by-elections of 1943–5, the effective electorate represented between 52 per cent and 78 per cent of its strength on paper. This may enable the exceptionally low turnout figures for wartime by-elections to be put in perspective. Thirty of the 75 contests resulted in a nominal turnout of over 40 per cent. In constituencies with one-third of the electorate absent, a common enough situation, this would imply effective turnouts of 60 per cent and over. Electioneering itself had to be carried on despite considerable handicaps, notably the absence of cars to take voters to the polling booth. In rural areas, farmers' hay wagons and pony traps were pressed into service – a slight feudal advantage accruing to the Conservatives. The candidates were allowed a ration of 200 gallons of petrol each for personal transport and often ran out in the more rambling constituencies.

One of the major distorting factors which complicate analysis was the strong moral sanction which the government and its candidates sought to bring to bear against the interlopers. After May 1940 every by-election bore a double aspect. On the one hand it was a matter of deciding which alternative the voter preferred. On the other it was a question of whether the voter, as a supporter of the government and adherent of one of the three parties which had signed the truce, should obey the advice given by all the party leaders, and vote for the government candidate regardless of his party label. Patriotic duty seemed to interfere with normal choice. At the Eddisbury by-election of April 1943 the government candidate made use of the slogan 'Hitler is watching Eddisbury'. The same month the government candidate at Daventry, Reginald Manningham-Buller, told one of his audiences: 'Three countries will be pleased if I am defeated – Germany, Italy and Japan'.[2] After losing four by-elections to Independents in the first half of 1942, the party leaders banded together and issued a joint message, signed by Churchill, Ernest Brown (the National Liberal leader), Attlee and Sinclair, to electors at subsequent by-elections. The text, apart from the name of the constituency, served for the rest of the war and read as follows:

> The verdict recorded by a single constituency is flashed round the world as though it were the voice of Britain that had spoken, and Barsetshire will realise that it has the responsibility at this moment of indicating to the United Nations, and to neutral countries, that we are united among ourselves in our unflinching determination to organise our total resources for victory.

Churchill usually sent an additional personal message to Conservative and allied candidates, commending their virtues. 'Let the electors ask themselves', he wrote to the candidate at Chelmsford in April 1945, 'what possible good it would do to the country to return to Parliament in these present times a member of a disintegrating political fragment such as the Common Wealth Party.'[3] Yet the electors returned the Common Wealth candidate. It may well be that this heavy hand jogging the voter's arm lost as much support as it gained. Perhaps the most outstanding fact about the wartime by-elections is that, despite the official line, the government lost nine contests in the period 1942–5, or 11 if the exceptional cases of Belfast West and the Combined Scottish Universities are taken into account. An opinion poll taken in April 1942 produced a notable majority in favour of by-elections being contested.[4] Whatever Coalition propaganda made out, voters knew that an expression of dissent implied no disunity about the will to victory, nor would it affect the course of the war. 'To labour that point', wrote the *East Anglian Daily Times*, 'would be to insult the intelligence and the patriotism of a people who know quite clearly that without victory all their high hopes for the eventual peace are simply chimerical.'[5] It is very likely indeed that one of the functions of by-elections, as Attlee argued in private, was 'the attraction to people, who have to submit to many Government regulations, of being able to act contrary to the wish of the Government with impunity. The more the Government expresses its support of a particular candidate, the greater is the attraction'.[6] Another very obvious problem in analysing voting behaviour is the difficulty of comparing results when the Independent candidates were of such variable quality and appeal. Only by comparing a large number of results can we expect that variables will tend to cancel each other out. For example, in the eight seats which the Conservatives defended after and including Hornsey, in 1941, their share of the poll increased on average by 5.6 per cent. The first half of 1942 was by contrast a phase of almost undiluted military disaster. Over the ten by-elections up to and including Salisbury in July 1942, the Conservatives suffered an average loss of 6.9 per cent. As these figures indicate, even at this point, when in theory party politics lay submerged by the urgencies of war, by-election results tended to fluctuate around the norm of the pre-war Conservative percentage of the vote, with the wartime opposition candidates picking up a share related to the pre-war Labour and/or Liberal vote. Several of the results from 1943–5, as will be argued, provide good evidence of a swing to Labour. But Tom Harrisson of Mass-Observation was almost alone in deducing that Labour would win the general election at the end of the war: contemporaries paid considerable attention to by-elections, and members of the government worried about adverse results, but hardly anyone seemed to understand what was happening.

Throughout the war there was no more depressing period than the opening nine months – the 'phoney war'. The Chamberlain government watched apprehensively for signs of anti-war feeling. Three British Union of Fascists candidates each failed to secure more than 3 per cent of the vote, and the Communists, who adopted an anti-war line after the Russo–German partition of Poland, fared little better. Only the ILP, providing an outlet for frustrated Labour voters at Stretford in December 1939 and Renfrewshire East in May 1940, appeared to evoke any response for peace. Lord Beaverbrook, who was also against the war at this time, toyed with the idea of financing ILP candidates.[7] It was difficult for local Labour caucuses to abandon the fight against the friends of Chamberlain, and at Glasgow Pollok in April 1940 the divisional party broke the rules, put up its own candidate and was disaffiliated. Had the 'phoney war' been prolonged, the truce would almost certainly have provoked a general revolt in the Labour Party. But on 10 May Churchill became Prime Minister, and the peril of the moment effaced party feeling.

It had always been a temptation for a party caucus in a safe seat to put up its own candidate without paying very much attention to the opinion of the rank and file. The electoral truce apparently made safe seats safer still, and there were two striking examples in wartime of a rank-and-file rebellion against a Conservative association. At Newcastle North in 1935 the Conservative majority was 17,990. In May 1940 the local association adopted H. Grattan-Doyle, the son of the retiring Member, as its candidate by a vote of 239 to 5. At the invitation of dissatisfied Conservatives, a rival candidate was nominated: Sir Cuthbert Headlam, a leading figure in the region, and experienced former MP. To the great annoyance of the electorate, these two candidates, supported by rival associations, campaigned against each other while the BEF struggled to escape from Dunkirk.[8] Headlam won a resounding victory. Brighton was still more certainly Conservative, a two-Member constituency where the majority in 1935 was 41,626. The local association adopted Flight-Lieutenant William Teeling as their candidate at the by-election of February 1944. Teeling had travelled the world as a writer and worker in the Roman Catholic cause, but he was almost unknown in Brighton. With a few minutes to go before nominations closed, a rival appeared: Bruce Dutton Briant, a well-known local barrister of undoubted Conservative loyalty. The Mayor of Brighton was his brother, and the Mayor of Hove signed his nomination papers. Briant alleged that the local party, in collusion with the party chiefs in London, had fixed up a rush election in order to get Teeling in without opposition. There seems to have been strong resentment in the local business community against the choice of an outsider. The hotel and boarding industry needed to be set on its feet again, and Briant belonged firmly in the town oligarchy whose interests were at stake. The local party arranged for Churchill to send down a thunderbolt, a letter condemning Briant's candidature as an 'attempted swindle'. This proved to be a *faux pas*, and after an outburst of local resentment Churchill sent another and more reasoned letter.[9] Briant, with 46 per cent of the poll, came close to upsetting Teeling.

These two contests were, however, only side-shows by comparison with the main theme of wartime by-elections, the radical assault on Conservative seats. Hardly anyone could have been more unsuitable as the pioneer of this development than Noel Pemberton Billing. One of the wild young men of aviation before 1914, Billing was a lone survivor of the jingoism of the Great War. A similar electoral truce had operated in the years 1914–18 and Billing had been the first Independent to defy it successfully, at the East Hertford-shire by-election of March 1916. He had stood as the champion of air power, and later in the war emerged as the hero of a libel case in which he alleged that the Germans possessed a black book containing the names of 47,000 perverts in high places in Britain. In the Second World War he stood for the defeat of Germany by bombing alone, and the defence of Britain by equally spaced upward-pointing lights which would confuse the enemy and enable the RAF's fighters to see the bombers against a background of light. For post-war policy, he argued that general elections should be replaced by the multiplication of by-elections, and an additional assembly of trades and professions be set beside the Houses of Parliament. There should also be a Woman's Parliament, 'to deal with domestic matters'. Billing fought four by-elections in the second half of 1941, and made quite an impression with his forceful speechmaking and yellow Rolls-Royce.[10] He was soon joined on the campaign trail by another diverting figure, Reg Hipwell, the founder and editor of the forces' newspaper *Reveille*, a vehicle for the grumbles of the ordinary soldier, and a never-failing source of pin-up girls. Hipwell announced at Scarborough in September 1941 that he was fighting for a 3s.-a-day minimum for servicemen, with £2 weekly for wives, 8s. 6d. for each child and an increase of at least 20 per cent in old-age pensions. He accused the president of the divisional Conservative Association of leaving Dunkirk ten days before the men under his command, and argued that although the Conservative candidate claimed to be unfit for service because he had only one leg, Douglas Bader had none and had still served his country. Hipwell's style was entirely uninhibited. He admired, he claimed, many of the planks in the Conservative platform, yet felt he also stood for the best that the Labour and Liberal parties had to offer. An observer for Mass-Observation thought it unlikely that Hipwell had ever read anything on economics or politics. 'For Democracy not Vested Interest' was one of his slogans, but he confided after his defeat: 'I only came up here for a holiday – something to make a change.'[11] Hipwell not only fought four by-elections himself, the last at Hartlepools in June 1943, but put up his *Reveille* assistant Winifred Henney at Harrow in December 1941, and acted as W. J. Brown's agent for his conquest of Rugby in April 1942. Both Billing and Hipwell were, in their different ways, irresponsible candidates. But they chalked up respectable polls, and *The Times* noted their emergence as an encouraging sign of a desire to ginger up the war effort.[12]

The first Independent to defeat a government candidate was Denis Kendall, who won Grantham in March 1942 with 50.8 per cent of the poll. The background was one of crisis in the war effort. In Russia the Red Army was barely holding its own, and a clamour was beginning in Britain for a Second Front. The Japanese had overrun the Far East, sinking the *Prince of Wales* and the *Repulse* on 10 December, and capturing Singapore on 15 February. The press and the House were obsessed by real or imagined deficiencies in war production, and Churchill had reshuffled the government, bringing Sir Stafford Cripps into the War Cabinet. Cripps, who had just returned from 18 months as Ambassador to Russia, appeared to be the long-awaited dispassionate brain who would introduce efficiency into all branches of the war effort. Kendall was Grantham's Cripps, as one of his leaflets boasted: 'Denis Kendall is another Stafford Cripps. Independent yet Churchillian.' A Yorkshireman who had made good in the United States, Kendall was the manager of a local engineering firm. He paid high wages and provided his workers with such additional welfare benefits as dances on Saturday night and services on Sunday morning – at which he read the lesson. He saw himself as a 'production man' who would go to Parliament 'not to learn politics but to teach members what production meant to the Country and the Empire'. Formerly a member of the local Labour Party, he had approached the Conservatives for nomination at the by-election, one reflection of a get-ahead approach which also included the demand that inefficient firms should be taken over by the government, and cost-plus – the system whereby government contractors were guaranteed a margin of profit above their estimate of cost – be abolished. His opponent, Sir Arthur Longmore, had recently been retired by Churchill from the command of the RAF in the Near East. Although the RAF was a great force in local society, it was also a divisive one, while Kendall could play the card of local man versus outsider. The local Communist Party, following the new line laid down since Hitler's invasion of Russia in 1941, produced a special pamphlet calling on the electorate to show their solidarity with the Red Army by voting for the government candidate. The local Labour Party decided, after much heart-searching, to lie low, and had to restrain their prospective candidate and other party workers from aiding Kendall.[13]

At Grantham the Conservative share of the vote fell by 8.9 per cent compared with 1935. At Rugby, W. J. Brown, a perfect stranger to the constituency, reduced it by 13.3 per cent. Rugby had been the seat of the former Conservative Chief Whip and Secretary for War, David Margesson, and was thought to be entirely safe. The Conservative candidate, Sir Claude Holbrook, had been chairman for 15 years of the local association. He not only declared that the electors of the division were against the holding of an election, but on the eve of poll wrote an article for the local press on 'Why I Won'. Brown had been a Labour MP in 1929–31, broke away to join Mosley's short-lived New Party, and subsequently fought bitterly against all the party machines. He was best known as the General Secretary of the major white-collar union, the Civil Service Clerical Association, which he had founded. His politics revolved around the idea of the general will as understood by W. J. Brown and thwarted by the party caucuses. In detail his programme ran as follows: '(a) Total efficiency in total war effort; (b) reconstitution of the Government on a non-party basis; (c) breaking through the contradictions in production, the Civil Service, politics and propaganda, which hinder the war effort; (d) maintenance of the freedom of the public Press and of public criticism against the growing tendency of the Government towards suppression; (e) democratization of the Army; (f) real equality of sacrifice.' The local Labour Party was split over Brown's candidature, while the National Council of Labour passed a resolution condemning him as a disruptive individual, not a fit and proper person to represent the working classes. At the last minute Brown came out in favour of the Second Front; and although Margesson himself warned voters that Hitler would gloat if Brown got in, Brown got in.[14]

The circumstances at Wallasey, where George Reakes defeated the government candidate at the by-election of April 1942, were again different. This time both the main candidates were local men. The Conservative, Alderman Pennington, had served on the town council since 1924; Reakes, who was formerly Labour, since 1922. A third candidate, the wealthy shipowner Major Leonard Cripps, the right-wing brother of Sir Stafford, issued one of the most unexceptionable manifestos of the war. He declared that he stood for victory, the support of competent Ministers such as Churchill and Cripps, the impartial examination of complaints and criticism, 'facing up to our mistakes' and avoiding 'hiding our heads in the sand'. Cripps received help from Liberal and Conservative quarters, but Reakes got none from Labour, unlike Brown and Kendall. During the Chamberlain period he had drifted away from the local Labour Party by championing conscription and rearmament, and praising the Munich agreement. 'The outstanding feature of the by-election at Wallasey', said *The Times* special correspondent, 'is the extent to which the Left has worked for the return of the National Government candidate...' Pennington and Reakes were old friends and, but for the intervention of Cripps, the contest would have been thoroughly cosy. According to the veteran Liberal campaigner Ivor Davies, Reakes was 'the local personification of the little man. Reakes had about him a wholesome humanity and real simplicity that made him impossible to dislike'.[15] He was good at canvassing in a saloon bar, and 'bore a remarkable resemblance to Arthur Askey'.[16] Reakes stood at the request of a group of local Conservatives who feared that an outside candidate would be foisted on the constituency. Once Pennington had been chosen, Reakes was left with little to say, apart from the fact that his own candidacy gave the electors a chance to vote against the party politicians. Nevertheless, the Conservative share of the vote fell by 35.7 per cent. Reakes attributed his triumph partly to the migration of Conservative voters from the constituency, partly to the stresses and strains of war, but above all to the revulsion against the appeasers, a curious argument from Wallasey's most notable man of Munich.[17]

The most common explanation of these results was popular frustration with the discouraging progress of the war, and Tom Driberg's victory at Maldon on 25 June was inevitably linked with the loss of Tobruk on 1 June, a frighteningly unexpected defeat. Driberg himself maintained that Tobruk was not decisive. Unlike the other Independents of 1942, he was consciously and openly on the Left, although not a member of the Labour Party. He was already well known as the author of the 'William Hickey' gossip column in the *Daily Express*, and continued to write it for a year after his election. It was Tom Hopkinson, the editor of *Picture Post*, who suggested to Driberg that he stand. Hopkinson belonged to a gathering of leftish public figures known as the 1941 Committee, which had devised in May 1942 a 'Nine-Point Declaration' as a platform for future by-election candidates. Driberg adopted the Nine Points as the basis of his campaign. Slightly abbreviated, these comprised:

(1) *Greater equality* of work, payment, sacrifice and opportunity; (2) *Transfer to Common Ownership* of services, industries, and companies in which managerial inefficiency or the profit motive is harming the war effort; (3) *Reform of the Government Supply Organisations*; (4) *Establishment of effective Works Councils*; (5) *Elimination of Red-Tape in the Civil Service*; (6)*Maximum freedom of expression*; (7) *British initiative in planning an Offensive Grand Strategy*; (8) *Repudiation of any policy of Vengeance*; (9) *Preliminary Post-war plans* for the provision of full and free education, employment and a civilised standard of living for everyone.[18]

Could the electors of Maldon have told the difference between Driberg's programme and Kendall's? Since they both concentrated on efficiency in the war effort, and described themselves as Independents, it must be doubtful. Nevertheless, Driberg's campaign had considerable significance behind the scenes. From the Left's point of view, Kendall, Brown and Reakes were rootless minor demagogues, stealing the by-election game from true progressives. The Nine-Point programme was designed to drive out irresponsible candidates.

Driberg's most important supporter at Maldon was the Revd Jack Boggis, the secretary of the Braintree Labour Party, who organized his campaign committee. But this was by no means confined to Labour supporters. The Conservative candidate, Reuben Hunt, was an elderly and uninspiring farmer who made little effort and the Independent Agricultural candidate remained obscure. Tom Wintringham, J. B. Priestley and Vernon Bartlett all spoke for Driberg. His luckiest break, he believed, was being the only candidate to appear for the opening of a new Anglo–Soviet bookshop in Braintree. On polling day the Conservative share of the vote was down 22 per cent on 1935.[19]

The election of four Independents could be interpreted as simply a patriotic response to bad war news, as part of a wider drift away from all party politics or, as Driberg saw his own success in retrospect, as part of the swing to the Left. All three explanations are compatible. Just as the Liberal Party declined in popularity during the Great War, as it became the chief scapegoat for everything that went wrong, so Dunkirk and the defeats of 1941–2 struck a blow at Conservative support. In the spring of 1942 Mass-Observation conducted a poll in three separate parts of the country in which people were asked who they thought would win the next general election. About half would express no opinion – understandably since there was no discussion whatever of the subject in the press or on the radio at that time. In the London area 12 per cent expected a Conservative and 27 per cent a Labour win; in the Midlands, 14 per cent a Conservative and 33 per cent a Labour win; in the North, 17 per cent a Conservative win, 26 per cent a Labour win.[20] These figures suggest that Conservatism was in far worse trouble then than in 1945, and the by-elections rather confirm this. Throughout the war, until April 1945, the out-of-date register, by excluding the growing number of new and certainly more left-wing voters, contained a built-in pro-Conservative bias. Despite this, the Conservative at Maldon did much better in the general election of 1945 than at the war-time by-election. But it is doubtful whether the swing away from the Conservatives meant a swing to Labour at this point. As late as the spring of 1943 Mass-Observation, commenting on the steady leftward trend of opinion during the war, also defined it as a trend away from all parties: 'This growing mass of politically leaderless people have no group in which to embody their aspirations and no clear idea as to how their hopes can be fulfilled.'[21] Obviously, however, the most likely implication of a leftward trend was a swing to Labour. The left-wing candidates of 1943–5 succeeded in providing a perfect half-way house between vague discontent with the status quo and a positive commitment to Labour.

The crystallization of pro-Labour feeling may be dated from the publication of the Beveridge Report in December 1942. Although commissioned by the government, this great landmark was in effect a one-man political manifesto, carefully publicized in advance. Beveridge had been asked to work out a plan for co-ordinating the various schemes of social insurance. He not only proposed a comprehensive social insurance plan for all, but ranged far beyond his original brief with demands for 'a comprehensive policy of social progress' to include a national health service and the maintenance of employment. The Report created profound popular interest and approval, but the government, like the Conservative Party and the leaders of industry, treated it with reserve.[22] In the debate of 16–18 February 1943 Ministers accepted most of the Report in principle, as the basis for working out their own proposals. But 97 Labour MPs rebelled and voted for an amendment demanding its implementation at the earliest possible moment. In effect, Labour had broken with the Conservatives on a major issue. In March an opinion poll registered 47 per cent of people dissatisfied with the government's response to Beveridge, as against 29 per cent who were satisfied.[23] It was not until September 1944 that the government's own social security plan was announced, and in the interval progressive politicians rode the Beveridge boom with the cry of 'Beveridge in full and at once'. Churchill had stressed that victory must come first; but victory was already in sight, and people's thoughts inevitably turned towards post-war life. Propagandists had often raised their hopes since 1940, but there was a strong collective memory of Lloyd George's promise of 'a land fit for heroes to live in', and the subsequent years of mass unemployment.[24] The Left warned that Toryism would put the clock back to 1939, and cited Churchill's involvement with the relics of Vichy France and Fascist Italy, Darlan and Badoglio. What kind of future would the troops come home to? Here was a climate of doubt in which Common Wealth and other progressive candidates could flourish.

Common Wealth was founded on 26 June 1942 by the merger of two organisations, the Forward March and the 1941 Committee. Forward March was the creation of the MP for Barnstaple, Sir Richard Acland, a member of an old-established Liberal family comparable with the Foots or the Trevelyans. He had been converted in 1936 to Socialism, and in 1940 to Christianity. His book *Unser kampf*, published in March 1940, called for the conversion of the war into a moral crusade; redemption and victory could be achieved only by the abandonment of private property, the root of all selfish behaviour. There must be a great change of heart leading to the establishment of common ownership. Acland wanted to found a mass movement; the 1941 Committee, by contrast, was a loose association of highly placed professional people whose main concern was the efficient conduct of the war. It arose out of a famous series of broadcasts given by the novelist J. B. Priestley after Dunkirk, with Edward Hulton, the owner of *Picture Post*, as its chief patron. The 1941 Committee was ready to accept Acland's demand for common ownership, at least for the sake of an efficient war effort, but most of its members shrank from the idea of establishing a mass political movement, and almost all the personnel of the 1941 Committee abandoned Common Wealth within a matter of weeks.

As a movement, Common Wealth therefore bore the dominant impress of Acland's own personality.[25] Its appeal was almost exclusively to the suburban middle class, and especially the professional employee. It attracted idealists who before the war might have worked for the League of Nations Union, but were put off the Labour Party by its cautious machine politics and rough-and-tumble atmosphere. The professional ethic and the ideal of service, rather than class interest, were the basis of its appeal, devolution ('Vital Democracy') as against the growth of state planning: managers and workers were to own factories and co-operate in running them. The moral flavour of Common Wealth is caught in the slogan of its candidate at Newark in June 1943, Flight-Lieutenant Moran: 'Human Fellowship not Inhuman Competition; Service to the Community not Self Interest; The Claims of Life not The Claims of Property.'[26] Typically, Common Wealth candidates were sincere young men who genuinely believed in a kinder and better world.

Acland and the majority of keen rank-and-file members imagined they were heading for a millennium in which the existing and corrupt old Labour Party would be transformed or displaced. But this was not the only view. One of the most prominent figures in the party was Tom Wintringham, the former commander of the British battalion of the International Brigade in the Spanish Civil War. Although detached from the Communist Party, Wintringham remained a Marxist and believed that Common Wealth's role was to be found within a Popular Front of left-wing parties. A still more realistic view of Common Wealth was taken by R. W. Mackay, who entered the party in 1943 and gradually gave it a viable central, regional and electoral organization. Mackay was a solicitor from Australia who had come to Britain and become a Labour Party stalwart. Apart from Labour, his chief causes were federal union and proportional representation. Like many people on the Left, Mackay was very alarmed that Labour, having entered the Coalition, would be persuaded by Churchill to arrange another 'coupon' election at the end of the war. The only way to prevent this, he argued, was to establish an effective opposition party in the country, 'carrying on electoral organisation against the Coalition or Tory Government in preparation for the General Election when it comes'.[27]

By September 1944 Common Wealth possessed 321 branches with 12,049 members. Sixty-eight prospective candidates had been listed in March. Ironically, the movement depended heavily for its finances upon its two rich men – Acland himself, and Alan P. Good, an industrialist and survivor of the 1941 Committee. In 1943 they contributed almost £17,000 of the party's total income of £20,000.[28] As the end of the war drew closer, Acland was obliged to recognize the limits of what Common Wealth could achieve. In the autumn of 1944 Common Wealth applied for affiliation to the Labour Party and was brusquely rejected. It fell back on the strategy of contesting seats where there was no Labour candidate, or where there was some special argument for putting up a candidate. In the end it fielded only 23 candidates in 1945, only one of whom, Wing-Commander Ernest Millington at Chelmsford, was elected. From the historical standpoint Common Wealth was a tiny tributary through which Acland himself, Millington, Desmond Donnelly, Elaine Burton, Raymond Blackburn and George Wigg passed eventually into the ranks of the Labour Party in the House, and a few thousand voters were added to its mass support in the country.

There were several by-elections between 1943 and 1945 at which there was clearly one Independent candidate of a Socialist or Labour character, a reasonable substitute from the elector's viewpoint for an official Labour candidate. The ILP succeeded in fulfilling this role with two of its nominees in the last months of the war, and if we include them with Common Wealth and Independent Labour candidates, we have 14 seats where a swing to highly unofficial Labour may usefully be calculated (see Table 7.2).

Table 7.2 Swings to Labour substitutes 1943–45 and to Labour 1945.

	Constituency	Candidate	By-election	1945
11 Feb 1943	Midlothian and North Peebles	Common Wealth	+11.0	+11.8
12 Feb 1943	King's Lynn	Independent Labour	+3.6	+12.2
16 Feb 1943	Portsmouth North	Common Wealth	+6.9	+18.4
18 Feb 1943	Bristol Central	Independent Labour	−4.5	+16.5
23 Feb 1943	Watford	Common Wealth	+11.5	+17.0
20 Apr 1943	Daventry	Common Wealth	+7.5	+12.0
9 June 1943	Birmingham Aston	Common Wealth	−6.7	+30.7
15 Oct 1943	Peterborough	Independent Labour	+4.2	+5.9
7 Jan 1944	Skipton	Common Wealth	+6.7	+3.6
17 Feb 1944	West Derbyshire*	Independent Labour	+16.2	+8.3
8 July 1944	Manchester Rusholme	Common Wealth	11.0	+16.6
20 Sep 1944	Bilston	ILP	+0.3	+19.2
26 Apr 1945	Chelmsford**	Common Wealth	+28.3	+22.6
17 May 1945	Newport	ILP	+4.6	+12.0

* Compared with the 1938 by-election, the Conservative being unopposed in 1935.
** Millington stood as Common Wealth in the general election.

Given the restricted character of the wartime register, most of these results co-ordinate well with British Institute of Public Opinion findings on voting intention at the next general election, which showed Labour leads varying between 7 per cent and 18 per cent at times between June 1943 and June 1945.

Studies in two particular constituencies, as well as overall constituency membership figures for the Labour Party, show that grass-roots organization was beginning to recover in 1942–43.[29] The Independent Labour candidates were another sign of this. Although the local Labour parties involved issued official statements declaring their support of the electoral truce, they were ready to break it on the quiet. Thus, Fred Wise at King's Lynn, a prospective Labour candidate jumping the gun, announced that he was still a member of the Labour Party, fighting on a good Socialist policy. He wanted the Beveridge Report to be implemented quickly, while Sir Thomas Cook, MP, supporting the Conservative candidate, thought it was 'early days yet to pass judgement upon such a scheme covering so many aspects'.[30] At Bristol Central, Jennie Lee announced that she was standing at the invitation of local Liberal, Labour and church leaders. The Borough Labour Party, reluctantly obeying Transport House and accepting the truce, expelled an alderman and six councillors for supporting her. 'I stand', she said, 'for every word, letter and comma in the Beveridge Report.' Her opponent Lady Apsley, in an article setting out her credo, would say nothing about the Beveridge Report except that social security could not come about without being earned.[31] The prospective Labour candidate for Peterborough, Sam Bennett, aided by Common Wealth, the ILP and local Labour workers, included freedom for India, total acceptance of the Beveridge Report and increased service pay among his campaign points. For once the Conservative nominee, Lord Suirdale, came out in favour of unbalanced budgets to create employment, and full support of Beveridge.[32] Of all these unofficial Labour fights, the most successful was the minor but choice political classic at West Derbyshire. This seat and its neighbourhood had been a family heirloom of the Cavendishes from the time of Good Queen Bess. Since the boundaries of West Derbyshire were drawn in 1885 it had passed out of the family's hands on only two occasions, when the Liberal C. F. White won it in 1918 and 1922. On 24 January 1944 the Duke of Devonshire told the local association that his brother-in-law, Lieutenant-Colonel Henry Hunloke, MP for the constituency, was retiring. The Duke's heir, Lord Hartington, was happily at that moment on leave and waiting outside the door. He was immediately adopted as the candidate, and two days later another of the Duke's brothers-in-law, the Government Chief Whip James Stuart, arranged for the moving of the writ in the House. This blue-blooded impudence met its match when Charlie White, the son of the Liberal MP of 1918–23, replied by standing as an Independent Labour candidate. Prior to this event, there had been a marked feud between Common Wealth and the Kendall–Brown–Reakes group, polarized at Newark in June 1943 with the adoption of rival candidates and a resultant slanging match during the campaign. Now a common front was achieved. Common Wealth sent in a team of six organizers, while Kendall, Reakes, Clement Davies and T. L. Horabin all spoke for White. Even the Communist Party renounced the truce and worked for his return. Among their other uses, by-elections were a source of light relief from grimmer affairs, and the comic aspects of West Derbyshire were played up by reporters, who were delighted when Lord Hartington said he was under the impression that the coalmines had already been nationalized.[33] One of the stranger features of his defeat was the uniquely depressed Conservative share of the vote for this period of the war: in 1945 the Conservative did considerably better – instead of even worse, as in most constituencies.

Three Common Wealth candidates won supposedly safe government seats in the last years of the war: Warrant Officer John Loverseed took Eddisbury in April 1943; Hugh Lawson, Skipton in January 1944; and Wing-Commander Ernest Millington, Chelmsford in April 1945. Loverseed, a former pilot for the Spanish Republic who had fought in the Battle of Britain, was a strong candidate who 'captured the imagination of the working classes and the young people and made a real stir and personal success'.[34] There was unusually strong local interest in the contest, despite the far-flung nature of the constituency. The government candidate, Thomas Peacock, laboured under an important disadvantage. The seat had been Liberal in 1929 and unopposed National Liberal since 1931; but Peacock, while standing as National Liberal, was known to be a Conservative. The Liberal label still counted, and Loverseed played on the issue by adopting a thoroughly Liberal stance with no hint of 'common ownership'. This was a wise tactic in a seat which had never been contested by Labour. Labour feeling in the area was, however, growing – farm wages were a major issue – and this must be part of the explanation of Common Wealth's success. For Liberals of the Sinclair variety, opposed to the National Liberals, there was an Independent Liberal candidate. Since a Sinclair Liberal retained a similar share of the poll in 1945, it looks as though Common Wealth was not benefiting from that quarter. The answer must lie in a defection by National Liberals who returned to the fold in 1945 – no doubt encouraged by the fact that Loverseed was by then standing as Labour – with the appearance of a true National Liberal candidate, Sir John Barlow. Eddisbury, then, does not fit into the pattern of swings to Labour: it voted Barlow in with a landslide majority in the general election.

Skipton was again an unusual constituency. On the normal swing between 1935 and 1945 it should have gone Labour at the post-war general election. But the swing away from the Conservatives seems to have gone instead to the Liberals, keeping Labour in second place. Common Wealth's victory in 1944 bore many hallmarks of Labour parenthood: the local Labour Party was persuaded by Lawson to back him, on the understanding that he would if necessary stand down for a true Labour candidate at the general election, and Tom Wintringham's wife Kitty wrote of the result: 'The hard core of the vote for Lawson came from Labour, the industrial workers of the wool industry.'[35] By this time Mackay had geared up Common Wealth's electoral machine to a fine pitch, and apart from full-time organizers, about 200 youthful volunteers arrived in the constituency to canvass, many of them schoolteachers making use of the Christmas holiday.[36] Lawson was determined to take his stand for the whole bible of Aclandism and nothing less; yet he seems to have picked up a few votes from farmers disgruntled with farm prices and ploughing-up policy.[37] Although Common Wealth won narrowly, there was comfort for the Left in the fact that Alderman Joe Toole of Manchester had stood as Independent Labour and split the vote. Why Skipton failed to follow through in 1945 is a puzzling question.

Chelmsford was the first English constituency fought on the up-to-date register. Millington was again a strong candidate, the commander of a famous heavy bomber squadron who allowed his political views to remain strangely vague during the campaign. His victory was simply a product of the Labour tide — although the intervention of a Liberal at the general election again damped down the Common Wealth rather than the Conservative vote.

Some of the younger Liberals of the war years, like their successors in the late 1950s, believed in the possibility of a fundamental Liberal breakthrough. 'The possibility was inherent in the situation of breaking the power of the caucus in British political life for ever', Ivor Davies argues.[38] The Radical Action Group founded by Donald Johnson in 1941 reflected a desire to ginger up the party leadership and led on to his own attempt to fight Chippenham as an Independent Liberal in August 1943, and Honor Balfour's stand at Darwen in December 1943. With precious little help from anyone, they achieved 49.4 per cent and 49.8 per cent of the poll respectively. Encouraged by these portents, Mrs Corbett Ashby put up at Bury St Edmunds in February 1944, and at last Liberals from outside the constituency rushed into the fray. Despite the backing of a local United Progressive Front of Liberal, Labour and Communist activists, and help from Common Wealth, she was not as successful.[39] Nor were any of these results meaningful for the future of Liberalism. All three of the seats were undergoing the transition from a Conservative–Liberal to a Conservative–Labour dichotomy: the war-time Independents here gathering a brief bloom of Lib–Lab co-operation in the seclusion of the electoral truce.

No by-election candidate, save perhaps the anti-war elements of 1940–41, ever publicly called for Churchill to be replaced as war leader. It is plain from every by-election that the very idea was unthinkable. The strongest line ever taken against him occurred, predictably, in May 1942 at the Chichester by-election, when Flight-Lieutenant Gerald Kidd, a protégé of Hipwell, made rude comments about the sinking of the *Prince of Wales* and called on Churchill to give up the post of Minister of Defence.[40] Equally, none of the by-election contestants of the more radical type supported Churchill as leader of the Conservative Party. By the last phase of the war, 1943–5, this had become a cardinal point in by-elections. Kay Allsop, Common Wealth's campaign organizer, noted the feeling at West Derbyshire:

> … speakers in support of White would make references to Churchill's war record and the debt owed him by the people of this country. Great and enthusiastic applause always greeted this. Then they would go on to say that despite his services to the nation no man, Churchill nor any other, had the right to dictate to the people of this country how they should use their vote. Invariably this brought louder applause.[41]

This distinction between Churchill the war leader and Churchill the party politician ran deep; as a post-war leader Churchill was not wanted. This was one of the reasons which Tom Harrisson of Mass-Observation gave, in a remarkable article in the autumn of 1943, for predicting a Labour victory at the general election. Commenting on the poor Conservative performance at by-elections, he wrote:

> It is hardly necessary to underline such results. No machine, no big names, no helpful register, no suitable 'political atmosphere', wartime difficulties, the current weight of status quo leaders, plus the much used argument of wartime disunity, can only just stem the success of independent, almost 'private' candidates, often of a quality lower than we expect after the war. Consider the difference with a nation-wide drive, a popular policy, backed by popular national figures, in an atmosphere of sanctioned rivalry.[42]

The assumption that Churchill had only to descend from Olympus and scatter the Left with a whiff of electoral grapeshot was almost universal. In March 1943, in a broadcast on postwar reconstruction, Churchill invited Labour to continue in coalition with the Conservatives after the war to carry out his 'Four-Year Plan' – a plan of which little was ever heard again. The Labour leaders were so incapable of believing they could ever beat him at the polls that they responded warmly. Dalton, Bevin and Morrison all raised the idea of a revised form of 'coupon' election at which the parties composing the Coalition would oppose each other in the constituencies, but go to the country pledged to continue in alliance after the general election, the Coalition reforming according to the new ratio of seats in the House. In September 1943 Hugh Dalton was telling the editor of the *New Statesman*, Kingsley Martin, that it would be 'total lunacy' for Labour to fight an election against Churchill while the laurels of victory were still fresh on his brow.[43] It was probably the rank and file of the party who determined the Labour leaders to go it alone.

The Labour Ministers were perhaps as displeased as Churchill himself by the defeat of government candidates, which gave the embarrassing impression abroad that people in Britain were fed up with their leaders, or even with the war effort. Lord Haw-Haw commented upon the striking results at Brighton and Skipton.[44] The government Whips cranked up their own by-election machine: 10 Conservative MPs spoke for Lady Apsley at Bristol Central in February 1943, while 25 were booked for Bury St Edmunds in February 1944.[45] The defeat of the government candidate at Skipton irritated Churchill considerably, and on 1 February 1944 the Cabinet revoked the pre-war rule preventing Cabinet Ministers from speaking at by-elections.[46] By this date there were signs of unease in all three parties, perhaps a sense that the party system itself was being eroded. Lady Violet Bonham Carter of the Liberals, Lord Hinchingbrooke of the Tory Reform Group, and Herbert Morrison (in private) for Labour, aired the possibility of a return to normal party warfare in the constituencies, without prejudice to the Coalition. But, as Attlee pointed out, party competition below would inevitably draw in the party leaders and disrupt the Cabinet; the idea faded away.[47]

Wartime by-elections served many purposes. The basic one was to replace 141 generally aged MPs by younger representatives, many of them acting servicemen. As Driberg suggests, the Independents by contesting Conservative seats at least gave the local caucus the incentive to select an able candidate. From the voters' point of view, contested by-elections were an opportunity to express a variety of frustrations. Chief of these was the absence of a candidate of the voter's party. Thus Conservatives were able to vote Scottish Nationalist rather than Labour at Motherwell in April 1945, giving Dr R. D. McIntyre enough extra votes to become the first Scottish Nationalist MP. No doubt the sheer frustration of enduring the war also expressed itself at the polls. But, as has been argued, mere protest of this kind easily shaded into an anti-Tory disposition. For hard-pressed Cabinet Ministers, operating an almost totalitarian system for the emergency, the high adverse votes were a tiresome but useful reminder that they were supposed to be democratic politicians. The press rubbed into them the kind of lesson it thought should be drawn. *The Times*, fairly typically, interpreted the Eddisbury result as 'a call, which cannot safely be neglected, for prompt and unequivocal measures to give effect to the great programme of social reform which has been embodied in a series of reports to the Government'.[48]

Historically, the by-elections provide valuable evidence of the role of the war in initiating a new leftward swing. David Butler has demonstrated, in an analysis of the by-elections of 1935–9, that there had been 'no very appreciable change in party support' since 1932.[49] Why did few people understand the new trend after 1940? 'No Tory agent need yet be seriously alarmed', said the *Observer* after West Derbyshire. 'It is certainly true', added the *Economist*, 'that there are no signs of any enthusiasm for Labour'.[50] 'Chips' Channon was relieved to hear from the editor of *The Times* in September 1944 that there was no serious swing to the Left: '... so much for the foolish prophecy of that very nice ass Harold Macmillan who goes about saying that the Conservatives will be lucky to retain a hundred seats at the election.'[51]

The failure to sense Labour's growing majority was a measure of the lack of communication between the world of Westminster, with its fixed assumptions, and the mood of the public. Mass-Observation sought to enlighten the situation, and the polls conducted by the British Institute of Public Opinion predicted a Labour victory on six occasions after June 1943. But the study of voting behaviour was only just beginning, and the professional pundits of the day ignored its conclusions.

Notes

1 G. L. Reakes, *Man of the Mersey* (1956) p. 78.
2 Mass-Observation Archive, University of Sussex, Mass-Observation file report No. 1669n (Eddisbury) and No. 1669m (Daventry).
3 *The Times*, 20 Apr 1945.
4 H. Cantril, *Public Opinion, 1935–1946* (Princeton, 1951) p. 195.
5 *East Anglian Daily Times*, 22 Feb 1944.
6 Attlee Papers, Bodleian Library, Oxford, box 7, note by Attlee on the electoral truce, for circulation to the Labour Party NEC, Feb 1944.
7 A. J. P. Taylor, *Beaverbrook* (1972) pp. 404–6.
8 Mass-Observation file report No. 195.
9 On Brighton, see *Sussex Daily News*, 27 Jan–3 Feb 1944; Mass-Observation file report No. 2020.
10 Mass-Observation file report No.725.
11 *Scarborough Evening News*, 10 and 23 Sep 1941; Mass-Observation file report No. 902.
12 *The Times*, 29 Sep 1941.
13 For Kendall, see *Picture Post*, 18 Apr 1942; for the Labour position, *The Times*, 23–24 Mar 1942; and, in general, Mass-Observation boxed material on Grantham, and the *Lincolnshire Echo*. I am very grateful to Dr O. Hartley for explaining the local political background to me.
14 For Brown's past and his account of the by-election, see his autobiography, *So far...* (1943); for his programme, *Birmingham Post*, 14 Apr 1942; in general, *The Times* 18–30 Apr 1942, and Mass-Observation's boxed material on Rugby.
15 I. Davies, *Trial by ballot* (1950) p. 155.
16 D. Johnson, *Bars and barricades* (1952) pp. 240–2.

17 For Reakes and Wallasey, see Reakes, *Man of the Mersey*, pp. 72–83; *Wallasey News*, 4, 11, 18, 25 Apr 1942; *The Times*, 8, 24, 25, 29 Apr 1942.

18 A. Calder, 'The Common Wealth Party, 1942–1945', PhD thesis (Sussex, 1967) part 1, pp. 90–1.

19 For Driberg and Maldon, see Tom Driberg, *The best of both worlds* (1953) pp. 81–5; Mass-Observation boxed material on Maldon; and Calder, op. cit., pp. 93–6.

20 T. Harrisson, 'Who'll win?', *Political Quarterly*, xv (1944) 27.

21 Mass-Observation, 'Social Security and Parliament', *Political Quarterly*.

22 For an excellent survey of reactions to the Report, see A. Marwick, *Britain in the century of total war* (1968) pp. 300–14.

23 Cantril, *Public opinion, 1935–46* p. 361.

24 This is one of the points stressed in Mass-Observation's study of attitudes towards reconstruction, *Journey home* (1944).

25 My comments on Common Wealth derive, except where otherwise indicated, from Angus Calder's thesis, already cited. This not only provides a definitive study of the movement, but includes an important analysis of wartime by-elections (see Part II, pp. 189). I have also consulted, by permission of the Secretary of Commonwealth, the minutes of the National Committee and Working Committee. I am also grateful to Sir Richard Acland for allowing me to examine his papers concerned with Common Wealth.

26 Calder, op. cit., p. 166.

27 R. W. Mackay, *Coupon or free?* (1943) p. 21.

28 National Committee Minutes, 2–3 Sep 1944; 11–12 Mar 1944; Common Wealth Conference Report, 1944, p. 30.

29 F. Bealey et al., *Constituency politics* (1965) pp. 91–2; A. H. Birch, *Small-town Politics* (Oxford, 1959) p. 61.

30 *Norfolk News and Weekly Press*, 23 Jan, 6 Feb 1943; *Norfolk Chronicle*, 22 Feb 1943.

31 *Bristol Evening Post*, 18 Jan, 8, 15, 16 Feb 1943.

32 Common Wealth Working Committee Minutes, 30 Sep 1943; *Peterborough Standard*, 24 Sep, 8 Oct 1944.

33 See the account of the contest in A. Calder, *The people's war* (1969) pp. 552–4. See also *Daily Mail*, 8 Feb 1944.

34 Mass-Observation file report No. 1669. My account of the contest is based on this report.

35 *Common Wealth Review* (Mar 1944) p. 8.

36 *Manchester Guardian*, 10 Jan 1944.

37 Appendix on the Skipton by-election in Calder, op.cit. *Sunday Express*, 9 Jan 1944.

38 Davies, *Trial by ballot*, p. 164 and throughout on the Liberal candidates. See also the account of Chippenham by Donald Johnson in *Bars and barricades*, pp. 229–48.

39 For Bury, see *New Statesman*, 26 Feb 1944; *Tribune*, 10 Mar 1944.

40 Mass-Observation boxed material on Chichester.

41 Kay Allsop, in *Common Wealth Review* (Mar 1944) p. 9.

42 Harrisson, 'Who'll Win?', *Political Quarterly*, xv (1944).

43 The diary of Hugh Dalton, 6 Sep 1943. For the coupon idea, see the diary for 22 Mar and 16 Sep 1943, and Hickleton Papers, diary of Lord Halifax, 18 Aug 1943.

44 *Reynolds News*, 5 Apr 1944.

45 *Bristol Evening Post*, 28 Jan 1943; *Yorkshire Post*, 28 Feb 1944.

46 Public Record Office, PREM 4–64/2.

47 *Observer*, 27 Feb 1944; *News Chronicle*, 12 Jan 1944; Attlee Papers, Morrison to Attlee, 9 Mar 1944, and Attlee to Bevin, 1 Mar 1944.
48 *The Times*, 9 Apr 1943.
49 D. Butler, 'Trends in British by-elections', *Journal of Politics*, xi 2 (1949) 396–407.
50 *Observer*, 12 Mar 1944; *Economist*, 4 Mar 1944.
51 R. Rhodes James (ed.) *Chips: The diaries of Sir Henry Channon* (1967) p. 393.

Note: 1945 to 1960

Chris Cook

The massive Labour victory in the 1945 general election produced a changeover of seats comparable only to the National Government victory of 1931. Labour emerged from 1945 with a net gain of 199 seats, compared with a net loss of 215 in 1931; the Conservatives finished with a net loss of 161 seats in 1945, having had a net gain of 202 in 1931.

Considering this tremendous switch of seats and votes, it is quite astonishing that so few constituencies changed hands at by-elections between 1945 and 1950. In the whole lifetime of the two Attlee governments, only the following constituencies changed hands:

Constituency	Date	Change
1. Combined English Universities	13–18 Mar 1946	Conservative gain from Independent
2. Down	6 June 1946	Unionist gain from Independent Unionists
3. Combined Scottish Universities	22–27 Nov 1946	Conservative gain from Independent
4. Glasgow Camlachie	28 Jan 1948	Conservative gain of seat won by ILP candidate in 1945, who had subsequently accepted the Labour whip

In no case had the Conservatives either gained a seat from Labour (except for the Camlachie result, in which the Labour–ILP feud makes comparisons impossible) or indeed had Labour gained a Conservative seat. For the record, the Liberals neither gained nor lost a seat, nor indeed did they look remotely like doing anything in particular. Between 1945 and 1950 Liberals fought only 14 of the 52 by-elections. Indeed, only in by-elections in the City of London and in Bermondsey Rotherhithe could they obtain over 20 per cent of the poll. Elsewhere, they forfeited 9 deposits from 14 candidatures.

Labour's ability to retain the seats won in the landslide victory of 1945 was nothing short of remarkable. Indeed, in the first few by-elections after 1945 there was a brief honeymoon period in which such seats as Smethwick (1 October 1945) and Ashton-under-Lyne (2 October 1945) actually swung to the government. Even in early 1946 there were swings to Labour at Preston (31 January), South Ayrshire (7 February) and Glasgow Cathcart (12 February).

A very different result occurred, however, at Bexley on 22 July 1946. At a by-election in which turnout fell from 76.7 per cent to 62.6 per cent, the voting, compared with 1945, was:

	1945			1946	
Labour	24,686	(56.9)	Labour	19,759	(52.5)
Conservative	12,923	(29.8)	Conservative	17,908	(47.5)
Liberal	5,750	(13.3)			

Even assuming that the bulk of the Liberal vote had moved to the Conservative, the fall in Labour's share of the total vote was an indicator that the political climate was turning cooler for the government. The growing economic difficulties of the Attlee administration produced a series of heavy swings to the Conservatives during 1947: 10.9 per cent at Liverpool Edge Hill (11 September), 8.5 per cent at Islington West (25 September) and 8.8 per cent at Epsom (4 December).

Apart from a few exceptional very heavy pro-Conservative swings during 1948, such as Glasgow Gorbals (17.0 per cent) and Edmonton (16.2 per cent), the by-elections during 1948 and 1949 settled down to show fairly consistent swings of between 4 per cent and 6 per cent away from Labour: in the last 12 by-elections of 1948–9, 6 of the contests showed a swing within these limits. There was relatively little in these by-elections to indicate the extent to which the Conservatives would recover lost ground in the general election of 1950.

After the 1950 election, although Labour retained all 8 seats it was called on to defend, in no case was there a swing in its favour. Nor did the climate get better for Labour; rather, it deteriorated considerably. From the autumn of 1950 (beginning with a 3.7 per cent swing against Labour in a by-election on 28 September at Leicester North-East), a fairly continuous swing to the Conservatives appeared, although swings were much higher in Conservative-held safe seats, as the following figures indicate:

Number of by-elections in
Conservative-held seats: 6.   Swing: 7.01 per cent.

Number of by-elections in
Labour-held seats: 8.   Swing: 2.45 per cent.

Unfortunately for analysis on these lines, no marginal-held seats really occurred after the Glasgow Scotstoun election of October 1950. It is thus hard to estimate the effect of Labour's divisions and resignations in by-election terms prior to the 1951 election.

The Conservative victory in the 1951 general election ushered in a period of remarkable electoral stability. Indeed, in the 45 contested by-elections up to the 1955 general election, only one seat changed hands – a Conservative gain from Labour in the highly marginal Sunderland South seat on 13 May 1953. Even more remarkable was the number of constituencies which, without changing hands, showed a quite definite swing to the Conservatives. Examples of this swing to a government in power at a mid-term by-election occurred at Canterbury (12 February 1953), Birmingham Edgbaston (2 July 1953), Ilford North (3 February 1954), Haltemprice (11 February 1954), Bournemouth West (18 February 1954) and Sutton and Cheam (4 November 1954). Even in early 1955 there was a swing to the government in four of the six contested by-elections; ironically, in view of events seven years later, the government's best result was at Orpington (20 January 1955).

It is true that, in the more safely Labour-held territory, there were swings against the government, but even here only two constituencies – Dundee East in July 1952 and Shoreditch and Finsbury in October 1954 – registered swings above 4 per cent. No doubt the improving economic climate was one important factor at work. Nonetheless, the achievement of the Churchill administration was quite remarkable.

Almost as remarkable – although for distinctly different reasons – was the Liberal performance. During these years the fortunes and morale of the party hit a new rock bottom. In the 45 contested by-elections, only eight Liberals were brought forward. Mercifully for the party, no Liberal seats fell vacant. Seven of the eight Liberal standard-bearers lost their deposit: indeed, only one of the seven achieved 10 per cent of the poll. However, in all this darkness there appeared one beacon. In a by-election in Inverness in December 1954 a Liberal who had not even contested the seat in 1951 took 36 per cent of the poll, sweeping Labour into third place. Admittedly, turnout was very low (down from 69.3 per cent to 49.2 per cent), but the by-election heralded, a decade in advance, the breakthrough the Scottish Liberals were to make in the Highlands in 1964 and 1966. Apart from 16 per cent of the poll for a Plaid Cymru candidate at Aberdare in October 1954, none of the other smaller parties achieved any success between 1951 and 1955.

After the return of the Conservatives again in 1955, the party did not enjoy a honeymoon comparable to the period after 1951. Partly, of course, the Suez affair served to disrupt the political scene, but equally the economy proved very soon to be a weapon that could increasingly be used against the government. In fact, however, the first feature of the by-election returns after 1955 was a series of impressive Liberal results. At Torquay on 15 December 1955 a Liberal took

23.8 per cent of the poll. At Hereford on 14 February 1956 the party took 36.4 per cent and on the same day achieved 21.6 per cent at Gainsborough.

Partly because the luck of the by-election draw gave the Liberals no likely territory to contest, this first semblance of a revival petered out during 1956: indeed, the party suffered its worst-ever humiliation when, at Carmarthen, Lady Megan Lloyd George won the by-election in February 1957 for Labour.

Long before this, however, the main feature of the by-elections during and after the summer of 1956 was a growing disenchantment with the Conservatives. At Tonbridge on 7 June 1956 there was a swing of 8.4 per cent to Labour. After the Suez episode, the by-election caused in the Melton division by the resignation of Anthony Nutting saw a 7.6 per cent swing.

Curiously, despite continuing fairly heavy swings against the Conservatives in 1957 – reaching 12.2 per cent at Warwick and Leamington on 7 March 1957 (Eden's old constituency) – only one Conservative seat was lost to Labour, the marginal Lewisham North. Meanwhile the Liberals had begun to achieve some impressive results during 1957, taking over 20 per cent of the poll at Edinburgh South (29 May), North Dorset (36.1 per cent of the poll on 27 June), Gloucester (12 September) and Ipswich (24 October).

Early in 1958 the Conservatives began the year with three consecutive and sensational by-election losses. Of these contests, Rochdale was perhaps the most extraordinary. In a straight fight in 1955 the Conservatives polled 51.5 per cent of the vote. For the by-election the Liberals waged a spirited campaign with Ludovic Kennedy, a well-known TV personality, as their candidate. The result was:

	1955		*Feb 1958*
Conservative	26,518 (51.5)	Labour	22,133 (44.7)
Labour	24,928 (48.5)	Liberal	17,603 (35.5)
		Conservative	9,827 (19.8)

The result was a humiliation for the Conservatives and a near-triumph for the Liberals – their final triumph coming on 26 October 1972 when a fortuitous by-election at Rochdale produced a Liberal gain (see below, p. 198).

After Rochdale, the Conservatives suffered a further rebuff when, on 13 March, the Kelvingrove division of Glasgow was lost to Labour on a swing of 8.6 per cent. Two weeks later the Liberals achieved the by-election breakthrough that had eluded them for a generation when they won Torrington from the Conservatives. Without detracting from Mark Bonham-Carter's individual triumph, the by-election was not quite the dawn of the promised land that many Liberals imagined. The seat had been held by George Lambert, sitting as a Conservative and National Liberal. No independent Liberal had fought in 1955, and clearly much of the traditional Liberal vote in this constituency had either abstained (turnout rose by 11.4 per cent to 80.6 per cent in the by-election) or found a temporary home in the Conservative ranks. As it was, the Liberals gained Torrington by the narrow margin of 658 votes – only to lose the seat again in 1959.

Torrington failed to inspire any similar Liberal breakthrough, although the party polled some impressive performances in a variety of residential and agricultural seats: 24.5 per cent at Weston-super-Mare and 27.5 per cent in Argyll (both on 12 June 1958), 24.3 per cent in East Aberdeenshire (20 November 1958), 24.2 per cent at Southend West (29 January 1959) and 25.7 per cent in Galloway (9 April 1959).

With the exception of these safe Conservative seats in which signs of a Liberal inroad were evident, the most significant feature of the by-elections was the marked lack of Labour success after the spring and early summer of 1958. As 1959 progressed, by-elections in such seats as South-West Norfolk (25 March 1959), Penistone (11 June 1959) and Whitehaven (18 June 1959) showed virtually no move from Conservative to Labour. Even without the summer sun and the even more comforting warmth of Macmillan's affluence, the Labour Party was in a weak position to face a general election.

For the whole period from 1945 to 1959 the degree of political stability witnessed in these by-elections cannot be overemphasized. During these 14 years only a handful of seats changed hands. The full statistics are set out below:

By-Elections, 1945–59

Total number of by-elections:	168
Number of contested by-elections:	163
Number of Conservative candidates:	163
Number of Labour candidates:	157
Number of Liberal candidates:	42

Seats Changing Hands at By-Elections, 1945–59*

13–18 Mar 1946	Combined English Universities	Conservative gain from Independent
22–27 Nov 1946	Combined Scottish Universities	Conservative gain from Independent
28 Jan 1948	Glasgow Camlachie	Conservative gain from ILP
13 May 1953	Sunderland South	Conservative gain from Labour
14 Feb 1957	Lewisham North	Labour gain from Conservative
28 Feb 1957	Carmarthen	Labour gain from Liberal
12 Feb 1958	Rochdale	Labour gain from Conservative
13 Mar 1958	Glasgow Kelvingrove	Labour gain from Conservative
27 Mar 1958	Torrington	Liberal gain from Conservative

*This list excludes, because of their peculiar nature, the by-elections in Down (6 June 1946), Mid-Ulster (8 May 1956), Liverpool Garston (5 Dec 1957) and Ealing South (12 June 1958). In both these last-named seats, Conservatives won seats in which the outgoing MPs had become Independent Conservatives.

The triumph of Macmillan in October 1959, and the third successive defeat at the polls of the Labour Party, was a watershed in British politics. The internal dissensions that were unleashed within the Labour ranks, and the subsequent Liberal revival that culminated in the summer of 1962, led to a markedly more turbulent period of by-election history than had occurred since war-time days.

Ironically, in the first by-election after 1959 a very small swing to the Conservatives was sufficient for the party to capture the highly marginal Brighouse and Spenborough seat from Labour. After this initial contest, however, the lesson of the by-elections became unmistakably apparent: a Liberal revival, quite unlike anything seen since the late 1920s, was under way. The causes and course of the road that led to Orpington deserve a separate study.

CHAPTER 8

Orpington and the 'Liberal revival'

Ken Young

General Election, 1959	(Electorate, 51,872)	
Sumner (Conservative)	24,303	*(56.6)*
Hart (Labour)	9,543	*(22.2)*
Galloway (Liberal)	9,092	*(21.2)*
Conservative majority	14,760	Turnout 82.8%

By-election, 14 Mar 1962	(Electorate, 53,779)	
Lubbock (Liberal)	22,846	*(52.9)*
Goldman (Conservative)	14,991	*(34.7)*
Jinkinson (Labour)	5,350	*(12.4)*
Liberal majority	7,855	Turnout 80.3%

General Election, 1964	(Electorate, 54,846)	
Lubbock (Liberal)	22,637	*(48.4)*
McWhirter (Conservative)	19,565	*(41.8)*
Merriton (Labour)	4,609	*(9.8)*
Liberal majority	3,072	Turnout 85.4%

For more than 50 years following the landslide victory of 1906, the Liberal Party suffered a slow, steady, seemingly inexorable decline in its Parliamentary representation. After the 1955 general election there seemed a possibility that the party might disappear from British politics altogether (see Table 8.1). Yet the decline was arrested, and the party in the post-Suez era was about to experience a change in its fortunes dramatic enough to create the illusion of revival.

The road to Orpington

In February 1958 came the Liberals' best by-election result since the war: 35.5 per cent of the poll and a good second place at Rochdale. The hoped-for breakthrough came just one month later, with victory at Torrington in

Table 8.1   The Liberal vote in post-war general elections.

	Candidates	Percentage votes cast	Deposits lost	Number of MPs
1945	305	9.0	76	12
1950	475	9.1	319	9
1951	109	2.5	66	6
1955	110	2.7	60	6

Devon. Increased party activity followed this success: the Liberals fought 19 of the 52 by-elections in the 1955–59 Parliament, and entered the 1959 general election with a new confidence.

This time 216 seats were fought, and the Liberal share of the poll more than doubled. North Devon was won and Torrington lost; but having fought almost twice the number of constituencies, the number of lost deposits was less than in 1955, and more Liberals finished second than at any time since 1945. The Liberal Party, it seemed, was seriously in national politics once more. The stage was set for a revival of Liberalism, aided by the internecine conflicts which racked the Labour Party in the years following the 1959 election.

While the party's by-election record continued to improve, equally significant results were to be seen in the local elections. In 1959 the Liberal Party was represented in local government by only 475 councillors and aldermen. The 1960 municipal elections increased this to 641. In 1961 came a great increase to 1,065, a figure which included a number of important gains in the county councils, while 1962 saw the number of local seats held increase to 1,603. Most of these gains were made in the south of England, and predominantly in the Home Counties; relative success in the suburbs and poor performance in the cities seemed to be the pattern.[1]

The importance of the local election campaigns was recognized by the Liberal Party as an essential base from which to build its Parliamentary strength. Mark Bonham-Carter's dictum that 'it is easier to change people's voting habits at local elections than at by-elections, and at by-elections than at general elections' was well-heeded.[2] The party leadership decided that the way to Westminster lay necessarily through town and county hall, and in 1960 appointed Pratap Chitnis to head a new local government department at Liberal HQ. The successes which followed, however, were not due simply to the increased interest of the party leadership and organization; the key to local success lay in the local communities where, tactically, 'Liberals were quicker to seize upon and exploit local dissatisfactions than were the other two parties'.[3]

Nowhere was this more true than in Orpington Urban District Council, a Kentish suburb in the south-east corner of Greater London, where the Liberal Party was building up an organization for the local elections which would eventually pay startling dividends in the by-election of 1962. In 1955 the Orpington Liberal Association had formed ward committees and resolved to fight the local elections. During the following year the Conservative-controlled council decided to seek borough status for the district, a policy which in Orpington, as elsewhere, brought a ratepayer reaction based on the expectation that municipal status would necessarily entail higher rates.

The Liberals campaigned on this issue, and also opposed the Conservative council's proposals to means-test council tenants. A substantial number of votes were won in wards with a high proportion of municipal housing, and Liberal candidates came second in four of the five Conservative-held seats contested. Although 1957 began with party membership at the low level of under 200, there was a clear ambition to become a major political force in the district. Accordingly, the 1957 elections were fought on the slogan of 'Labour Can't Win', and election literature presented the Liberals as the second party of the district. Membership trebled during the next 12 months, as the Liberals continued to campaign on such skilfully chosen local issues as the council's failure to plan for more multiple stores to serve the district's rapidly growing population.

In 1959 the party won two council seats, a significant achievement in a year when the Conservatives did rather well in local elections throughout the country. Although the Conservative vote increased, a Liberal candidate won the Biggin Hill ward – at his fourth attempt – with a majority of 113, while another Liberal won the Goddington South ward. The party's advance at the local elections continued in 1960. The St Mary Cray ward was won from the sitting Labour councillor with a majority of 384. A subsequent win in a local council by-election gave the Liberals seven members on the council. In 1961 further gains were made, Liberals winning a majority of the votes cast (see Table 8.2) to bring their representation up to 12 on the 33-member council, while a by-election in September 1961 gave the Liberals their first seat on Kent County Council.

In the late summer of 1961 the sitting Conservative MP, Donald Sumner, announced his resignation from Parliament on being appointed as a county court judge. The Liberals were ready for the by-election, although, despite their local election successes and the excellent fettle of their election machinery, there was little ground for expecting that the seat could be won.

Table 8.2 Orpington UDC election results, 1956–61: votes cast.

	1956	1957	1958	1959	1960	1961
Conservative	9,903	9,509	9,763	11,828	8,882	11,009
Liberal	2,443	2,460	3,584	6,716	8,046	11,771
Labour	5,123	6,297	5,348	2,580	1,570	1,725

Table 8.3 Orpington division Parliamentary election results, 1950–59.

	1950	1951	1955 (by-election)	1955 (general election)	1959
Conservative	56.7	No Liberal	No Liberal	59.9	56.6
Labour	32.8	stood	stood	27.6	22.2
Liberal	10.5			12.6	21.2

The percentages of votes cast for the parties at parliamentary elections since 1950 (Table 8.3) told their own story of a solid Conservative seat in which a good second place was a reasonable ambition.

The candidates at Orpington

Jack Galloway, the prospective Liberal candidate, was an experienced and popular man who had nursed the seat since before the general election, when he had achieved a close third place to Labour. But Liberal headquarters, alive to the possibility and importance of a good result at Orpington, no longer felt him to be a suitable candidate for the by-election. They had come to know of a change in his personal circumstances which, if it became public, could mean political disaster. Liberal Whip Donald Wade pressed Galloway to withdraw, which he declined to do.

Further pressure from other members of the Liberal Parliamentary Party and the officers of the local association only stiffened Galloway's resolve to fight. A general meeting was called, at which the officers appealed to the party membership to withdraw their support, alluding to, but never revealing, the information in their possession. This ruse failed. The local party was split, and the majority backed the candidate. Nevertheless, two months and several meetings later Galloway reluctantly stood down, sensing that the tide of opinion, fed by suspicion and rumour, was turning against him. Conservative Central Office, who at that stage were baffled by the rumours surrounding Galloway, noted with satisfaction the departure of 'the idol of the local Liberals', calculating it could only work to their advantage.

Expecting a writ for the by-election to be moved at any time, the Liberals moved quickly. An emergency meeting of the executive officers sought the advice of Donald Wade, who insisted that they adopt a local man. The choice fell upon Eric Lubbock, a local councillor and an engineer. It did not seem at the time to be a particularly momentous decision. In Lubbock's own words

My political experience was very limited, but as the most we could expect was a good second, nobody thought it mattered. My employers, after a perfunctory look at the 1959 voting figures, with the Liberals at the bottom of the poll, generously agreed to let me have three weeks' paid leave for the campaign.[4]

As local candidates went, Lubbock was unusually strong, with a family connection in Orpington that stretched back 150 years. He soon recovered the ground lost by the dispute over Galloway.

The Orpington Conservatives adopted Peter Goldman as their candidate from a glittering shortlist of aspirant MPs, several of whom were later to become major figures in Conservative politics. Goldman was undoubtedly the leadership's, and Central Office's, candidate. He was a close associate of party chairman Iain Macleod, for whom he had ghost-written a biography of Neville Chamberlain. A former President of the Cambridge Union, and latterly Director of the Conservative Political Centre, Goldman was arguably the brightest of the Party's 'back-room boys', and was widely regarded as being of Cabinet calibre. His campaign literature featured him in intimate, if respectful, conversation with the prime minister. Yet, for all his contribution to shaping party policy since 1951, Goldman's electoral experience was limited to having previously fought West Ham South, an East End unwinnable seat of the type on which young hopefuls were expected to cut their teeth. The Labour Party chose as their candidate Alan Jinkinson, a NALGO official, and at 27 the youngest of the candidates.

The campaign

The writ was not moved in the few weeks following the resignation of Donald Sumner. Rather, the government preferred to wait until the new electoral register was ready in February. At first sight the effect of this decision was to hamper the Labour Party, for the problems of tracing voters who have changed their address and of organizing the postal votes is generally handled more capably in the Conservative Party. Yet, insofar as the delay put a premium upon organization, it happened to benefit the highly efficient Liberal machine even more, Martin Redmayne warning Central Office in August that an early writ would be advisable in view of the gathering strength of the Liberals in local government.

Paradoxically, the party split over Galloway's candidature also resulted in improved Liberal organization in the wards. The heightened emotions and sharpened rivalries engendered by the affair intensified the efforts of the party workers, so pro- and anti-Galloway factions each determined to outshine the other in ward organization and canvassing effort. In addition, delay in moving the writ fostered a local resentment which was skilfully exploited by the Liberals, who collected 3,500 signatures on a petition deploring the disenfranchisement of the Orpington constituents. This was delivered to the House of Commons with appropriate publicity by Jeremy Thorpe and Eric Lubbock.

Once the campaign began, the differences in style and stance between the two candidates in what was evidently a two-horse race became immediately apparent. On the issues, Goldman ran a cerebral, policy-oriented campaign, emphasizing national and international issues, and attacking Lubbock as a 'little Englander'. On the one local issue on which he took a position – that of the proposed integration of Orpington into a larger London Borough of Bromley, and its inclusion in an expanded Greater London – Goldman could hardly dodge unpopularity.[5] Nor were his concessions to localism likely to convince. He promised, if elected, to live within the constituency, and stressed his wife's Kentish connections. More significantly, he met head-on the largely unspoken racial prejudice that Central Office had anticipated at the time of his adoption: while the briefing notes provided to his canvassers pointed out that 'by religion, he and his wife are Church of England', they also asserted that the candidate himself was 'proud of his Jewish ancestry'.

In terms of style rather than substance, Goldman's campaign was confident, if remote. His long experience at the centre of British politics stood him in good stead, the regular area agent's reports on his meetings uniformly recording that they were 'first class' and 'well-received'. At his adoption meeting he 'spoke brilliantly', although he later proved to suffer the back-room boy's affliction of being better and more comfortable on radio than television. Importantly, he had heavyweight support. Leading figures in the government and party debated how they could best lend a hand to his campaign, Sir Toby Low urging that 'Peter Goldman does deserve something special of us'. At least in the early stages, the canvassing efforts of Mr and Mrs Goldman were praised for their cheerfulness and enthusiasm. The criticisms were to come after polling day.

Eric Lubbock's campaign also began well, seeming consistently to hit the right note, but in different and less formal settings. The Conservatives thought his public meetings unimpressive, poorly attended, and his speaking style dull. Lubbock's strengths lay elsewhere. Identification with the candidate was the cornerstone of the Liberal appeal, and the campaign literature put heavy stress upon his young family with whom he was photographed in several appealing domestic poses. It stressed his professional standing as an engineer and added, for good measure, that he was heir to the Avebury peerage. Liberal propaganda also bore the effective message that, having established 12 Liberal councillors upon the UDC, the electors of Orpington should now cap this with the election of a Liberal MP. Eric Lubbock's meetings centred upon the kind of grievance likely to strike a chord among the relatively hard-pressed owner-occupiers, as was the case with his call for consumer representation upon the newly created NEDC and the abolition of Schedule A tax. As early as November 1961, a Central Office report rated their Liberal opponent 'a formidable candidate'.

Press interest in the campaign was considerable. The *Daily Mail* gave particularly full coverage, and was the only national daily to see the potential significance of Orpington. On 14 December the *Mail* asked:

> Will the word Orpington be engraved on the coffin of the Macmillan government? At the moment the outer London dormitory consti-tuency is only a very small cloud on the horizon – and most politicians have scarcely considered that it could become the name of a famous disaster. There is a distinct possibility that Lubbock might beat Goldman – in which case the word Orpington would become the beacon to set the Liberals alight all over Britain.

The *Mail* followed up this speculation six weeks later with evidence that their prescience had been soundly based. The Conservatives were shown by the latest NOP poll to have a slender 1.1 per cent lead over Lubbock, with the Labour candidate trailing a very poor third. 'The pending by-election', prophesied the *Mail* on 26 January, 'could provide the Liberals with their most spectacular victory for years. And the Tories with their most damaging defeat.'

By 1 February the Daily Mirror was prepared to concede that 'Orpington is, according to every report, far from the good Tory consti-tuency it was'. *The Times*, unwilling to stoop to vulgar speculation, assured its readers on 23 February that Peter Goldman was 'confidently astride a thumping majority [and] is planning a first-class ride to Westminster'.

Goldman's plans, however, seemed increasingly likely to go awry. He was fairly widely regarded as an outsider, foisted upon a constituency which had a long tradition of local members. His executive committee had short-listed from 99 applicants, and had been forced to add two local candidates to the short-list in order to placate the strong localist sentiment within the association. Significantly, on 25 February, James Margach discussed in the *Sunday Times* 'the twilight of the carpetbaggers', adding that they were 'at a discount these days'. Peter Goldman, however, did little to counter the criticism, doing little canvassing in person. As the days passed, the contrast became more marked: the personable accessible local Liberal against the remote (and, to some, pompous) Conservative. The final stages of the campaign were clarified by the withdrawal of two Independent candidates, Francis Pym, who clearly withdrew in the Liberal interest, and Harry Onslow-Clarke, representing the British Radical Party, who withdrew for family reasons ten days before the poll.

The Conservatives meanwhile concentrated the full force of their campaign upon the Liberal Party. The Labour campaign assumed decreasing relevance, and reports of Labour activists supporting the Liberal cause as the best means of blocking Goldman were rife. The local Conservative magazine proclaimed that 'the forthcoming by-election will be a test of the Government and the strength of the local Liberals'. Campaign literature claimed that 'the political opposition in the Division is now almost entirely Liberal', a claim which was largely self-fulfilling, and served to concentrate attention upon Lubbock as the main contender for the seat.

This was not however a matter of mistaken tactics, but of fore-thought. During Rab Butler's chairmanship of the party, the rising Liberal vote in by-elections had been carefully scrutinized for the lessons it offered. In the past, wrote Butler, the Liberals had been ignored. Now was the time to define the line the party should take in opposing them. Macleod followed through on this work, demanding a detailed analysis of the Liberal vote. In March 1961 the Conservative agents were warned that a change of campaign was necessary. Conservative tactics had been traditionally geared to fighting the Labour Party, who tended to play the early stages of a contest quietly and 'hold their fire until the last four days'. These tactics had proved useless against the Liberals, who were being allowed to run away in the initial weeks, seizing the political initiative and leaving the Conservatives trailing in their wake. A shift to early and direct attack was indicated, and Orpington was to be a test of the new tactics.

National political figures were prominent at campaign meetings, George Brown and Bessie Braddock appearing on Alan Jinkinson's behalf, and Iain Macleod and Enoch Powell supporting their fellow Tory intellectual. But Jo Grimond's meetings pulled the largest crowds, and Eric Lubbock was also backed up on the doorsteps by Jeremy Thorpe, Donald Wade, Frank Byers and Mark Bonham-Carter. On polling day itself Grimond toured the constituency, ensconced in the boot of a vast white Chevrolet.

Lubbock's only moment of real political danger came when both Peter Goldman and the Gaitskellite Alan Jinkinson attacked him (reasonably enough, given his unilateralist election address) for displaying overt sympathies with CND. At the height of the bewildering period of accusation and ambiguous denial the three candidates were scheduled to take part in a television discussion. Liberal Party headquarters, anxious about charges of irresponsible unilateralism, advised Eric Lubbock to withdraw. This he did, presenting both opponents with the opportunity to put the worst possible construction upon his reticence. They were quick to do so, and further implicit criticism came from academics David Butler and Robert McKenzie who, in a joint letter to *The Times*, urged amendment of the Representation of the People Act to prevent a single candidate vetoing broadcast discussions. Locally, however, Lubbock's tactical evasion showed no sign of harming him.

The Conservatives' canvass returns were promising, and offered a degree of reassurance in the face of the Cassandras of the press. Running an intense and efficient organization, the Conservatives managed an 86 per cent canvass in the week following 5 March. Conservative promises amounted to more than 20,000, with the Liberals at about half that level and Labour trailing an insignificant third. Just a whiff of anxiety was engendered by the registering of more than 10,000 doubtfuls in the responses to Conservative canvassers. In the last two days of the campaign the opinion polls confirmed that a remarkably large proportion of voters had yet to decide how to cast their vote. Conservative agent Brian Wilcox declared that 'on anything above a 65 per cent poll we are home and dry' and directed his efforts to organizing a high turnout. The Liberal returns also suggested that a high poll would aid them, as their own promises of support, although a fallible guide, indicated that they had sufficient potential supporters to win the seat.

On 13 March, the day before Orpington polled, the electors of Blackpool North had their opportunity to pronounce upon the performance of the Macmillan government. The result, in a seat vacated by Sir Toby Low on his elevation to the peerage as Lord Aldington, was better than the Liberals expected, the Conservative majority being cut from nearly 16,000 to 973. The Liberal candidate increased his share of the vote from 20.6 per cent to 35.3 per cent. The NOP poll, published the previous day in the *Daily Mail*, had slightly underestimated Liberal strength, while being otherwise highly accurate; the result suggested that a last-minute effort by the Blackpool Liberals, encouraged by the NOP prediction, had brought them close to victory.

The Blackpool result, coupled with the large proportion of uncommitted voters in Orpington, meant that the eve-of-poll survey there by NOP was to be crucial. It clearly showed a probable Liberal win, and the enterprising Pratap Chitnis, drafted in as Lubbock's agent, secured several thousand copies. These he used for free distribution to the homecoming commuters at Orpington's Southern Region station on polling day and flooded the normally Labour-voting council estates with copies. When polling ended at 9.00 p.m. Chitnis was optimistic. Everything he saw and heard told him that the Liberals would win, although 'my common-sense tells me we cannot'. The result, when announced by the returning officer, was sensational, Eric Lubbock's own exact figures being drowned in the exultant roar from the many Liberal supporters present at the count.

The Liberal majority was 7,855. In the television studio, Jo Grimond registered honest bewilderment: 'My God! an incredible result!' was his spontaneous reaction. Equally bewildered was Peter Goldman, unable to believe that he had been so resoundingly defeated. Eric Lubbock, chaired by his supporters, drank exultantly from a convenient bottle and toasted, with understandable hyperbole, 'the next government'.

Why Orpington elected Lubbock

The Orpington result was universally regarded as being of quite unprecedented significance. The lessons which were drawn, correctly or incorrectly, from the result had a discernible impact on the shape of British politics during the next few years. Perhaps the Conservatives were the least surprised. The first report submitted to Central Office by the area agent in November 1961 recognized that this once-sound suburb was no longer a safe seat and that 'it is not beyond the bounds of possibility for the Liberals to win Orpington'. In January he warned that 'we can be under no illusion that this by-election is going to be an easy one.' In his post-election final report he ventured the chilling conclusion that 'I do not think we could have held Orpington under any circumstances'.

The finality of that judgement warns against a single-cause explanation of the Orpington result. Local sentiment, the changing social structure, the effect of published opinion polls, the unpopularity of the Macmillan government, virulent anti-Semitism and the collapse of Labour in Orpington were variously cited as 'causes' of Peter Goldman's defeat. Orpington was also closely analysed after the event by social surveys carried out on behalf of both the Conservative and Liberal headquarters. With the benefit of the Liberals' survey and the Conservatives' own inquest, it is possible to go beyond speculation and offer some reliable evidence on the behaviour of the Orpington electorate.

'The two candidates', remarked the authors of the Liberal post-election survey, 'were antithetical to a remarkable degree.' Goldman was not favourably regarded, except by a minority of Conservative voters, who stressed his ability and his professionalism. Little more than one-fifth of all electors rated him a 'good' or 'very good' candidate. He was widely seen as over-confident and remote, with an 'unfortunate' manner. That Peter Goldman was not a local man was deeply resented, but more so among those Conservatives who nevertheless voted for him than among those who defected to the Liberals. It was not in itself a decisive factor in the shift of votes.[6]

More important was Goldman's lack of identifiability; few electors thought him 'one of us'. Jewish by birth, Peter Goldman was to some degree a victim of anti-Semitic sentiments. Although the precise effect of the prejudice he encountered is hard to gauge, the Liberal survey indicates that consciousness of his Jewishness was the leading feature of Conservative voters' perceptions of the contest. Having previously fought an East London seat without success, Goldman was regarded by some electors as 'from the East End' and, by association, 'not a gentleman'. Conservative evidence, although anecdotal, confirmed the Liberal survey finding, and attributed the anti-Semitic reaction to vicious campaigning on the Liberals' part. In the aftermath of defeat, the armchair campaigners of the Conservative associations across the country reached for their pens, and party chairman Iain Macleod received a stream of vitriolic and sometimes deranged tirades of racial abuse. Macleod stood by his protégé, and defended him stoutly on every occasion, not just from the slurs, but from the criticism that he had not been a suitable candidate.

Macleod's loyalty was honourable, but in truth the qualities that make a potential cabinet minister differ from those needed to win a difficult seat against a sure-footed opposition. Quick-tempered, Peter Goldman was reported by his area agent as having 'neither the aptitude, nor the experience, nor did he appear to have the inclination to get himself well-liked'. 'His self-presentation was dreadful' agreed one Conservative MP who had taken part in the campaign. Cruelly, these judgements – which were widely repeated – spelled the end of Goldman's political chances. On 23 March he and his wife attended a meeting of the finance and general purposes committee of the Orpington Conservative Association, where he announced that he did not expect to be asked to fight the seat at the general election. His correspondence with the association chairman was published in early May, the usual pleasantries doing little to disguise the brutal reality that he was no longer wanted. Nor was Peter Goldman ever to fight another Conservative seat. His once-glittering career in the Conservative party was terminated for good by the electors of Orpington.

The evidence shows that Eric Lubbock, on the other hand, was almost universally popular. Electors regarded him as likeable and sincere. Well known locally, both by family association, residence and his activities on the UDC, he was, with his young family (and children at a local school), an easy candidate with whom to identify. Although regarded by a very large majority of electors as 'one of us', he also picked up votes from the deferential, who appreciated his connection with the peerage, and he thus paradoxically benefited from displaced Conservatism. He was, in more senses than one, the man Conservatives wanted to elect as their own. Central Office officials admired his qualities and noted ruefully that 'he was the type of candidate normally selected by Conservatives'.

The Liberals' post-election survey shows that a curious aura of hope surrounded the Liberals. Voter approval was consistently couched in terms of what it was hoped Eric Lubbock and the Liberal Party would achieve. He was, it seems, given the benefit of every doubt, while these benefits were equally consistently denied to Goldman. The only count against Lubbock was his seeming lack of a strong personality. But, significantly, 70 per cent of all electors rated him a 'good' or 'very good' candidate.

The party images were by no means as dichotomous as those of the candidates. Both the Labour and Conservative parties had clearly distinct images, expressed usually in terms of social class and socialist/capitalist stereotypes. But Orpington voters found it difficult to describe what the Liberal Party meant to them. The predominant impression was of a party of youth, distinct from the other two parties on an age rather than a class continuum, an impression doubtless heightened by the saturation of the constituency by young activists during the campaign itself. Lacking a class image, the Liberals were readily seen as 'the middle way', a party both of all classes and of none. Such vagueness and novelty could only be given form in terms of expressed hopes of the party's future; by and large, voters projected onto the party their own particular favoured policy proposals as being measures which, it was imagined, Lubbock and his parliamentary colleagues would promote. Recognition of these factors had, as we shall see, an important impact upon the party's subsequent electoral strategy.

Disappointment and disillusion with the Conservative government was naturally a factor in influencing voting behaviour, particularly among voters normally supporting the Conservative Party. Specific objections were made to the pay pause, rising prices and high and inequitable taxes. Letters to Central Office confirm this post-election survey finding. The economy ranked first as an issue, although immigration, colonial policy and Europe also served to disturb Conservative supporters. Discontent is always fairly readily apparent where it exists, and the election was widely read as a judgement on the Macmillan government. But perhaps the most curious fact about the Orpington voter is that this discontent was by no means commensurate with the turnover of votes. Of the Liberal voters who, it might be expected, were judging the government harshly, a relatively modest 46 per cent thought the government was doing 'a bad job'. More than one-fifth of all Liberal voters questioned approved the government's performance, while a further third were unable to offer either a positive or a negative verdict. It is the more ironic, then, that Macmillan should have written to Peter Goldman, assuming personal responsibility for the defeat. If the Liberal majority had been one of eight votes, confessed the abject Prime Minister, the loss of the seat would have been the candidate's fault; at 8,000, it must be counted as his own.

The Liberal victory might not have been possible without the collapse of the Labour campaign and the defection of Labour supporters to the Liberal camp. Lubbock's victory was based, it was estimated, upon a numerically large transference of voters from the middle classes from Conservative to Liberal, and upon a numerically smaller but proportionately very high transfer of support by working-class electors, who deserted the other parties to support Lubbock. Of the 24,000-odd electors who voted for Donald Sumner at the general election, an estimated 7,500 switched to Eric Lubbock in 1962. Of the 9,000 Labour voters at the general election, some 3,500 deserted their party for the Liberals. The Labour loyalist rump that remained was overwhelmingly a middle-class intelligentsia; it was the working-class Labour voters on the council estates who supported Lubbock, partly out of dissatisfaction with their own party, but largely, it seems, because Labour was seen as having no chance of winning. Labour, not the Liberals, were on this occasion the victims of the third-party squeeze.

Finally, it is clear that the local elections had provided a passage for electors to transfer their allegiance from the Conservatives to the Liberal Party. In politics, electoral success is vital; the last result shapes electors' perceptions of the possibilities of the next. The Liberals had shown they could win the by-election by polling in the 1961 UDC elections more votes in total than the Conservatives. Mark Bonham-Carter's dictum was borne out by the Orpington experience, for there was a close correspondence between Liberal voting in the by-election and at previous UDC elections; in the words of the Liberal survey: '... the Council elections may have been a stepping-stone into the Liberal camp for some voters who were not, therefore, voting Liberal for the first time in 1962.'

In the aftermath of the by-election it became apparent that Orpington was no Torrington. Liberal support was firmly founded and looked like enduring; Orpington Conservatives warned Central Office that they did not expect to recover the seat at the next general election. The Liberal survey lent this prediction support. Asked about their future voting intentions, 50 per cent of all voters declared themselves for Lubbock. Only two per cent of those who had voted Liberal expected to return to the Conservatives. This support was given notwithstanding the recognition that the Conservative Party was likely to win a majority of seats nationally. Again, in the words of the Liberal survey:

> Few people now regret voting as they did, and few intend to go back to their former parties at the next general election. The Liberal position seems reasonably secure. The majority thought the Liberals would win next time in Orpington...

And win they did, in 1964 and again in 1966. The Liberal Party was in a position to capture and retain the seat because of its inherent local strength. But why *was* the Liberal Party so strong in Orpington?

The sources of Liberal strength

The answer which comes first to mind is that given by Donald Newby, one-time chairman of the Orpington Liberals, that Orpington's strength lay in the dedication and determination of a small band of activists, whose aim was eventually to overturn the massive Conservative majority.[7] But such an explanation is inadequate. Committed Liberals exist in many constituencies, and the ambition is a common enough one, if rarely achieved. It merely raises the further question of how the Orpington Liberals were able to succeed, and why no further seats, vulnerable on Orpington form, fell to the Liberals in the months which followed.

Other, more sophisticated, explanations were offered at the time. Foremost among these was the view of Orpington as the home of a new social group, the young professional middle-class, aspirant, upwardly mobile, committed to neither major party nor to class stereotypes. Soon after the Orpington result, Philip Goodhart, Tory MP for neighbouring Beckenham, ascribed the loss of Orpington to the tensions of social mobility which themselves derived from Conservative social policy: 'now the extent and the growth of this social mobility can be seen for the first time', he lamented in a letter to the *Daily Telegraph* on 23 March. *The Spectator* ran a leader that same day on social mobility and 'the new men', posing the question: 'Is the new middle-class radical in its temper?' Certainly it seemed so. A survey by Mark Abrams, carried out in the aftermath of Orpington in suburban constituencies in north-west and south-east London and in the suburbs of Manchester, found the most striking feature of 'the new Liberals' to be their classlessness; an unusually large proportion refused the interviewers' questions about self-assigned class.[8] Thus, Orpington was to be explained in terms of an almost fortuitous concentration of the new men (and their wives) in a commuter suburb to which they were attracted. The weakness of the 'new men' theory is that other constituencies could easily be identified in which the socio-economic profile closely resembled that of Orpington, and yet which failed to give the Liberals an Orpington-type result.

A further explanation derives not from political sociology but from social ecology. Consider the position of Orpington: not an established residential suburb, like neighbouring Bromley or Beckenham, but a new, raggedly growing suburb within the outer metropolitan/rural fringe area. Orpington UDC contained more green belt land than any other of the areas soon to be included within Greater London. Yet the northern end of the district also contained a considerable amount of modern industry, producing in the main consumer durables, and housing its workers in the pre-war overspill estates built by the London County Council.[9] Much of the remainder consisted of large tracts of cheaply-built pre-war private houses and bungalows. Very little of Orpington matched the description given it by the *Daily Mirror* as 'the home of the well-to-do stockbroker, the higher grade civil servant, the "comfortable" business man...' Such stereotypes serve only to mislead. Suburbs are various in form and function, and what was distinct about Orpington proved a potent electoral factor.[10]

Orpington's distinctiveness lay in its substantial and continuing rate of suburban 'colonization'. This is readily apparent from a comparison of the intercensal growth figures for the district and its neighbours. Between 1931 and 1951 Orpington grew more rapidly than any other part of suburban Kent, with the exception of Chislehurst–Sidcup. Orpington's annual growth rate during those two decades was 4.59 per cent. After 1951 it was the outer metropolitan ring, beyond the Green Belt, which grew more rapidly than Greater London as a whole; yet in the politically crucial decade 1951–61 Orpington's annual rate of growth was still considerably higher at 2.39 per cent than any of its suburban neighbours, and indeed higher than any other district in Kent with the exception of Strood, in the depths of the rural county.[11] In numerical terms, Orpington's population grew by almost 17,000 during the 1950s, from 63,364 to 80,293. Significantly, the anti-Conservative element of Liberal success was predominantly in the rapidly growing areas of the district, as the figures in Table 8.4 show.

How is this correspondence between population growth and the Liberal vote to be explained? The suggestion put forward here is that the politics of Orpington were largely the politics of the established versus the newcomer. Certainly, the kind of issues used by the Liberals to mobilize their vote – unmade roads, and the lack of provision of shopping facilities to serve the rapid population growth, for example – suggest a conscious preoccupation with the problems of the newcomer and his family.[12] The Conservatives, in Newby's view, 'were the local establishment.... They were obviously insensitive to the aspirations of their rapidly expanding population and failed to keep abreast of its social needs'.[13] Conservative sources confirm this view. The area agent, surveying the prospects for the by-election in November 1961, reported with alarm that there was

> a great deal of dissatisfaction with the Conservative-controlled Orpington UDC, particularly with regard to the making up of unadopted roads. The state of the roads in the Biggin Hill area is quite shocking. The Council has kept rates low, but there is a strong demand on the part of the younger families for more local facilities than are at present provided.

The Liberal vote in the UDC elections was strongest amongst these disenchanted newcomers, whose demands for services were at odds with the

Table 8.4 Some originally Conservative-held wards in Orpington.

	1951 pop.	1961 pop.	Political history
High-growth wards			
Goddington South	5,164	7,709	Liberal win 1959
Goddington North	4,692	7,844	Liberal win 1961
Green Street Green	6,987	8,247	Liberal win 1961
Crofton South	5,963	10,404	Liberal win 1961
Knoll	4,894	6,052	Liberal win 1962
Stable wards			
Petts Wood	6,779	6,880	Conservative held
Farnborough	4,125	4,828	Conservative held

minimalist policies of the earlier settlers. Orpington was, then, a classic case of a local regime conflict. Such may well occur where rapid expansion generates friction between the established, long-resident ruling group and the recent arrivals. It is in part a contest over policies and provision; but it is also a contest over 'what kind of place this is'.[14] More often, these conflicts are fought between an established political party and a non-partisan or 'ratepayer' group.[15] Such an interpretation suggests that the challenge to the local establishment in Orpington might well have taken the form of a 'ratepayer' movement, had not the small band of resident Liberals been already in existence, ready and able to channel dissent in a more avowedly partisan direction. Thus the local politics of growth and change would have threatened Conservative control of the urban district council in any event. The fact that the beneficiaries of this protest were a national political party, rather than a purely local group, ensured that their momentum carried the challengers through into Parliament.

In time, Orpington matured, its roads were gradually metalled, its facilities expanded. The newcomers put roots down, weight on, and grew into their destined place as solid Conservative burghers. Deprived of the opportunity to maintain a local power base when the Orpington UDC was swallowed up by the new London Borough of Bromley in 1965, Orpington Liberals gradually reverted to type: a dwindling band of enthusiasts. In 1970 Ivor Stanbrook, a hard-edged Conservative with little regard for 'the best local councillor at Westminster', took back the seat for the Conservatives.

'Orpington man', as a synonym for a suburban classless Liberalism, arose from a misunderstanding of the variety and complexity of suburban life-styles. Orpington in 1962 was no archetypal prosperous middle-aged established suburb, but an area of growth, conflict and change. The political sub-culture of Orpington comprised a more unusual pattern of attitudes than has been realized. But without the Orpington myth, the history of the three major political parties might have been very different. It is to the impact of Orpington on the Conservative, Labour and Liberal parties that we must now turn.

The impact of Orpington

Orpington, *The Times* pronounced on 15 March, was 'the most severe blow the Conservatives have suffered since they returned to office in 1951'. The day following the by-election, senior ministers were due to address a meeting of the Central Council of the Conservative Party in London. Unexpectedly, the Prime Minister himself turned up to steady the nerves. Iain Macleod had already been dismissive, describing Orpington as a second Torrington; when Harold Macmillan rose to placate his troubled followers he conceded that Orpington was 'a disappointment, even a shock', but:

> What has happened is that Conservative voters have abstained, or voted Liberal as a by-election protest against some things they don't like, some things they don't understand, and some things where perhaps they are not patient enough to look to the end. I do not blame them. I am sorry about it but I understand it. I suppose the lesson to us is that if it is due to lack of knowledge and understanding, I and my colleagues … who have the task of explanation must set about it with new endeavour … [16]

The new endeavour was, however, tempered with prudence; the *Sunday Express* on 18 March revealed that a new creation of life peers was to be delayed to avoid any unnecessary by-elections in even the safest seats.

The tensions in the cabinet were clearly mounting, and the party rank and file were restless. In the following three months other by-election results, at Middlesbrough West, Stockton-on-Tees, Derby North, Montgomeryshire and West Derbyshire, all showed Conservative stock to be at its lowest. Then, on 12 July, came Leicester North-East, where the Conservative ran third to the Liberal candidate. On the following day Harold Macmillan announced the reconstruction of his cabinet, dispensing with the services of seven of its members, including the Chancellor, Selwyn Lloyd, to whose 'pay pause' so much of the Conservative unpopularity was ascribed.

None of these events is directly attributable to Orpington, and yet Eric Lubbock's victory was the most threatening of the spate of by-election results which boded ill for the Conservative Party. One particular policy response that has been attributed to Orpington, not least by Lubbock himself in a radio broadcast, was the abolition of the Schedule A property tax, announced in the budget speech of 8 April. Schedule A had been thought to be a significant issue at the by-election, but it is certain that its abolition had been long planned and owed nothing to Peter Goldman's defeat. At a lower level within the party, the carpetbagger's stock fell even further. In the aftermath of Orpington, neighbouring Conservative associations absorbed the lesson that failure to adopt a locally known candidate was an unacceptable political risk. [17]

Just as reformers within the Conservative Party were concerned at their failure to attract 'the new men', so also were the middle-class progressives within the Labour Party. There is no doubt that Orpington, and recognition of the new forces it appeared to herald, greatly strengthened Labour's liberal wing. Although the *Daily Worker* could explain Labour's failure at Orpington in terms of Jinkinson's reluctance to proclaim a Socialist message, the contrary conclusion was more widely drawn. Orpington conveniently illustrated the Crosland and Abrams's thesis that traditional social divisions were being eroded, and that Labour must adapt to these fundamental changes in society. Woodrow Wyatt warned his Constituency Labour Party in a speech a few days after the by-election:

> There is a new social group emerging. It is young. It is white collar. It is skilled. It is ambitious to advance socially and economically. It will decide the next election. It does not want the Tories but it does not want a cloth cap Labour Party either.[18]

The message was repeated in the leading revisionist journal, *Socialist Commentary*. In an article contributed to the May issue, college lecturer Geoffrey Rhodes warned that

> the Labour Party must take account of this new factor in British politics or be ultimately replaced as the principal opposition party ... time will not be on the side of a party which plods along as though no major social changes have taken place since the 1930s.[19]

Socialist Commentary continued to promote this interpretation of the Liberal success and the failure of the Labour Party to make a political breakthrough at a time when the government's popularity was low. Despite the gradual fall-off in support for the Liberal Party which occurred in the midsummer of 1962, the August issue of *Socialist Commentary* carried a leader devoted to the subject of Liberal support. This dealt mainly with the findings of Mark Abrams's survey in the London and Manchester suburbs, which had appeared in the *Observer* on 1 July. Unless Labour adapted to the patterns of social change, it warned, and ceased 'to think in class terms where these have become irrelevant...there will be no stopping the Liberals' advance'. The sceptical voices were few, but they included a leading writer on the English middle classes, who claimed that major party panic over the rediscovery of a neglected middle class was no new phenomenon.[20]

With the election of Harold Wilson to the party leadership following the death of Hugh Gaitskell, and his adoption of a technocratic appeal, exemplified in his Scarborough speech on science, Labour left and Labour right united behind a revisionist programme and a 'new class' image. Wilson himself, with an oblique reference to Orpington, declared his aim to be 'acceptability in the suburbs'. The message, if there was one, had been read and heeded.

Owing perhaps to their predisposition to believe that the tide of social change was flowing in their favour, many in the Liberal Party also accepted the 'new men' interpretation of Orpington. The Liberals claimed both too little and too much; too little in the sense that Lubbock's support already had a broader base than the rising middle class; too much, in the sense that there was no sign of a repeat performance in any other Home Counties constituency.[21] It was a serious error. The major parties, each with a solid bedrock of class-based support, could compete for the uncommitted vote of the young professional middle class in the knowledge that whichever party succeeded in winning it could have a majority at the next general election. But the Liberal Party, even if successful in its aim to monopolize the support of this group, was unlikely to win a single parliamentary seat on that support alone. One of the Liberal Party's leading historians surely got it right:

> The Liberals have been obsessed for ten years with the belief that they, like the Congregational Church, have a vocation to serve the 'new' middle class. This is market research gone mad. It has got them precisely nowhere... The Liberals set their cap at the London commuter and ended up with the Ross and Cromarty crofter. They tried to win by spotlighting a particular social group. They should have spotlighted place.[22]

In order to win Parliamentary seats, it is necessary to attract majority or very substantial minority support in a number of specific constituencies. The 'new men' on whom the Liberal revival was to be based were fairly evenly distributed throughout the country, with a strong bias towards the affluent south-east, and something of a concentration in Orpington. Their support, if gained, could provide the Liberal Party with a respectable vote in a large number of areas, but nowhere – not even in Orpington – would it be sufficient by itself to elect a Liberal MP. And in October 1964 this social group gave their vote largely to a Wilsonian Labour Party.

The significance of Orpington in the fatal misdirection of Liberal electoral strategy which followed should not be underestimated. The survey carried out for the Liberal Party Organisation was more than just an analysis of the factors leading to Lubbock's triumph. It was also read for the formula which would produce more Orpingtons elsewhere. The party's most vulnerable point, the survey showed, was its vague image, which had contributed little of positive value at Orpington. In the words of the survey report:

> While people may have quite clear beliefs about the party [for example that young people support it] they find it difficult to put into words just what the party stands for, when they can easily describe the others in terms of class and socialist/capitalist stereotypes. It seems likely that doubt about the party would diminish if it could be associated explicitly with young people, their problems and approach – a feature of this approach being rejection of class...

The problem of the Liberal (and Liberal Democrat) image is of course a perennial one. The solution offered, however, turned out to be no solution at all. Perhaps it was a mistake to seek a positive image. Orpington, after all, had been won without one, and the 'image' never reflected the substance of Liberal support. The Liberal publicity campaign in the following general election was schizophrenic, combining Celtic fringe and West Country appeals to local and agricultural interests, with a national television campaign to win the support of the 'new man'. It was the former that brought such results as were achieved.

Was there a Liberal revival?

The success at Orpington 'gave an enormous but dangerous fillip to Liberal plans and activities. Electorally, everything thereafter seemed a disappointment.'[23] That this was so is attributable in some degree to the press, who predicted further unrealisable 'Orpingtons' in the subsequent by-elections. Middlesbrough West in June 1962 was breathlessly awaited, with the press billing a repeat Liberal triumph. But the local candidate polled only a respectable 25.8 per cent of the votes – a good result, comparable with Tiverton, Moss Side, Bolton East or Carshalton, but, given the inflated expectations, a disappointment. And although the seemingly marginal seat of Montgomeryshire was held comfortably in May, the Liberals failed to win West Derbyshire, Chippenham or Colne Valley, all seats which they could reasonably have expected to capture. From March 1963 electoral decline set in, and the deteriorating by-election results – average vote 17 per cent, as against 28 per cent in 1962 – were matched by the inexorable decline in Liberal support as indicated by the opinion polls.

Orpington was, of course, merely one event, though an important one, in the period of the Liberal 'revival'. Although the downturn in publicly expressed support for the party came within two months of Orpington (and after the sensational NOP poll which indicated hypothetical majority support for the Liberal Party), the steady improvement in the more immediate aspects of the party's well-being continued for some time. Most notable was the growth in membership, income and full-time agents.[24]

Less tangibly, the Liberals enjoyed the heady period when for a while it was 'smart' to profess a Liberal allegiance, and especially smart to do so in normally non-political circles. Moreover, the party seemed to have monopolized the political commitment of the young. This illusion was largely attributable to the social visibility of an articulate young elite and the blurring of the distinction between the activist and the ordinary voter. Liberal Party activists were overwhelmingly young; but young voters were not overwhelmingly Liberal. The number of Young Liberal branches rose from around 150 to some 500 in the years 1959–63. It claimed, in that

Table 8.5 Liberal party membership, finance and full-time agents.

	1959	1964
Paper membership	150,000	300,000
Annual income	£24,000	£70,000
Full-time agents	32	60

latter year, to be the fastest-growing youth organisation in the country. And as Abrams and Little remarked, 'a significantly high proportion of Young Liberals came from white collar and professional families with a tradition of civic or political activity'.[25]

The influx of activist youth into the party was, however, a transient phenomenon. So long as by-election results and opinion polls were encouraging, the 'revival' was largely self-confirming. But in late 1962 and 1963, support began once again to coalesce around the major political parties. Liberal support now dwindled, and the Young Liberals became the fastest-declining political youth organization in the country. From 1964 they suffered an annual rate of decline in the order of 20 per cent, as compared with rates for the Young Socialists and Young Conservatives of five and 2.5 per cent respectively. More important than the entry and exit of activists was the failure of the Liberals to make any inroads into the political commitment of the younger voter. The young, as Abrams and Little in a separate study discovered, were neither more radical nor more conservative – nor indeed more Liberal – than their elders. They pointed out that 'the young do not give the Liberals more support than other age groups. This reflects a direct failure of a major campaign by the Liberal Party in 1962–3 to identify itself with the interests of the young ...'[26]

Given, then, the decline of popular support after Orpington, and the failure to secure the support of the special 'target' groups of voters, the general election, when it came, was no revivalist occasion, although the results were an improvement on 1959. The gains – and especially the untabulated second places – do perhaps illustrate the one long-term consequence of Orpington: that the Liberal Party was once again taken seriously as a national political institution. On 16 March 1962 the *Daily*

Table 8.6 Liberal performance in the 1959 and 1964 general elections.

	Candidates	MPs elected	Deposits forfeited	Total votes	% of UK total
1959	216	6	55	1,640,760	5.9
1964	365	9	52	3,099,283	11.2

Mirror had announced that it would henceforth present the Liberal viewpoint to its readers 'as a public service'. The Liberals were news, and in the words of the party's then Director of Research,

> almost every national newspaper has given the Liberals space to answer the Tory charge that Liberals have no constructive programme. The result has been a crystallisation of Liberal policy in terms of the problems of today.[27]

The concomitant of this crystallization was that every Liberal candidate had now to face the opposition of both major parties. All existing electoral arrangements were abrogated. From now on, the Liberal Party would have to fight for survival. Its credit had expired.

Notes

1 R. H. Pear, 'The Liberal Vote', *Political Quarterly*, 33 (3), July/September 1962, pp. 247–4.

2 Quoted in A. Watkins, *The Liberal dilemma*, (Plymouth, McGibbon & Kee, 1966).

3 Watkins, *Liberal dilemma*, p. 109.

4 E. Lubbock, MP, 'My first campaign', BBC Radio 4, 3 April 1970.

5 The Macmillan government's white paper proposing these mergers had just been published, and found little favour in the outer suburbs. See G. Rhodes, *The new government of London: the struggle for reform*, (London, Weidenfeld and Nicolson, 1970).

6 *The Orpington by-election: report on a survey by the political research unit*, Liberal Party Organisation, 1962. All quotations from Conservative Central Office papers are from the Conservative Political Archive in the Bodleian Library.

7 D. Newby, 'The Orpington Story', *New Outlook*, March, 1963, pp. 3–18, 27–42. The author is indebted to Newby's account for much of the pre-election background of the Orpington Liberals.

8 M. Abrams, 'Who are the New Liberals?' *Observer*, 1 July 1962.

9 J. T. Coppock, 'Dormitory settlements around London', and J. H. Johnson, 'The suburban expansion of housing in London, 1918–39', in J. T. Coppock and H. T. Prince (eds), *Greater London*, (London, Faber and Faber, 1964).

10 For perspectives on suburban diversity see B. M. Berger, 'The myth of suburbia', *Journal of Social Issues*, 1961, pp. 38–49, and L. Schnore, 'Urban form: The case of the metropolitan community', in W. Z. Hirsch, (ed.) *Urban life and form*, (New York, Holt, 1963).

11 *Census 1961, England and Wales, county reports: Kent* (London, HMSO, 1963).

12 For the social and familial factors that drive the politics of suburbia, see E. Mowrer, 'The family in suburbia', in W. M. Dobriner (ed.) *The suburban community*, (New York, Putnam, 1958), and D. Chapman, *The home and social status* (London, Routledge and Kegan Paul, 1965). Their impact upon the growth and politics of the London suburbs, and suburban Kent in particular, is dealt with in K. Young and J. Kramer, *Strategy and conflict in metropolitan housing* (London: Heinemann, 1978), pp. 21–31 and 226–34.

13   Newby, 'The Orpington Story', p. 29.
14   See generally, Young and Kramer, *Strategy and conflict.* A rare analysis of community conflict between such groups is given in N. Elias and J. L. Scotson, *The established and the outsiders* (London, Cass, 1965).
15   See W. Grant, 'Local' parties in British local politics: a framework for empirical analysis, *Political Studies*, June 1971, pp. 201–12, and more generally the same author's *Independent local politics in England and Wales*, (Farnborough: Saxon House, 1977).
16   *The Times*, 16 March 1962.
17   M. Rush, *The selection of parliamentary candidates*, (London, Nelson, 1969), pp. 105–6.
18   *Observer*, 18 March 1962.
19   G. Rhodes, 'Labour and the young professionals', *Socialist Commentary*, May 1962, pp. 12–14.
20   J. Bonham, 'The middle class revolt', *Political Quarterly*, 33 (3), July–September 1962, pp. 238–46.
21   Watkins, *The Liberal dilemma*, p. 120.
22   J. Vincent, 'What kind of third party?' *New Society*, 26 January 1967. See also M. Steed's reply in *New Society*, 3 February 1967.
23   D. E. Butler and A. King, *The British general election of 1964*, (London, Macmillan, 1965), pp. 101–2.
24   C. Cook, 'The Liberal and Nationalist revival', in D. McKie and C. Cook (eds), *Decade of disillusion*, (London, 1972). For a discussion of local developments in the Liberal Party in the following years, see A. Brier, 'A study of Liberal party constituency activity in the mid-1960s', Exeter University PhD dissertation, 1967.
25   P. Abrams and A. Little, 'The young activist in British politics', *British Journal of Sociology*, 16 (4), December 1965, p. 325.
26   P. Abrams and A. Little, 'The young voter in British politics', *British Journal of Sociology*, 16 (2), June 1965, p. 99.
27   H. Cowie, 'Liberalism's new deal', *Political Quarterly*, 33 (3), July–September 1962, p. 255.

CHAPTER 9

By-elections of the Wilson Government

David McKie

Until 1966, it had for many years been a rare exception for a seat to change hands in a by-election. The Labour Governments of 1945-51 lost only one seat. The Conservatives survived over five years after their return to power without any casualties, and actually picked up a seat from Labour in May 1953 – the first time since 1924 that the government had captured a seat from the opposition at a by-election. In the whole of their thirteen years the Conservatives lost only 10 seats – 8 to Labour, 2 to the Liberals.

The astonishing thing about the by-elections of the 1966 Parliament was that, far from being an exception, the loss of seats by the government became for a time the almost invariable rule. In one ten-month period alone, September 1967 to June 1968, Labour lost almost as many seats as the Conservatives had in their 13 years.

The first shock was Leyton. Patrick Gordon Walker, Harold Wilson's choice for Foreign Secretary, had been defeated in the 1964 general election at Smethwick, a seat he had held since 1945, after a contest in which the race issue had been heavily against him. Reginald Sorensen had first been elected for Leyton West in 1929. He was 73 years old when it was first put to him that he might move conveniently aside and enable Gordon Walker to occupy Leyton; he was, by all accounts, shocked and horrified. 'Heavens above! God forbid!' he is said to have exclaimed. He was opposed to peerages on principle. But pressure was applied, and Sorensen duly resigned his seat to go to the Lords.

Leyton was one of those suburbs of London which once used to regard itself as a self-contained township but was now sinking more or less resignedly into metropolitan anonymity. Nearly 30 per cent of the electorate were aged 60 or over. The campaign was a bleak affair. The weather was not cruel, as it might have been for a January election, only cheerless. Gordon Walker campaigned from the back of a furniture van, haranguing half-empty street corners.

The immigration issue had unseated him at Smethwick; there were those determined to use it against him here as well. Colin Jordan, leader of the National Socialist movement, moved in on Leyton. He invaded an early press conference. Then two Labour meetings, one addressed by Denis Healey, the other by George Brown, were interrupted by demonstrations involving Jordan and his associates.[1] There had been no history of racial disturbance in Leyton. There was, at the 1966 census, a coloured population of some 3,000; as one voter told a reporter: 'There are quite a lot of dark people round here. There didn't seem a lot of animosity. We heard nothing about it at the General Election. We never had fighting and that sort of thing before. We've always been a very peaceful borough, up to now.'

The Conservative candidate was Ronald Buxton, a civil engineer and a local employer who campaigned in a curious ginger overcoat. He called for tougher immigration controls, but denounced allegations that his canvassers were using the race issue on the doorstep.

On the face of it, Labour should not have been in trouble at Leyton. The opinion polls were favourable: Gallup put them 9 points ahead in December, with 48 per cent satisfied with the government's record – though the January lead fell to 3.5 per cent. But on 21 January, Gordon Walker lost the seat by 205 votes.

The swing at Leyton was 8.7 per cent. Not, perhaps, very spectacular compared with some of those the Conservatives had suffered in the late days of Harold Macmillan. But it came so soon after Labour's general election victory, at a time when, despite unpleasant economic measures, they had still seemed to have a solid backing of public support, it was a major political sensation. Yet at least there were special circumstances to explain it: the eviction of Sorensen, the failure of Leyton to take Gordon Walker to its heart. Subsequent by-elections produced nothing to match it. There were seats where the Labour vote slumped, but these were places where it didn't really matter anyway; it was widely noted that the beneficiaries seemed to be the Liberals. Much speculation broke out as to whether the voters were constructing a series of informal 'radical alliances', supporting whichever of the leftward parties was challenging the Conservatives.

The emergence of this pattern gave the Liberals an excellent chance at Roxburgh, Selkirk and Peebles, which polled in March. This was a ripe slice of luck for the Liberals. It had been a Liberal seat from 1950 to 1951. Their candidate, David Steel, was young, energetic, fluent and familiar from frequent television appearances, and he had a ready-made issue. The Borders, he said, were falling into neglect. Successive governments had ignored them and had stood by while the whole area fell into decline. The Conservatives had chosen Robert McEwen, a lawyer, who suffered a double disadvantage: he was a laird, and he was also a Catholic – a marked misfortune for a man involved in Border politics.

In the last few days of the campaign, Labour workers were urging on the doorsteps: 'If you can't vote for our man, make sure you vote for Steel.'

On 24 March, Roxburgh sent Steel to Westminster with a 4,607 majority on a swing from Conservative to Liberal of 7.3 per cent. Meanwhile Labour was still picking its way along the tight-rope of its tiny majority. There was always the fear of death or accident creating a difficult by-election. The Labour Member for Falmouth (majority 6.9 per cent) was known to be in very poor health. The seat which eventually came on to the market was precarious. Henry Solomons, who died on 7 November 1965, had taken Hull North from the Conservatives at the 1964 general election by a mere 1,181 votes (2.5 per cent).

The Conservatives moved in on Hull with every sign of confidence. Newspaper dispatches from the battleground were virtually unanimous in reporting that they were setting a cracking pace. Their candidate, Toby Jessel, adopted the practice of campaigning on the trot and occasionally at the gallop, rushing from house to house, hands outstretched, with a troupe of presentable young women panting along behind him. Labour's chances of holding the seat were also complicated by the arrival of Richard Gott, until then a leader-writer on the *Guardian,* who wanted to restore Labour to a more aggressively radical position and who was particularly opposed to the government's acquiescence in America's involvement in Vietnam.

Yet, in reality, Labour's candidate Kevin McNamara was building himself a strong position. He was much more in keeping with the provincial sobriety of the place than were Jessel and his acolytes, invading the quiet of the terraced streets with the confident well-polished accents of the posher London suburbs. While the *Guardian* might declare in a headline on 19 January: 'Mr Gott a highly important factor at Hull North', there was no evidence that the ordinary voters of Hull North attached any significance to him at all.

On the day, Richard Gott collected just 253 votes; and Kevin McNamara earned himself a double claim to space in the record books. It was the biggest pro-government swing in a by-election since Ilford North in February 1954, nearly 12 years before. It was the sign Harold Wilson needed that the time was right to call the general election for which everyone had been waiting.

One of the less remarked features of Harold Wilson's electoral triumph in 1966 was the advance made by the Scottish Nationalists. Their average vote increased from 10.7 to 14.3 per cent, and in one region, around the Forth and Tay, they fought every seat and did not lose a single deposit. In West Lothian they took more than 35 per cent of the vote, and in three other constituencies their vote topped 20 per cent. In Wales, results were disappointing. But there was one exception to this pattern, and it was to outweigh in significance everything else which happened to the Nationalists in 1966.

Carmarthen was the largest constituency in Wales: there were 820 square miles of it. It was mainly farming country, but there was mining in the Gwendraeth and Amman valleys. It had a highly individual political history: Liberal from 1923 to 1929; Labour until 1931; then Liberal again until 1935; Labour from 1935 to 1945; then regained and held by the Liberals until the death of Sir Rhys Hopkin Morris in November 1956. The Labour candidate in the subsequent by-election was Megan Lloyd George, who had herself been a Liberal MP (for Anglesey) for 22 years up to 1951. She had joined Labour in 1955. Her selection in 1957 helped convert a Liberal majority of 3,333 (6.8 per cent) into a Labour majority of 3,069 (6.1 per cent). In each case, no Conservative stood; Plaid Cymru (or the Blaid as it was known in Wales) took 7.8 per cent in 1955 and 11.5 per cent in the by-election. In 1966 Lady Megan had her biggest majority yet: 9,233, (20.1 per cent) over the Liberals. But she was by now a very sick woman, and took no part in the campaign. She died six weeks later on 14 May.

The candidate whose performance in the 1966 general election had done so much to light up the general Nationalist gloom was Gwynfor Evans, president of the party since 1945 and far and away its most commanding personality. His vote in 1966 – 7,416 (16.1 per cent) – was the second-best in Wales, and a steady advance on the 5.2 per cent of 1959 and the 11.7 per cent of 1964. Evans had assembled a fine collection of local fears and grievances and he hammered away at them with vigour and enthusiasm. His meetings were packed (though opponents liked to point out that many of his most devoted supporters were too young to vote for him) and he returned time and again to the same theme: you must choose, he declared, between Wilson and Wales.

Events played into Evans's hands. The selective employment tax, introduced in Callaghan's post-election budget, was particularly unwelcome in a constituency of this kind. It didn't help when Callaghan, anxious to offset the damage the issue was doing to Labour, told a local farmer that he was tired of this kind of complaint from farmers who 'spend as much on an afternoon at Ascot as they would on SET'. Farmers in Carmarthenshire do not customarily spend much time at Ascot, or much money either. The closure of the Carmarthen – Aberystwyth railway line, too, was a perfect symbolic issue for the Nationalists.

Labour said Evans was 'parochial'. Parochial? He picked up the taunt and paraded it like a flag. 'In the present by-election', reported Adam Hopkins and Peter Tinniswood in the *Western Mail* on 12 July, 'the government is not on trial as the government of Britain, but as the government of Carmarthen and nowhere else.' And, as the government of Carmarthen, it got a resounding vote of no confidence with Gwynfor Evans's victory on 14 July. Evans had laid claim to 15,000 votes; he passed his target with more than a 1000 to spare.

Though the other parties did their best to minimize it, it was difficult to challenge the Blaid's contention that this was a historic result. 'Throughout Great Britain', reported the *Carmarthen Journal* proudly, 'his history-making win put news of the increased bank rate and stringent financial measures into second place.'

For eight months Labour escaped further by-elections. Then on 9 March 1967 they fought three. One was Nuneaton, now vacated by Frank Cousins, a seat subjected for the second time to the need to stage an election because of the internal needs of the Labour Party, and therefore likely to be dejected and apathetic – but not on anyone's card a likely loss. The other two were more serious: Rhondda West and the Pollok division of Glasgow. In both, all normal rules ceased to apply: Labour was once more facing the challenge of the now rampant Nationalists.

Rhondda West was a constituency in decline. People were leaving the valley at an estimated rate of 800 a year. Housing conditions were bad, and had not been notably improved either by three years of Labour government or by decades of Labour control in local politics. But the one over-riding and inescapable preoccupation of people in the Rhondda in the early months of 1967 was unemployment, which stood at more than 9 per cent and showed every sign of being chronic. It was twice the average for Wales, and four times the average for Britain as a whole.

The Nationalist candidate of 1966, Victor Davies, had remained active in Rhondda politics and was readopted now. Labour chose the secretary of its local party, Alec Jones, teacher, who had grown up in the area, moved away to London and then returned. Jones wanted to widen the campaign, but found it virtually impossible. 'You kept on coming up against unemployment. It was like a wall', he recalled later.

Labour brought in their regional organizer, J. Emrys Jones, to run the campaign, as they had at Carmarthen. His ideas, though conventional in British politics, were not in keeping with the peculiar inbred traditions of the Rhondda. There must, he said, be a canvass. 'A canvass?' exclaimed an astonished local loyalist. 'We *never* canvass in Treherbert.' Since the lowest majority since 1950 had been 55 per cent, in 1959, they had never really needed to. The headlines were as bad as they had been in Carmarthen. Bank Rate was down, which helped; the wage freeze was over, but celebrations were muted by the knowledge that it had been replaced by a period of severe restraint. The Nationalists failed; but they cut the Labour majority in one of the most cast-iron of all Labour seats to a desperately marginal 2,306 (9.1 per cent). The increase in the Nationalist vote was far greater even than in Carmarthen.

Simultaneously, the Scottish Nationalists struck their own blow at Pollok. The Scots, as the 1966 election results indicated, had been far ahead of the Welsh in electoral terms. As early as November 1961 they had polled 18.7 per cent of the vote in a by-election at Glasgow Bridgeton; in the West Lothian by-election of June 1962, fighting a seat not previously contested, they had taken second place.

Pollok had once been a Conservative stronghold. But then the Labour-controlled Glasgow council began, as Labour councils did, to build large council estates in the midst of Tory territory. The 1966 census showed that 55.7 per cent of homes in the constituency were council tenancies. It was clear that there was much disaffection on the estates about the record of Labour government. The unemployment rate in Glasgow stood at 4.3 per cent – far below that in the Rhondda, but still twice the national average. There was general awareness of the threat to the economy of south-west Scotland in the decline of traditional industries.

Labour imported Dick Douglas, a 35-year-old economics lecturer from Dundee who had formerly lived in the city. The Conservatives, hurriedly dispensing with the candidate who had fought the seat for them in 1966, brought in Esmond Wright, Professor of Modern History at Glasgow University. The Nationalist was George Leslie, a leading figure in SNP politics in the city and a veterinary surgeon. They staged a lively and eventful campaign on the model which the party was then evolving, featuring much singing of Scottish songs, both topical and traditional, and a showbiz flavour.

In the event it was Esmond Wright who went to Westminster, but the Nationalists who could fairly claim to have put him there. The Labour vote fell by 9,000, the Conservative vote by only 5,000, which meant the Conservative was in. The Nationalist, fresh to the constituency, took 28.2 per cent of the vote. Anxiously, the party awaited another chance to show its paces. In September 1967, when Tom Fraser, who had been dropped by Wilson as Minister of Transport at Christmas 1965, took the post of Chairman of the North of Scotland Hydro-Electric Board, it came.

The Hamilton division of Lanarkshire must, even after Pollok, have seemed a reasonable risk to Labour. It was the ninth safest seat in Scotland; Fraser's 1966 majority had been 16,576 (42.4 per cent). The Nationalist track record was unimpressive: 6.2 per cent of the vote in 1959 and no candidate since. They had done well in the county areas at the municipal elections but not in the burgh.

But once again the Labour campaign immediately ran into difficulties. There was a bitterly contested selection: among those rejected was the chairman of the local party. The choice fell on a miner, Alex Wilson, from Forth; now fifty, he had worked in the pits from the age of 14. It seemed to some a backward-looking choice. This had once been a mining consti-tuency. Fraser had been a miner; so had his predecessor, Duncan Graham. But Hamilton was changing. Only 4.5 per cent of the work-force were now employed in the pits. There was a new breed of bright, ambitious middle-class voter in the constituency who would not be attracted by this appeal to tradition. The Nationalist candidate, on the other hand, a vivacious, original and infectiously enthusiastic woman lawyer of 37, Winifred Ewing, looked tailor-made for them. She was basically Left in politics (which could not by any means be said for her party as a whole); she was witty and inventive; she had a good eye for publicity. The campaign was full of the crowd-pleasing gimmickry which became the hallmark of Nationalist politics.

Labour were now trailing the Conservatives in the polls (Gallup gave the Conservatives a 5-point lead in October, widening to 6 per cent in November) and trouble was raining in on the government thick and fast. The platform had suffered defeats at conference; unemployment remained extremely serious (though at least, by polling in November, Labour avoided the peak period of winter unemployment). There were crisis situations in the docks and in the railways. Reading the signs one could only assume that things were going to get worse.

All this was exactly the diet on which Nationalism fed. There were even signs that religious differences were working in their favour. The available statistical evidence suggests that Catholics stayed more faithful to Labour in the troubles of the 1966–70 Parliament than did Protestants. Certainly, in Hamilton, there was believed to be an 'Orange vote', and the signs were that Mrs Ewing was collecting it.

On the night of 2 November 1967, Hamilton passed into the hands of the Scottish Nationalists in a result which set the experts searching vainly for precedents. Here was a seat, not even contested 18 months before, in which 46 per cent of voters, 33.9 per cent of the total electorate, had turned out for Mrs Ewing.

Opinions differed about how long the phenomenon would last; but it was difficult to dispute that after Hamilton, as the government staggered on from crisis to crisis (the parity of the pound survived Hamilton by only 16 days) and Labour's support in the polls sank to a mere 30 per cent, the Nationalists were now a serious and potentially a decisive political force. Nor were they merely conducting a kind of spoiling operation on other people's votes. They were mobilizing previous non-voters too. Their supporters did not predominantly want to see Scotland independent; there was undoubtedly force in the view that many who advocated a complete cut-off from England might have changed their views very sharply had that ever become a real political possibility. But they wanted to register the fact that Scotland and Wales, after electing Labour Governments for years, only to be frustrated by the Conservative English, were gravely dissatisfied with the Labour Government which was now directing their fortunes from faraway London.

Certainly, it still remained possible, even now that Carmarthen, Pollok and Rhondda West had been capped by Hamilton, to regard it all as a Poujadist wave which, if treated with appropriate disdain, would eventually go away. There was no such consolation over the ground which was now being lost to the Conservatives. Judged against Nationalist successes, the damage the Conservatives had been doing to Labour in by-elections was unspectacular. But judged by the normal standards of seats lost and swings between the parties, it was very serious indeed.

At Walthamstow West the swing against the government was 18.4 per cent, nearly 5 points higher than anything the Conservatives had suffered in the worst of the Macmillan years. At Cambridge the turnout fell, compared with the general election, by 14.2 per cent and the swing to the Conservatives was 8.6 per cent. At Walthamstow the drop in turnout was 17 per cent and the swing 18.4 per cent. So apathy did go some way to explain it; but there was more to it than that. Most unusually, the Liberals, third at Walthamstow with 14.1 per cent at the general election, substantially improved their position in a contest in which a seat was changing hands, taking 22.9 per cent of the vote at the by-election. Still more significantly, the Conservatives, for the first time in this Parliament, recruited a larger proportion of the total electorate than they had at the general election. The turnout had dropped by nearly one-fifth; but even so, the Conservative vote was numerically up on 1966. This result reflected more than abstention: it meant that 1966 Labour votes were crossing over in significant numbers to other parties.

After Walthamstow it was clear that Manchester Gorton and Leicester South-West, which polled on the same day as Hamilton, were going to be hard to hold. Gorton, which became vacant on the death of Konni Zilliacus, its Labour MP since 1955, would be lost on a swing of 10.1 per cent. The Leicester seat, vacated by Herbert Bowden, the Commonwealth Secretary, who was leaving politics to become chairman of the ITA after 22 years as an MP, would change hands on a swing of 8.7 per cent.

In Leicester, where municipal elections had signalled massive disaffection on the vast council estates which contained some 44 per cent of all homes in the constituency, Labour drifted towards disaster. But in Gorton Labour was putting up a very solid fight. Gorton was a dour, self-respecting Manchester suburb: by no means affluent, but a cut above the living conditions of a division like Exchange. More than half its households were owner-occupied. The Labour candidate was Kenneth Marks, a headmaster in nearby Blackley, a cheerful, rubicund, common-sense man who seemed just right for the constituency. The Conservative, whose selection had caused much excitement, was Winston Churchill, grandson of the former Prime Minister.

From the start there were doubts about whether Churchill's selection had been the right one. 'Churchill is green in rough-and-tumble politics' wrote Joseph Minogue, of the *Guardian,* who had known Gorton all his life. 'He has matured considerably during the campaign, but Gorton is the wrong kind of seat for him...' Churchill was 27, without previous experience, and out of character with the constituency: compared with Marks, his selection seemed almost to have about it a certain un-Gortonian levity.

The issues were unremittingly the economic ones; it was difficult for anyone, candidate, agent or voter, to get his mind away from them for long in the circumstances of late 1967. The electorate was generally reported to be apathetic. Yet in fact, unlike any of the other English contests so far, this one had actually managed to get the voters involved. The turnout was 72.4 per cent – only 0.2 per cent short of the general election figure.

That was what saved Gorton for Labour: they got out the vote. It was easy to say afterwards, comparing the 9.4 per cent swing at Gorton with the 16.5 per cent which put the Conservatives in at Leicester, that the choice of Churchill had cost the Conservatives the seat. Yet, in fact, the Conservatives increased their numerical vote. They pulled out over 3 per cent more of the total electorate than they had at the general election, against a decrease of 0.9 per cent at Leicester.

So, at the end of just over 19 months of Labour government, the by-election scoreboard looked like Table 9.1.

A pattern was emerging: party workers reluctant to work, disillusioned not only by the government's economic record but also in many cases by its behaviour over defence and Vietnam; and voters who saw no reason to turn out for a party which in their view had brought down upon them a cruel collection of miseries.

Devaluation, the veto on British entry into Europe, the painful convolutions within the party over South African arms and Harold Wilson's leadership, prescription charges, the end of free milk in secondary schools, cuts in housing programmes, deferment of the raising of the school-leaving age: the winter months of 1967–8 were punctuated by a stream of enforced decisions all damaging to the government's standing in the country and especially bitter for the Labour faithful to swallow. Many could not swallow them at all.

Three crucial by-elections were arranged for 28 March 1968: at Dudley (where George Wigg had left politics to become Chairman of the Horserace

Table 9.1 By-elections, July 1966–November 1967.

	Defended	Attacked	Held	Lost	Gained	Lost deposit	Change
Labour	9	2	3	6	–	–	–6
Conservative	2	9	2	–	4	2	+4
Liberal	–	9	–	–	–	4	–
Nationalist	–	4	–	–	2	–	+2

Betting Levy Board), Acton and the Meriden division of Warwickshire, where the Labour incumbents had died. (A third West Midlands seat, solidly Conservative Warwick and Leamington, was to poll the same day.) Meriden would be lost on a swing of 3.7 per cent, Acton on a swing of 7.7 per cent. Dudley could be lost on a swing of 9.1 per cent, though Wilson was said to have had firm assurances that it could be held before he let Wigg go.

Dudley was a curious double-yolked constituency: it comprised the borough of Dudley (an island of Worcestershire marooned in a sea of Staffordshire) to the north, and the borough of Stourbridge five miles to the south. George Wigg had represented Dudley since 1943, and he had a reputation for fighting constituency battles which few MPs could match. As at Leicester, there were vast council estates (44 per cent of households were council tenancies) which had been giving Labour a hard time in municipal elections. Unemployment – 3.3 per cent in Dudley, 2.2 per cent in Stourbridge – had reached levels to which the prosperous West Midlands were not accustomed; factories were going on to short-time; everywhere there was the bitterness of disappointed expectations.

Labour selected, not a local candidate as might have been expected, especially in view of George Wigg's extra-party appeal, but John Gilbert, an accountant and economist who had fought Ludlow in 1966 and who had assiduous support from within Transport House. The strategy in the Labour camp was to stress the continuity between George Wigg and Gilbert: 'I'm John Gilbert', the candidate would announce himself on the doorstep, 'I'm the man in George's place.' But unfortunately he did not look or sound the part. Assured, urbane and speaking in the accents of South Kensington, where he lived, rather than of the West Midlands, he was obviously hard placed to deliver a line like that and sound convincing.

There were clearly several issues working against him. One was race. Dudley's black community – about 2.2 per cent of the population – was modest by West Midlands standards, and despite a frightening outburst of racial violence in 1962, the town had mostly been peaceful. But Dudley is only six miles from Wolverhampton. It reads the Wolverhampton papers. Many go there to work. Enoch Powell's Birmingham speech was still a month ahead, but what was said in that speech was already commonplace in the political discussion of that part of the Midlands. In January and February, the threat of coloured invasion, so-called, had been dramatically advertised by the plight of the Kenya Asians: day after day the voters of Dudley had seen on their TV screens pictures of the congregations at Nairobi airport, of immigrants thronging into Heathrow. On three occasions, Gilbert's appearance in a local pub was the signal for shouts of abuse directed at his and his party's allegedly pro-immigrant associations. The only other issue which produced quite the same virulence among voters – judged by the writer's own experience of many hours on Dudley doorsteps – was the level of social benefits. Everyone, it seemed, knew that most of these fell into the hands of scroungers.

Thirteen days before the election there was George Brown's resignation: embarrassing to any party in a by-election, infuriating for party workers slogging away in an unpopular cause only to read in their newspapers about such antics, such divisions, such personal jealousies, uncontrolled and unconcealed, at the top. On top of it all came Roy Jenkins's budget of 19 March, the most savage in peacetime history. Over £900 million was to be taken out of the economy. Cigarettes, spirits (though not, as punch-drunk party workers somehow remembered to bring out, beer), petrol and purchase tax were all affected. Worst of all, the road fund licence went up to £25. That hit people in Dudley two ways. It damaged the motor industry, to which many owed their employment, and it directly affected them as motorists.

The swing at Dudley was 21.2 per cent: not since the mid-1930s had there been a comparable swing from the government to its principal opponents. The Conservative vote was 20 per cent above the 1966 figure – by far the biggest increase in any by-election so far. Here was a result which, unlike those before it, looked at least as much pro-Conservative as anti-Labour. It confirmed what one had found in traditional Labour areas: some of the former faithful had become so disillusioned with the government, especially for its economic failures (and the West Midlands tends to think about life in terms of economic success perhaps more than any other region in the country), that abstention was no longer enough.

In fact, Dudley can be seen in retrospect as the worst moment for Labour in all its tribulations. Two more seats were lost in June – Oldham West, on a swing of 17.7 per cent, and Nelson and Colne on a swing of 11.4 per cent; but at Bassetlaw in October, a seat which had looked in perilous danger (it was vulnerable on a swing of 11.6 per cent) was held by 740 votes (1.7 per cent). Encouragingly for Labour, Bassetlaw and Nelson paralleled Gorton. On turnout not far short of general election level, the swing was satisfyingly down.

The message from Caerphilly, too, had a certain bleak, though entirely negative, comfort. The Nationalist threat, 16 months after Rhondda West, had certainly not receded. On the other hand, it had not actually got worse. The Blaid had been stronger here than in the Rhondda. They had polled 11 per cent of the vote in 1964 and again in 1966. Now, on 18 July 1968, they cut the Labour majority from 21,148 votes (59.7 per cent) over the Conservatives in the 1966 election to 1,874 votes (5.2 per cent), pushing the Conservatives into third place and costing them their deposit. The proportion of the total electorate voting Plaid Cymru had been pushed up by 22 per cent – a bigger achievement than at Carmarthen, though just short of Rhondda West. At the end of 1968 the by-election scoreboard looked like Table 9.2.

Table 9.2 By-elections, July 1966–November 1968.

	Defended	Attacked	Held	Lost	Gained	Lost deposit	Change
Labour	17	6	6	11	–	1	−11
Conservative	6	17	6	–	9	3	+9
Liberal	–	18	–	–	–	9	–
Nationalist	–	5	–	–	2	–	+2

One party had fallen short of the heady achievements which the smaller battalions had been notching up in Wales and Scotland. The Liberals had failed to turn Labour's unpopularity to their own account in the way they had done with the Conservative misfortunes of the early 1960s. A sudden stroke of luck put them back on the map. Birmingham Ladywood did not have the immediate statistical desirability of the two predecessors. It was far from being the most marginal Labour–over–Liberal seat: the Labour majority in 1966 had been 35.2 per cent. But the Liberal candidate in Ladywood, Wallace Lawler, had recently led the Liberals into a succession of impressive local election successes. He was attacked for his attitude on race, but critics were unable to prove their charges against him. It was said that he was not a Liberal, but a Lawlerite: a populist successfully practising under a Liberal label. His 2,713 vote (28.8 per cent) victory over Labour's Mrs Doris Fisher on a swing from Labour to Liberal of 32 per cent was a triumph for all those in the party who had claimed that hard slogging at local issues was the way in which the party could fight itself back into a strength not entirely dependent on the Celtic fringes.

The loss of Ladywood, on 26 June 1969, was the last of the great Labour disasters. By autumn the trend in the polls was dramatically improved; Gallup put the Conservative lead at 12.5 points in August, 9.5 in September, then 2 per cent in November. On 30 October five Labour seats were defended: Islington North and Paddington North, in London, both greatly reduced in numbers since 1966; Newcastle-under-Lyme, in Staffordshire; Glasgow Gorbals, the safest seat in Scotland; and Swindon, where Francis Noel-Baker had finally resigned after months of anxious speculation. The result was both a relief and a disappointment. Only Swindon fell: the three other English seats were held, and the Nationalist challenge was beaten off in the Gorbals. (Even so, the Nationalists polled 25 per cent of the vote and took second place, which would have been sensational progress up to the time of Pollok.) And the swings, though not in the 1968 class, were still too big for comfort: 9.2 per cent at Islington, 11.4 per cent at Paddington, 10.7 per cent at Newcastle, 12.9 per cent at Swindon. No echo here of the message of the polls that the gap between the main parties had now been closed.

In December, Labour lost Wellingborough on a swing of 9.7 per cent and were on the wrong end of a 14.3 per cent swing at Louth, though this was probably inflated by bad weather. The swing against them dropped to 8.6 per cent at Bridgwater on 12 March – the first by-election in which 18-year-olds were able to vote. But it was not until South Ayrshire, on 19 March, that the party really had something to celebrate. The swing against them was assessed on normal calculations at 3 per cent. But even this probably exaggerated the extent of the damage. On a two-party calculation, there was a swing to Labour of 0.6 per cent.

Those who at the height of the Nationalist tide had given the advice 'stand firm' were now waiting about with hopeful faces expecting to be congratulated. Yet the Nationalists had left their mark. There was always a cynical note in Labour's dismissal of Nationalist politics. 'They'll come to their senses when we get to a general election' it was said, as if the views people expressed three years out of four could be taken as an aberration, and the only criticism which deserved attention was that which might eventually turn you out of power. Had Labour won the 1970 election, this complacency would have been rewarded, would have become a sanctified part of conventional political wisdom: the significance of by-elections as a force for administering shocks to unpopular governments would have been diminished. But on 18 June 1970 the nation reserved its right to behave unpredictably at general elections as well as in between them.

There was, it seemed, a new volatility in the electorate; a new willingness to abandon traditional patterns of voting – or, among the younger voters, a greater disposition to regard such traditions as irrelevant; a new readiness to cross, as so many people did on the council estates of Dudley and Leicester and elsewhere, from one's normal allegiance to that directly opposed to it; there was, too, at a time when none of the established parties had much to boast about, an unusually strong advantage in fielding a candidate who, like Kenneth Marks at Gorton, seemed in sympathy with the spirit of the people whom he aspired to represent.

There was, in this series of by-elections, a certain element of unchannelled emotion, a compound of disappointment, frustration, even despair; on this score, Labour could fully argue that its worst punishments were out of any real proportion to its crimes. But there was also, one suspects, something else: a mood of rampant pragmatism unusual in British politics. Harold Wilson, as the prophet of political pragmatism, had the least right of anyone to complain about that.

Notes

1 This meeting also produced a memorable piece of heckling. After the clashes on immigration were over, Reginald Sorensen was explaining to the audience that,

although they might be surprised to see him going to the Lords, the peerage and democracy were not incompatible. After all, we had just been celebrating the anniversary of the birth of British democracy, which we owed to Simon de Montfort, who was a baron. Voice from the back: 'And *he* was a bloody immigrant, too.'

CHAPTER 10

Lincoln and the Liberal surge, 1972–73

Richard Jay

General Election 1970	Electorate 52,243	
Taverne (Labour)	20,090	*51%*
Alexander (Conservative)	15,340	*39%*
Blades (Independent)	3,937	*10%*
Labour majority	4,750	Turnout 74.5%

By-election 1 March 1973	Electorate 51,199	
Taverne (Democratic Labour)	21,967	*58.2%*
Dilks (Labour)	8,776	*23.3%*
Guinness (Conservative)	6,616	*17.5%*
Simmerson (Independent Conservative)	198	*0.5%*
Waller (Independent)	100	*0.3%*
Justice (Independent)	81	*0.2%*
Democratic Labour Majority	13,191	Turnout 72.6%

In the 1970 general election, the logic of two-party competition between Conservatives and Labour appeared to have reasserted itself decisively. Jo Grimond's much-vaunted bid for a political realignment of the Left in the early 1960s had failed. Liberals had performed well in the mid-term of an unpopular Conservative government, most spectacularly at Orpington; they had made little impact under subsequent Labour administrations. Rudderless and financially troubled, the party was increasingly split between its parliamentary establishment, representing a scattering of half a dozen, mainly rural, constituencies, and radical grass roots activists inspired by the new philosophy of community politics. After 1967, the tide of opinion ebbed from Labour to the primary benefit of Nationalists and the Conservative Party. In 1969–70, it coursed in again, though, to the surprise of both the pollsters and the Labour leadership, insufficiently to produce a third term of office.

It was part of the conventional wisdom by 1970 that the electorate was becoming more volatile, less firmly committed in its loyalty to the two main parties, and perhaps also more disillusioned and alienated. The development of tactical voting was recognized, though little understood. By-elections were increasingly subjected to media scrutiny, not because they represented a choice between candidates or a test of specific public policies, but to set alongside regular national opinion polls in tracing the increasingly erratic movements of public opinion. But in 1970, though turnout had drifted down to 72 per cent, Labour and Conservatives continued to capture almost 90 per cent of the vote between them. Whatever signals the electorate might wish to send out between general elections, at the moment of truth it appeared content to participate in engineering marginal swings between the big two parties.

That conclusion was brought into sharp question between 1972 and 1974. A run of Liberal by-election victories revived the spirit of Orpington; nationalism, at least in Scotland, gained a second wind; and events in Lincoln, where the Labour MP, Dick Taverne, having been deselected after a long-standing row with his local party, won a triumphant by-election victory as an independent Democratic Labour candidate, provided a focus for speculation about a fundamental realignment of party politics. The results of the February 1974 election, called prematurely by Edward Heath to secure a mandate for dealing with the miners' strike, and its successor in October, seemed to suggest that, uniquely in post-war politics, mid-term by-election results and opinion polls might not be mere transient events, but pointers to a fundamental change in party relations. In February 1974, turnout shot back up to 78 per cent, and third parties won 25 per cent of the vote and 37 seats. Liberals gained six million votes and a post-war record 19.5 per cent share of the vote. Two Labour independents, Taverne in Lincoln and Eddie Milne in Blyth, beat the party machines. For the first time since 1931, no party held an overall majority in the House of Commons.

The national background

By the autumn of 1972, Edward Heath's government had been bruised by a series of damaging political encounters and economic problems. Inflation rose inexorably, despite an early promise to cut price rises 'at a stroke' through tax reductions. Unemployment also rose to the unprecedented level of one million. A new term, 'stagflation', entered the vocabulary. Edward Heath had promised a new style of non-interventionist government sympathetic to private enterprise. A series of U-turns, often incomprehensible to supporters, and certainly poorly communicated by a Prime Minister addicted to a distant, technocratic style of government, ensued. The proclaimed intention of allowing 'lame duck' industries to be tested against the forces of nature was replaced by a disbursement of costly financial crutches. After August 1971, sterling was allowed to float on an increasingly turbulent financial sea. The first phase of a statutory prices and incomes policy was initiated in September 1972.

Unlike its predecessor, the cabinet kept its internal differences within house: Reginald Maudling was the only front-rank casualty, resigning in July 1972 over his connection with the Poulson corruption scandal. On the backbenches, right-wingers, in the main identified with Enoch Powell's views on race, free markets and Europe, were troublesome but not openly rebellious. Far more the focus of media attention than Conservative divisions were those within the Labour party, where electoral defeat had unleashed the pent-up bitterness of the last years of the Wilson government. The Left, reinforced by a shift at the top of the big trade unions and the conversion of Tony Benn, demanded vigorous opposition to what was presented as an ideologically-driven attack from the government upon the unions, local government, and working class interests. The Industrial Relations Act (1971) and Housing Finance Act (1972), in particular, stimulated occasional acts of non-co-operation. In February 1972, the Government conceded defeat to the National Union of Mineworkers after a bitter and protracted industrial dispute.

In 1971, entry into the Common Market increasingly became the focus of conflict between Labour's Left and Right, the parliamentary leadership and the extra-parliamentary organization. As Wilson moved rapidly to cover his left flank by adopting a more sceptical posture, pro-Europeans whom he had brought to the fore in the late sixties preparatory to a bid for membership and whose figurehead was the deputy leader, Roy Jenkins, felt isolated and betrayed. 'Entry on Tory Terms' became increasingly unacceptable in a party more virulently anti-Conservative than it had been for a generation. With the prospect of Conservative anti-Market defections, the European issue was not only a focus of Labour's ideological differences, but offered an opportunity to defeat a 'divisive' and 'socially irresponsible' government. Heath's shrewd offer of a free vote on the principle of entry into the EEC split the parliamentary Labour party, and, on 28 October 1971, 69 Labour MPs voted with the Government, enough to outweigh its own defectors. Labour's internal wrangles became increasingly bitter when the Second Reading of the European Communities Bill was carried by five Liberal and four Labour supporting votes, and pro-European Labour MPs indicated that they would ensure that the Bill survived the Committee stage.

A gap opened up on the centre-right of the party. After being unsuccessfully challenged for the Deputy Leadership in the autumn by Michael Foot and Tony Benn, Jenkins resigned in May 1972 against the acceptance of Benn's proposal for a referendum on the terms of entry. He was followed by other pro-Marketeers – George Thompson, Harold Lever, Bill Rodgers, David Owen, Dickson Mabon and the MP for Lincoln, Dick Taverne, among others in what, according to Wilson's biographer[1] 'appears in retrospect as a dress rehearsal for the SDP defections nine years later'. The old Gaitskellites, however, were split: Shirley Williams, Roy Hattersley and Tony Crosland retained their posts, the last leading to a permanent personal breach with Jenkins.

The possibility that this Adullam's cave might prove to be the foundation of a political realignment of the centre-left was widely canvassed. The various manoeuvres of Jenkins and his followers had been extensively reported, and in the main favourably treated, by the media after 1970. But in the latter part of 1972 they became the focus of much more intensive attention, in particular in the pages and editorials of *The Times* under its editor, William Rees-Mogg, and the writings of its astringent columnist, Bernard Levin. Labour was accused of having become an irreconcilable mix of social-democracy and marxism; the two main parties, it was said, had been pulled away from the political centre and a concern for the national interest by their ideological extremes, and a disillusioned electorate was seeking a new political alignment. There were two potential problems with this proposition – that the Jenkinsites might not aspire to the role in which they were being cast and that the evidence of support from the electorate was, at best, speculative.

Certainly, the Jenkinsites appeared to be presenting a rather different message. In the Spring of 1972, a series of speeches from Jenkins, interpreted by Wilson and his allies as preparing a bid for the leadership, emphasized the need for Labour to reunite as a party of constructive, radical reform rather than being locked into mere Tory-bashing. In the main his theme was one of Labour revival: a return to consistent policy-making, greater autonomy for the parliamentary leadership from the dictates of the extra-parliamentary party; and a retrieval of the traditional centre ground of politics, increasingly reoccupied by the Conservative about-face. His capacity to regain the initiative, however, was limited. Europe remained a running sore, splitting the old Gaitskellites, with the main beneficiaries from the divisions appearing to be the party pragmatists, Callaghan and Healey. Many MPs, under pressure from local constituencies, sought to accommodate to the shifting balance of power and opinion in the party. Lever returned to Shadow Cabinet in the Autumn, and George Thompson resigned his seat at Dundee to take up the post of Britain's European Commissioner. It was only in the Lincoln constituency of Dick Taverne that a different kind of outcome seemed to be on the cards. Since the general election, Taverne's relations with his local party management, always prickly, had deteriorated badly, and in July he was deselected as party candidate for the next election. On 6 October 1972, in a challenge to the superficial facade of party unity on the last day of the Labour conference, he announced his resignation to fight a by-election as an Independent Labour candidate.

Elections and polls over the previous 18 months had presented a mixed picture. The government lost Bromsgrove (27 May 1971) on a 10.1 per cent swing; it was consistently behind in the polls, and Conservative candidates were routed in the local elections of 1971 and 1972. But, given continuing price rises and unemployment figures topping one million, the overall picture was by no means disastrous from the Government's viewpoint. If Bromsgrove was lost, Marylebone, Enfield West, Macclesfield and Kingston-upon-Thames were held, and there was even a swing towards the government in Arundel and Shoreham. Labour's lead in the polls remained generally steady at around 7 to 10 per cent. Over 15 contests, turnout fell sharply in all but two, and support for Liberal candidates remained steady at the 1970 level. Significant, though little noted, events were the substantial shift of S. O. Davies's Independent Labour votes in the Merthyr by-election to the Welsh nationalists, and the rise of the SNP vote in Stirling and Falkirk at the expense of the Conservatives.

There was no indication from the electorate, therefore, of any great turbulence other than a sharp turn against a Government which had, in any case, never been expected to win in 1970. Even after a Liberal victory in the Rochdale by-election of 26 October 1972, the mood was relaxed. Their candidate, Cyril Smith, had run second to Labour in 1970. His local standing made Rochdale one of the party's most winnable seats. More media coverage was given to Smith's size (over 20 stone) than to the significance of the result.

In Sutton and Cheam, however, Liberals recognized a constituency closely mirroring Orpington a decade before. Its suburban, middle-class electorate, alienated and confused by the government's policy reversals and inability to control prices, provided a perfect target for the mass army of Liberal volunteers pouring into the area. On 7 December, Graham Tope easily won the seat on a swing which made Orpington look tame. Disillusioned Conservatives responded well to the appeal to deliver a slap on the wrist to their government and Labour voters to exploit a once-in-a-lifetime chance to oust the Conservatives. The impact of Sutton, however, was partly mitigated by the declaration which came a few minutes later at Uxbridge: here, the Conservative scraped home in a highly marginal seat, and the Liberal lost his deposit. No obvious conclusions about the national political context could easily be drawn from these results. Liberals and Labour each lost a deposit, the Conservatives lost a safe seat, but also survived a Labour challenge. Sutton was also claimed as a triumph for the new-style community politics, managed by the leader of Liverpool Liberalism, Trevor Jones, and deploying radical activists to highlight local grievances and problems. Community politics had its electoral roots in the Birmingham, Ladywood by-election of 1969, and had proved effective in challenging the local dominance of Labour machines in inner-city areas of Birmingham, Leeds and Liverpool suffering from urban neglect or technocratic housing redevelopment. Many leading Liberals attributed the failure at Uxbridge to a concentration of activity upon Sutton; they were far less ready to accept the claim from their radical wing that it was the message of populist anti-establishment politics which had swept Sutton. The electoral mood, therefore, remained unclear as the next round of by-elections at Lincoln, Dundee and Chester-le-Street came round on 1 March 1973.

The Lincoln by-election

The 'Lincoln Affair' had begun to engage the national media even before Taverne voted with the 69 Labour dissidents on 28 October. Three days before, ITV's *World in Action* had conducted an investigation into relations between Taverne and the local party leadership, ending in debate among Taverne, his supporters and opponents which rapidly degenerated into a slanging match. The incident revealed both Taverne's flair for focusing favourable publicity upon his role as an innocent victim, and his opponents' flair for handling controversy as if driven by a form of political road-rage.

The roots of the controversy went back as far as Taverne's nomination to fight the by-election which took place six days before Orpington in 1962. Taverne, then Treasurer to the Gaitskellite Campaign for Democratic Socialism, was selected from a short list of three right-centre candidates to succeed Sir Geoffrey de Freitas, recently appointed as High Commissioner to Ghana. A left-wing minority, led by a young radical, Leo Beckett, walked out of the nominations committee in protest at being out-manoeuvred in the selection process, and, in a series of coups, succeeded in establishing themselves at the heart of the local organization. By 1971, Beckett was the party chairman; his ally, Ralph Wadsworth, was leader of the Lincoln council. They were backed by Don Gossop, district secretary of the AUEW, the powerful engineering union, as vice-chairman of the party and chairman of the council's Industrial Committee, and increasingly by Pat Mulligan, the party agent after 1964. Taverne later claimed that 'I was a Gaitskellite MP with a left-wing management committee'.

The troubled years of the Wilson government, when Taverne was a junior minister, saw regular sniping between the MP and his party, which grew increasingly sharp after 1970. In 1971, Labour regained control of Lincoln Council, and the radical group took the opportunity to tighten its hold on the local party machine. Added to the political differences were ones of personality and class. Taverne was a product of Charterhouse, Balliol and the Bar, a close friend of William Rees-Mogg, the editor of *The Times*, since their days at the Oxford Union. Self-confident, intellectual, seemingly well-heeled, and the owner of a private catamaran, he was a far cry from the cultivated proletarianism of the Beckett group. 'The problem Dick Taverne has is that he lives on a different plane from what we do,' said Leo Beckett, 'and when you get people like myself who are nothing more or less than a foundry worker, we speak different languages, we live different lives. He seems to find it very difficult when he arrives and is in our company to be at ease.' Taverne's local appeal was very much to the older party worker, middle-class professionals living 'up the hill' in Lincoln's Cathedral area, and to the city's business class as they searched for alternatives to its ailing economic base – his opponents' political roots lay in sections of local unions radicalized by a declining engineering industry, high unemployment and fears of further rationalization.

With the emergence of entry into the Common Market as the central issue in the party, Taverne was warned that his support for the Government's legislation would lead to a challenge. At the Labour Party Conference in October 1971, statements from Ian Mikardo, the Conference Chairman, and Harold Wilson himself, that MPs who fell out with their local parties would receive no assistance, provided the necessary legitimacy. At a special meeting of the General Management Committee of Lincoln Labour Party on 16 November 1971, a censure motion on Taverne was passed by 54 votes to 50 with 5 abstentions, and approval was given for assembling a new selection committee. This initiated a period of trench warfare. Taverne's supporters were mobilized to quash the vote at a subsequent meeting on 6 December, but new elections to the GMC, and from there to the Executive Committee in March, strengthened the hands of the Left as moderates and Taverne supporters were ousted. Taverne's resignation from the front bench with Roy Jenkins in April brought to an end an uneasy truce that had held since December, and the temperature rose dramatically when the Left tightened its control on Lincoln Council after the local elections in May, removing a number of long-serving notables from their committee posts. 'The sacking of the chairmen' became a major issue in the local media, which had increasingly begun to focus upon the grip of Labour's inner caucus – commonly termed 'Grafton House' after the name of the party headquarters – upon Council business, and polarized internal party divisions. On 15 May, the GMC decided to vote on Taverne's position at its next meeting. On 19 June, after a bitter debate, Taverne was deselected on a vote of 75–50. A subsequent appeal to the National Executive Committee, on the grounds of irregularities in the conduct of ward committee business between the two GMC meetings, was supported by a special NEC subcommittee and the Organisation Committee, but rejected in July by the full NEC. On 6 October, after a series of well-publicized leaks, Taverne resigned his seat to fight a by-election as an independent Democratic Labour candidate.

Of all the 69 rebels from October, Taverne was the only MP to end up in such an open confrontation. Several were fully supported by their local parties. A number yielded to pressure and gave promises of future good behaviour. Some left quietly either at the next election or, like George Thompson, appointed as Britain's European Commissioner, to take up other posts. Taverne's unique circumstance undoubtedly stemmed in part from a long-standing, in some cases personal, local feud. Taverne took the view that he had a choice 'between fading or fighting. I am not the fading type. If I do not get in, I will at least go out with a bang rather than a whimper'. Rather than pragmatic accommodation with his local party leaders, he adopted a strong ideological posture in support of the independence of MPs, and the morality of political consistency. Tony Crosland, one of the few former Gaitskellites to visit Lincoln and speak against Taverne during the by-election, took a more critical view: 'if Dick Taverne had been a bit more understanding,' he said, 'he would still be Labour MP for Lincoln.' But there were also other factors: the split, for instance, was not merely between Taverne and his party, but within the Labour group on Lincoln Council under the impact of what was presented as a left-wing take-over. At the national level, Taverne found few protectors. Many of the Jenkinsites, while sympathizing with his predicament, found his robust stance a political embarrassment and sought to deter him from fighting a by-election: indeed, Taverne reported that only Jenkins thought he could win. On the NEC, Shirley Williams stood up for him, but Barbara Castle and Tony Benn had little difficulty winning the argument for rejecting his appeal. The views of the party faithful in the face of Taverne's truculent stance were probably best expressed in a remark attributed to Jim Callaghan: 'We must find some way to execute Dick Taverne.'

Taverne's resignation was timed deliberately to coincide with the end of the Labour Conference in October. However, it had long been public knowledge that he was determined to stand as an independent, and the ground was carefully prepared. *The Times* ran a full news-spread and editorial on 30 September outlining the case for a new centre party, including a specially commissioned opinion poll showing that a party of Liberals and Labour moderates would command the support of almost half of the electorate. Though widely commented upon, and whatever the current electoral strength of the Liberals, the unhappy fact was, however, that only Taverne was potentially available among Labour moderates to help forge this new party. Even he was in no way anxious to set out such a case in public. In his resignation press release, he attacked Labour's European policy, the 'sham democracy' of the party, which allowed autocratic caucuses to rule the consciences of MPs; and the pursuit of 'slovenly politics, the politics of tactics, manoeuvres, compromise and double-talk which means all things to all men, but in reality means nothing'. The battle of Taverne versus Grafton House had turned into Taverne versus the party, but his principle theme was the need for Labour to review its character and organization, and assert itself as a party of principle, to regain the respect and support of the electorate.

Most political commentators, accustomed to the disappearance of Independents in post-war British politics, took a pessimistic view of Taverne's chances. S. O. Davies, the ejected Labour MP for Merthyr, had stood successfully against his party in 1970, but the result (even where anyone noted), was said to arise from his age, long-tenure and local roots. Taverne's position was very different. However, early opinion polls suggested considerable local support. The row with Grafton House had been long-drawn-out and widely publicized. Taverne had shrewdly discerned the high moral ground, and firmly planted himself there. His appeal was to consistency, principle, the conscience of MPs and personal honour. The image of the Man against the Machine gained wide publicity – the bitter TV confrontations of October 1971; denial of access, even before his resignation, to his surgery in Grafton House; a hasty decision to put his bicycle out on the street (' "They even threw out my bicycle", says Dick Taverne' was the local headline: it actually turned out to be the wrong bike); the dismissal of pro-Taverne Council Chairmen in May 1972; a refusal to renew the party membership of Taverne supporters in December 1973, thereby excluding the longest serving member of the party, one Jack Goodman.

The image of being hard-done-by was sustained after October by temporization, as Taverne presented it, over issuing the writ. Taverne resigned as a Labour MP, and hence it was the party whip who determined the date of the by-election. While the delay between early October and 1 March was not excessive in comparison with earlier by-elections of the parliament, it was widely believed that Labour hoped to let the sheen fade from Taverne's dramatic announcement and his campaign to run out of steam. A Liberal attempt in November to move the writ was abandoned. In fact, both Labour factions probably benefited. Only one ward committee out of 10 defected with Taverne, but individuals left from all party and union branches. Grafton House, therefore, needed to reconstruct its organization and come to grips with a new electoral register while Taverne himself had virtually no organization at all. His headquarters, presidentially entitled 'Taverne House' and located 150 yards from Grafton House was a decrepit billiard hall, rented for £4 a week and converted for a cost of £300. He claimed to have 100 active supporters at his resignation and the first meeting filled a large hall to overflowing. Many supporters who came forward were relatively inexperienced, attracted by Taverne's stand, but his agent, Tony Elkington, himself a novice, also claimed support from young Liberal and Conservative activists.

Meanwhile, national events continued to stir the political pot. The results of the Uxbridge, and Sutton and Cheam by-elections in December were as significant for the criticisms of Labour's performance launched by Lord George-Brown and others as for their indication of potential Conservative problems. In January 1973 Wilson launched a series of 'new-look' speeches, which led the *Daily Mirror* to speak of 'The Second Coming of Harold Wilson'. But the tenth anniversary of Hugh Gaitskell's death on 18 January also elicited speeches from Jenkins and other followers which emphasized the need for a 'broad based responsible party of power', and were perceived in the Wilson camp as sustaining a bid for the leadership. David Steel, the Liberal Chief Whip, suggested in an interview on 21 January that 'not very much divided Liberals from, say, Mr Roy Jenkins or Mr Dick Taverne,' which quite obscured relations between Taverne and his former party.

Taverne's problems in his constituency lay in forging a plurality from among an electorate accustomed to choosing between party labels, and whose response to novelty was entirely unpredictable. Wisely, he did not seek to invest his Democratic Labour Party with any coherent political philosophy or strategy. He sought to define himself as the man of principle rather than party, making a virtue of the fact that no major national political figure could be found to give him local support: his main political backer remained *The Times*, and the only notables who spoke for him in Lincoln were Bernard Levin and Mervyn Stockwood, the Bishop of Southwark. He appealed to political consistency, at a time when both parties had shifted ground from their pledges in the 1970 election, claiming that the established parties were losing credibility, or, as he once put it, 'the fact is that nobody believes a bloody word that any politician says any more'. In both politics and industrial relations, at a time when days lost in national strikes reached the highest level since 1926, he espoused moderation and accommodation. He attacked the Conservative government for failing to accord Lincoln the status it merited as a region of high unemployment, and the Labour Council for failing to represent the city's case effectively. At times, he was happy to point out that he remained a Labour candidate, committed to supporting a broad-based Labour Party; indeed, to the consternation of his Labour opponents, it began to emerge as election day approached that many electors still saw him *as* the Labour candidate. Only the intrusion of leading Jenkinsites to attack Taverne on his home ground could have effectively challenged this ambiguity, but they remained resolutely absent. Taverne also, however, needed to woo non-party and Conservative voters, and in mid-February he began to flirt with the idea that Lincoln might be the catalyst to the formation of a new, centrist Social Democratic-style grouping distinct from the two main parties.

In putting across his message, Taverne was helped by his opponents' decisions on candidate selection. Overriding the opposition of Peter Hain and the Young Liberals, flush from Sutton and Cheam, the Liberal Party chose not to fight and muddy the middle ground: 'Our Watchword, No Enemies in the Centre', a Bernard Levin headline demanded. Patrick Furnell, who had gained 6,579 votes for the Liberals in 1964, came out for Taverne, while a deal of Taverne's election materials in the early days came from the local Liberal party. Labour's choice of John Dilks fitted the Taverne stereotype superbly: working-class origins, now a Co-op executive, a left-winger, and the local party boss in Derby. Though an effective party man, he had little style to throw against Taverne's glamour campaign, and his emphasis upon the importance of party loyalty glued him to the increasingly beleaguered local Labour machine. A declaration at a public meeting that he was not a tool of Grafton House, invited the heckle 'you'll be out then'. The Conservative choice of candidate was, at best, idiosyncratic. Jonathan Guinness, a scion of the brewing family and Chairman of the right-wing Monday Club, was an elegant figure, witty, but quite unsuited to the task of exploiting the Labour split to bring the Conservatives home. Though capable of sharp one liners – most famously describing Taverne as a 'pinchbeck Kennedy with his Camelot of plastic gnomes' – his unpredictable utterances (for instance, on giving razor blades to convicted murderers) and appalling performance among the general public meant that his campaign was increasingly confined to whatever safe Conservative areas that could be found. Rumours abounded, though they were strongly denied, that he had been selected by the local party as a weak candidate to encourage the Labour split, helping Taverne who was popular in local Tory business circles, and was approved by Central Office, to create difficulties between moderates and hard-liners in the Monday Club.

Both main parties had hoped that the Lincoln public would have grown tired of Taverne by the time that real campaigning began in January, and that they could return to the time-honoured battle. The host of journalists and TV crews who were drawn in by the prospect of analyzing a novel political experiment found both main parties refusing to admit that this was the issue in the campaign. Undoubtedly, this appeared to be their best strategy. But the headlines continued to focus upon the battle of the lone figure: 'Dick's got glamour, but will he win?'; 'The machines close in on Lincoln's Lochinvar', figured among the fruitiest. A different kind of campaign, attacking Taverne's claims about his role as an MP, his character, the sources of his political, and perhaps even financial, support might have proved more damaging. However, it was only in the final week of the campaign, when it became clear that Dilks and Guinness were both in serious difficulties, that they turned upon him. Interestingly, both chose to define their charges in traditional terms – for Dilks he was 'just a Tory', for Guinness still a socialist and a Labour candidate. But it is difficult to believe that, in turning up the heat at this stage, they did anything other then reinforce the picture of innocent victim painted by Taverne himself. Dilks accused Taverne of pretending to be a political virgin ravished by a party machine from which he had benefited for years. The charge misfired; but, compared with his opponents, Taverne had experience, slickness in personal skills which charmed the media, and an ego capable of carrying him through the hard knocks.

By-elections in which third parties suddenly intervene invariably pose problems in relation to canvassing and campaigning, and not just for the incomer. Taverne's agent, Tony Elkington, abandoned organizing on a ward-basis, and relied upon returns coming directly to him from areas based upon loyal Taverne supporters. Both main parties had the problem of trying to identify and lobby those in their 'natural' territory who might be potential defectors. Whether as a result of overcanvassing loyal supporters or not, neither party appears to have anticipated the scale of the disaster about to overwhelm them until the last moment, when polls by Gallup and NOP, published on 1 March, caught the local mood and showed over 50 per cent support for Taverne.

The announcement of the result at Lincoln Town Hall proved devastating for Labour. On a 73 per cent poll, Taverne won 58.2 per cent of the vote, Dilks 23.3 per cent, Guinness 17.5 per cent and other parties a mere 1 per cent. He had plundered the support of both parties to establish his credentials as a genuinely independent centre party candidate, but enough voters had remained loyal for him to avoid being tarred as merely a Labour or Conservative figure. Labour activists were outraged by the result, and violent scenes broke out, relayed via the evening's television by-election programme to the nation at large, as police struggled to clear a passage for him and his supporters through the mob.

Comment on Lincoln was inevitably bracketed with Chester-le-Street, where Labour held a very safe seat with a reduced margin over the Liberal, and Dundee East, which Labour held narrowly against the Scottish National-ist. In all three, Labour came under pressure on high turnouts in seats that it had held since the war, and the Conservatives came last. Whether Conserva-tive defectors were signifying disappointment with the Government's performance or switching to third parties capable of overturning Labour incumbency, was not easy to establish. However, the Conservative vote held up best in the most marginal seat, Dundee, where the Liberal lost his deposit. The two Labour victories could not conceal the fact that its fortunes remained in the doldrums, but, even so, the result in Lincoln could not be seen as indicative of the electorate's aspiration for a new politics. Paradoxically, the uniqueness of the split in the locally dominant party, and Taverne's success in personalizing the battle, minimized the extent to which generalizations could be drawn from what was clearly a resounding individual victory.

After Lincoln

The Spring by-elections of 1973 lay just beyond mid-term in the antici-pated life of the 1970 Parliament. Experience from the 1959–64, and 1966–70, parliaments suggested that, in the normal course of events, the wave of anti-government feeling would continue on its trajectory for a period, and then fade away as the General Election became imminent. A strategy meeting of senior ministers at Chequers on 18 March, for instance, took an optimistic view of the government's prospects. The present policies of economic expansion, price and wage control, and toughing out industrial action would lead, it believed, to an escape from stagflation, while the disarray of Labour revealed by Lincoln, and a closing of the opinion poll gap, indicated the Opposition's continuing problem of mounting an effective challenge. On 12 April elections to the new county councils in England and Wales were held. When all voters had a chance to go to the polls in a unique 'general' election, they elected 1772 Conservatives, 1835 Labour and 782 other candidates, results which showed neither Conservative collapse, nor massive disillusion with the main parties.

Within the Labour Party, the Lincoln result had not so much opened up the question of the shape of the party as closed it down. A week after the result, Jenkins categorically rejected ideas of a new or third party, and *The Times* reluctantly accepted his decision. Taverne was left with only minimal tacit encouragement to establish a firmer local political base. Democratic Labour candidates won 5 out of Lincoln's 11 seats on the new Lincolnshire County Council on 12 April 1973, and in the city council elections of 7 June, swept to power taking 20 out of 30 seats. Only one Labour councillor was left, winning by one vote on the third recount. In October, plans to widen Taverne's support were brought to fruition when he undertook a speaking tour to launch the formation of a Campaign for Social Democracy, which, with customary panache, was timed to coincide with the Labour Party Conference. During the period, the Labour Party justified his stance by moving inexorably to the Left, adopting a programme of widespread nationalization and industrial regulation at the conference. However, mainstream Jenkinites, rather than looking to Taverne's new movement as a political refuge, instead retreated further under the party umbrella in the hope of ensuring that a broad-based Labour party might later re-emerge. Even *The Times* by October was providing only a few column inches to Taverne's initiative. In November, Jenkins himself, despite profound unhappiness at the state of the party, stood for election to Shadow Cabinet and came fifth out of 12 successful candidates.

The attempted reconstruction of left-centre politics, therefore, was pushed off onto future parliaments. The crucial issue does not, however, appear to have been apprehension by the Jenkinsites that the electorate would not support such a strategy. The simple fact was that Labour politics, however distasteful it was becoming, remained sufficiently widely-based to provide them with a secure niche from which they might hope to re-establish their former position within the leadership. What led Taverne to talk of a new party was not intellectual conviction so much as the simple fact that he had been unable to avoid being thrown out. And undoubtedly his execution was at least partially designed *pour encourager les autres.*

However, while the right wing of the Labour Party became increasingly weary and cynical, convinced that Labour was unelectable, the morale of the Liberals, and of the Scottish Nationalists, rose dramatically. Another major ORC opinion poll, timed to coincide with the Labour conference, observed that the Liberal revival was now longer and more powerfully sustained than the post-Orpington surge, and was within $1\frac{1}{2}$ per cent of its high point. By contrast, the Conservatives, who had briefly overtaken Labour in the polls earlier in the summer, had slipped back to third place, with the Liberals second – all the parties being within a few percentage points of each other. As the end-game of the Heath administration came nearer, blown off course by external economic shocks and irreconcilable conflict with the trade unions, the electoral prospects of the Liberal Party as a third force in its own right came centre stage.

Post-Lincoln by-elections

Post-Lincoln by-elections fell, broadly, into three blocks. Labour-held seats were contested at West Bromwich and Westhoughton (24 May) and Manchester Exchange (27 June). On 26 July, elections took place at the Isle of Ely and Ripon. Finally, on 8 November, Hove, Berwick-upon-Tweed, Edinburgh North, all Conservative, and Glasgow Govan, a solid Labour seat, were fought. Worcestershire South remained vacant at the general election.

The by-elections of May and June created few waves. Labour held three solid urban strongholds. Significantly, in the first two, where Liberals did not stand, the Labour share of the vote remained broadly comparable to that of 1970. The only significant deviation was at West Bromwich, where turnout fell from 62 to 44 per cent, and the National Front candidate gained 16 per cent to cut the Conservative share down from 45 to 25 per cent. Manchester proved to be more revealing.

The result almost exactly paralleled that at Chester-le-Street in March, though on a much reduced turnout. A Liberal intervention into decaying urban working-class territory caused a collapse of the Conservative vote and a major loss of support for Labour, bringing in a Liberal vote of over 36 per cent. The Liberal candidate, Michael Steed, an electoral analyst at the University of Manchester and party adviser, wrote up an account of his contest.[2]

The most significant factors, he suggested, about the current Liberal surge were, first, that it manifested itself not just in constituencies with a history of Liberal representation or recent intensive local revival, but in new territory; and, secondly, that the party was attracting support equally from both main parties. The implication of this was that electorates were not merely registering a protest against the government of the day by delving into folk-memories of earlier party alignments, but registering new political concerns. Offering his own impressions of the Manchester campaign, he highlighted the effectiveness of Trevor Jones's saturation strategy in stimulating voter interest (though not necessarily in stimulating a dialogue between the party and the voters); the centrality of housing redevelopment issues in engaging constituents and media attention; but also the decline in support as polling day drew near, when the traditional loyalties of working-class male electors asserted themselves over the home-bound voters whom Liberal canvassers had earlier tempted. Class, one might say, will out. However, Steed felt that, beyond class politics, a different dimension was emerging, crucial to Liberalism's drawing capacity, which was that of *powerlessness*. Now, of course, this was a central item in contemporary Liberal philosophy; and there is no reason to believe that Steed, any more than the established parties, was able to read the electorate's mind rather than to project his own philosophy on to it. However, clearly, at least one key Liberal strategist was convinced that the success of third parties was more than merely a negative protest against the established parties, and represented a positive vote capable of restructuring the political map.

In terms of the broad character of the constituency, Manchester bore comparison with Glasgow, Govan, one of the four November contests. Here was another Labour rotten borough, where industrial decay and indiscrimi-nate poor-quality housing development had created a landscape of urban blight. Early press reports dismissed the possibility of an upset for the Labour candidate, Councillor Harry Selly, aged 60, a self-proclaimed revolutionary socialist in the tradition of Red Clydeside, whose stated aim was to cap a life of service to the movement with a seat in the highest tribunal of the land. Having failed at Dundee in March, it seemed unlikely that the Nationalists would break through in Govan. But Labour and media complacency was misplaced. Internal party investigations in the late 1960s had pointed to the frighteningly weak structure and membership of Glasgow's Labour party. It proved hopelessly incapable of countering a vigorous, lively and dynamic campaign from the SNP's 'blond bombshell', Margo Macdonald, who won with a margin of 3 per cent over her Labour opponent, in virtually a rerun of Winifred Ewing's victory at Hamilton in 1967. Macdonald had the advantage over Steed in Manchester, not just of personal attractiveness and charisma, but of the appeal to Scotland's Oil as a resource for regenerating Clydeside, and of the publication, in the week before the contest, of the Kilbrandon Commission Report recommending Scottish devolution. In both Manchester and Govan, the main challengers represented the local Labour machine's mismanagement, exclusiveness and indifference to popular needs as metaphors for the fundamental inability of the national party to create an effective and responsive alternative government.

For the Conservatives, the dog days lay in the month of July. The Isle of Ely and Ripon were blue-chip county constituencies, vacated by the deaths of two stalwart Tory squirearchs, Sir Harry Legge-Bourke, MP for Ely since 1945, and Sir Malcom Stoddart, whose Ripon seat was regarded as amongst the safest 40 Conservative seats in the county. *The Times's* headline of 28 July on the result said everything: 'Double Liberal win – a shattering blow for Government'. At Ely, the television personality, cook and petfood advertiser, Clement Freud, won by over 1,200 votes on a 71 per cent poll; at Ripon, the local candidate, a long-standing active councillor and campaigner, David Austick, scraped home by 946 votes. The Liberals had poured everything into these contests, convinced that they could repeat Sutton and Cheam, and were overjoyed by the results. Jeremy Thorpe, comparing them with the Liberal victories in Eddisbury and Holland with Boston in March 1929 (which prefigured substantial Liberal gains in the subsequent General Election), declared this 'a dramatic turning-point in British politics'. He immediately announced that Liberals would be putting up 500 candidates in the next General Election, and that the party intended to establish a 'bridgehead' in the new parliament.

Most commentators attributed the Conservative disaster to the failure to control prices: 'The housewives whom we courted in 1970 have now turned on us,' a backbencher was reported as saying. But candidates and history also played their part in the Liberal victories. Austick was a well-established local figure; Liberals had held Ely between 1929 and 1945, and dug deep into the Tory majority when they last fought in 1966; and the somewhat idiosyncratic Clement Freud, though dismissed at the start as a frivolous media personality whose press conferences were notable more for their jokes than serious political comment, soon established a presence, proving that wit could be effective over party rhetoric. The Conservative candidates, though able, lacked the same panache: in Ripon, Keith Hampson, later Michael Heseltine's *aide-de-camp,* was a respected academic from Edinburgh University, while John Stevens, Edward Heath's personal assistant in the mid-sixties, was characterized in the press as having been 'plucked down from the "Grocer's" shelf' by Central Office.

Heath's response to the fear and trembling which set in even among senior figures in the Government was to keep a cool head. The best internal advice remained that the party was on course for a majority next time, and the task, he claimed, was to concentrate upon putting the Government's message about the economy across more effectively to allay the anxieties of the electorate. Labour, coming in third, could glean little comfort from the results. Ian Mikardo, the Labour leftwinger, declared them mere protests against price rises, and described the Liberal victors as 'lightweights'. But Roy Jenkins had no qualms in declaring the result as a blow to both main parties. Rather than persuading him into further public reflections upon its implications for future party relations, however, he simply went on to attack the Chancellor of the Exchequer's mismanagement of the floating pound.

209

Jeremy Thorpe, however, was prepared to be far bolder, and spoke openly of the possibility of a hung parliament after the General Election. The upshot of that might entail a Lib–Lab compact, he foresaw, though the Liberals would 'paddle their own canoe' and wait to be approached for their support. These reflections opened up a major debate within the party. A leader in *The Times* commented that one 'cannot regret the development of Liberal power', and claimed that it was not necessary to be a Liberal to welcome a strong Liberal presence in the next parliament. It also carried a letter from Graham Tope, the victor of Sutton and Cheam, aimed at 'correcting' the impression conveyed by Thorpe's canoe analogy: it was still the hope, he said, that 'thoughtful' Labour figures would continue looking to a relationship with the Liberals.

After the July results, the three November by-elections in the Conservative-held seats of Berwick, Edinburgh North and Hove were approached by the government with some trepidation. The loss of three seats at this stage would be a substantial blow to morale, and, in more practical terms, narrow a parliamentary majority already reduced by by-election losses and the periodic absence of a dozen Conservative MPs in the European Parliament, which Labour was boycotting. There was much manoeuvering between the whips over Berwick, where the Liberals were expected to do exceptionally well, and Govan. Berwick had been vacant since May, but local Conservatives were searching for a strong candidate, and the decision was eventually taken to pair it with Edinburgh in the hope of dividing the energetic Liberal forces in David Steel's constituency of Selkirk and Peebles. (The writ was finally moved by Dick Taverne.) Pairing Edinburgh with Govan, by contrast, was expected to help Labour in the latter by splitting the nationalists' resources.

In the event, Berwick fell to the Liberal, Alan Beith, a Politics lecturer at Newcastle University. The margin, however, was a mere 57 in a seat vacated by the resignation of the naval minister, Lord Lambton, as a result of revelations about his relations with prostitutes. In July Thorpe had said that 'we need to be shot' if Liberals failed to win here. In Edinburgh, the opposition fragmented among Labour, SNP and Liberal candidates to produce a comfortable Conservative victory on a much-reduced turnout. And at Hove, where the local Conservative party had recently been in severe financial problems, a forceful Liberal assault from the charities fundraiser and campaigner, Des Wilson, was beaten back by Timothy Sainsbury, in an increasingly robust and vituperative campaign that produced a clear 10 per cent Conservative margin of victory. The Conservatives, therefore, were recognized as having done remarkably well in all three seats, not least in the midst of an oil crisis and petrol shortages arising from the Yom Kippur war.

Of all the parties, Labour was the only one to come away with nothing from the four contests. Organizational sclerosis in Govan; poor candidate selection in Hove, where their choice fell upon a look-alike for the *Private*

Eye parody of radical leftism, Dave Spart; strong Liberal traditions in Berwick, where, as in Ely, Liberals had held the seat until the unexpected defeat of William Beveridge in 1945; and the proliferation of anti-Government parties in the commercial and professional heart of Edinburgh; there were individual factors that could account for Labour's difficulties in each contest. But for the official Opposition at this stage to be, at best, prey to such specific accidents, and at worst incapable of harnessing any coherent electoral response to a profoundly unpopular government, was deeply disturbing. Left-wingers claimed that the new radical policies adopted at the October conference still had to get across; sceptics observed that they might be coming across all too well.

Nor, however, could the Liberals take great comfort. The optimism of July had persisted through the summer, and at the party conference in September John Pardoe succeeded in opening up a debate about general election tactics, Pardoe himself advocating a broad frontal attack contesting every constituency, others arguing for the concentration of limited resources upon a smaller number of winnable seats. On that issue, both David Steel and Dick Taverne were publicly associated with the second view. But an ORC national opinion poll of 3 November had shown Liberals falling back into third place over recent months, and the November results seemed to reveal a levelling-off of support, not an upward movement in the surge. In an analysis for *The Times* on 9 November, Richard Rose set out the barrier which, given the nature of the electoral system, the Liberals would have to cross in a general election to establish a real parliamentary presence. An overall 23 per cent vote should bring them at least 50 seats, and every 1 per cent beyond that could net an additional ten seats. However, the average in the by-elections, 13 per cent, would bring a mere 14 MPs. The most likely result, therefore, given Labour's continuing inability to engineer a swing in their own favour, remained a small Conservative majority.

The by-elections also revealed other Liberal weaknesses. One was the difficulty of concentrating forces for a campaign. As the Conservatives had hoped, Liberal workers had been in short supply in the far-flung Berwick constituency, until supporters were latterly bussed in from Yorkshire. A belated and unwise decision to stand in Govan, where neither membership nor organization had previously existed, further dissipated energy, without averting a lost deposit along with the Conservative. Although press reports described Berwick as a 'battle of the machines', elsewhere results seemed to be closely bound up with the character of individual candidates. Freud had done surprisingly well at Ely, but in Hove Des Wilson's aggressive campaigning on housing issues was met with a counter-attack focusing upon his personal credibility and political consistency. (The Conservatives issued a pamphlet in which Wilson was not only shown to have once stood as a Labour candidate for Twickenham Council, but to have written to the *Guardian* in 1969 stating that he was not a Liberal, and had never voted

Liberal.) Finally, in Scotland, the SNP posed a substantial threat to Liberalism's ability to capture the anti-establishment vote. The three Scottish by-elections in 1973 suggested that, in a four-cornered fight, at least where they lacked the benefits of incumbency, Liberals risked coming off worst.

The secret of success for both main parties in any future general election lay in winning traditional supporters back from the Liberals; and after the November elections, Benn gained approval for Labour MPs to absent themselves from the Commons to fight the Liberals at their own game in the constituencies. But the best chances still seemed to lie in showing that Liberals were irrelevant to the outcome of the contest. The development of a crisis atmosphere surrounding the miners' decision on 8 November to start industrial action, followed by the Government's declaration of a State of Emergency on 13 November, promised to do so. Opinion polls pointed to a slide from 30 per cent to 20 per cent in Liberal support by the New Year. As election fever rose with the growing confrontation between government and miners, and the economic statistics deteriorated, the question of who governs Britain was pushed to the fore, promising to undercut third-party support.

The results of the by-elections of the period appear to have played, in themselves, little role in influencing the timing of the general election. Conservative party whips had some concern about their declining parliamentary majority in relation to potentially controversial proposals on company law and the third London airport, but this was not sufficient to sway their calculations. The results of the November by-elections and subsequent opinion polls made an early election less menacing for the government, and the likelihood that the economic and political climate could only worsen undoubtedly led party managers to prepare for an election that might be earlier rather than later. However, it was the onset of the confrontation with the miners which brought the issue of a general election on to the agenda. In the early stages, the prospect of an election was as much part of the political manoeuvering as a genuine intention on Heath's part – indeed, throughout, the Prime Minister appeared concerned to avoid holding a crisis election which it was likely would be characterized by bitter antagonism. The first two weeks of January 1974, however, saw intense speculation that the issue could only be resolved by a government armed with a new electoral mandate. The Heath administration was, by now, almost completely exhausted by its unsuccessful battles to control the economy, contain the crisis in Northern Ireland, and deal with a rapidly changing international environment. Eventually, facing the challenge of an all-out strike, the decision was announced on 7 February to go to the polls on the 28th.

How far did the by-election results of 1972–73 shape the results? In a broad sense, the success of the Liberals in securing six million votes and 19 per cent of the poll – though, to their intense disappointment, only 14 seats – reflected earlier, local, successes, and represented an extension of the trajectory of public opinion during the previous year. Liberal support did not simply dissipate as the election drew near. The proximity of a successful run of by-election results and the high political drama surrounding them clearly had an impact in disorienting sections of the electorate and loosening their traditional allegiances. The air of confrontation in which the election took place, rather than squeezing out the centre ground, instead played to voters dismayed by the historical failures of the main parties and prepared to call down a plague upon both their houses. What was not clear was whether a firm new basis of political support had been established.

The Liberals had been lucky in both the timing and the location of the by-elections. They could point to five seats gained within the course of a single year, outstripping their performance in the early sixties, almost doubling their representation, and distracting attention from the 25 contests they failed to fight or lost, sometimes disastrously after 1970. It was clear, though, that they had yet to develop a clear idea of how to translate these results into a successful national campaign. In an unsuccessful bid to break through the magic barrier of 23 per cent, the party eventually threw in over 500 candidates. It was not obvious that this was rational for a party whose main electioneering strengths lay in intensive campaigning in select winnable constituencies. Nor was Jeremy Thorpe's overall political strategy at all easy to perceive. During the outburst of election fever in January, he had ordered the destruction of a document prepared by the party's leading academic advisers, Michael Steed and William Wallace, which set out options in the event of a hung parliament. But in responding to Edward Heath's proposal for parliamentary co-operation after the results were announced, Thorpe found himself faced with an internal revolt, from a party whose mood was predominantly anti-Conservative and whose main electoral achievement was to consolidate a position as the main anti-Conservative party in the South of England. Throughout the period, those such as David Steel who advocated a *rapprochement* with the Labour Right were quite unable to show how this was to be achieved.

One main problem for the Liberals was that of continuity. Its support in the opinion polls was seen to fade away after the summer of 1973, revive in the early stages of the election campaign, and then drop off in the final days when the two main parties directed their fire against a party whose only impact, it was argued, would be to muddy the eventual result. The disappointing outcome of February 1974 was followed by a fall in the number of votes to just over five million in the October election. By contrast, nationalist votes in Wales and Scotland rose from 800,000 to over one million. Far more revealing were the results of detailed panel surveys of voters published later in the decade, which suggested that, during the period, while many voters were tempted to vote Liberal, only half actually did so.[3] One half of Liberal supporters in the February election abandoned the party in October, to be replaced by new deserters from other parties, or abstainers. These floating supporters had only a shadowy idea of Liberal policy, and, if they were motivated by positive factors rather than negative reactions to the two main parties, these revolved around amorphous ideas of the party's image and the personality of its leader, rather than close identification with its stated aims and objectives.

Heath's failure to secure an arrangement with the Liberals after the February election allowed Labour to take power as a minority government, and instigated renewed, often hysterical, speculation in sections of the press about the need for a new national party or 'government of national unity' that could command the political centre and contain the allegedly radical left-wing thrust of the Labour Government. But in the event, substantial political reconstruction had to await Labour's next electoral defeat in 1979, and an even more determinedly radical Conservative administration. In the political turmoil of the early 1980s, it was possible to look back on Dick Taverne's act of defiance as a perhaps premature foreshadowing of the SDP breakaway. In February 1974 he put up five candidates in seats which the Liberals chose not to fight, but all failed badly. Having lost Lincoln in October 1974 and watched his local party disintegrate, Taverne retreated to private business and the shadowy world of the think-tanks (and eventually, in 1996, to the House of Lords). Coincidentally, his old protagonist from Lincoln, Leo Beckett, had also retreated from the limelight to the political backroom. Captivated by Taverne's sparkling young female Labour opponent in the February and October elections, Beckett went on to become her political adviser, style-guru and, in 1979, husband. As Margaret Beckett, she entered Labour's front ranks in the early 1990s, briefly as Shadow Chancellor, then as President of the Board of Trade in the 1997 Labour Government. Grafton House's 'sinister' influence upon political life, it appeared, was more than capable of surviving the romantic assault even of Lincoln's Lochinvar.

Notes

1   B. Pimlott, *Harold Wilson* (1992).
2   M. Steed, 'My own by-election', *Government and opposition* ix (1974).
3   J. Alt, I. Crewe and B. Salvik, 'Angels in plastic', *Political Studies*, xxv, 3, 1977.

CHAPTER 11

The Wilson–Callaghan Government of 1974–79: by-elections (eventually) bring down a Government

Peter Rose

The general election of October 1974 gave Harold Wilson a tiny overall majority of three. Labour won 319 seats, the Conservatives 276 and the Liberals 13. It was the performance of the minor parties, principally the SNP with 11 seats and the Ulster Unionists with 10, that made the arithmetic so tight for the Labour Government. During the Parliament 30 by-elections were held, the final contest not taking place until the very day the 1979 General Election was announced. Because the Government was in a minority for much of this period, the loss of by-elections – in theory at least – should have gravely threatened its ability to survive. That it did last so long (longer than some majority governments) despite suffering major defeats during its mid-term is the underlying theme of the survey which follows. Several reasons can be found for this tenacity: early unwillingness of the small parties to band together with the Tories and strike, the Lib–Lab Pact which guaranteed the Government against defeat in confidence votes for 18 months and the skill and cunning of that old survivor, the Prime Minister, James Callaghan. It is interesting to note that the Government was defeated 42 times in the House of Commons before finally losing a vote of confidence in March 1979.[1]

Repeated Conservative by-election successes such as the huge swings in the rock-solid Labour fortresses of Walsall North and Ashfield, proved very frustrating for the new Conservative leader, Margaret Thatcher. After the celebrations were over, she found herself each time no nearer 10 Downing Street. For the Liberals it was a bleak time – the only period in recent years when they consistently achieved a worse performance in by-elections than in the previous general election. They lost votes in every contest but two.[2] The SNP too, after the triumphs of the 1974 general election, failed to use the three by-elections in Scotland as a springboard to further success. Significantly, at Berwick and East Lothian in November 1978 there was a pro-Government swing.

The first by-election of the Parliament, which was held on 26 June 1975, was caused by the death of the Labour MP for Woolwich West, William Hamling. Not only was it to be a stern test for the Wilson Government with its tiny majority but also for Margaret Thatcher who had been elected Conservative leader only four months before. Labour had held the seat at the general election with a majority of 3,541, which Mrs Thatcher must have been confident of overturning because she broke precedent and campaigned personally in the constituency. It was a bold step, for defeat would have been a major blow so early in her leadership, giving comfort to her critics in the Tory party still smarting from the ousting of her predecessor Edward Heath. For Labour, however, the by-election came at a bad time. Raging inflation was damaging the Government's reputation. Indeed a headline on polling day declared 'Pound Sinks to New Low'.[3] Though observers had felt that the result was too close to call, the victorious Tory candidate, Peter Bottomley, won by a majority of 2,382, a swing of 7.6. per cent. The *Daily Telegraph*, the following morning, hailed the result as a personal victory for Mrs Thatcher and a vote of no confidence in the Labour Government. Its veteran political correspondent, Harry Boyne, saw the swing to the Tories as a clear warning that 'inflation is the dominant issue in politics today'. If inflation continued at the present rate, he noted prophetically, Labour would lose more by-elections and possibly the following general election.[4] For the Liberals though there was no consolation. They received less than 2,000 votes – only five per cent – and lost their deposit.

The result could have been taken to mean that Harold Wilson now ran a minority government because of the disappearance of the Labour MP John Stonehouse. In practice the position was not so precarious because nearly 40 of the Opposition MPs were split among minor five parties and rarely all turned up to vote at once. The Scots and Welsh Nationalist parties in particular were not ready to unseat a government which was likely to be more sympathetic to their aims than a Thatcher administration.

No further by-elections were held for nine months. During that time the Labour Government's fortunes worsened. In July 1975 Harold Wilson brought in Phase One of his pay policy. The inflation rate had risen to an alarming 26 per cent. (Between February 1974 and the end of 1978 the cost of living doubled.) In July, the unions accepted a voluntary income policy: pay increases were to be limited to £6 per week for one year.[5] Three days later unemployment passed the one million mark. The damage done to Labour was made clear by the batch of three by-elections held in March: Coventry North West which polled on 4 March, Carshalton and Wirral, a week later. In Coventry the Labour candidate, Geoffrey Robinson, held on to the seat with a swing against the Government of 5 per cent, a respectable result in the circumstances. But it was a different story in the other two, which the Tories held with greatly increased majorities. The swing to the

Tories in Wirral, one of their safest seats, was 13 per cent. Between these setbacks and the next contest at Rotherham in the summer, a sudden and unexpected transformation of the Government took place triggered by Harold Wilson's resignation on 16 March. James Callaghan, the Foreign Secretary, won the subsequent leadership election with relative ease but was to face a turbulent 12 months during which the Government lost their majority. Unemployment rose from 1.2 million to 1.5 million and the pound crashed by nearly 50 cents to just over $1.50.[6]

The next contest, at Rotherham, was held on 24 June. Journalists covering the campaign in this rock-solid Labour seat reported considerable apathy and the result suggested that the change of leadership had done nothing to lessen the Government's unpopularity. Labour's majority slumped from 17,000 to 4,000, a swing to the Tories of more that 13 per cent. This verdict on the new Prime Minister and his beleaguered government was confirmed three weeks later, on 15 July, at a by-election at Thurrock where Labour's majority was cut by more than 14,000, a swing of more than 10 per cent.

Summer and early autumn provided a respite from the anger of the voters as no further by-elections were held until November. However, during this period the Government suffered its greatest humiliation of the Parliament. As a result of the collapse of sterling Britain had to ask the International Monetary Fund for a loan of $3.9 billion to save the pound. In return the IMF demanded savage cuts in public spending. This was hardly the best backdrop for three more by-elections held on 4 November in Walsall North, Workington and Newcastle Central, all Labour seats. It proved a disastrous night for Labour with the Tories seizing both Workington and Walsall North. The two defeats meant that the Government now had only a majority of one, and even that was assuming that the two independent Northern Ireland MPs and two Scottish Labour Party MPs continued to support them. The swing at Workington was over 13 per cent, bad enough, but the swing of 22.5 per cent in the Walsall contest which had been caused by the imprisonment of the former Labour MP John Stonehouse was one of the largest for years. Both lost seats had been considered Labour fortresses and even Newcastle Central almost fell, coming close to giving the Tories a hat trick. There the Labour majority fell from just over 8,000 to 1,838 thanks to a swing to the Tories of 13.7 per cent. The seat provided the Liberals with their one bonus of the night: their candidate came second, pushing the Tories into third place. The analysis of these results the following day inevitably questioned the Government's ability to survive for more than a few months particularly as the huge swings to the Tories suggested that Labour would have difficulty in retaining any constituencies in subsequent by-elections. A by-election in the Tory-held seat of Cambridge on 2 December provided a crumb of comfort for Callaghan. The Tory candidate, the historian Robert Rhodes James, had a solid majority but the swing of 9.95 was at least considerably smaller than in the November contests. Two months later on 24 February a by-election in the City of London and Westminster South constituency was held by the Conservatives with a similar swing.

By then a vacancy had occurred in Labour-held Grimsby as a result of the sudden and tragic death of the Foreign Secretary Anthony Crosland. Though the swing against Labour at recent by-elections had been reduced, there was still a clear danger that Grimsby could fall. It would only need a swing of 7.6 per cent to the Tories. As a result the Government found itself in a desperately vulnerable position. In December 1976 the Chancellor, Denis Healey, had announced deep cuts following the IMF loan. Roy Jenkins, the Home Secretary, had resigned as an MP to become President of the European Commission, creating yet another by-election at Birmingham, Stechford. The latest Gallup poll gave a Tory lead of more than 16 per cent, enough for a Tory landslide in a General Election. The slightly better performance in the Cities of London and Cambridge contests caused little cheer in the Parliamentary Labour Party. Indeed the left-wing Labour MP Ian Mikardo, the 'MPs' Bookie' prophesied that after an election Labour would be down to a mere four seats (with 'Mik' as party leader). As David Butler and Dennis Kavanagh wrote later '...it is no wonder that the Government did not want to face the electorate early in 1977...' When Margaret Thatcher suddenly tabled a motion of no confidence 'there was a danger that for the first time since 1924 such a vote might succeed'.[7] As a result of the by-election losses Labour now had only 310 MPs out of 635. The Government needed the support of at least some of the smaller parties. The Scottish Nationalist Party were not in the mood to put their 11 MPs behind Callaghan nor were the 10 Ulster Unionists. Neither party at that time feared a General Election. Luckily for Callaghan, however, the Liberals were even more vulnerable than Labour. Their dismal performance in by-elections has already been recorded. Add to that a poor showing in the opinion polls and the bizarre and widely reported events surrounding their former leader Jeremy Thorpe, and they feared that an early general election might reduce the party to the tiny rump it had been in the 1950s and early 1960s. It became clear that the way out for the two battered parties was to cobble up an agreement which would at least keep the Government going until it reached the safer shores of the summer recess. Callaghan, in fact, had argued that he needed 18 months to two years to complete the national recovery.[8]

On 23 March, 1977 Callaghan and the Liberal leader, David Steel agreed a 'Pact' which ensured that Labour would win any vote of confidence at least until the end of the summer. For their part the Liberals would be consulted on all major policy initiatives. In addition the Government was to relaunch its plans for devolution with the Bill amended to take account of Liberal ideas and would press ahead with direct elections to the

European Parliament. As one commentator wrote later Callaghan 'must have realized the ease with which he bought Liberal support.'[9] And armed with his 'Pact' Callaghan duly won the confidence debate called by Mrs Thatcher by a comfortable 24 votes.

Only a week later Labour's disastrous showing at the Stechford by-election (31 March) made it clear that the Pact would have to last much longer than the summer. A swing of 17.5 per cent handed victory to the young Tory candidate Andrew Mackay, the third 'safe' Labour seat to be lost in less than six months. Mackay had a majority of nearly 2,000 over his Labour opponent. Several reasons were given for Labour's dismal showing: voters' fury over Roy Jenkins' desertion to advance his own career, the increase in the price of petrol in the Budget earlier in the week and, in the view of Mrs Thatcher, the Lib–Lab pact. She said that Stechford was the people's verdict on Lib–Lab dealing. Certainly for the Liberals it was an appalling result. With a mere 8 per cent of the poll they lost their deposit and had the indignity of being forced into fourth place by the National Front. Steel had visited the constituency twice during the campaign – unwisely, given the result which he must have known was unlikely to be good for his party whatever his own efforts.[10] However, 'the galling irony' of the result for Mrs Thatcher, as one political commentator put it, was that the Tory victory was too handsome for Callaghan to risk an early general election. A 17.5 cent swing would threaten Labour with a 1931 débâcle giving the party just 72 seats. In addition the Liberals now had no incentive to limit the Pact's life to the end of the summer recess.

Three weeks later a pair of by-elections were held, in Grimsby and Ashfield, with results that stunned the pundits. This was not because the Labour slide had suddenly halted, but because neither seat behaved as it was supposed to but exactly opposite. The contest in Ashfield had been caused by the decision of the Labour MP, David Marquand, to follow his mentor Roy Jenkins to Europe, that in Grimsby by the sudden death of Anthony Crosland. Ashfield, a staunchly Labour mining constituency, was considered impregnable even in these miserable times for the Government. In Grimsby defeat seemed inevitable. In the event an enormous swing of nearly 21 per cent to the Tories wiped out Marquand's majority of nearly 23,000. In Grimsby where the swing was only 7.1 per cent, miraculously Labour held on. The following day commentators agreed that the results were baffling. It was true that in Ashfield the Labour candidate, Dr Michael Cowan, an intellectual and writer on local government, was chosen against the wishes of local miners, and the National Front's 1,734 votes must have included many former Labour supporters. But these were minor points when set against a collapse of the Labour vote from more than 35,000 to below 20,000.

The victorious Labour candidate at Grimsby, Austin Mitchell, who for some years had been a lecturer in politics at universities in Britain and New

Zealand, has provided a personal assessment of the paradoxical outcome of the two contests.[11] Mitchell was known in the constituency through his work as a television journalist with Yorkshire Television. However, he discounted that as a reason for his success. People, he said, were just as likely to vote against you just because they had seen you on TV and had taken a dislike to you. At the time of his selection for Grimsby, he had watched the Stechford result on television and seen the bitter hostility to Labour but from the start did not believe that it would be repeated to the same extent in Grimsby. His optimism was confirmed by a confidential opinion survey carried out during the campaign for the Labour Party's Director of Publicity, Percy Clark.

> What it showed was that while there was some hostility to the Government in Grimsby, it wasn't hatred, it wasn't bitter and it hadn't turned sour. It was rather a kind of rueful feeling that the Government hadn't succeeded. Whether that was unique to Grimsby I don't know. The crucial point was that Grimsby was a low wage economy where women's work is very important, exactly the sort of place which benefited from the £6 incomes policy.

'If you are proposing a basic increase for everybody which is the same across the board then it benefits the low paid rather than the high paid.' The real hostility to Labour came from skilled manual workers in places like Stechford and from the miners of Ashfield, the high earners whose industrial muscle would have entitled them to improve their position. But they had been held back by incomes policy. However, said Mitchell, the picture was quite different in Grimsby. 'The Labour Government had worked hard to keep social spending high with the result that tax was higher but in a low wage area like Grimsby tax is less of an issue.'

Mitchell said that in contrast to Ashfield the cause of the by-election had not harmed Labour. Crosland had died serving his constituency and was well-loved. 'He hadn't deserted like Marquand in Ashfield to a well-paid job in Europe and said "sod you" to the constituents.' Mitchell also believed that he had been helped because his vigorous anti-Common Market stance was appreciated in a town which felt aggrieved about the EEC's fishing policy.

At one point in the campaign, however, he nearly came unstuck because of his opposition to his own Government's policy. 'The Foreign Secretary, Dr. David Owen, that passionate pro-European, came to speak for me.' Somebody from the audience got up and asked wasn't Dr Owen's view, particularly on the Common Fisheries Policy, different from that of the candidate. Owen had to admit that was the case but that the 'Labour Party was a broad church'. Mitchell admitted that this was an embarrassment but added, 'I did not notice because I was blithely setting my own agenda'. This independence that he had been allowed by party HQ had been a feature of the campaign. 'They keep candidates under much closer control now,' he said when interviewed. 'Perhaps the party was a bit in awe of me because they assumed I would know what was going on because of my experience on television. I didn't actually, but I was thankfully left pretty much on my own. Nobody told me what kind of line to take on the issues.' He thought the Tories had picked a weak candidate in Robbie Blair who was local in the sense that he had been in Grimsby a long time and was an executive with a frozen food company in the town. But that could be a disadvantage because employers were not particularly popular among their employees.

A myth had grown up that, because it seemed so certain that it was Grimsby that was at risk, Labour supporters deserted Ashfield to help him. Mitchell said this was not true. However, the political journalists took a gloomy view and one of them, James Fenton of the *New Statesman*, wrote about 'the air of death that hangs over Grimsby'. Mitchell, however, had never thought that he was going to lose. He had been selected immediately after the Lib–Lab Pact and had felt that this was the turning of the tide in the Government's favour. Proof of this was the much better result in another Midlands seat, Birmingham Ladywood, later in the year. 'Grimsby was unique in that there were local factors that meant that anti-Government hostility was not as strong there as elsewhere but it was also on the cusp of the Government's recovery.' On election night, despite his optimism, and partly as a result of an exit poll, he began giving interviews to the press on the assumption that Labour would win Ashfield and lose Grimsby. Then his wife came up to him and said: 'Shut up, you are doing better than you think. You might well win.' He did just, after two recounts by a majority of 520. Over in Ashfield, after one recount the Tory majority was even smaller at 264. As they surveyed the results the following day, the Prime Minister and his Cabinet colleagues were reported to be 'kicking themselves' for not doing more to conserve the rock-solid mining seat.

The three remaining by-elections of the year, Saffron Walden on 7 July, Birmingham Ladywood a month later and Bournemouth East in November, gave a mixed picture. Mitchell's view that Grimsby had shown the Government to be 'on the cusp of the Government's recovery' did not seem to be borne out by the local elections in May when Labour was annihilated in Greater London and in most of the other big cities it had controlled three years earlier. Gallup showed Labour nationally 10 per cent behind. The Tories held Saffron Walden comfortably and Labour, who came third, only just saved their deposit. However, the Liberals who were about to renew their Pact with the Government had reason to be relieved. Their share of the vote had fallen only slightly from 30 per cent to 25 per cent and as one account of the Pact put it later 'for the first time it looked as if Steel's dream of tactical voting to win Liberal seats at the expense of the Tories might be coming true'.[12]

At Birmingham Ladywood held on 18 August, unusually in the middle of the summer holiday period, there was some good news for the Government. The contest had been caused by the decision of Labour MP Brian Walden to become a full-time TV interviewer. Labour's candidate, John Sever, held the seat with a majority of just under 4,000, and the swing of 8.8 per cent to the Tories was well below the massive swings the party had achieved at a number of previous by-elections. For the Liberals it was a different story. They were humiliated by being driven into fourth place again in Birmingham by the National Front which snatched nearly 6 per cent of the vote. With the Tory lead in the national opinion polls falling into single figures for the first time for a long time, it did look as though the worst was over for the Government. Shortly after the Labour Party conference in October, Callaghan told Tom McNally, his political secretary, to make arrangements for an election which might come at any time from spring 1978. He did not think it was possible or desirable to continue the Lib–Lab pact into the fifth year of the Parliament'.[13] The last by-election of 1977 at Bournemouth East on 24 November did not dent the optimism. In one of the safest Tory seats their candidate David Atkinson as expected substantially increased the majority. At the General Election the Liberals had come second and Steel considered Bournemouth East as just the kind of seat where the party could look for gains. During the campaign he made the mistake of saying that it would be a very serious setback if the party lost second place to Labour. It did and was lucky to save its deposit.[14] Over the next few weeks several leading Liberals, including Cyril Smith MP, demanded an end to the Pact, which they were convinced was inflicting heavy damage on the party. However, at a special conference in Blackpool in January 1978 delegates voted by an overwhelming majority to keep it alive for a few more months.[15]

With Callaghan now considering the possibility of going to the country early the by-election to be held on 2 March in Ilford North (caused by the sudden death of the Labour MP Millie Miller) was bound to be considered a pointer to the timing of the national poll. It would be all the more significant because it was highly marginal and something of an electoral bell-wether. The Tories had managed to hold on to the seat at the February 1974 election but then lost it by a mere 778 to Mrs Miller in October. The emotive issue of immigration dominated the headlines during the by-election. In January Mrs Thatcher had put it firmly back on the political agenda when she had said on television that 'people can feel rather swamped by immigration'. She was accused by Labour ministers of playing the race card during the by-election campaign. Whether the row helped the Tories is arguable. They won the seat with a majority of more than 5,000. The swing against Labour was held to just under 7 per cent, better than in constituencies lost previously in the Parliament. However, Labour were helped marginally by the intervention of the previous Conservative MP, Tom

Iremonger, whom Mrs Miller had ousted. He stood as an Independent Conservative receiving 671 votes. The National Front who might have been expected to do well, but for Thatcher's remarks, came in fourth, narrowly behind the Liberals, polling just over 2,000.

Looking back nearly 20 years later, the triumphant Tory candidate, Vivian Bendall, was convinced that immigration was not the main reason for his success.[16] It was true that he was a right-winger, in his own words 'a Thatcherite before Thatcher,' and he had been briefly banned from the Conservative Candidates' list because he was thought too extreme during the Heath years. He, in turn, insisted that Heath should not be invited to speak during the by-election campaign. However, said Bendall, given the unique nature of the constituency it would have been counter-productive to have made immigration the main issue even if he had wanted, because a large proportion of voters in Ilford North were Jewish, many of them taxi-drivers. 'The Jewish population was about 20 per cent. Many had moved out of the East End where their fathers had been tailors working in the sweat shops – they would have been natural socialists. But now they were small entrepreneurs owning their own cabs.' Just before the campaign started, said Bendall, 'immigration became a hot potato because Mrs Thatcher had made her speech about swamping. The line I was taking on immigration was that if we continued to allow the same number into Britain we certainly would become rather swamped and I was calling for stiffer controls.' But at the same time, bearing in mind the number of Jews who had come from Eastern Europe to escape persecution, he stressed that they must not 'completely close the doors to genuine political refugees'. He had also called for the banning of a National Front march during the campaign because he recognized the sensitivity of the issue with the very large Jewish vote in the constituency. He had been seen originally as a right-wing anti-immigration candidate. 'But' he said, 'that changed the percep-tion of me to someone who realized the dangers of what could occur in a constituency like Ilford North which I hoped to represent. I think Jewish voters realised that and in the end it helped me considerably.'

It was the media, in his view, who were trying to play up immigration, but after the early days of the campaign it was clear that they had failed. 'We tried to keep the main issue Labour Government failures, stressing the number of strikes, high taxation and the charge that the economy was no longer being run by the Government but by the IMF.' The economic policy he put before the electorate was that of Mrs Thatcher and Keith Joseph not of Ted Heath. Bendall, an estate agent, said that he tried to explain things to voters from the point of view of a practical businessman. 'Being in a small business myself I could see what was wrong. I had seen the Heath administration move from "Selsdon man" and completely stand on its head. Heath had bad luck but the U-turn on the economy did not help.' Bendall said that he had also benefited from his call for capital punishment and tougher sentencing by the courts in a constituency where voters were very alarmed by rising crime. Also Ilford's large Roman Catholic community had welcomed his opposition to abortion. He had campaigned hard on local issues demanding, for example, that Ilford should have a Jewish secondary school. He was fortunate in Labour's choice of candidate, Tessa Jowell, who though she later went on to have a successful political career herself, was at that time, he claimed, inexperienced and 'out of her depth'. A minor problem had been caused by the decision of Iremonger to stand against him because he had not been re-selected. 'He claimed to be the true Conservative of the Heath mould, but it did him no good,' said Bendall.

The contest had received enormous coverage by the press and television partly because of the immigration issue but also, said Bendall, because it was thought likely to be the last by-election before the general election. Perhaps for this reason Bendall received massive support from Conservative helpers throughout the campaign. 'Coachloads came in night after night from all over London,' he said. On polling day his taxi-driver supporters, working for him voluntarily, took voters to polling stations, particularly useful when torrential rain started to come down at about 4.30 pm. When the result was announced, he recalled, the general conclusion was: 'Margaret Thatcher's on her way. She is going to be the next Prime Minister. It was only a matter of time and I think she was very disappointed that it did not come earlier.'

The by-election the following month in Glasgow Garscadden would be the first Scottish contest of the Parliament and thus the first test of SNP strength. Devolution for Scotland and Wales had, according to Butler and Kavanagh, 'permeated the Parliament'. The SNP's achievement in getting 30 per cent of the Scottish vote and 11 seats in the October 1974 election convinced the Government, with 41 of its 319 seats coming from Scotland, that something must done to meet the Scottish urge for self-government'. In the 1977–78 session separate measures were introduced for Scotland and Wales with the provision for referendums before they could take effect.[17]

The voters of Glasgow Garscadden went to the polls on 13 April after a campaign in which much went wrong for the Labour candidate, Donald Dewar, who had briefly been MP for Aberdeen South (1966–70). During the campaign nearly 2,000 job losses were announced. However Dewar, who was to prove one of Labour's most able Front Benchers, conducted a powerful campaign against the SNP's promise of an oil-rich independent Scotland. His reward was to hold the seat for Labour with a majority of 4,552. The swing to the SNP had only been 3.6 per cent. The following day, a London newspaper carried a report with the headline 'Callaghan Cools Poll Fever'. Its political correspondent reported:

Most Labour MPs were banking on an October General Election as they savoured their party's undoubted success ... in beating the SNP challenge. But the Prime Minister said he did not feel 'like rushing to the country'. But the Government was in a minority and we are living dangerously.

Labour MPs were jubilant that in this nineteenth and possibly the most crucial contest since the general election the Government had the smallest swing against it since October 1974.

Three more by-elections were held in April 1978 which sent mixed signals to Callaghan. On 20 April Labour held on to Lambeth Central in London but the vote was well down and the substantial swing to the Tories (9.4 per cent) suggesting that despite Labour's performance in Scotland the previous week the Ilford factor was still alive and well in England. The National Front again came third pushing the Liberals into an ignominious fourth place. A week later (27 April) the Tories held on to Wycombe and to Epsom and Ewell with increased majorities largely at the expense of the Liberals. The swing to the Tories at Wycombe was 7.9 per cent and at Epsom 6.2 per cent – the second smallest since the General Election. Five weeks later on 31 May, Scotland was to give Labour another big boost when the voters of Hamilton went to the polls. In the party's best result of the Parliament its candidate, George Robertson, doubled Labour's majority from 3,332 to 6,492 as a result of a swing from the SNP of 4.5 per cent. Callaghan, who was visiting the United States, received the news at the White House. It seemed certain that he would decide on early polling days for two key tests of the English electorate at the Labour-held seats of Manchester Moss Side and Penistone. The extra pleasure for Labour at Hamilton was that it was there in the 1960s, during the first Wilson administration, that Winifred Ewing's by-election victory began the relentless rise of the SNP. Until George Robertson's triumph, the SNP had seemed poised to snatch many seats from Labour at the General Election.

When Labour decided to call the two outstanding contests on 13 July, they were on equal terms with the Conservatives in the opinion polls. That, and the fact that Steel had announced in May that the Pact would not be renewed at the end of the session, meant, MPs thought, that good by-election results would make an autumn General Election likely. When the results came in they made a case for going to the country in October. In Penistone the Conservatives achieved a swing of 8.8 per cent, reducing Labour's majority from 15,135 to 5,371. However, at Moss Side the swing to the Tories of 3.47 per cent was the lowest in England since the General Election. Finally the economy itself seemed to provide clinching evidence for consulting the electorate at once rather than risking a downturn during the winter. There had been an annual advance of 6 per cent in living standards, the largest single increase for 20 years. Other countries expected a slowdown in growth and Britain faced a menacing wage round.[18] All three parties assumed that Callaghan was ready to fire the starting pistol, so there was general amazement among MPs and journalists when on 7 September he went on television to say that a 1978 election would not be in the national interest. Callaghan had calculated, wrongly, that the unions would not harm Labour's prospects over the winter by pushing for excessive pay rises. (But Labour's private polls had apparently provided gloomier evidence than those published in the press.)

The result of the by-election at Berwick and East Lothian two months later on 26 October must have made many Labour MPs wish that the Prime Minister had decided to go ahead after all. Given all that had gone before in this Parliament it was a remarkable victory for the party. The Tories needed a swing of only 2.8 to snatch the seat, which would have posed no problem over the previous four years. Instead the victorious Labour candidate, John Robertson, achieved a swing to the Government, albeit less than 1 per cent. The former party leader, Edward Heath, took much of the blame for the Conservative defeat. He was accused of opening up a split in the party. While Mrs Thatcher had firmly rejected incomes policy, during the campaign Heath endorsed it in two speeches. The fact that there had been a by-election the same day in Pontefract where the Labour majority had slumped badly with a swing to the Tories of nearly 8 per cent tended to be overlooked by both parties.

There were to be no more by-elections for four months, but in that time the Government's fortunes were transformed once more. In the autumn Labour were confident that they had a real chance of seeing off Mrs Thatcher. However, two by-elections at Clitheroe and Knutsford on 1 March 1979 suggested that the Conservatives would sweep to victory in the General Election now at most only eight months away. The swing against the Government at Clitheroe was nearly 10 per cent while at Knutsford it was over 13 per cent. What had happened to bring about such a sharp change? Quite simply the 'winter of discontent'. The trouble had started when the Government proposed a 5 per cent guideline for pay settlements. However, as *The Times* correspondent, George Clark, pointed out in a special survey of the pre-election period, 'the reaction of the TUC and the Labour Party annual conference showed there was not the slightest chance of this being accepted'. A winter of strikes and disruption followed and finally on 28 March the Government lost a confidence vote and a May General Election was announced the next day. Tory by-election winners provided the Conservative majority in a very close vote and so both brought down a Government in the House for the first time since 1924, and forced a contest when Labour was unpopular. This allowed Thatcher to win office with all that entailed for the future of British politics.

When it was all over, Clark wrote, and he had accepted the verdict of the people, Callaghan confessed sadly: 'Memories of the winter have been too great for many people and undoubtedly that handicapped us ... I have a feeling that people voted against last winter rather than for Conservative proposals.'[19]

There is an ironic footnote to this chapter on the by-elections of the October 1974 Parliament. On 29 March, the very day the General Election was announced, a by-election was held in Liverpool, Edge Hill. The Liberals had failed to achieve the by-election successes of previous Parliaments. Now with a month to go before the General Election they won Edge Hill with an enormous swing of 32 per cent. The triumphant candidate, David Alton, would be an MP for one week only. The Conservatives lost their deposit but a month later began 18 years in office.

Notes

1   *The Times*, 11 April 1996.
2   Pippa Norris, *British by-elections* (Oxford: Clarendon Press, 1990), p. 38.
3   The *Daily Telegraph*, 26 June 1975.
4   The source for the political reaction to by-election results throughout this chapter is the *Daily Telegraph*.
5   D. Butler & D. Kavanagh, *The British general election of 1979* (London: Macmillan, 1980), pp. 24-6.
6   Ibid., p. 31.
7   Butler & Kavanagh, p. 34.
8   A. Michie & S. Hoggart, *The pact: the inside story of the Lib–Lab Government, 1977-8* (London: Quartet Books, 1978), p. 37.
9   Ibid., p. 50.
10   Ibid., p. 42.
11   Austin Mitchell in an interview with Peter Rose at Westminster, 21 November 1995.
12   Michie & Hoggart, p. 131.
13   Butler & Kavanagh, p. 42.
14   Michie & Hoggart, p. 153.
15   Butler & Kavanagh, pp. 35–6.
16   Quotes from an interview with Vivian Bendall at Westminster, 10 July 1995.
17   Butler & Kavanagh, pp. 35-6.
18   Ibid., p. 43.
19   *The Times guide to the House of Commons 1979* (London: Times Books Ltd, 1979), p. 26.

CHAPTER 12

'Breaking the mould?' The Alliance by-election challenge, 1981–82

John Stevenson

The early 1980s saw the testing of the prospects for an effective third force in British politics. The creation of the Social Democratic Party in March 1981 and the rapid establishment of the Alliance with the Liberals seemed to promise a credible alternative political grouping, one sufficiently popular to establish a sizeable bloc of seats in competition with the other parties or possibly even to displace one of them altogether, most likely the strife-torn Labour Party. The crucial test of these expectations was the series of critical by-elections during 1981–82 at Warrington, Croydon North-West, Crosby and Glasgow Hillhead. They were to be the crucible in which the most serious attempt to establish a new party since the War was to be forged. Out of them, it will be argued, the Alliance was able to establish itself as a credible third force, but one which, in spite of the often spectacular results obtained, indicated some of the elements which were to limit an Alliance breakthrough and prevent a radical reshaping of the contours of British politics. These elections, too, were to be raked over subsequently by protagonists in the controversy about the nature of the SDP–Liberal Alliance. Occurring as they did at the inception of a new party and when the relationship with the Liberal Party was still being determined, they were to be viewed as crucial elements in the battle for the identity and leadership of the new third force in British politics and to its fate.

The Conservative victory at the 1979 general election certainly marked the beginning of one of the most dramatic periods of post-war British politics. Initially, Mrs Thatcher's election victory seemed to have broken the near stalemate of party politics since the mid-1970s by obtaining a clear majority for her brand of Conservatism. But as Britain plunged deeper and deeper into recession, apparently compounded by the unorthodox economic policies of the Thatcher administration, its popularity plummeted. By the end of 1980, the Thatcher administration was already beginning to experience some of the lowest opinion poll ratings seen by any government in recent times. On the left, however, the discomfiture of the Conservatives was overshadowed by the effects of defeat, bringing to a head the strains within the Labour Party and the bitter conflicts between left and right. Out of this ferment, the formation of the Social Democratic Party in March 1981 was the most important breakaway by a group of MPs and senior figures from a major Party since the war. The formation of an Alliance between the SDP and the Liberals created for the first time since 1945 what had been talked about but absent for so long, a credible, alternative third party which seemed to have the potential of becoming a party of government.[1]

This was especially significant in the context of the position the Liberal Party found itself in after the 1979 election. By the late 1970s the Liberal Party had already been the beneficiary of several spectacular by-election successes and spurts in support which had ratchetted up the Party's profile and presence since the 'dog days' of near oblivion in the 1950s.[2] Liberal revival – the struggle to avoid extinction – had been marked by a series of increases in support fuelled by by-election successes, almost as regularly followed by a falling away of support and the loss of by-election gains at the subsequent general election. The late fifties revival, based on the Torrington by-election, and the Orpington revival of the early sixties, was followed in the mid-sixties and the early seventies by further peaks of support in which by-elections were won and the Party registered an overall advance in terms of a modest increase in MPs and share of the vote. By the February 1974 election the Liberals had achieved 14 MPs in the Commons, their highest total since the 1930s, on the basis of over 19 per cent of all votes cast. In between general elections, however, the Liberals depended very heavily upon the 'oxygen of publicity' given to them in by-election contests. In a political world heavily weighted towards a two-party system, by-elections were one of the few opportunities for the Liberals both to attract publicity and to compete on something like equal terms with the major parties. By the late 1970s the Liberal by-election upset was a regular feature of the political scene and the party was recognized as having a formidable by-election team capable in the right circumstances of achieving remarkable results. By-elections also provided the opportunity for the Party to nullify somewhat the advantages of the larger parties in resources and personnel by concentrating their resources on a single constituency. The concentrated 'narrow-front' of the by-election campaign gave the Liberal Party one of its few chances to operate in the political big league.

But by the beginning of 1979 the Liberal by-election record had somewhat faded. No seat had been won since Berwick-upon-Tweed in 1973; rather the Party had a string of by-election failures behind them. The Party languished at single figures in the polls and faced very uncertain prospects in any forthcoming election. As it turned out, the Party which emerged from the 1979 general election was fairly battered and bruised. The gamble of Liberal leader David Steel that going into a Pact with Labour, the Lib–Lab Pact of 1977–78, would bolster the Party's credibility, had left them a somewhat ambivalent legacy. While Steel had asserted his authority within the Party by winning a vote of confidence on the Pact, there was clear dissent from many rank and file for an arrangement which apparently had gained the Party little in real terms but had identified it with all the failings and unpopularity of the Labour Government. As the Party prepared in the autumn of 1978 for a general election it stood as low as 4.5 per cent in the polls. But Callaghan's fateful delay in calling an election gave the Party a chance to recapture its old by-election credentials as the country experienced the impact of the 'winter of discontent'. Virtually on the eve of the general election, on 29 March 1979, David Alton won the Liverpool Edge Hill seat largely as a result of a collapse of the Labour vote, foreshadowing the problems for Labour in the larger contest.[3] The question was whether the Liberals could succeed where they had failed so often before, by converting by-election success into a good general election performance.

In the event, the 1979 election was a setback for the Liberals who could, realistically, up to that point claim a significant degree of advance since the revival of the late 1950s and early 1960s. In spite of praise for their manifesto, the Liberals found themselves swept away by the anti-Labour tide which carried Mrs Thatcher to outright victory. It was relatively easy for the Conservatives to brand the Liberals as part authors of the country's misfortunes for their role in the Lib–Lab Pact. Whatever disclaimers Steel could try to provide, those seeking a clear alternative to the Labour Party had turned not to the Liberals but to the fresh and abrasive Conservatism offered by Mrs Thatcher. The Liberals lost another million votes and were reduced to only 11 MPs; the share of the vote was only 13.8 per cent, well down on October 1974. Moreover, the Party had a huge toll of lost deposits, 284 out of 577 candidates, the largest number of lost deposits since the infamous 'massacre of the innocents' back in 1950.[4] What was particularly depressing for the Liberals, well summed-up in the title of a post-election academic study of the Liberal performance as 'Too old to cry, too hurt to laugh', was that the 1979 result blocked off all the obvious routes whereby it might gain the long-awaited share of power.[5] Incremental advance in the number of seats to build up a sizeable bloc in Parliament had been frustrated. There had been a fall in the number of MPs since 1974 and a significant drop in the share of the vote. The hopes of the 102 Liberals fighting seats where the Liberals had come second in 1974 were dashed. Moreover, a clear majority for Mrs Thatcher meant that hopes of holding the balance of power were further away than ever. Debates about with whom the Party might most appropriately ally and the terms on which deals might be struck were effectively redundant. Though they were to resurface over the course of the next decade, in practice the hopes of holding the balance of power had to be put aside in the medium-term. More than 20 years after the Liberal revival became evident in the late

1950s, the Party was forced to take stock of a position which left them with less than a dozen MPs and still remote from the exercise of effective power. As Steel put it later, somewhat ruefully, 'We had survived, but the Thatcher era had begun'.[6]

Apart from survival, one of the few things in which the Liberals could still retain pride was their ability to win by-elections. However disappointing their performance in general elections and however frustrating the failure of the electorate to respond to their appeal in sufficient numbers across more than a handful of constituencies, the Edge Hill result had demonstrated once again that the Party retained the capacity to achieve dramatic and startling results on a narrow front. The Party also retained its reputation as a highly effective force in local politics. A decade or more of community politics had given the Liberals considerable faith in the incremental build-up of support at local level. Liberals could persuade themselves that whatever the disadvantages and drawbacks of the existing party or electoral system, they still had the prospect of by-election success and a special talent for bringing local activism to a point where a by-election victory was possible. Hence following a decade of what could be deemed as larger failures, the Liberal Party carried into the 1980s a conviction that it had a particular expertise for local campaigning and by-election upsets. This view of themselves, sharpened and hardened, particularly at grass-roots level, by the failure to achieve a bigger parliamentary breakthrough, did much to explain their attitude to the dramatic events of the departure of the 'Gang of Four' from the Labour Party and the creation of the Social Democratic Party.

The tensions in the Labour Party following the defeat in 1979 were reaching crisis point by the winter of 1980–81. The potentially explosive re-entry into British politics of Roy Jenkins, former deputy leader of the Party, after his period in Europe had been signalled by his Dimbleby Lecture of 22 November 1979 in which he had argued the need for a new centre party with a programme of radical, social and constitutional reform. He envisaged a new party which would seek to attract support from left and right, from disillusioned moderates of all parties, as well as from those who had hitherto played little part in politics, alienated by the adversarial nature of the Labour–Conservative contest and seeking a more constructive and consensual approach. Jenkins, with all the authority of senior politician seeking to rise above the apparent petty squabbling of the major parties, tapped into a tradition of 'centre party' sentiment which had appeared recurrently in British politics at varying points since 1945, most recently with Dick Taverne's short-lived career as a breakaway Democratic Labour victor in the Lincoln by-election in 1973. But Jenkins's call was translated from vague aspiration to practicalities by the increased leftward drift of the Labour Party in response to defeat and the reaction to this drift by some of its leading members. One formation which articulated this concern was the centre-right grouping, Campaign for a Labour Victory, formed in 1977. Concerned initially with modernizing the Labour Party, its founder members, Ian Wrigglesworth, John Cartwright, William Rodgers and Alec McGiven were to become part of the movement for consideration of a breakaway from the Labour Party. As the Labour left began to exercise increasing influence on the Party, the CLV began to make noises about the possibility of forming a new democratic socialist party. The election as leader of Michael Foot, a long-standing supporter of unilateral nuclear disarmament, on 10 November 1980 marked a shift in the balance of power in the Party, followed by an acrimonious dispute over the method to be adopted for choosing the leader of the Party in future. The question of whether to adopt a one-member, one-vote system, as opposed to the proposed electoral college system which gave a strong weighting to the trade unions, became the issue on which a group of MPs decided they could no longer stay within the Labour Party.

A week after the Special Labour Conference at Wembley in January 1981 reaffirmed the electoral college decision, the so-called Gang of Four, Roy Jenkins, David Owen, William Rodgers and Shirley Williams, issued the Limehouse Declaration (25 January 1981) setting up an interim body called the Council for Social Democracy. Initially designated a pressure group rather than a separate party, the Declaration attracted the support of nine Labour MPs. Events moved rapidly in the spring of 1981, with the Liberals under Steel giving encouraging support for the creation of a non-socialist alternative to Thatcherism. An opinion poll in the *Sun* gave a putative Liberal–Social Democratic arrangement 51 per cent of popular support; a hundred prominent people gave their backing to the Council for Social Democracy in an advertisement in the *Guardian* and called for funds and members; Shirley Williams resigned from Labour's National Executive and, on 2 March, 12 Labour MPs resigned the Party Whip. On 26 March the new Social Democratic Party was formally established, consisting initially of 14 MPs, 13 Labour and one Conservative. It was the largest defection of MPs from the Labour Party since 1931. Headed by a group of talented and experienced figures with Cabinet experience it completely transformed in the short-term the electoral position: at a step, the SDP became the third party in British politics.

Almost immediately the question of an alliance with the Liberals arose. Actual discussions between the Liberals and the SDP proceeded informally: while Steel had close relations with Roy Jenkins, he had less direct links with the other members of the Gang of Four. On the face of it, the formation of a separate SDP was something of a rebuff – why had the dissenting MPs not simply joined the Liberals? Here Jenkins's view that a separate Party was the best interim vehicle for a realignment of British politics, bringing in hitherto uncommitted potential activists and voters, was important. But it was not necessarily shared by other members of the

SDP. In the short-term, however, a fortuitous opportunity came in April for Steel to consult with Shirley Williams and Bill Rodgers at the annual Anglo–German conference in Germany in April 1981. In what insiders called the 'Königswinter Compact' the ground rules for the Alliance were laid, including the decision to issue a joint statement of principles, arrangements to contest alternate by-elections as they arose, and some kind of agreement on a share-out of constituencies in the event of a general election. On 16 June the SDP and the Liberals issued a joint statement of policy, *A Fresh Start for Britain.* Its main proposals included parliamentary reform and proportional representation, a Freedom of Information Act, devolution, industrial partnership, support for NATO and continued EEC membership. These policies were later to form the core of the party's 1983 manifesto.[7]

The immediate question was whether the new Party could prove its credentials at the ballot box rather than in the hothouse atmosphere of London and the metropolitan media. There was already some criticism that the Party had not made an issue of testing its electoral support already by sitting MPs resigning and putting themselves and the country through a mini general election. The auspices looked favourable, for whereas the Liberal Party on its own had attracted about 14 per cent of support in Gallup throughout 1980, by the spring of 1981 Gallup had registered as high as 33 per cent for a putative Alliance between the Liberals and the SDP.[8] This level of support, registered in March and April, was already slipping slightly by May and June, and it was a matter of urgency for the SDP in particular to put itself into a position where it could prove that the momentum of its launch and the high expectations it had generated would not be dissipated. Fortuitously for the newly-fledged SDP an opportunity arose at this crucial time with the first of the series of Alliance by-elections, at Warrington.

The resignation of Sir Tom Williams from his seat late in May 1981 to become a judge provided the occasion for a by-election to be held in summer or autumn. The difficulty was that Warrington was not, on the face of it, promising territory. It was a safe Labour seat, held by Williams for 20 years, and by Baroness Summerskill before him, in which Labour had taken 62 per cent of the vote and a 33 per cent majority.[9] To fight the seat Labour had in 1981 chosen Douglas Hoyle, a member of the NEC and an experienced candidate who had held Nelson and Colne until 1979. If Labour was in a strong position, the track record for the Liberals was correspondingly weak. They had taken only 9 per cent of the vote in the 1979 general election and were not very active locally with only one ward contested in the recent local elections. Warrington was in many respects typical of scores of fairly solid Labour seats where the Liberal presence was marginal. For the SDP, however, there was little choice but to go ahead and fight the seat, however unpropitious Warrington might look. The coming by-election put the SDP in a position where it had to justify its claims to be a national party, not just one of the metropolitan south. Many of the SDP's founders aimed to replace Foot's Labour Party with a reconstituted party appealing to traditional Labour voters on the basis of moderate, up-dated policies. If that strategy was to have any realistic chance, it had to be pursued in seats like Warrington and by proving the SDP's ability to win over working-class Labour supporters in open competition with the existing Labour Party. As a result, as early as the end of May, the SDP Steering Committee had firmly decided to contest the seat and had commissioned a poll to see how it might be fought to the SDP's best advantage.[10]

Had they but known it – and few of the leading SDP members had the remotest idea about Warrington prior to the by-election – the prospects were more auspicious than they thought. Warrington was a politically moderate and relatively prosperous constituency, one that prided itself on its varied industrial base which had meant that it escaped the worst effects of the run-down of major northwestern industries like mining and textiles. It had no strong traditions of trade union militancy and a significant conservative Catholic working-class presence. The town had seen a relatively successful post-war development of new housing estates on the fringes of the old centre, and had benefited from the network of new motorways to become a significant distribution centre, assisted by being designated in 1968 one of the later wave of New Towns.[11] It had claims to be just the sort of test-bed for a moderate alternative to the Labour Party that the SDP needed.

The major difficulty for the SDP was that the most obvious candidate for the seat, one of the most electorally attractive founder members of the SDP, Shirley Williams, was reluctant to take on the challenge for a mixture of reasons, partly personal, partly political.[12] Although a poll in the *Sun* suggested that if Shirley Williams was the SDP/Liberal candidate she had every chance of winning, she issued a press statement in early June saying she could not stand. In her place, Roy Jenkins took up the challenge on behalf of the SDP. Widely regarded as a brave and bold move, it gave added credibility to the SDP that its most senior figure was prepared to risk his reputation in what was still regarded as an uphill struggle, estimated on one calculation as 551 in order of hopefulness for the new party amongst the 635 constituencies in the United Kingdom. Jenkins had the benefit of a private survey by his wife to sound out the possibilities. He records in his memoirs that while he was attending an international bankers' conference in Switzerland, his wife was engaged on a private reconnaissance of Warrington.

So on that night of effective decision [4 June] I stayed in the Hotel Beau-Rivage, Lausanne, and looked out from the balcony of my suite across a moonlit Lake Geneva to the Savoy Alps. She stayed in the

Patten Arms Hotel, Warrington, and looked out, without a balcony I think, over the railway station and the soap works which had been a founding pillar of the first Lord Leverhulme's massive combine.

His wife's report was not particularly favourable; a solidly industrial town with most of the most prosperous middle-class areas in other constituencies, it looked 'a hard nut to crack'.[13] Nonetheless on 11 June, Jenkins was acclaimed as the SDP's candidate at an enthusiastic meeting, staking his claim as having represented 'one of the most industrial seats in Birmingham for 27 years'.[14]

Seeking to deprive the new Party of the chance to build up any further momentum, the Labour chief whip called the election for 16 July. On the whole, in spite of the exceptional circumstances of the launch of the Party in the spring, the campaign was surprisingly uneventful. As Norris has shown, the majority of polls gave Labour a lead of about 30 per cent over the Alliance at the outset and these figures remained largely unchanged during the campaign. In the final poll, four days before the election, MORI estimated that Labour remained ahead with 56 per cent of the vote, followed by the SDP with 23 per cent and the Conservatives at 10 per cent.[15] Jenkins campaigned forcefully with support from the rest of the Gang of Four and from David Steel, the Liberal leader. The enthusiasm of the SDP campaign team and the good relations of the new Party with the press were assets, while the Warrington electorate seemed to be giving Jenkins and the other members of the Party an encouraging degree of support.[16]

When the result was announced, Labour had held the seat, but its 1979 majority had shrunk from 10,274 to 1,759, while its share of the vote had fallen from 62 per cent to 48 per cent. Jenkins had captured 12,521 votes, 42 per cent of the total. The Conservatives lost their deposit, with the minor parties polling fewer than 600 votes between them. The declaration of the results was treated as a barely concealed triumph for Jenkins and the new Party, Jenkins responding to a sour acceptance speech by Hoyle by declaring the result 'My first defeat in thirty years in politics, and it is by far the greatest victory in which I have ever participated'.[17] The basis of such a good result was the *de facto* Alliance picking up approximately a quarter of the former Labour vote and almost three-quarters of the Tories. In what was, in effect, a classic by-election squeeze, the Alliance had mopped up most of the opposition to Labour in Warrington and added to it a significant portion of the Labour vote. It had just failed to mobilize sufficient support to defeat Labour, but the result was dramatic enough even without the bonus of victory; the flag-bearer for the new third force in British politics had come a close second in a seat which all the pre-election polls suggested it had no hope of winning.

The result at Warrington had a number of important effects. First, it undoubtedly boosted the electoral credibility of the new party. It remains a matter of speculation what a lesser share of the vote, still more an ignominious defeat, at Warrington would have done to the future history of the SDP and of the Alliance. As it was, the near miss allowed the SDP to break out of the cycle of media publicity followed by electoral failure which had dogged other attempts to create new parties in British politics. For those interested in canvassing the possibilities of electoral realignment, Warrington was highly significant. Thus immediately after the Warrington result, the *Guardian* wrote: 'There have been false dawns before; but there has been no time when a fundamental change in the pattern of British politics looked more likely to come than it does this morning'.[18] Experienced political scientists were just as ready to see the result as of more than temporary importance, Ivor Crewe commenting that the result was 'worse than a government's normal mid-term unpopularity: it was a collapse of unparalleled proportions'.[19] The momentum which had appeared to be faltering was taken up again; the by-election was followed by a renewed surge in third party support, Gallup giving a putative Alliance 32 per cent of support in August, 6 points up on the previous month.[20] At a point where the novelty of the new force was beginning to fade, Warrington came as a vital shot in the arm.

Second, the result massively boosted Jenkins's prestige and position with the SDP, still nominally run by a collective leadership. His somewhat patrician, possibly to some even dilettante image, had been dispelled by his vigorous campaigning at Warrington, but his candidature and performance together also put him firmly in place as the most likely leader of the SDP. David Owen was later to ascribe momentous significance to the combined effect of Shirley Williams's decision not to stand and of Roy Jenkins's to do so. One effect was to decide the leadership question, as Owen trenchantly put it: 'It effectively put paid to Shirley's chance of becoming Leader of the SDP and ensured that Roy Jenkins would be its first Leader.' For Owen this had an even more powerful and determinative effect upon the future of the SDP and marked a turning-point in the relationship between the SDP and the Liberals, indeed in the entire history and fate of the Alliance. Where Jenkins celebrated Warrington as a vital first step on the road to a credible challenge to the two major parties and as a dry run for later co-operation between the SDP and the Liberals, warmly recognizing Liberal assistance during the campaign, Owen was to put on record that Williams 'having ducked the fight' at Warrington was decisive not only for her own chances of leadership, but also for the history of the SDP as a whole. According to his scenario, Shirley Williams would have won at Warrington 'with dramatic consequences for the SDP and for the country':

> She would have fought a predominantly SDP campaign and we would
> in consequence have been able to negotiate a far better seat deal with
> the Liberals than the miserable one we ended up with. Shirley would

have been the Leader of the SDP and Bill and I would have buttressed her position. There would have been no question but that it was a Social Democratic Party, standing in its own right as one of four parties in British politics. But it was sadly not to be.[21]

The Warrington by-election thus gave birth to a kind of 'black legend' about the 'wrong turning' taken by the SDP at its infancy. According to Owen and like-minded members, Jenkins's candidature and 'triumph in defeat' set the new party along the course of its fateful Alliance with the Liberals rather than a more independent and less compromised future, one, it is always implied, which might have been more successful. But however enticing this prospect might seem in retrospect, as subsequent studies have shown, an independent SDP would still have faced an uphill struggle against the operation of the existing electoral system.[22]

If the Warrington by-election was seen subsequently by some as a lost struggle for the soul of the SDP, the Croydon North-West by-election in October 1981 was in practice the first fully-fledged Alliance by-election. The encouraging result at Warrington had helped to create a strong surge of support for the prospects of breaking the mould of the British political system. At the Llandudno Liberal Assembly in September, the unratified Alliance with the SDP received overwhelming support in an almost euphoric atmosphere, culminating in Steel's closing words to his address to the Assembly: 'Go back to your constituencies and prepare for government.'[23] The Alliance was then endorsed at the first SDP conference, a three-part event held in Perth, Bradford and London. Initially, the question of the candidature for Croydon North-West had again proved an issue. That Croydon would be fought became apparent while the Warrington by-election was being conducted. The tensions between those, like Owen, who were still keen to preserve the independence of the SDP and those prepared to accept joint selection of candidates with the local Liberals were just beneath the surface and demonstrated themselves in attempts to prevent a premature selection of the sitting Liberal candidate and local activist, William Pitt. The infant SDP was in the difficult position that, as part of the agreement over Roy Jenkins fighting Warrington, the Liberals would have first refusal over the next by-election, as it happened, Croydon. With Shirley Williams now ready to enter the fight, there was wide support, including from David Steel, for William Pitt to stand down and allow Williams to run 'out of turn' so to speak, for as David Steel later put it: 'we had very few members and again a poor track record. Shirley was willing to fight. I had to try to persuade our previous candidate who had polled only 4,000 votes in 1979 to stand aside since I did not believe he could possibly win.' While it made sense to almost everyone in the leadership of the Liberal Party and the SDP for Pitt to stand aside and allow Shirley Williams to run, every attempt to persuade him failed. Instead, with the backing of the local Party and the benefit of the publicity surrounding the possibility of bringing Shirley Williams in to contest the seat, Bill Pitt was himself transformed into something of a local hero bravely resisting the machinations of the Party bosses. Faced with the stubborn refusal of Pitt and the local Liberals to stand aside, Pitt's candidature went ahead.[24]

The Alliance's difficulty in Croydon was that it was a Labour–Conservative marginal in which the Liberals were usually squeezed. As Steel and everyone else had noted, the track record of the Liberals was almost as bad as at Warrington. Pitt had lost his deposit in the 1979 general election and the council election record both for Pitt and the local Liberals was unpromising, Pitt having taken only 23 per cent of the vote in the May 1981 GLC elections. The local Liberal organization was also weak, with only 40 members. Although an early poll had suggested that with Williams as the candidate the Alliance might gain the seat, the campaign was not to be led, as at Warrington, by a nationally-known figure. None the less, the momentum of the early Alliance was maintained into the early polls, which showed a three-horse race in which Pitt was just in the lead by a few percentage points. The losers in this situation were primarily the Conservatives who had seen a 20 point fall in their national poll ratings from the 1979 general election by the summer of 1981. The Alliance was thus able to capitalize upon a huge drop in Conservative popularity and some weakening of Labour's position. Thus, instead of Labour being the natural beneficiaries of what was, in effect, the classic mid-term unpopularity of the government, the actual gainers were the Alliance. The result when declared on 22 October was a triumph, the first win for the Alliance, with a majority of 3,254, almost quadrupling the share of the vote from 1979 to 40 per cent. Labour was forced into third place, though easily held their deposit.[25]

The outcome of Croydon was significant in many ways. It proved that the Alliance could win in almost any environment, including hitherto difficult marginals; it could also win without national celebrities to lead the campaign; and it could build up support rapidly in seats where organization was weak. The outcome seemed to reinforce the attraction of Alliance co-operation; with Steel's words at the end of the Liberal Assembly still ringing in their ears, it was possible to believe that the Alliance could win almost any seat that came their way. For those amongst the SDP who still regretted the Alliance with the Liberals, it was clear that, for good or ill, the die was now cast, the result at Warrington and the events of the conference season in September had shaped an Alliance in which the SDP would have to learn to live with the very considerable autonomy of local Liberal associations. Predictably, the Croydon result saw a further surge in popularity for the Alliance in Gallup, rising from 29 per cent in September to 42 per cent in November.[26]

The third in the early Alliance by-election quartet was Crosby, a safe Conservative seat of Liverpool commuter suburbs and farming villages north of Liverpool on the way to Southport. With over 81 per cent of the electorate owner occupiers in 1981, a tiny minority ethnic population, and virtually none of the usual problems associated with Merseyside, Crosby was not just safe, it was a Tory stronghold with a 19,272 majority in 1979. Fortunately for the Alliance, Shirley Williams was now available and willing to stand. Although it was not entirely clear who was entitled to take the lead in determining the candidature, pending a formal agreement about seat allocation between the Parties, the local Liberals showed less inclination to make an issue of it than those in Croydon. Accordingly, Williams was adopted as Alliance candidate on 19 October 1981 with the full support of the previous Liberal candidate.[27] Her campaign was immediately boosted by the Croydon result and, in what took on something of a carnival atmosphere, Williams entered the by-election contest with a lead in the polls from the outset. Once again there was a huge slump in Conservative support in the polls on 1979, of the order of 20 points, with Labour's 25 per cent share of the poll in 1979 being squeezed by the Alliance. Once again the Alliance was able both to generate considerable local enthusiasm and to flood the constituency with volunteers. With the polls consistently registering a Williams victory, the result on the day (26 November) was a triumph of major proportions. The Conservative majority of over 19,000 had been converted into an Alliance majority of 5,289. Williams more than tripled the Liberal vote in 1979, the Conservatives' share of the vote fell from two-thirds to less than half, while the Labour candidate fell from a quarter of the vote to less than a tenth.[28] The impact of Williams's victory at Crosby was to propel Alliance expectations into the stratosphere. Gallup in December 1981 showed Alliance support at 50 per cent in the polls, historically its highest ever rating, while the cover of *The Economist* for the second week in December showed Jenkins, Steel and Williams with the simple title 'Her Majesty's new Opposition'.[29]

The period from autumn 1981 to early spring 1982 marked the high point of Alliance support. By that time some at least of the Thatcher government's difficulties were moderating; inflation was falling, and unemployment ceasing to rise as rapidly, and real incomes and expectations for those in work beginning to revive. Alliance support in the polls was down to 39 per cent in January 1982 and to 36 per cent by February. Although still ahead of the other parties in the latter month, the Alliance was only two points ahead of Labour who remained stubbornly in the field in spite of their internal squabbles. Already expectations that the Alliance would replace the Labour Party looked at best a medium-term objective rather than a short-term one. Dissent between Liberals and Social Democrats over seat allocation was also beginning to tarnish the cosy image built up since the autumn.[30] Moreover there was little occurring to attract publicity in the aftermath of Crosby, so that the Alliance was beginning to suffer from the familiar problem that had affected the Liberal Party in the past, a reduction in media interest once by-election victories were over. As a result, the last of the four by-elections which marked the establishment of the Alliance as a credible third force occurred on the ebb tide of Alliance popularity. Glasgow Hillhead became vacant on the death of Sir Thomas Galbraith on 2 January. In this case, the determining factor over the candidature was the need for Roy Jenkins to have a seat in parliament if he was to be eligible for the leadership contest due in the summer of 1982. Jenkins was the only one of the original Gang of Four not to have a seat and it was necessary for him to find one sooner rather than later. Glasgow Hillhead was promising Alliance territory and on the list of target seats with a Conservative majority of only 7 per cent. The seat was socially mixed with both poor working-class neighbourhoods and some very affluent areas. What made it most attractive was its large professional middle class and many students and teachers at Glasgow University. By all measures this suggested a seat in which there were likely to be many of the kind of people who would support an Alliance candidate.[31] After some initial hesitation by Jenkins, fearing a second near-miss, and a difficult negotiation with the local Liberals who had a candidate in place, Jenkins went ahead.[32] The by-election proved a stiffer contest than either Croydon or Crosby, with some of the initial polls showing the Alliance in third place. The electoral position was confused by fringe candidates and a Scottish Nationalist presence. During the campaign the polls showed each of the parties in the lead at different points. The Alliance had a particularly low point 11 days out from polling, on 14 March, when three polls were published, none of them showing the Alliance in the lead. As late as the day before polling a Gallup poll gave Labour a 7 per cent lead with Jenkins in third place. But the hard campaigning of the last few days of the campaign paid dividends with three polls showing the Alliance in the lead on the morning of the election, 25 March.[33]

In the event, Jenkins won with 33 per cent of the vote and a narrow majority of 2,038. He had more than doubled the Liberal vote in 1979, showing once again the Alliance's ability to win in seats where the Liberals had failed in the past. By any objective measure, a third party win in a Tory–Labour marginal in Scotland, with an SNP intervention to boot, was a remarkable result. It was clear, however, that if the Alliance bandwagon had continued to roll, it was rolling more slowly than during the euphoria of the autumn. With support dropping rather than rising, it was evident that the Alliance was unlikely to sweep to the victory prophesied in the winter opinion polls. Jenkins on the other hand had confirmed himself again as an effective and hard-working campaigner, not only getting himself back into the House of Commons but also establishing an irresistible claim for the leadership, duly confirmed in his victory over David Owen in the summer of 1982.[34]

The Alliance had fought four by-elections since the summer of 1981, scoring one near-miss and three victories. It had effectively established the

Alliance as a significant political force, one which would present a serious rather than a marginal challenge to the two other parties. But it was equally the case that the Alliance would never achieve such a clear run of success again. The improvement in Conservative fortunes evident in the spring of 1982 was to be massively reinforced by the effects of the Argentinian invasion of the Falkland Islands on 2 April, a week after the Hillhead result. The events of late spring and early summer in the South Atlantic were to transform the position of the Conservative Party. Between November 1980 and April 1982 the Conservatives' standing in the Gallup Poll never rose above 40 per cent; between May 1982 and June 1983 it never fell below that figure; in the four months before Argentina invaded the Falklands the Conservatives' average standing in the polls was 30 per cent; in the following four months, it was 45 per cent. As David Steel put it:

> ... the political momentum of the Alliance was stopped dead in its tracks by an event over which we had no control ... Fate dealt us a cruel blow. With the sending of the task force, British domestic politics were virtually swept aside. We had to back our boys and our Maggie, leader of the War Cabinet.[35]

The Falklands Factor came into play when the Alliance momentum, as shown at Hillhead, was, in fact, slowing down. Following it the Alliance by-election record became much more patchy. The government was even able to gain Mitcham and Morden from the SDP in June 1982, and then avoid the usual anti-government swing in contests at Beaconsfield and Coatbridge. Labour was able to win Birmingham Northfield from the Tories in October, exactly the kind of seat the Alliance would have triumphed in 12 months earlier. Some successes were still possible, as at Bermondsey in February 1983, but the tide of irresistible success was clearly gone for good.[36]

In retrospect, the surge in support for an electoral third force in 1981–82, hugely boosted by the creation of the SDP and the formation of the Alliance, looked much like the latest version of the Liberal revivals witnessed since the late 1950s. It had similar characteristics: spectacular by-election success, a dramatic increase in poll support, and an almost equally rapid decline. As in earlier instances, it left support at a somewhat higher level than before the revival, though vulnerable to erosion and slippage, as seen before. But it also, on this occasion, left a third party which was capable of winning almost a quarter of the popular vote at the general election of 1983 and not much less in 1987. Whatever the criticisms surrounding its failure to realign British politics, the Alliance lasted long enough to give birth to a credible merged party, the Liberal Democrats in 1988, and one capable of securing a fifth of the popular vote in 1992.

But the early Alliance by-elections are haunted by the spectre of 'might-have-beens', in particular Owen's belief that a fateful wrong turning was taken by the SDP at Warrington and that it should have fought separately to establish itself as an independent fourth party, a decision which doomed the whole SDP enterprise to failure. However, Crewe and King in their detailed assessment of the failure of the SDP have judged Owen's 'go-it-alone' scenario 'not remotely credible':

> It might have worked in a country that already had proportional representation and a multi-party system, but it was utterly unsuited to the realities of Britain's first-past-the-post-system. It is inconceivable that the Liberals would have taken Owenite bullying lying down. For them, of all parties, bottom place and lost deposits in by-elections held no terrors; they had been there too often before. The outcome in 1981-2 would have been what it was in fact after the merger fiasco: two centre parties competing for the same vote and denying each other victory as a consequence … Once the decision was taken to establish a separate party, the logic of the first-past-the-post system required an electoral pact with the Liberal party and therefore *ipso facto* an agreed policy programme.[37]

Thus the early Alliance by-elections occupy not only a place in the conventional psephological history of postwar Britain, but they also have a place in the contentious historiography of the most dramatic attempt to realign British politics seen since the Second World War.

Notes

1   See I. Crewe and A. King, *SDP: the birth, life and death of the Social Democratic Party*, (Oxford, 1995), pp. 27–127 for the fullest account.
2   C. Cook, *A short history of the Liberal Party, 1900–88* (London, 1989) pp. 137–62; J. Stevenson, *Third party politics since 1945: Liberals, Alliance and Liberal Democrats*, (Oxford, 1993) pp. 44–73.
3   Stevenson, *Third party politics*, pp. 60–65; Cook, *Short history*, p. 166. The Liberal vote increased from 27 per cent to 64 per cent; Labour's vote collapsed from 52 per cent to 24 per cent.
4   The Party lost 319 deposits in 1950 out of 461 candidates.
5   J. Rasmussen in H. R. Penniman (ed.) *Britain at the polls, 1979; a study of the general election*, (London and Washington, 1981) p. 170.
6   D. Steel, *Against Goliath: David Steel's story*, (London, 1989) p. 152.
7   See Crewe and King, *SDP*, pp. 167–78.
8   Gallup poll figures from D. Butler and G. Butler, *British political facts, 1900–1994*, (London, 1994) p. 256.
9   See P. Norris, *British by-elections: The volatile electorate*, (Oxford, 1990) p. 44.
10 D. Owen, *Time to declare*, (London, 1991) pp. 519–20.
11 The *Stockport Messenger* dispute of 1983 which occasioned some serious picket line violence was not linked to any of the town's traditional industries.
12 For her reasons, see Crewe and King, *SDP*, pp. 136–7.

13 R. Jenkins, *A life at the centre*, (London, 1991) pp. 539–40.
14 *Daily Telegraph*, 12 June 1981.
15 Norris, *British by-elections*, pp. 44–5.
16 See Jenkins, *Life at the centre*, pp. 541–3 for the carnival-like atmosphere of the campaign.
17 Jenkins, *Life at the centre*, p. 544.
18 *Guardian*, 18 July 1981, cited in Crewe and King, *SDP*, p. 138.
19 Cited in Norris, *British by-elections*, p. 45.
20 Butler and Butler, *British political facts*, p. 256.
21 Owen, *Time to declare*, p. 520.
22 Jenkins, *Life at the centre*, p. 544; Owen, *Time to declare*, p. 520–1; See Crewe and King, *SDP*, esp. pp. 457–65.
23 Steel, *Against Goliath*, pp. 225-6. On the atmosphere of the Llandudno Assembly see also Jenkins, *Life at the centre*, pp. 546–7.
24 *Ibid.*, pp. 226–8; see also Owen, *Time to declare*, pp. 522–3.
25 Norris, *British by-elections*, pp. 45–7.
26 Butler and Butler, *British political facts*, p. 256.
27 For the seat negotiations, see Crewe and King, *SDP*, p. 143; Steel, *Against Goliath*, pp. 228–9.
28 See Norris, *British by-elections*, pp. 47–9.
29 Butler and Butler, *British political facts*, p. 256; *The Economist*, 5–11 December 1981.
30 This phase is discussed in detail in Crewe and King, *SDP*, pp. 146–9.
31 See R. Waller, *The Almanac of British politics*, 4th edition, 1991, pp. 594–5.
32 See Crewe and King, *SDP*, pp. 153–4.
33 Norris, *British by-elections*, pp. 49–51; Steel, *Against Goliath*, pp. 230–1.
34 Crewe and King, *SDP*, p. 155.
35 Steel, *Against Goliath*, p. 231.
36 Crewe and King, *SDP*, pp. 191–2.
37 *Ibid.* p. 458.

CHAPTER 13

By-elections since 1983: did they matter?

Ivor Crewe

On the day of the Monmouth by-election in May 1991 a *Times* leader began:

> Today's by-election in Monmouth is unimportant. A new member of Parliament will be returned to Westminster. That is all. The voters will have experienced a deluge of campaigning. The evidence of by-elections past is that they will react in a way wholly unrepresentative of the national electorate in a general election. Nobody should deduce any wider conclusions, except that wider conclusions should not be deduced from by-elections.[1]

The 56 by-elections held in Great Britain during the Conservative governments of 1983 to 1997 offer ample support for such sober scepticism.[2] Their most striking feature was the consistently dismal performance of the Conservatives. The party held on to only eight of the 26 six seats it defended, losing ten to the Alliance or Liberal Democrats, seven to Labour and one to the Scottish Nationalists. Hitherto impregnable Conservative fortresses – Christchurch, Eastbourne, Newbury, Ribble Valley, Ryedale – were captured by the Liberals and in three cases – Mid-Staffordshire, Wirral South and Staffordshire South East – by Labour. The Conservative share of the vote fell every single time, on 15 occasions by more than 20 percentage points. In the 28 by-elections defended by Labour, the Conservative candidate slipped from second to third place or worse in all but seven. By-elections, to an even greater degree than local elections, were occasions on which the electorate invariably gave the Conservative government a bloody nose.

At by-elections the Conservative vote almost always collapsed; but at the following general election it almost always recovered. The Tayside seat of Kincardine and Deeside provides a striking example. It had been Conservative since 1923, but in 1987 the Liberals, building on local election successes and their strength elsewhere in Grampian, had come within 2,063 votes (4.3 per cent) of winning. In the November 1991 by-election caused by the death of its long-standing MP, Alick Buchanan Smith, the Liberal Democrats, fielding an experienced local candidate, comfortably gained the seat with an 18.4 per cent majority on a high turnout. Yet at the general election only five months later, the Conservatives regained the seat with a larger majority (8.6 per cent) than in 1987. The by-election had left not a trace.

The same could be said for most by-elections. In the 16 by-elections of the 1983–87 parliament the Conservative share of the vote averaged 29 per cent, behind both the Alliance (38 per cent) and Labour (31 per cent). Yet they went on to win the 1987 general election with a majority of 102 and a mere 0.1 percentage point decline in their vote. They also recaptured three of their four by-election losses – Portsmouth South, Fulham and Ryedale – and came within 57 votes of recovering the fourth, Brecon and Radnor (which fell to them in 1992). The pattern of slump and recovery was even more pronounced in the 1987–92 parliament. The Conservative share of the vote averaged 23 per cent across the 23 by-elections, well behind Labour (43 per cent) and not far ahead of the then divided Centre (19 per cent). Yet the 1992 general election returned the Conservatives for an unprecedented fourth term of office with a share of the vote virtually identical to that in 1983 and 1987. It also returned Conservative MPs in every one of the seven seats they had lost in by-elections since 1987. By-election 'sensations' turned out not to be sensational after all. As indicators, let alone predictors, of the general election result the post-1983 by-elections, like all post-war by-elections, signified nothing.[3] In these circumstances the comments of the *Independent*'s political columnist shortly before the first by-election of the 1992 parliament were understandable:

> Uncle George can enjoy shocking the aunts by admitting that he defected to the Lib Dems: 'And frankly, if Major doesn't pull his socks up the blighter might have lost me for good'. Uncle George glares at himself in the mirror and feels considerably better. He is not, perhaps, such a stick-in-the-mud fellow after all, hmm? (But come 1995–6, as all present know full well, Uncle George's views on income tax will return him to the Tory fold.) Because of Uncle George we can discount most midterm Tory losses at by-elections and be disproportionately surprised when the ruling party holds onto its seats. Meanwhile it is in everyone's interests to pretend that by-elections are more interesting than they really are.[4]

A straightforward explanation exists for the huge disparity between by-election and general election results: by-elections are ideal for protest voting. On the one hand, a protest vote at a by-election is cost-free because the existence of the government (or the local council) is not at stake. On the other hand, the benefits of protest are maximized by the strong signal that

245

can be sent to the government (or occasionally the Opposition) by an upset result. The question posed to the voter at a by-election is not 'Do you want a Conservative or Labour government?' but 'Do you want a Conservative or Labour (or Liberal Democrat) MP?' As a result, the question the voter chooses to answer is 'Do you approve or disapprove of the current government's record?' Most voters find something to disapprove of.

The media play a crucial role, applying a magnifying glass to a by-election, thereby maximizing the protest vote and grossly exaggerating its significance. By-elections provide the perfect conditions for media attention: a single, usually compact, geographical area; politicians and parties vying for attention; the excitement of the horserace, aided by the local polls; the cheers and tears of the final result; a spot of colour in the drab routine of party politics. Local elections are arguably of more consequence but campaigning is low-key and media attention unfocused. National opinion polls are a superior measure of the public mood, but statistical abstractions; by-elections involve real (national) politicians, real campaigns and real voters. They put the drama into politics.

Sceptics argue that the one-of-a-kind nature of by-election results strips them of any political significance at all. A by-election is no more than an arrangement for democratically replacing a constituency MP who has died or resigned. If the media, the psephologists and, most important, the politicians take by-elections seriously, more fool them. The descent of national politicians to the by-election hustings, the ranks of cameras following the candidates, the self-important morning press conferences, the bizarre *galère* of fringe candidates, the clan gathering of activists from the four corners of the nation, *Newsnight By-Election Special* with Peter Snow's computer graphics – are all hoop-la. By-elections have become an excuse for carnival. But they signify nothing.

The sceptics' case forms the backdrop to the rest of this chapter. Part I provides an analytic summary of the 56 by-elections since 1983. It shows that, while by-elections offer few clues to the following general election result, they do provide a useful albeit rough measure of the public's changing political mood and party preferences. Part II highlights the political impact of some of the by-elections and shows that their significance for British politics during the period was wider than sceptics allow.

Part I: electoral analysis

A summary of the period

The three parliaments of 1983–87, 1987–92 and 1992–97 provide an appropriate division of the period since 1983. They constitute distinct periods in British party politics, although the last needs to be sub-divided at mid-1994, when Tony Blair was elected leader of the Labour party.

246

Tables 13.1 and 13.2 summarize the by-election results in the three periods. In 1983–87 the Conservatives defended nine seats, losing three to the Liberal/SDP Alliance (Portsmouth South to the SDP and Brecon and Radnor and Ryedale to the Liberals) and one to Labour (Fulham). Of the five seats they held, two were saved by a whisker: Penrith and the Border by 552 votes (1.4 per cent) and Derbyshire West by 100 votes (0.2 per cent). Labour held four of its five seats, losing Greenwich to the SDP. The period was marked by the success of the Liberal/SDP Alliance, which increased its share of the vote in every seat bar Cynon Valley and took first or second place everywhere but Fulham. The mean three-party division of the vote was Conservative 29.2 per cent, Labour 30.5 per cent, Liberal/SDP 38.0 per cent: in by-elections, at least, three-party politics thrived.

The 1987–92 parliament was marked by Conservative losses on a larger scale. They lost seven of the ten seats they defended, four to Labour (Vale of Glamorgan, Mid-Staffordshire, Monmouth and Langbaurgh) and three to the Liberal Democrats (Eastbourne, Ribble Valley and Kincardine and Deeside). They might have lost two more – Epping Forest and Richmond – had the rival candidacies of the SDP and Liberal Democrats not split the Centre vote. Labour defended thirteen seats, comfortably holding all but Glasgow Govan, which it lost to the Scottish Nationalists. An important difference from the 1983–87 period, however, was Labour's advance at the expense of the Liberal Democrats in the battle for the non-Conservative vote.

The results of the 17 by-elections held since 1992 bore a superficial resemblance to those in the preceding parliament, with the Conservatives losing badly and Labour and the Liberal Democrats sharing the spoils. The Conservatives lost all of the eight seats they defended, three to Labour (Dudley West, Wirral South and Staffordshire South East), four to the

Table 13.1 Summary of by-election results, 1979–97.

	No.	Conservative			Labour			Centre*			Other		
		Hold	Lose	Gain	Hold	Lose	Gain	Hold	Lose	Gain	Hold	Lose	Gain
1979–83	(17)	3	4	1	8	1	0	–	1**	4	–	–	–
1983–87	(16)	5	4	0	5	1	1	1	0	4	–	–	–
1987–92	(23)	3	7	0	12	1	4	–	–	3	–	–	1
1992–97	(17)	0	8	0	8	0	3	–	–	4	–	–	1
1983–97	(56)	8	19	0	25	2	8	1	–	11	–	–	1

*Liberal, 1979–March 1981; Liberal–SDP Alliance, July 1981–87; Liberal Democrat, 1988–97.
**Bruce Douglas-Mann, who was elected as a Labour MP, but resigned to fight a by-election in his seat of Mitcham and Morden as an Independent Social Democrat and lost to the Conservatives.

247

Table 13.2 Summary of by-election voting patterns, 1979–97.

		1979–83 (17)	1983–87 (16)	1987–92 (23)	1992–97 (17)
Mean share of	Conservative	27.1	29.2	22.5	17.3
vote (%)	Labour	37.3	30.1	43.3	51.1
	*Centre	27.2	38.0	18.5	21.6
Mean change in	Conservative	−11.4	−13.9	−11.1	−19.9
vote share	Labour	−10.9	+0.4	−1.0	+7.5
(percentage points)	*Centre	+18.3	+12.3	−0.3	+6.0
Mean vote	Conservative	51.6	55.0	50.7	29.8
retention (%)	Labour	61.1	90.7	74.9	79.0
	*Centre	276.6	133.7	79.8	81.6
Mean swing (%)	Conservative to Labour	0.3	7.1	4.6	13.7
	Conservative to Lib Dem	14.8	13.1	5.4	12.9
	Steed swing (Con/Lab 2-party)	2.7	9.7	6.3	17.7
Mean turnout	Level (%)	56.8	63.4	57.5	53.0
	Change (% pt change)	−14.5	−9.6	−16.9	−23.6

* see first footnote to Table 13.1.

'Change' is measured against the previous general election results in the same constituency.

Liberal Democrats (Newbury, Christchurch, Eastleigh and Littleborough and Saddleworth) and one to the Scottish Nationalists (Perth and Kinross). Labour held the nine seats it defended, everywhere with comfort except in Monklands East, where the Scottish Nationalists reduced Labour's general election majority of 15,712 (43.3 per cent) to 1,640 (4.9 per cent). As in 1987-92, Labour and the Liberal Democrats appeared to be equal beneficiaries of Conservative misfortune, yet there was a qualitative difference to the pattern of voting. First, turnout was substantially lower. Secondly, partly as a result, the Conservative collapse was far more serious. In the three previous parliaments, the Conservative share of the vote fell by an average of 11.4, 11.0 and 13.9 percentage points respectively; in the 1992 parliament it fell by almost twice as much – 19.9 points. Thirdly, ruthless tactical voting by anti-Conservatives was more apparent, although it did not always occur. Finally, Tony Blair's succession as Labour leader in July 1994 heralded a marked improvement in Labour's by-election performance.[5]

The number and cause of by-elections

The number of by-elections held after 1983 was itself significant, marking a further stage in their long-term decline. Between the wars there were on average 18 by-elections a year; the annual frequency fell to 12 between 1945 and 1964 and nine between 1964 and 1979. Thereafter it fell further to 4.1 in 1979–83, 4.0 in 1983–87, 4.8 in 1987–92 and a record low of 3.4 after 1992. One reason was that far fewer MPs were the heirs to hereditary peerages and thus obliged to resign on the death of their father.[6]

Another was that the House of Commons was younger, and thus fewer by-elections arose from the deaths of MPs. The 1959 election, for example, returned 117 MPs over the age of 60; in the 1987 election the number was only 75. But this was only a minor factor: the declining age of MPs has been entirely a Labour phenomenon (reflecting the gradual replacement of older working-class trade unionists by middle-class professionals) while the incidence of by-elections has fallen as much in Conservative as Labour seats. The main reason was that by the 1980s the party whips came to regard by-elections as politically dangerous and to be avoided if at all possible. In the 1950s and 1960s the party whips would put few obstacles in the way of MPs wishing to resign for career or health reasons; indeed they frequently used their influence to appoint MPs to the bench, boardroom and governor's mansion. In the 1980s and 1990s the whips blocked an MP's wish to resign before a general election whenever they could.

The very first by-election of the 1983–87 parliament was a warning of what could go wrong. Mrs Thatcher insisted on elevating William Whitelaw, her loyal deputy prime minister and trouble-shooter, to a hereditary peerage. His far-flung rural constituency of Penrith and the Border was an ultra-safe Conservative seat, which had elected him with a 15,421 majority. In the by-election seven weeks later, his Conservative successor, David Maclean, a Scottish farmer, scraped home with a majority of 552 over a Liberal. There had been no political events since the general election to provoke the 14.8 per cent swing from Conservative to Liberal. The whips concluded that voters resented being foisted with an unnecessary by-election to suit the convenience of the MP (why didn't Whitelaw retire at the general election?) and punished the incumbent party. Thus the overwhelming majority of by-elections after 1983 – 47 out of 56 – were caused by the death of the sitting MP; of the remainder, seven were caused by resignation and two by elevation to the Lords. Moreover, of the seven MPs who resigned, only three – Leon Brittan, Bruce Millan and Neil Kinnock – moved onto posts in the whips' gift (the European Commission, in all three cases); the other four changed career and were beyond the whips' grasp.[7] The impact of the whips is illustrated by a statistical comparison of the causes of by-elections: between 1945 and 1979, 52 per cent were caused by death and 31 per cent by resignation; after 1983, 84 per cent were caused by death and only 13 per cent by resignation (see Table 13.3). (The figures for 1979 onwards are 81 per cent and 14 per cent). Had resignation and elevation to the peerage played as large a role after 1983 as they did in most of the post-war period there would have been an additional 30 to 35 by-elections.

Turnout in by-elections[8]
Turnout is generally lower in by-elections than general elections, reflecting the much lower stakes of the contest, but is generally higher than in local

Table 13.3 Causes of by-elections, 1945–79 and 1979–97.

	1945–79		1979–97		1983–97	
	(N)	(%)	(N)	(%)	(N)	(%)
Death	167	52	59	81	47	84
Resignation	98	31	10	14	7	13
Peerage:						
Succession	8	3	–	–	–	–
Elevation	45	14	3	4	2	4
Other	3	1	1	1	–	–
Total	321	100%	73	100%	56	100%

Note: Percentages total between 99 and 101 due to rounding
Sources: F.W.S. Craig, *Chronology of British parliamentary by-elections, 1833–1987* (Chichester, Sussex: Parliamentary Research Services, 1987); P. Norris, *British by-elections: the volatile electorate* (Oxford: Clarendon Press, 1990), esp. Chapter 1; author's own files.

elections or European elections, reflecting the capacity of all but the most predictable by-elections to attract the focused attention of the national media and politicians. By-election turnout over the whole period averaged 57.9 per cent, 16.6 percentage points below the constituency turnout at the previous general election, which was broadly in line with that for the 1970–83 period (down 13.1 points to 56.6 per cent) but slightly lower than for the 1945–70 period (down 15.2 points to 62.9 per cent).

There was a rough partisan pattern in the variations of turnout. It was higher and fell by less in Conservative seats (down 12.2 points to 66.7 per cent) than Labour seats (down 19.3 points to 49.7 per cent). Perhaps surprisingly, marginality was not a consistent factor: in the eight Conservative seats with a general election majority of under 15 per cent turnout actually fell more sharply (17.0 points) than in the 18 safe Conservative seats (10.1 points). The one constant pattern was the particularly low turnout in Labour's inner city and council estate heartlands. Except where there was locally organized Liberal or Nationalist opposition to Labour-dominated town halls, the inevitability of a Labour win combined with the widespread civic apathy of the poor produced turnouts of below 40 per cent (Tyne Bridge, Knowsley South, Bootle (November 1990), Barking, Dagenham, Newham North East and Hemsworth (February 1996)). But there were marked disparities within categories of seat. Intense coverage by the national media could produce general-election levels of turnout, indirectly by attracting party workers from outside the constituency as well as directly by its impact on the local electorate. In solidly Labour Chesterfield (March 1984), for example, where Tony Benn was seeking to re-enter Parliament after losing his Bristol seat in the 1983 general election, turnout was 4.3 percentage points higher than at the general election. Turnout almost reached general election level in a number of other particularly newsworthy by-elections, such as Brecon and Radnor (down 0.7 points), a three-way marginal in a particularly scenic area of rural Wales; Greenwich (down 0.4 points), a close Labour–SDP contest fought on the issue of 'London's Loony Left'; Mid-Staffordshire (down 1.9 points), a normally safe Conservative seat perceived to be vulnerable to Labour on the issue of the poll tax; and Monklands East (down 3.8 points), where the Scottish Nationalists mobilized deep rooted anti-Catholicism with well-founded allegations of Labour–Catholic nepotism on the local council. Yet in other colourful by-elections, which aroused intense media interest – Newbury (the first post-1992 by-election, where the Liberal Democrats were strong challengers), Perth and Kinross (a traditionally close Conservative–SNP battle), Littleborough and Saddleworth (a three-way marginal), Staffordshire South East (a Conservative marginal, regarded by government and commentators alike as a test of an initial upturn in Conservative fortunes) – the fall in turnout was at or above the average. The media did not invariably mobilise the voters.

These latter by-elections all took place in the 1992–97 parliament. After 1983, by-election turnout was successively lower, and the fall in turnout successively sharper, in each parliament (see Table 13.2). In 1983–87 it averaged 63.4 per cent (down 9.6 points); in 1987–92 it averaged 57.5 per cent (down 16.9 points) and after 1992 it ebbed down further to a mere 53.0 per cent (down 23.6 points).[9] The explanation for this trend is unclear. It is not an artifact of a concentration of by-elections in safe Labour seats: in Conservative seats, by-election turnout fell by 9.8 points in 1983–87 and 10.8 points in 1987–92 but by as much as 18.4 points after 1992. Nor can it be plausibly attributed to a demoralization among Conservative supporters brought on by dismal opinion polls, since the turnout falls were increasingly sharp in Labour seats too, where the same opinion polls might have been expected to buoy up Labour supporters. One can but speculate: perhaps the long recession and constant reports of 'sleaze' made the public increasingly disillusioned with party politics; perhaps the narrowing of ideological differences between the three main parties made voters feel that less was at stake; perhaps it reflected the eroding social basis of partisanship. Whatever the reason, substantially fewer people thought it worth voting in by-elections in the course of the 1983–97 period, especially after 1992.

The fall in turnout in by-elections was commonly cited as a key factor in the result, especially by government sympathizers attempting to explain the loss or near-loss of Conservative seats. A classic instance was the December 1994 by-election in the West Midlands marginal of Dudley West, where Labour took the seat on a huge 29.1 per cent swing – the largest Conservative-to-Labour by-election swing since East Fulham in

1933.[10] The collapse in the Conservative vote from 34,729 (48.8 per cent) to 7,706 (18.7 per cent) was by far the heaviest in any post-1992 by-election.[11] The decline in turnout (from 82.1 per cent to 47.0 per cent) was by far the sharpest in any Conservative by-election seat since 1992. The Conservative party chairman, Jeremy Hanley, predictably put two and two together: 'It was not that people switched in large numbers to the Labour party ... our voters stayed at home. The jury is out.'[12]

Whatever the facts about Dudley West (unknowable without a panel survey), the statistical correlation between the percentage point fall in turnout and the percentage point fall in the Conservative vote in Conservative seats was only a weak +0.2. Poor turnout accompanied relatively good Conservative performances such as Southgate (turnout down 19.0 points; Conservative vote down only 8.5 points) whereas high turnout did not prevent Conservative humiliation in Brecon and Radnor (turnout down 0.7 points; Conservative vote down 20.5 points, and from first to third place) and Mid-Staffordshire (turnout down 1.9 points; Conservative vote down 18.3 points). The connection between turnout and the Conservatives' by-election fortunes was very weak.

The decline in the Conservative vote

The Conservative vote fell at every single by-election. But the degree to which it fell varied hugely. In Paisley North and Paisley South it slipped by a mere 1.3 and 1.0 percentage points respectively. The by-election campaigns coincided with the leadership challenge to Mrs Thatcher and her subsequent resignation, and John Major became the new prime minister the day before polling; the stability of the small Conservative vote was almost certainly an expression of solidarity of a beleaguered minority given fresh hope by the party's change of leader. At the other end of the range, the Conservative share of the vote collapsed by fully 30.4 percentage points in Dudley West and 32.1 percentage points in Christchurch.

How might the variation in the decline of the Conservative vote be best explained? Shifts in turnout, we have seen, had a negligible impact. To what degree did it reflect national variations in the public mood, paralleling trends in the opinion polls? To what degree did it result from a unique combination of local factors, thus signifying little about the national parties' true level of support? Sceptics stressed the latter:

> each by-election appears to be a law unto itself. By-election swings are scattered all over opinion poll graphs. There is no rhyme or reason to them. While talk of tactical voting clearly explains the choice of protest voters, it cannot explain their numbers. A dozen other elements are also at play ... a local school may be opting out; there may have been a swingeing increase in the local water rate; the candidate may wear ghastly shirts; a motorway route may be unpopular. Such factors are suppressed

at a general election, when a government is being selected. But a by-election is Liberty Hall. It can be analysed only by chaos theorists.[13]

Judged in terms of the Conservative vote, the by-election results were not quite that haphazard. For purposes of analysis two measures of the Conservative vote are useful. The first is *per cent decline*: the percentage point change in the Conservative share of the vote between the general election and the by-election. This is the conventional measure and has two drawbacks. First, it ignores turnout and thus does not measure the rate at which the Conservatives held on to their general election vote: a 10 percentage point decline when turnout has plummeted to 40 per cent is much more serious than a 10 percentage point decline when turnout holds steady at 75 per cent. Secondly, the measure is inevitably skewed by a 'floor effect' where Conservative support is weak: since the Conservative share of the vote cannot fall below zero, by-elections in hopeless seats might artificially understate the haemorrhaging of the Conservative vote in by-elections generally. For example, in the post-1992 by-elections the mean drop in the Conservative vote was 19.9 percentage points. But in three by-election seats – Monklands East, Islwyn and Hemsworth – the Conservative vote at the previous general election was already below 21 per cent: even if the Conservative vote in these by elections had fallen to zero (as it almost did in the first two), the average per cent decline for the whole period was spuriously reduced. The second statistic, the Conservative *vote retention rate*, circumvents both problems. It is the Conservative by-election vote (in raw numbers) expressed as a proportion of the Conservative general election vote, and therefore measures the success with which the Conservative party retained its general election vote at the by-election: the lower the rate, the more serious the collapse.[14]

The extent to which the Conservative vote fell in by-elections was not random: as Table 13.4 shows, it was clearly connected with the Conservative government's general popularity at the time, as measured by the national opinion polls. The two statistics of Conservative decline in by-elections correlated 0.67 and 0.68 with 'approval of the Government's record' and 0.66 and 0.64 with 'intention to vote Conservative at the next general election' (the standard opinion poll measure of party preferences). The proportion of the variance in the by-election decline of the Conservative vote that can be explained by the Conservative government's national popularity is the square of the correlation, i.e. in the range of 41 to 46 per cent. The rest of the variance can be attributed to special factors, most of them local. The sceptics are only half right.[15]

Broadly speaking, Conservative fortunes in by-elections moved in tandem with their position in the polls. For example, in July 1988 they held Kensington fairly comfortably, with only a 5.5 point drop in their vote; at the time they were 6 per cent ahead of Labour in the polls, enjoying the

Table 13.4 Correlations of decline in Conservative vote at Conservative-defended by-election seats, 1983–April 1996.

	Per cent decline in Conservative vote[1]	Conservative vote retention rate[1]
Measures of public opinion in same month as by-election		
Intention to vote Conservative at general election[2]	0.66	0.64
Approval of government's record[3]	0.67	0.68
Personal economic optimism[4]	0.56	0.47

Source: 1983–87: monthly Gallup Poll; 1987–96: Gallup 9000, in *Gallup political index*
Notes: 1 For definitions, see text (p. 253).
    2 Per cent answering 'Conservative' to the question: 'If there were a general election tomorrow, which party would you support?'
    3 Per cent answering 'approve' to the question: 'Do you approve or disapprove of the Government's record to date?'
    4 'How do you think the financial situation of your household will change over the next 12 months?' (Per cent saying 'a lot' or 'a little' better *minus* per cent saying 'a lot' or 'a little' worse).

electoral fruits of the Lawson boom. In March 1990 they lost Mid-Staffordshire to Labour with an 18.3 point drop in their vote, but by then the public outcry at the poll tax was at its height and they were trailing Labour by 23.5 per cent in the polls. The Conservative decline in by-elections was usually worse than its decline in the opinion polls – on average by 8 percentage points, a measure of the additional protest effect of by-elections. But there were anomalies: in the three by-elections held on 7 November 1991 the Conservatives retained 79 per cent of their vote in Langbaurgh, 67 per cent in Kincardine but only 35 per cent in Hemsworth. Local factors clearly mattered.

One indicator of those by-elections where special local factors reinforced or (more rarely) counteracted the Conservatives' national popularity at the time is a per cent decline in their vote that was appreciably more (or less) than the 8 percentage points 'protest norm'. These are listed in Table 13.5. Five by-elections registered dramatically larger falls in the Conservative vote, even after taking the national polls and the protest factor into account: Penrith and the Border, Epping Forest, Richmond (Yorkshire), Ribble Valley and Christchurch. As regards Penrith, reference has already been made to voters' possible resentment at having a by-election for Lord Whitelaw's convenience; a similar factor may have been at work in Richmond, where the by-election was caused by the appointment of the sitting MP, Leon Brittan, as a European Commissioner. In addition, in Richmond, like Epping Forest, a 'continuing' SDP candidate as well as a Social and Liberal Democrat contested the seat, possibly attracting

Table 13.5 Unusually 'good' and 'bad' Conservative by-election performances in Conservative-defended seats, 1983–96.

Seat	(a) Change in Conservative support in polls compared with general election	(b) Percentage point decline in Conservative vote share in by-election	'Adjusted' decline in Conservative vote at by-election (a)–(b)
'Bad' performances			
Richmond	−2.3	−24.0	−21.7
Ribble Valley	−2.1	−22.4	−20.3
Epping Forest	−1.2	−21.4	−20.2
Christchurch	−17.4	−32.1	−14.7
Penrith	+1.7	−12.8	−14.5
'Good' performances			
Perth and Kinross	−21.5	−18.8	+2.7
Langbaurgh	−3.8	−2.6	+1.2
Fulham	−11.2	−11.3	+0.1

Note: The percentage decline in the Conservatives' by-election vote share was, on average, 8.1 points worse than its decline in the national polls in the month of the by-election. The standard deviation was 6.2. The table lists those by-elections in which the Conservative decline was greater than our standard deviation, i.e. more than 14.3 points or less than 1.9 points.

Conservative voters who would otherwise have stayed loyal – although the impact of two Centre candidates earlier in Kensington and later in Mid-Staffordshire was quite the opposite. In Ribble Valley, a rural area of owner-occupied cottages and small houses paying low rates, the poll tax hit voters particularly hard and dominated the campaign; moreover the Conservatives were still riding high in the polls under their new leader John Major and after the successful conclusion to the Gulf War. Another anti-tax protest – this time against the 1993 budget's extension of VAT to fuel – probably explains the Conservatives' spectacular collapse in Christchurch, a retirement area with many elderly people paying large fuel bills. It should be stressed that these are the probable explanations; one cannot be sure.[16]

Even more uncertainty surrounds the three seats where the per cent Conservative decline was appreciably less than the national polls combined with the protest factor would have predicted: Fulham, Langbaurgh, and Perth and Kinross. Paradoxically, the Conservatives lost all three seats, but all were marginals and this may partly account for the relative containment of Conservative losses. The Fulham by-election took place when the Conservative campaign against 'London's Loony Left' was having maximum impact (although the Labour candidate, Nick Raynsford, was a conspicuous moderate). The Langbaurgh election took place when the 1992 general election was known to be imminent and voters may have already switched from a by-election to general election frame of reference; the Conservatives might also have benefited from some quiet prejudice against the Asian origins of the Labour candidate. For Perth and Kinross there is no obvious explanation.[17]

The beneficiaries of the Conservative decline

Conservative performance in by-elections broadly paralleled the government's popularity, as measured by the polls. The Opposition parties' performance in by-elections bore much less resemblance to their position in the polls, because there were two main Opposition parties (three in Wales and Scotland) competing for the non-Conservative vote. Which opposition party benefited from the ineluctable decline in the Conservative vote depended on the type of seat. Generally, Labour gained more than the Centre party where it was the clear challenger to the Conservatives, typically in Conservative–Labour marginals in urban England. Similarly, the Centre gained more than Labour where it was the main challenger, typically in suburbia, the resorts, small towns and rural areas. Where both opposition parties were in equal contention, both advanced, although not in equal measure. In Labour seats, the collapse in the Conservative vote tended to help the Centre in English seats and the Nationalists in Scotland and Wales, although the pattern changed after 1994.

This pattern was at its clearest in the 1983–87 parliament. Of the nine Conservative by-election seats, only one was a clear Conservative–Labour seat, Fulham, which Labour gained on a 10.9 per cent swing, with the Centre vote static. Five were safe Conservative seats in which the Alliance had come second, albeit well behind, in 1983: Penrith and the Border, Surrey South West, Enfield Southgate, Ryedale and West Derbyshire. At the by-elections the Centre vote increased sharply in all five and the Labour vote fell further from its low 1983 level except in Derbyshire West (thereby enabling the Conservatives to hold on by 100 votes). In the three other seats – Stafford, Portsmouth South and Brecon and Radnor – the two Opposition parties came almost equal second in 1983 and it was difficult for either to establish the claim of being the true Opposition. At the by-elections both increased their share of the vote although in every case the Centre advanced more that Labour. Exactly why the relative performance of the two Opposition parties differed from one three-party marginal to another depended on local factors. In Brecon and Radnor, where the percentage increase in the Labour vote (9.4 points) almost matched that of the Liberal (11.4 points), the Labour candidate was probably helped by a misleading MORI poll close to the election which showed Labour well ahead.[18] In Portsmouth South, a seat with many naval personnel and defence workers, the Labour candidate was probably handicapped by her support for unilateral nuclear disarmament: her vote rose by 3.9 points whereas the SDP's vote rose by 12.1 points.

In the 1983–87 by-elections the average swing from Conservative to Liberal Democrat (13.1 per cent) was much higher than that from Conservative to Labour (7.1 per cent). In the 1987–92 by-elections, by contrast, they were much the same (4.6 per cent and 5.4 per cent respectively). In 1983–87, the Liberal Democrats established themselves as the main contender in practically every Conservative and Labour seat. But the fragmentation of the Liberal/SDP Alliance in 1987–89, and the modernization of the Labour party under Neil Kinnock enabled Labour to replace the Centre as the main (and successful) challenger in traditional Conservative territory, notably Mid-Staffordshire in March 1990 and Monmouth in May 1991, both constituencies in which the Alliance had pushed Labour into third place in 1983. Not until Eastbourne in October 1990, five months after David Owen had effectively wound up the SDP, did the Liberal Democrats re-establish themselves as the leading challenger in Conservative seats, but then only in those without a Labour presence on the ground.

In the post-1992 by-elections Labour and the Liberal Democrats again appeared to share equal honours in terms of share of the vote (up by 7.2 and 7.1 percentage points respectively) and swing from the Conservatives (14.1 and 14.0 per cent respectively). But these averages mask a much sharper variation in both parties' performance. Each of the seven Conservative seats were lost to whichever party came second in the preceding general election, and in four cases the Opposition party was squeezed to a negligible vote. The Labour vote was reduced to 2.0 per cent in Newbury and 2.7 per cent in Christchurch; the Liberal Democrat drained to 7.6 per cent in Dudley West and, more spectacularly, to 4.7 per cent in Staffordshire South East (where the SDP had come second with 26.7 per cent as recently as 1987). Tony Blair's impact as leader was reflected in Labour's substantially increased share of the vote in Labour seats, something it had very rarely managed in previous by-elections going back to 1979.[19] Blair's success in capturing the Centre ground for his party is well reflected in the changing pattern of Opposition party performance in by-elections after 1994, and Labour's win at Wirral South in February 1997 clearly prefigured the surge in the party's national vote that was to sweep him into office in May 1997.

Part II: The political impact of by-elections since 1983

The political significance of by-elections is typically judged in terms of their record of predicting general election results and of measuring public opinion. By these criteria they fail. Even when held shortly before a general election, they conspicuously mis-forecast its result, whether for the country as a whole or the constituency in question. They are at best a rough measure of the public mood, a measure distorted by the protest opportunity of a by-election and affected by strictly local factors in unpredictable ways; undoubtedly opinion polls provide the superior measure.

Yet these are narrow criteria of significance. Perceptions define reality; if politicians, parties and commentators believe that by-elections matter, then by-elections have political consequences that matter. We may grasp these consequences by seeking answers to two counterfactual questions. First, how would British politics after 1983 have been affected if the by-election results had been different? Secondly, how would they have been affected if no by-elections had been held at all?

Certainly in most cases a different result would have had no lasting consequence. Had the Liberal Democrats won rather than lost the West Derbyshire by-election by 100 votes, the constituency would have been represented by a (surprised) Liberal Democrat for 12 months before it reverted to a Conservative at the general election. Had the SDP not unexpectedly defeated the Conservative in the Portsmouth South by-election, the unfortunate Conservative candidate, Patrick Rock, would have had a promising rather than blighted political career. Otherwise little would have changed: most by-elections have lasting consequences only for individual candidates.

However, a minority of by-elections can alter, or help to alter, the course of British politics, and the institution of by-elections shapes important elements of the political structure. This argument is best expressed as a series of propositions, supported by evidence from the period since 1983.

By-elections affect the timing of elections

Prime ministers time general elections to maximize their party's chance of re-election and they scrutinize all the evidence available, including by-elections, in arriving at their decision. No by-election after 1983 played as decisive a role as the January 1966 Hull North by-election did in persuading Harold Wilson to dissolve parliament, then only in its fifteenth month. Mrs Thatcher relied on private polling and the May local election results, not on by-elections, in calling general elections for June 1983 and June 1987, in each case a year earlier than required.

But two by-elections influenced John Major. He was anxious to dissolve parliament sooner rather than later, because he felt that only victory at a general election could legitimis his succession as prime minister and entrench his position as party leader. An opportunity presented itself in March 1991, after victory in the Gulf War and when the national polls showed his government a few points ahead; but he backed off after the Conservatives' humiliating loss of Ribble Valley, a by-election held only a week after victory in the Gulf War yet fought almost wholly on the issue of poll tax. There was another opportunity in the summer, but the loss to Labour in mid-May of Monmouth, where the NHS was the dominant issue, as well as the disappointing local election results, persuaded him that the Conservatives' recovery in the polls was too fragile to risk a khaki election. A strong Conservative performance in Ribble Valley and Monmouth, or the absence of by-elections altogether, would almost certainly have led to a snap election in spring or summer 1991.

By-elections affect the position of party leaders

By-election defeats demoralize parties and may be blamed by activists and MPs on the policies or personality of the party leader. In a divided party, factions opposed to the party leadership seize on by-election losses to spread dissension. After Labour was crushed in its impregnable inner London fiefdom of Bermondsey by the Liberals in February 1983, Michael Foot's leadership came under sharp and semi-public attack from the Labour Right who were exasperated by his ineffectual handling of the selection of the hard-Left Peter Tatchell as the Labour candidate. Foot was rescued by the Darlington by-election a month later, which Labour held against expectations, helped partly by a conspicuously weak SDP candidate (though Labour then lost Darlington as well as Bermondsey at the general election). By-election defeats also put John Major's leadership under pressure, although public criticism from Conservatives was usually coded. Conservative MPs attributed the loss of Newbury to Britain's bungled membership and sudden departure from the ERM, for which they publicly blamed the Chancellor of the Exchequer, Norman Lamont, even though he was carrying out his prime minister's policy. Lamont did not help himself by declaring 'Je ne regrette rien' at a Newbury campaign press conference; three weeks after the by-election, Major dismissed him from the cabinet to satisfy the critics. The defeat at Christchurch was pinned on the Conservative party chairman, Sir Norman Fowler, but 'it was conceded by some critics that the 'real' target was the Prime Minister; it was only a matter of time before they turned their fire on him'.[20] After the Conservatives' landslide defeat at Dudley West, critics were bolder, with leading backbenchers on the Right calling in chorus for 'a return to true Conservative policies', a thinly disguised call for a change of leader.[21]

The most notable victim of by-election defeats was Margaret Thatcher. The circumstances leading to her resignation as prime minister in November 1990 were complex, but the by-elections at Eastbourne on 18 October and Bradford North on 8 November were crucial.[22] In 1990 the mood on the Conservative backbenches changed. Numerous Conservative MPs, especially in marginal seats, believed for the first time since being elected that the government would go down at the general election and they with it. The government's showing in the polls in 1990 was its worst since Margaret Thatcher became prime minister in 1979. In March and April the Labour lead rose to 24 per cent, a margin corroborated by its stunning by-election victory in March in Mid-Staffordshire. Conservative MPs blamed the poll tax demands that hit voters' doormats that spring and noted Margaret Thatcher's resolute commitment to continuing with the tax. Their slight encouragement from the Conservatives' better than expected performance in some London borough elections and from a small recovery in the polls was dashed by the two by-elections. Eastbourne proved that the Liberal Democrats were still a threat where they had local strength; Bradford North was equally dispiriting because, although a Labour seat, the Conservatives were relegated to third place in a seat they had actually won in 1983. Conservative MPs returning to Westminster from a spot of canvassing – especially Northern MPs helping in the Bradford North campaign – were convinced that Mrs Thatcher as well as the poll tax was the problem: on the doorsteps the two were inextricably linked. To win the next election, many believed, they would have to get rid of both. Without the doorstep evidence of the two by-election campaigns fewer Conservative MPs would have voted for Heseltine in the first round of the leadership election and thus triggered the sequence of events that led to Mrs Thatcher's resignation.

By-elections affect parliamentary party management
Whenever the government loses a by-election its parliamentary majority is reduced by two. The smaller its majority at the general election, the more vulnerable it is to by-election losses. Since 1983, as this chapter has shown, by-elections have put every government seat, however safe, at risk. As a result government whips have engineered a sharp decline in the number of by-elections in government-held seats (see pp. 248–9); even so, compared with the earlier post-war period, a government now needs to be elected with a larger overall majority in the Commons to be sure of surviving a full parliament, let alone passing its measures without being in thrall to maverick backbenchers. The overall majority of 21 with which the Conservatives were re-elected in 1992 was considered a modest but sufficient majority for a full parliament; in the event the seven by-election losses (plus three backbench defections) reduced that majority to one within four years. From the spring of 1996 the government's overall majority depended entirely on actuarial luck. Had the post-1983 rate of by-election losses applied to earlier parliaments, the Churchill government elected in 1951 would have seen its overall majority of 17 disappear within three years and the Heath government of 1970 would have seen its majority of 30 dwindle to single figures had it lasted into a fifth year.

A small Commons majority now makes the management of government business in parliament much more difficult. Disproportionate concessions can be extracted by a handful of backbenchers, who may bear personal as well as ideological grudges against the government, and by the small Opposition parties who have different priorities and may not even be committed to government by Westminster. A desperate MP can successfully threaten resignation – and thus a by-election.[23] The divisions over Europe would probably have plagued the 1992 Conservative government whatever its majority, given the association of European issues with Thatcherism and the ignominious departure from the ERM in September 1992; but the government's diminishing majority in the Commons undoubtedly exacerbated the whips' problems and made it impossible for them to impose a consistent policy.

By-elections can affect party policy

Most by-elections are mid-term referendums on the government's record, which generally means its economic record; few by-election campaigns are dominated by a specific issue and in even fewer does the result turn on one. When they do, the government can respond in three ways. First, it can plough on regardless. The Christchurch by-election was dominated by the unpopularity of the 1993 budget's extension of VAT to domestic fuel but the government made no concessions.[24] Secondly, the government can redouble its efforts to present a policy in a more favourable light. The main issue at the Monmouth by-election was the reform of the NHS; smarting from what it believed to be blatant misrepresentation by the Labour party, it proceeded with the reforms but overhauled its public relations on the Health Service. Finally, the government can change policy. The commitment to reform the poll tax by all three contenders for the Conservative leadership after Mrs Thatcher's resignation was influenced by the by-election defeats in Mid-Staffordshire and Eastbourne; Michael Heseltine's decision, as the responsible minister in John Major's government, to return to a property-based rather than per capita tax was a direct response to the Ribble Valley result in March 1991. Opinion polls, riots and non-payment all made clear the public's antipathy to the poll tax, but it was the electoral evidence of the by-elections that pressured the government into abandoning the policy.

By-elections are particularly important for the minor parties

In the British electoral system minor parties live and die by their credibility as election winners.[25] Between general elections their only media coverage is at their annual conference (where it is as likely to be critical as favourable), after the annual local elections (if they performed well) and during by-elections. For minor parties by-elections are an intermittent oxygen pump of publicity and credibility, without which they would be invisible to all but a small, politically aware, minority. Success at by-elections raises party morale, boosts party membership and leads to a surge of support at the polls; disappointment in by-elections has the reverse effect.

During the 1983–87 parliament, the Liberal/SDP Alliance used by-elections in their claim to be the 'real' opposition to the Conservatives. At the 1983 general election it had taken second place in two thirds (262 out of 397) of the Conservative seats and come only 2.2 percentage points behind Labour in the national share of the vote. By winning or taking second place in every Conservative by-election seat other than Fulham the Alliance convinced not only itself but the two major parties and many in the media that it had a real prospect of electoral breakthrough in the 1987 election. Its gain at Greenwich and comfortable re-election in Truro in quick succession in early 1987 produced strategic reappraisals in both main parties; in the Conservatives' case the party chairman, Norman Tebbit, went onto the offensive with the (traditional) warning that a vote for the Alliance would allow Labour to win through the backdoor. During the disintegration of the Liberal–SDP Alliance in 1987–88, by-elections became the chief battleground between the rival claimants for the inheritance of the Centre vote – the Liberal Democrats (briefly called the Social and Liberal Democrats) led by Paddy Ashdown and the continuing SDP under David Owen. In Kensington (July 1988) and Epping Forest (December 1988) the SDP took almost one-third of the combined Centre vote and in Richmond (February 1989) it took three-fifths; moreover, the Epping Forest and Richmond results suggested that a single Centre candidate could have won the seat. This encouraged tentative discussions between the two parties about a new electoral pact; only when they failed did voters punish rival Centre candidates with derisory votes in the Vale of Glamorgan (May 1989) and Glasgow Central (June 1989). A creditable performance by the Liberal Democrats in Vauxhall (June 1989), where the SDP did not stand, and a four-to-one split of the (much reduced) Centre vote in the Liberal Democrats' favour in Mid-Staffordshire in March 1990 convinced Ashdown that his party would eventually see the SDP off. In the Bootle by-election of May 1990 the SDP candidate polled a derisory 155 votes, coming well behind an independent Liberal (474 votes) and, even more embarrassingly, a 'Monster Raving Loony' candidate (418 votes). Bootle proved what previous by-elections were increasingly suggesting: the SDP had lost its battle with the Liberal Democrats and had no future. David Owen promptly announced that he was winding up the party.

The nationalist parties in Scotland and Wales are equally dependent for their credibility on by-elections. They made their post-war parliamentary breakthrough in the late 1960s through by-election victories, Plaid Cymru in Carmarthen in July 1966 and the SNP in Hamilton in November 1967. Unlike the Liberal Democrats, however, they are at the mercy of by-election geography. There were no by-elections in Wales between 1979 and 1983 and none in Scotland between 1983 and 1987. The Scottish Nationalists' capture of Glasgow Govan from Labour (scene of an earlier SNP triumph 15 years earlier) re-established their electoral credibility after a long fallow period as Scotland's fourth party following the failure of the devolution referendum in March 1979. Thereafter the SNP became a contender with the Conservatives as Scotland's second party and the only serious opposition in Labour's extensive Scottish heartlands.[26] Its capacity to outflank Labour as the defender of Scottish interests against an English Tory government pushed Labour towards a devolutionist position. After the 1992 general election, when the SNP vote rose to 21.5 per cent (despite winning only three seats and losing Govan back to Labour) the Labour party formally committed itself to a tax-raising Scottish parliament, subject to referendum. Labour had embraced devolution before, notably during the Callaghan government of 1976–79; but then many Scottish Labour MPs were opposed. This time the policy commanded virtually united and often passionate support. Scotland's experience under an increasingly centralized Conservative government was part of the reason; but the SNP's electoral strength, demonstrated in by-elections, was also responsible. In Wales, as in Scotland, the Nationalists filled the vacuum left by the collapse of the Alliance after 1987. In industrial Wales it became the preferred party of protest against Labour hegemony at the expense of the Conservatives who suffered as the party of government and of the Centre, who were divided. Plaid Cymru jumped from fourth to a (still distant) second place in Pontypridd (February 1989) and Neath (April 1991). Although a far less serious threat to Labour than the Nationalists were in Scotland, the Labour party's gradual acceptance of an elected assembly for Wales was a response to Plaid Cymru's modest but growing strength, as revealed in by-elections.

By-elections affect parliamentary recruitment

The media spotlight focuses on by-election candidates much more than on parliamentary candidates at a general election, let alone candidates in local or European elections. As a result the selection of the candidate, although formally in the hands of the local party, is increasingly subject to influence from the national office, including direct intervention to preclude anyone headquarters considers undesirable. The characteristics of by-election MPs have been affected in three ways. First, Conservative candidates in Conservative seats have been political heavyweights. The eight Conservative candidates elected at by-elections since 1983 comprise (in August 1996) three cabinet ministers (Virginia Bottomley, William Hague and Michael Portillo), one junior minister (David Maclean), one ex-junior minister (Steven Norris),[27] one whip (Patrick McLoughlin) and one leading backbencher (the campaigning Eurosceptic, Bill Cash). Secondly, the Labour party has excluded left-wingers. After 1983 candidates of the radical or Marxist Left came to be regarded as electoral liabilities by Labour headquarters. The hero of the Labour Left, Tony Benn, contested Chesterfield; the Labour vote slipped a further 1.6 percentage points from its already low level at the 1983 general election, despite Labour's 11-point recovery in the national polls. In February 1987, the Labour leadership blamed its defeat at Greenwich on the far Left views of the Labour candidate, Deirdre Wood, a former GLC councillor with apparent sympathies for the IRA and PLO. After 1987 every Labour by-election candidate was loyal to the party leadership. Thirdly, by-elections have brought proportionately more women into Parliament than a general election does. Women made up 24 per cent of the by-election winners (13 out of 54), which compares favourably with their 9 per cent share of all MPs elected in 1992 and their 15 per cent share of newly elected MPs in 1992. There is no obvious explanation.[28]

By-elections affect parties' electoral management

By-elections influence the timing of elections and the selection of parliamentary candidates. The involvement of party headquarters makes them a campaign laboratory for the general election. Much of the new technology of campaigning has had its first outing in by-elections.[29] For example, in 1985–86 the SDP invested in the development of computer-based differential direct mailing to electors, angled according to the social group being targeted. The technique had its first outing in Tyne Bridge in December 1985 and a full dress rehearsal in Greenwich in February 1987, where it appeared to be highly effective. Throughout the post-1983 period, the Centre parties used by-elections to refine their (sometimes dubious) methods for encouraging tactical voting by supporters of the weaker of the major parties in the constituency. In Littleborough and Saddleworth, a Conservative–Liberal Democrat marginal, the Labour party, under the direction of Peter Mandelson, tested a new tactic for resisting the tactical squeeze: blatantly tendentious attacks on the Liberal Democrat, reminiscent of the 'negative advertising' techniques fashionable in the United States. Many in the Labour party were left uneasy; yet the result suggested that dirty-tricks campaigning of this kind had some success.

Conclusion

The by-elections held since 1983 confirmed, if any confirmation were needed, that the results were meaningless as predictors of the general election that followed. By-elections differ markedly from general elections as electoral institutions – in the outcome at stake, in the attention of the media and thus in voters' frame of reference. As a result, the incentive for protest and tactical voting is much stronger and the government always suffers, sometimes spectacularly, only to recover at the general election. Commentators interpret the results to excess while politicians are unduly depressed or buoyed up.

Yet by-elections matter for British politics. They do not make or break governments, but as the post-1983 period shows, they can make or break politicians, including the prime minister, and shape the outer contours of the party system. Their effect on government policy is rare but can be decisive. Their impact on party morale is profound, with consequences for internal party management and organization. In the river of British politics most by-elections are mere pebbles; but among them are rocks that capsize the canoeists and the occasional boulder that alters the course of the flow.

Notes

1 'Meaningless Monmouth', *The Times*, 16 May 1991.

2 This chapter excludes Northern Ireland, because its politics and party system are so different from the rest of the United Kingdom. There were 17 by-elections in the province during the period, 15 of them resulting from the concerted resignation of all Protestant MPs in December 1985 against the Anglo–Irish Agreement. In the quasi-referendum of 23 January 1986, the Protestant community's hostility was made clear: all the MPs were comfortably re-elected except for James Nicholson, who lost the highly marginal Newry and Armagh to Seamus Mallon of the SDLP. The death of Harold McCusker, the Ulster Unionist MP for Upper Bann, led to a by-election on 17 May 1990 at which the Ulster Unionist's David Trimble was elected; he was to become leader of the party in 1995. The death of Sir James Kilfedder, the independent Unionist for Down North led to a by-election on 16 June 1995, which was won on a low turnout by another independent Unionist, Robert McCartney, standing against an official Unionist.

3 A minor qualification to this general law of by-elections is that in seats that change hands the swing at the following general election deviates appreciably from the national average. For example, in 1987 the average decline in the Conservatives' vote was 5.1 percentage points in the four by-election seats they lost, compared with 0.1 points in the five by-election seats they held and 0.2 points in Great Britain as a whole. In 1992 the average decline in the Conservatives' vote was 2.0 percentage points in the seven by-election seats they lost compared with 0.5 points in Great Britain as a whole. In the four Conservative by-election seats lost to Labour the Conservative–to–Labour swing averaged 5.4 per cent, compared with the 2.5 per cent mean for the country as a whole. In the three Conservative by-elections lost to the Liberal Democrats the Conservative–to–Liberal Democrat swing averaged 7.5 per cent, compared with the 2.5 per cent mean in the opposite direction in Great Britain as a whole. The general tendency for by-election results to have a distinctive impact on the following general election result in the constituency is analyzed in detail in S. J. Stray and M. S. Silver, *Do by-elections demonstrate a government's unpopularity?*, 33 (3), pp. 264–70, 1980; and G. J. G. Upton, 'The impact of by-elections on general elections: England, 1950–87', *British Journal of Political Science*, 21 (1), January 1991, pp. 108–18.

4 Andrew Marr, 'Newbury will be a non-event, unless ...', *The Independent*, 4 May 1993.

5 There was an anticipatory Blair effect. John Smith died in May 1994 and Tony Blair was elected in July 1994. Both the manner of the election and the widespread expectation that Blair would win appears to have boosted Labour's vote in the five by-elections (and European elections) that occurred during the interregnum on 9 June 1994.

6 The option of renouncing a hereditary peerage was only available after Anthony Wedgwood Benn's successful by-election campaign on the issue in 1963.

7 Eric Varley (Labour, Chesterfield), the Secretary of State for Energy and then for Industry in the 1974–79 Labour government, resigned in 1983, after Labour's

massive defeat, for a new career in industry; Matthew Parris (Conservative, Derbyshire West) resigned in 1986 for a career in journalism; Stuart Holland (Labour, Vauxhall), academic economist and author of the Bennite economic strategy of the early 1980s, resigned in disillusion in 1989 for a career in research consultancy; and the shadow minister Bryan Gould (Labour, Dagenham), increasingly isolated in John Smith's Labour party, quit politics in 1994 for a vice-chancellorship in New Zealand.

8 In this and the next section I am indebted for many of my ideas to Pippa Norris, *British by-elections: the volatile electorate* (Oxford: Clarendon Press, 1990).

9 By-election turnout in 1979–83 averaged 56.8 per cent (down 14.5 points). The 1983–87 parliament is therefore arguably an artificially high start point for analysis of trends.

10 The Conservative to Labour swing in the February 1935 Liverpool Wavertree by-election was 35.0 per cent, but this by-election is not comparable because an Independent Conservative split the Conservative vote.

11 In Christchurch the percentage point fall in the Conservative share of the vote was slightly larger (32.1 points) than in Dudley West (30.4 points) but from a higher base; the *proportional* loss was considerably worse in Dudley West.

12 'Poll misery puts Tories in a panic', The *Guardian*, 17 December 1994.

13 Simon Jenkins, 'Ashdown's empty victory', *The Times*, 5 May 1993.

14 This does not mean that all Conservative voters at the by-election necessarily voted Conservative at the previous general election: a minority will have voted for other parties or not voted at all; some will have been too young to vote or have lived in a different constituency. A third measure of the decline in the Conservative vote is *proportional vote loss*, the Conservative percentage share of the by-election vote expressed as a proportion of the Conservative percentage share of the general election vote. Unlike *vote retention rate* this measure does not take account of changes in turnout and did not prove particularly useful in analyses of the results. All three measures suffer from one drawback: they are affected by the baseline established at the previous general election. This drawback is negligible for changes in Conservative support between 1983 and 1996 because the general election baselines barely changed; but it matters more for measures of change in Labour and Centre party support. Between 1983 and 1992 the general election baselines rose on average by 7 percentage points for Labour and fell on average by 8 percentage points for the Centre.

15 Attempts to model statistically the by-election decline in the government party's support are notable for their weak results. See, for example, Anthony Mughan, 'Toward a political explanation of government vote losses in mid-term by-elections', *American Political Science Review*, 80 (3), September 1986, pp. 761–75.

16 One possibility is that the additional protest vote encouraged by by-elections will be magnified when traditional *Conservative* supporters are particularly disenchanted with their government and dampened when they are particularly supportive. This can be roughly measured by the extent to which the proportion saying they intend to vote Conservative exceeds the proportion saying they 'approve of the (Conservative) government': the bigger the gap, the larger the number of angry Conservatives. There was no overall association between the size of the gap and the Conservatives' 'good' and 'bad' by-elections, but it is worth noting that two of their 'bad' by-elections, Ribble Valley and Christchurch, occurred when the gap was much larger than normal.

17 It cannot be explained by the technicality that the Conservatives won the seat with only 40 per cent of the vote and thus had a smaller proportion of the vote 'at risk'.

An equivalent analysis based on proportional vote loss produces a very similar list of 'bad' and 'good' results for the Conservatives; Perth and Kinross remains on the 'good' list.

18   The MORI poll, published in the *Daily Mirror* on the day before the election, gave Labour an 18-point lead. In the event, the Liberal won by 1.4 points over Labour. For an account of why the MORI poll was inaccurate, see R. M. Worcester, 'Brecon: how we got it wrong', *The Times*, 17 August 1985.

19   For example, in the one Labour-defended by-election when John Smith was leader, Rotherham, Labour's share of the vote fell from 63.9 to 55.6 per cent and the Liberal Democrats' rose from 8.8 to 29.7 per cent. In the three East End by-elections (in Barking, Dagenham and Newham North East) held a month later, after John Smith's death and when Blair was widely expected to be the new leader, the mean percentage point change in the vote was Labour: +18.9, Liberal: −4.2.

20   Anthony Bevins, 'Tories target Fowler as scapegoat for defeat', The *Independent*, 31 July 1993.

21   The critics included the former minister, Sir Rhodes Boyson; the recent member of the 1922 Executive, Sir George Gardiner; the Eurosceptic Teresa Gorman; and the chairman of the backbench finance committee, John Townend. See S. Bates, 'Poll misery puts Tories in a panic', The *Guardian*, 17 December 1994.

22   For accounts of Mrs. Thatcher's downfall, see B. Anderson, *John Major: The making of the prime minister* (London: Fourth Estate, 1991) and A. Watkins, *A Conservative coup* (London: Duckworth, 1991).

23   The Conservative member for Reigate, Sir George Gardiner, a Eurosceptic and persistent critic of John Major, was de-selected by the executive committee of his association in June 1996. After threatening to resign his seat and provoke a by-election – which the Conservatives would almost certainly have lost – the Conservative whips successfully put pressure on the local association to readopt him. He was eventually de-selected, joined the Referendum Party and fought the May 1997 election for them.

24   The second stage of the extension, introduced in the 1994 budget, was defeated by a Conservative backbench rebellion in the Commons in December 1994, but the rebels were more influenced by their own constituents than by the Christchurch result.

25   This proposition is convincingly argued in P. Norris, 'By-elections: their importance in Britain', *Contemporary Record*, 4 (2), November 1990, pp. 19–21.

26   In Glasgow Central (June 1989) the SNP jumped from fourth to second place, raising its vote share from 10 to 30 per cent, at the equal expense of Labour and the Liberal Democrats; in the twin by-elections at Paisley (November 1990) the SNP made the same jump, increasing its vote share from 12.9 to 29.4 per cent in Paisley North and from 14.0 to 27.5 per cent in Paisley South.

27   Norris was returning to Parliament. He was elected for Oxford East in 1983 but lost the seat in 1987.

28   The well-known tendency for women to have a better chance of selection in seats that are normally difficult to win is not the explanation: most of the women Labour MPs returned at by-elections were elected in safe Labour seats.

29   See K. Swaddle, 'Ancient and modern: innovations in electioneering at the constituency level', in I. Crewe and M. Harrop, (eds) *Politial Communications: the general election campaign of 1987* (Cambridge: Cambridge University Press, 1989), pp. 29–40.

APPENDIX A

The results of contested by-elections

The following is a list of all contested by-elections from 1919 to the general election of 1 May 1997, excluding only Irish, University and double-Member constituencies. Irish seats (1919–22) and Ulster seats (from 1923) are not comparable because of the different structure of parties; University seats and double-Member seats are not comparable because of different voting systems. Nor were any of these categories in themselves a continuous run of comparable results covering the whole period of the book. The seats excluded are listed in chronological order on pp. 298–9.

For actual numbers of votes cast, for an explanation of party allegiances and for the results of succeeding general elections, information can be found in F. W. S. Craig's *British parliamentary election results, 1918–1970*, 2 vols. (1969, 1971), and *Britain votes 1974–88*, 2 vols. (1980, 1988). In the following table, only official Labour, Conservative and Liberal candidates are listed in these columns. Coalition Liberals (1918–23), National Liberals (1931–45), National candidates (1931–45), Scottish and Welsh Nationalists, Communists and all minor party candidates or Independents are list as 'Others'. Where the votes of more than one candidate are aggregated in the 'Others' column, a superior numeral shows the actual number of other candidates. Where a seat changed hands at the by-election, it is marked *, and where the by-election was a second contest in the same seat in a single Parliament it is marked †.

All swing figures are calculated between Conservative and Labour candidates only, a plus figure being a swing to Conservative and a minus figure being a swing to Labour. Whenever Conservative and Labour were not first *and* second at both the preceding general election and at the by-election, the swing figure is printed in italics.

Butler swing (also called 'conventional swing') is calculated from the mean shares of total votes cast at the preceding general election and at the by-election which were cast for Conservative and Labour candidates. *Steed swing* (also called 'two-party swing') is calculated from the mean shares of the Conservative and Labour votes cast at the preceding general election and at the by-election which were cast for the Conservative and Labour candidates.

It is possible, and relatively easy, to calculate a Butler swing between any two parties that contested both the preceding general election and the by-election, from the figures printed below. This is done using the following formula:

Where X_1 is the percentage gained by X at the preceding general election, X_2 the percentage gained by X at the by-election, Y_1 the percentage gained by Y at the preceding general election, and Y_2, the percentage gained by Y at the by-election:

$$\text{Percentage swing from } X \text{ to } Y = \frac{(X_1 - X_2) + (Y_2 - Y_1)}{2} \text{ per cent.}$$

For example, at Manchester Rusholme on 7 October 1919 the swing from Conservative to Liberal was:

$$\frac{(65.1 - 47.7) + (19.1 - 19.3)}{2} = 8.6 \text{ per cent.}$$

In the same by-election the swing from Labour to Liberal was:

$$\frac{(15.6 - 31.2) + (19.1 - 19.3)}{2} = -7.9 \text{ per cent.}$$

Previous General Election					By-Election and Date	By-Election Result					Swing to Con.	
Con. %	Lab. %	Lib. %	Others %	Turnout %		Con. %	Lab. %	Lib. %	Others %	Turnout %	Butler	Steed
67.4	32.6	–	–	55.1	Liverpool, West Derby — 26 Feb 19	56.5	43.5	–	–	34.3	–10.9	–10.9
67.5	–	32.6	–	49.9	*Leyton, West — 1 Mar 19	42.7	–	57.3	–	42.5	–	–
80.1	–	19.9	–	54.9	*Kingston-upon-Hull, Central — 29 Mar 19	47.2	–	52.8	–	51.9	–	–
52.6	–	47.4	–	47.3	*Aberdeenshire, Central & Kincardine — 16 Apr 19	36.1	26.4	37.5	–	50.2	–	–
–	36.4	–	63.6	64.1	Swansea, East — 10 July 19	–	46.9	–	53.1	64.0	–	–
50.9	49.1	–	–	69.2	*Lanarks., Bothwell — 16 July 19	–	68.8	–	31.2	71.9	–	–
59.6	40.5	–	–	63.0	*Lancs., Widnes — 30 Aug 19	47.7	52.3	–	–	71.1	–11.8	–11.8
–	37.1	–	62.9	45.6	Yorks., Pontefract — 6 Sep 19	–	46.0	–	54.0	61.5	–	–
65.1	15.6	19.3	–	62.9	Manchester, Rusholme — 7 Oct 19	45.7	31.2	19.1	4.0	67.5	–17.5	–21.2
Unop.	Unop.	–	–	–	Durham, Chester-le-Street — 13 Nov 19	–	77.1	–	23.0	63.7	–	–
71.8	28.2	–	–	55.0	Croydon, South — 14 Nov 19	55.2	–	44.8	–	45.5	–	–
Unop.	–	–	–	–	Kent, Isle of Thanet — 15 Nov 19	57.9	–	42.1	–	52.8	–	–
66.0	20.6	13.5	–	59.7	Plymouth, Sutton — 15 Nov 19	51.9	33.3	14.8	–	72.5	–13.4	–15.3
Unop.	–	–	–	–	Herts., St Albans — 10 Dec 19	45.8	42.4	11.8	–	62.8	–	–
79.5	–	20.5	–	52.0	Bromley — 17 Dec 19	52.5	47.5	–	–	48.9	–	–
–	44.4	–	55.6	49.4	Yorks., Spen Valley — 20 Dec 19	–	39.4	33.8	26.8	76.5	–	–
58.3	–	–	41.7	68.4	Ashton-under-Lyne — 31 Jan 20	43.2	39.6	17.1	–	82.3	–	–
–	–	–	Unop.	–	*Shrops., Wrekin — 7 Feb 20	–	38.4	–	61.6[2]	71.0	–	–
–	33.5	34.0	32.5	57.6	Paisley — 12 Feb 20	12.5	39.1	48.4	–	77.6	–	–
54.3	–	45.7	–	68.2	Lincs., Horncastle — 25 Feb 20	44.5	18.8	36.7	–	77.1	–	–
–	–	–	100.0[2]	52.0	Argyll — 10 Mar 20	–	35.0	–	65.0	50.2	–	–
36.1	28.6	–	71.4	47.9	*Kent, Dartford — 27 Mar 20	15.6	50.1	16.8	17.5[2]	61.3	–	–
64.1	–	–	63.9	36.5	Camberwell, N.-West — 31 Mar 20	–	32.1	23.0	44.9	47.9	–	–
–	35.9	–	–	55.2	Hants., Basingstoke — 31 Mar 20	44.2	27.8	28.0	–	60.0	–5.9	–2.7
–	37.4	62.7	–	62.5	Northampton — 1 Apr 20	–	44.4	–	55.6	67.2	–	–
63.0	–	37.0	–	53.0	Edinburgh, North — 9 Apr 20	44.8	17.1	38.1	–	62.3	–	–

271

Previous General Election					By-Election and Date	By-Election Result					Swing to Con.	
Con. %	Lab. %	Lib. %	Others %	Turnout %		Con. %	Lab. %	Lib. %	Others %	Turnout %	Butler	Steed
75.0	—	25.0	—	61.8	Edinburgh, South — 9 Apr 20	57.8	—	42.3	—	59.3	—	—
54.5	—	45.5	—	60.3	*Lincs., Louth — 3 June 20	42.7	—	57.3	—	63.1	—	—
—	62.0	38.0	—	52.3	Nelson & Colne — 17 June 20	30.1	49.6	20.4	—	65.2	—	—
—	35.7	64.3	—	55.8	*Norfolk, South — 27 July 20	—	45.7	19.8	34.5	58.5	—	—
55.9	—	44.2	—	51.0	Suffolk, Woodbridge — 28 July 20	53.2	46.8	—	—	61.4	—	—
60.8	19.5	13.7	—	58.3	Ilford — 25 Sep 20	54.4	22.9	22.7	—	66.2	-7.9	-7.1
—	—	—	Unop.	—	†Shrops., Wrekin — 20 Nov 20	—	42.1	—	57.9	78.3	—	—
—	Unop.	—	—	—	Mon., Abertillery — 21 Dec 20	—	66.4	—	33.6	70.8	—	—
—	Unop.	—	—	—	Rhondda, West — 21 Dec 20	41.5	58.5	—	—	70.2	—	—
75.8	24.2	—	—	54.6	Herefs., Hereford — 11 Jan 21	56.6	—	43.4	—	62.5	—	—
68.7	—	31.3	—	46.6	*Kent, Dover — 12 Jan 21	43.7	—	—	56.3	71.0	—	—
—	—	—	Unop.	—	Cardiganshire — 18 Feb 21	—	—	42.7	57.3	80.1	—	—
—	Unop.	—	—	—	*Woolwich, East — 2 Mar 21	51.3	48.7	—	—	78.5	-10.8	-10.8
60.2	39.9	—	—	60.4	*Dudley — 3 Mar 21	49.3	50.7	—	—	79.9	—	—
—	—	—	Unop.	—	*Kirkcaldy Burghs — 4 Mar 21	—	53.4	—	46.6	65.6	—	—
36.2	24.4	39.4	—	58.4	*Yorks., Penistone — 5 Mar 21	—	36.2	33.7	30.1	71.7	-11.3	-11.3
72.4	27.6	—	—	60.4	Somerset, Taunton — 8 Apr 21	61.1	39.0	—	—	73.5	—	—
Unop.	—	—	—	—	Worcs., Bewdley — 19 Apr 21	89.6	—	10.4	—	63.8	—	—
—	—	—	100.0[2]	45.2	Beds., Bedford — 23 Apr 21	—	40.3	—	59.7	73.3	-11.3	-7.7
75.9	24.1	—	—	59.2	Hastings — 4 May 21	54.7	24.5	19.9	—	78.0	—	—
Unop.	—	—	—	—	Cumberland, Penrith & Cockermouth — 13 May 21	50.1	—	49.9	—	74.0	—	—
90.2	—	9.8	—	39.9	*Westminster, St George's — 7 June 21	42.5	—	—	57.5	39.8	—	—
—	32.4	—	67.6	52.2	*Lancs., Heywood & Radcliffe — 8 June 21	—	41.7	17.6	40.7	80.9	—	—
—	9.1	—	90.9[2]	57.4	Herts., Hertford — 16 June 21	31.1	—	—	69.0	55.2	—	—
—	54.8	45.2	—	64.0	Glam., Caerphilly — 24 Aug 21	—	54.3	—	45.7[2]	73.2	—	—
Unop.	—	—	—	—	Westminster, Abbey — 25 Aug 21	43.6	—	21.5	34.9	38.5	—	—
Unop.	—	—	—	—	Lewisham, West — 13 Sep 21	39.0	—	25.6	35.4	59.3	—	—

Constituency	Date												
†Lincs., Louth	22 Sep 21	54.5	–	45.5	–	60.3	38.3	19.5	42.2	–	72.1	–	–
Lancs., Westhoughton	5 Oct 21	–	63.9	36.1	–	61.6	–	57.8	–	42.2	84.7	–	–
Hornsey	10 Nov 21	Unop.	–	–	–	–	53.4	–	46.6	–	65.7	–	–
*Southwark, South-East	14 Dec 21	–	27.4	–	72.6	36.1	–	57.0	–	43.0[2]	38.5	–	–
Warwicks., Tamworth	17 Jan 22	Unop.	–	–	–	–	68.8	31.2	–	–	60.0	–	–
*Manchester, Clayton	18 Feb 22	61.6	38.4	–	–	57.5	43.0	57.1	–	–	73.7	–18.7	–18.7
*Camberwell, North	20 Feb 22	58.0	21.0	21.0	–	39.2	46.1	53.9	–	–	50.8	–22.4	–27.3
*Cornwall, Bodmin	24 Feb 22	58.4	–	41.6	–	69.1	43.6	–	56.5	–	74.8	–	–
Wolverhampton, West	7 Mar 22	56.8	43.3	–	–	63.3	54.9	45.1	–	–	80.0	–1.9	–1.9
Cambridge	16 Mar 22	75.3	24.7	–	–	61.0	48.7	31.1	20.2	–	80.4	–16.5	–14.3
Inverness	16 Mar 22	–	–	–	100.0[2]	37.3	–	49.0	–	51.0	50.1	–	–
Surrey, Chertsey	24 Mar 22	80.7	19.3	–	–	48.0	55.5	44.6	–	–	55.4	–	–
*Leicester, East	30 Mar 22	–	27.1	–	72.9	65.6	–	52.9	14.4	32.8	71.3	–	–
Nottingham, East	29 June 22	65.7	19.4	–	14.9	49.5	52.3	27.3	20.4	–	66.3	–10.7	–11.5
Glam., Gower	20 July 22	–	54.8	45.2	–	62.2	–	57.5	–	42.5	73.1	–	–
*Glam., Pontypridd	25 July 22	1.1	42.8	–	56.1	68.3	–	57.0	–	43.0	72.9	–	–
*Hackney, South	18 Aug 22	–	–	–	100.0[2]	55.4	50.2	49.8	–	–	56.3	–	–
*Newport	18 Oct 22	–	41.0	–	59.0[2]	62.2	40.0	33.8	26.2	–	79.2	–	–
Portsmouth, South	13 Dec 22	68.7	–	31.3	–	73.7	62.9	–	–	37.1	57.7	–	–
Newcastle-upon-Tyne, East	17 Jan 23	–	43.2	30.0	26.9	73.7	26.8	45.7	27.6	–	76.4	–	–
Stepney, Whitechapel	8 Feb 23	22.4	40.2	37.4	–	64.1	–	57.0	42.1	0.9	60.5	–	–
Darlington	28 Feb 23	49.7	33.8	16.5	–	88.0	56.6	43.4	–	–	85.4	–1.4	–2.9
*Surrey, Mitcham	3 Mar 23	65.0	–	35.0	–	52.7	34.1	38.0	15.2	12.7	66.2	–	–
*Willesden, East	3 Mar 23	52.8	–	47.2	–	58.4	39.4	–	60.6	–	60.2	–	–
*Liverpool, Edge Hill	6 Mar 23	59.8	–	40.2	–	70.5	47.3	52.6	–	–	58.1	–	–
*Anglesey	7 Apr 23	–	54.2	–	45.8	80.5	16.2	30.5	53.3	–	76.4	–	–
Shrops., Ludlow	19 Apr 23	66.4	–	–	33.7	71.6	55.0	7.8	37.2	–	73.0	–	–
*Northumberland, Berwick-upon-Tweed	31 May 23	–	–	38.1	61.9	66.2	55.0	18.2	26.8	–	74.9	–	–
*Devon, Tiverton	21 June 23	46.9	6.6	46.5	–	80.1	48.1	2.1	49.8	–	88.1	2.9	8.3
Morpeth	21 June 23	19.5	48.4	32.2	–	72.1	–	60.5	39.5	–	76.9	–	–
Leeds, Central	26 July 23	50.1	27.8	22.2	–	66.1	47.6	41.4	11.0	–	64.3	–8.0	–10.8

273

Previous General Election					By-Election and Date	By-Election Result					Swing to Con.	
Con. %	Lab. %	Lib. %	Others %	Turnout %		Con. %	Lab. %	Lib. %	Others %	Turnout %	Butler	Steed
68.7	–	31.3	–	73.7	†Portsmouth, South	54.9	–	45.1	–	54.9	–	–
61.8	38.3	–	–	73.0	Somerset, Yeovil	46.6	28.7	24.8	–	80.8	−2.8	0.1
46.8	32.9	–	20.3	81.2	Rutland & Stamford	57.1	42.9	–	–	71.5	0.2	−1.6
31.8	37.8	30.4	–	87.3	Burnley	41.6	58.4	–	–	82.4	−5.4	−4.1
Unop.	–	–	–	–	Westminster, Abbey	35.9	27.0	1.3	35.8	61.6	–	–
50.3	49.7	–	–	66.1	*Liverpool, West Toxteth	45.7	54.3	–	–	76.2	−4.6	−4.6
42.9	39.0	18.1	–	68.2	Glasgow, Kelvingrove	55.3	39.8	4.9	–	70.5	5.8	5.7
43.9	–	56.1	–	83.5	*Oxford	47.8	13.1	39.1	–	80.3	−0.2	1.5
59.6	40.4	–	–	58.1	Sussex, Lewes	52.0	33.2	14.8	–	67.3	5.3	5.7
45.9	54.1	–	–	68.8	*Lincs, Holland-with-Boston	39.6	37.1	23.3	–	77.2	−3.5	−6.3
30.1	24.8	45.1	–	78.3	Carms, Carmarthen	27.2	28.8	44.0	–	78.9	–	–
37.9	28.7	31.8	1.6	86.2	Walsall	38.2	30.0	31.8	–	83.4	*−0.5*	*−0.9*
62.3	37.7	–	–	73.5	Ayr Burghs	46.3	35.2	18.6	–	71.0	−6.7	−5.4
67.9	16.0	16.1	–	77.6	Sussex, Eastbourne	58.4	16.9	24.7	–	65.5	−5.2	−3.4
46.9	53.2	–	–	70.0	Gloucs., Forest of Dean	35.9	48.4	15.7	–	80.9	−3.1	−4.3
53.1	–	46.9	–	76.8	Galloway	43.4	16.9	39.7	–	83.3	–	–
63.1	–	36.9	–	81.8	Suffolk, Bury St Edmunds	62.8	–	37.2	–	74.0	–	–
Unop.	–	–	–	–	Yorks, Ripon	59.0	–	41.0	–	74.6	–	–
55.8	44.2	–	–	75.6	Dunbartonshire	48.0	43.9	8.1	–	75.0	−3.7	−3.6
55.7	44.3	–	–	83.5	Renfrewshire, East	52.0	48.0	–	–	75.2	−3.7	−3.7
53.8	46.2	–	–	86.1	*Darlington	43.3	44.4	12.3	–	87.6	−4.4	−4.5
43.7	56.3	–	–	79.3	Lanarks, Bothwell	35.2	59.7	5.1	–	74.2	−5.9	−6.6
39.4	35.8	24.6	–	77.6	*East Ham, North	34.5	40.6	24.9	–	71.7	−4.9	−6.6
56.0	–	44.0	–	82.3	Yorks, Buckrose	48.7	8.8	42.5	–	81.7	–	–
54.1	45.9	–	–	74.2	*Hammersmith, North	38.6	53.3	8.0	–	72.2	−11.4	−12.1

Constituency	Date	Prev 1	Prev 2	Prev 3	Prev T%		By 1	By 2	By 3	By 4	By T%	Swing	Swing2
Wallsend	21 July 26	47.6	52.4	—	85.4	—	30.1	57.7	12.2	—	82.9	-11.4	*-13.3*
Cumberland, North	17 Sep 26	54.2	10.9	34.9	86.0	—	47.5	15.1	37.1	—	82.0	-5.3	*-7.2*
Yorks., Howdenshire	25 Nov 26	Unop.	—	—	—	—	54.2	11.8	34.0	—	73.6	—	—
*Kingston-upon-Hull, Central	29 Nov 26	45.9	—	—	77.1	—	37.6	52.9	9.5	—	82.8	—	—
Essex, Chelmsford	30 Nov 26	54.7	10.0	54.1	77.1	—	47.9	22.0	30.2	—	70.5	-9.4	*-16.0*
Smethwick	21 Dec 26	47.7	52.3	35.3	78.2	—	33.7	57.1	9.2	—	78.6	-9.4	*-10.6*
*Worcs., Stourbridge	23 Feb 27	39.5	34.8	25.7	83.7	—	34.0	41.9	24.1	—	79.8	-6.3	*-8.3*
Leith	23 Mar 27	—	40.4	59.6	70.5	—	15.7	42.0	42.4	—	73.9	—	—
*Southwark, North	28 Mar 27	17.9	43.9	38.3	71.5	—	19.2	36.9	43.9	—	62.8	4.2	*5.3*
*Leics., Bosworth	31 May 27	34.9	31.5	33.6	80.8	—	24.5	37.3	38.2	—	84.6	-8.1	*-12.9*
Wilts., Westbury	16 June 27	44.2	18.1	37.7	84.9	—	40.1	20.4	39.5	—	84.6	-3.2	*-4.6*
Lambeth, Brixton	27 June 27	56.6	25.9	17.5	69.4	—	48.1	28.0	23.9	—	53.9	-5.3	*-5.4*
Southend-on-Sea	19 Nov 27	62.5	8.4	29.1	79.3	—	54.7	12.3	30.7	2.4	73.2	-5.9	*-6.5*
Kent, Canterbury	24 Nov 27	70.3	—	29.7	65.9	—	57.3	—	42.7	—	60.8	—	—
*Northampton	9 Jan 28	40.0	37.2	23.3	87.0	—	36.1	37.5	23.7	2.7	84.2	-1.9	*-2.5*
Kent, Faversham	25 Jan 28	46.9	29.9	23.2	73.9	—	41.6	36.2	18.6	3.5	72.4	-5.8	*-7.7*
Bristol, West	2 Feb 28	79.0	21.0	—	75.1	—	57.2	26.0	16.8	—	67.6	-13.4	*-10.2*
*Lancs., Lancaster	9 Feb 28	47.8	17.5	34.8	82.9	—	38.2	18.1	43.7	—	82.7	-5.1	*-5.4*
Ilford	23 Feb 28	58.4	21.7	19.9	74.8	—	44.8	21.9	33.4	—	67.5	-6.9	*-5.8*
*Cornwall, St Ives	6 Mar 28	53.0	—	47.0	69.1	—	39.4	18.1	42.6	—	77.4	—	—
Middlesbrough, West	7 Mar 28	—	—	Unop.	—	—	27.8	36.0	36.3	—	82.2	—	—
*Linlithgowshire	4 Apr 28	51.1	48.9	—	80.0	—	31.5	49.1	19.4	—	81.5	-9.9	*-12.0*
Stoke-on-Trent, Hanley	23 Apr 28	47.0	53.1	—	73.5	—	26.3	60.2	13.5	—	69.9	-13.9	*-16.6*
St Marylebone	30 Apr 28	73.5	26.5	—	65.5	—	56.2	29.4	14.5	—	43.1	10.1	*-7.8*
Holborn	28 June 28	75.5	24.6	—	55.1	—	59.7	21.0	19.3	—	39.0	-6.1	*-1.5*
*Carms, Carmarthen	28 June 28	—	31.5	68.5	67.9	—	29.1	35.4	35.5	—	76.6	—	—
Surrey, Epsom	4 July 28	79.5	20.5	—	67.1	—	60.3	16.8	23.0	—	51.2	-7.8	*-1.3*
*Halifax	13 July 28	—	—	Unop.	—	—	26.4	42.9	30.8	—	78.7	—	—
Sheffield, Hallam	16 July 28	63.7	36.3	—	77.8	—	53.7	30.8	15.5	—	54.7	-2.2	*-0.1*
Aberdeen, North	16 Aug 28	39.2	60.8	—	64.4	—	23.1	52.5	11.5	12.9	56.8	-3.9	*-8.6*
Cheltenham	26 Sep 28	56.6	—	43.4	82.7	—	49.5	18.8	31.7	—	80.3	—	—
Devon, Tavistock	11 Oct 28	52.8	—	47.2	77.7	—	45.2	10.3	44.5	—	77.3	—	—

Previous General Election					By-Election and Date	By-Election Result					Swing to Con.	
Con. %	Lab. %	Lib. %	Others %	Turnout %		Con. %	Lab. %	Lib. %	Others %	Turnout %	Butler	Steed
39.5	32.8	27.7	–	88.3	*Ashton-under-Lyne	29 Oct 28	30.3	40.5	29.1	–	89.1	–8.4	–11.8
55.2	44.8	–	–	79.2	*Midlothian, North	29 Jan 29	36.9	42.0	16.6	4.5	66.0	–7.8	–9.9
57.7	42.3	–	–	76.5	*Battersea, South	7 Feb 29	43.4	45.6	11.1	–	57.7	–8.8	–8.9
–	55.1	44.9	–	80.9	Durham, Bishop Auckland	7 Feb 29	13.0	57.2	29.9	–	74.4	–	–
47.2	52.9	–	–	79.4	Northumberland, Wansbeck	13 Feb 29	27.3	58.0	14.7	–	65.3	–12.5	–15.1
60.0	24.6	15.5	–	76.4	Liverpool, East Toxteth	19 Mar 29	43.2	29.2	27.6	–	61.7	–10.7	–11.3
54.1	–	45.9	–	86.9	*Cheshire, Eddisbury	20 Mar 29	46.6	–	53.4	–	80.6	–	–
55.8	13.6	30.6	–	84.6	Bath	21 Mar 29	45.1	25.7	29.3	–	70.1	–11.4	–16.7
47.5	32.8	19.7	–	75.9	*Lincs, Holland-with-Boston	21 Mar 29	24.2	27.3	38.1	10.4	75.6	–8.9	–12.1
53.9	46.1	–	–	79.9	*Lanarks, North	21 Mar 29	33.4	57.5	9.1	–	82.3	–16.0	–17.2
24.8	75.2	–	–	62.6	Leeds, South-East	1 Aug 29	–	95.8	–	4.2	25.9	–	–
48.5	34.8	16.7	–	69.8	Middx., Twickenham	8 Aug 29	47.7	46.1	6.2	–	49.5	–6.1	–7.4
30.4	48.2	21.4	–	77.8	Ayrshire, Kilmarnock	27 Nov 29	40.0	55.7	–	4.4	71.7	1.1	3.2
67.4	32.6	–	–	73.6	Warwicks., Tamworth	2 Dec 29	64.8	35.2	–	–	60.3	–2.6	–2.6
26.8	55.2	18.0	–	77.3	Sheffield, Brightside	6 Feb 30	34.6	46.4	14.7	4.4	52.4	8.3	10.1
38.7	44.9	16.4	–	71.3	*Fulham, West	6 May 30	50.4	49.6	–	–	63.6	3.4	4.0
41.8	33.2	25.1	–	77.4	Nottingham, Central	27 May 30	54.3	28.8	16.9	–	61.1	8.5	9.6
39.6	60.4	–	–	76.9	Glasgow, Shettleston	26 June 30	43.8	45.5	–	10.7[2]	55.8	9.5	9.4
41.4	47.5	11.1	–	78.0	Norfolk, North	9 July 30	49.7	50.3	–	–	75.0	2.8	3.2
47.2	18.7	34.1	–	73.1	Bromley	2 Sep 30	32.5	15.1	28.4	24.1	53.4	–5.5	–3.3
Unop.					*Paddington, South	30 Oct 30	34.3	26.6	–	39.1[2]	57.3	–	–
31.2	42.3	26.6	–	85.0	*Yorks., Shipley	6 Nov 30	36.0	32.1	30.2	1.7	80.0	7.6	10.6
52.2	47.8	–	–	77.8	Renfrewshire, East	28 Nov 30	53.6	33.4	–	13.1	69.0	7.9	9.4
16.0	63.1	20.8	–	60.3	Stepney, Whitechapel	3 Dec 30	17.1	39.2	34.1	9.6	59.0	12.5	10.2
–	65.8	34.2	–	78.2	Bristol, East	16 Jan 31	25.4	61.7	12.9	–	66.6	–	–
48.0	26.9	25.2	–	75.5	Liverpool, East Toxteth	5 Feb 31	75.4	24.5	–	–	45.6	14.9	11.3

19 Feb 31	Islington, East	34.1	38.0	27.9	–	66.4	23.5	34.7	14.6	27.2	50.0	−3.6	−6.9
20 Feb 31	Hants., Fareham	54.2	22.1	23.7	–	68.0	65.6	22.1	12.3	–	50.3	5.7	3.7
11 Mar 31	Wilts., Salisbury	47.3	13.4	39.3	–	81.9	53.9	13.4	32.7	–	71.1	3.3	2.1
19 Mar 31	Westminster, St George's	78.1	21.9	–	–	53.3	59.9	–	–	40.1	53.1	–	–
19 Mar 31	Glam., Pontypridd	10.1	53.1	36.8	–	82.0	15.9	59.9	24.2	–	73.6	−0.5	5.0
15 Apr 31	Woolwich, East	36.8	63.2	–	–	75.6	43.3	56.7	–	–	66.6	6.5	6.5
30 Apr 31	*Ashton-under-Lyne	33.0	44.5	22.6	–	85.9	44.5	39.5	–	16.0	80.2	8.3	10.5
6 May 31	Yorks., Scarborough & Whitby	48.3	10.8	40.9	–	79.7	52.7	–	47.3	–	75.5	–	–
7 May 31	Glasgow, St Rollox	36.3	61.8	–	2.0	72.0	39.0	45.2	–	15.8	54.1	9.6	9.3
19 May 31	Glam., Ogmore	10.3	56.7	29.2	3.8	82.8	–	78.8	–	21.2	50.8	–	–
21 May 31	Gloucs., Stroud	44.5	26.1	29.5	–	81.6	49.6	30.0	20.4	–	71.4	0.6	−0.8
21 May 31	Lanarks., Rutherglen	36.5	52.2	8.8	2.5	75.7	48.7	51.4	–	–	69.6	6.5	7.5
8 June 31	Gateshead	21.6	52.5	19.1	6.8	73.9	48.4	51.6	–	–	60.8	13.9	19.4
22 June 31	Manchester, Ardwick	39.7	60.3	–	–	72.0	49.5	50.5	–	–	64.1	9.8	9.8
23 June 31	Liverpool, Wavertree	40.0	32.2	27.8	–	78.1	65.1	35.0	–	–	51.7	11.1	9.6
9 Feb 32	Croydon, South	80.3	19.7	–	–	68.3	67.6	32.5	–	–	38.2	−12.8	−12.8
9 Feb 32	Hants., New Forest & Christchurch	83.3	16.7	–	–	71.9	82.0	18.0	–	–	48.0	−1.3	−1.3
25 Feb 32	Oxon., Henley	72.3	11.5	16.3	–	68.6	69.9	–	30.1	–	48.9	–	–
17 Mar 32	Dunbartonshire	63.6	36.4	–	–	82.8	43.5	35.6	–	20.9[2]	70.5	−9.6	−8.6
21 Apr 32	*Wakefield	57.4	42.6	–	–	85.5	49.4	50.6	–	–	83.0	−8.1	−8.1
28 Apr 32	St Marylebone	86.7	13.3	–	–	63.5	52.3	–	–	47.7	30.8	–	–
8 June 32	Camberwell, Dulwich	71.5	15.6	12.9	–	70.7	61.0	19.3	19.8	–	47.1	−7.1	−6.1
28 June 32	Montrose Burghs	–	23.0	77.0	–	74.6	–	41.4	46.9	11.8	56.7	–	–
22 July 32	Cornwall, North	45.3	5.6	49.2	–	85.7	47.6	–	52.4	–	80.8	–	–
26 July 32	*Wednesbury	54.5	45.5	–	–	89.0	45.3	54.7	–	–	78.0	−9.2	−9.2
16 Sep 32	Middx., Twickenham	74.0	26.0	–	–	71.3	56.2	43.8	–	–	51.9	−17.8	−17.8
22 Sep 32	Cardiganshire	–	24.0	76.0	–	67.5	32.1	19.2	48.7	–	70.4	–	–
19 Jan 33	Liverpool, Exchange	68.8	31.2	–	–	69.0	55.1	45.0	–	–	55.2	−13.8	−13.8
2 Feb 33	Fife, East	–	–	–	Unop.	–	–	22.0	–	70.4[3]	65.6	–	–
27 Feb 33	*Rotherham	50.8	49.2	–	–	82.6	31.0	69.1	–	7.6	73.5	−19.9	−19.9
17 Mar 33	Kent, Ashford	58.7	–	–	41.3	75.9	47.7	18.4	33.9	–	70.9	–	–

Previous General Election					By-Election and Date	By-Election Result					Swing to Con.	
Con. %	Lab. %	Lib. %	Others %	Turnout %		Con. %	Lab. %	Lib. %	Others %	Turnout %	Butler	Steed
–	68.1	–	31.9	73.7	Rhondda, East — 28 Mar 33	–	47.4	26.3	26.3	67.3	–	–
75.7	24.3	–	–	71.2	Herts, Hitchin — 8 June 33	58.4	41.6	–	–	51.3	–17.2	–17.2
Unop.	–	–	–	–	Cheshire, Altrincham — 14 June 33	52.2	16.8	32.0	–	63.4	–	–
35.4	64.6	–	–	74.6	Derbys., Clay Cross — 1 Sep 33	19.9	69.3	–	10.8	71.2	–10.1	–13.1
68.7	26.1	5.2	59.6	66.1	*Fulham, East — 25 Oct 33	42.1	57.9	–	37.8[2]	59.5	–29.1	–30.3
–	40.4	–	–	79.5	Ayrshire, Kilmarnock — 2 Nov 33	34.8	27.4	21.8	1.7	77.3	–	–
68.2	31.8	–	–	80.3	Yorks., Skipton — 7 Nov 33	43.0	33.5	–	–	82.7	–13.5	–12.1
71.9	28.1	–	–	75.3	Rutland & Stamford — 21 Nov 33	53.3	46.7	–	–	77.2	–18.7	–18.7
69.3	17.7	13.0	–	80.4	Manchester, Rusholme — 21 Nov 33	50.7	40.2	9.1	–	60.8	–20.6	–23.9
74.5	25.5	–	–	78.1	Leics., Harborough — 28 Nov 33	50.9	32.9	16.2	–	72.3	–15.4	–13.9
73.2	26.8	–	–	75.6	Cambridge — 8 Feb 34	51.2	41.9	7.0	–	67.8	–18.5	–18.2
67.8	32.3	–	–	70.8	Suffolk, Lowestoft — 15 Feb 34	47.9	42.1	10.0	–	67.9	–14.9	–14.5
68.4	31.6	–	–	74.5	Portsmouth, North — 19 Feb 34	59.6	40.4	–	–	55.7	–8.7	–8.7
69.7	12.2	18.1	–	74.2	Hants, Basingstoke — 19 Apr 34	53.7	15.5	30.8	–	64.4	–9.6	–7.5
59.2	37.3	–	3.6[2]	69.6	*Hammersmith, North — 24 Apr 34	41.9	55.7	–	2.4	56.7	–17.8	–18.4
58.5	41.5	–	–	70.4	*West Ham, Upton — 14 May 34	40.1	56.4	–	3.5	50.5	–16.7	–16.9
–	69.4	–	30.6	80.8	Merthyr Tydfil, Merthyr — 5 June 34	–	51.9	28.9	19.3[2]	81.2	–	–
70.9	29.2	–	–	78.0	Mon., Monmouth — 14 June 34	65.0	35.0	–	–	69.2	–5.8	–5.8
74.0	26.0	–	–	71.3	†Middx., Twickenham — 22 June 34	56.1	43.9	–	–	55.5	–17.9	–17.9
85.7	14.4	–	–	71.8	Somerset, Weston-super-Mare — 26 June 34	61.5	16.6	21.9	–	57.3	–13.2	–6.9
72.1	27.9	–	–	77.8	Notts., Rushcliffe — 26 July 34	48.8	38.0	13.2	–	56.5	–16.7	–15.9
–	34.9	65.1	–	64.6	*Lambeth, North — 23 Oct 34	–	57.9	25.5	16.6	52.6	–	–
55.9	44.1	–	–	85.5	*Wilts, Swindon — 25 Oct 34	46.6	53.4	–	–	81.8	–9.3	–9.3
81.6	18.4	–	–	66.3	Wandsworth, Putney — 28 Nov 34	54.7	45.3	–	–	57.5	–26.9	–26.9
77.9	22.1	–	–	75.2	*Liverpool, Wavertree — 6 Feb 35	31.2	35.4	9.5	23.9	72.3	–30.0	–31.0
81.0	19.0	–	–	63.9	Lambeth, Norwood — 14 Mar 35	51.0	40.5	–	8.5	53.4	–22.8	–22.6
50.2	9.7	40.1	–	81.4	Perthshire, Perth — 16 Apr 35	68.7	31.3	–	–	53.0	–1.6	–15.2

Constituency	Date	Con	Lab	Lib	Turnout	Con	Lab	Lib	Other	Turnout	Swing	Swing
Edinburgh, West	2 May 35	71.2	28.8	–	79.2	53.0	33.9	13.1	–	51.2	-11.6	-10.2
Aberdeen, South	21 May 35	83.7	16.3	–	75.8	66.0	34.0	–	–	56.6	-17.6	-17.6
*Liverpool, West Toxteth	6 July 35	57.9	42.1	–	76.2	39.1	60.9	–	–	53.9	-18.9	-18.9
Dumfriesshire	12 Sep 35	–	22.3	77.7	77.6	–	39.7	60.3	–	58.8	–	–
Ross & Cromarty	10 Feb 36	–	23.3	76.7	50.8	13.4	33.0	4.1	49.5	65.2	–	–
*Dunbartonshire	18 Mar 36	50.3	42.0	7.8	80.5	45.7	48.1	–	6.2	68.6	-5.3	-5.8
Carms., Llanelly	26 Mar 36	Unop.	–	–	–	–	66.8	–	33.2	68.4	–	–
*Camberwell, Peckham	6 May 36	51.3	48.7	–	64.8	49.8	50.2	–	–	56.6	-1.5	-1.5
Sussex, Lewes	18 June 36	70.0	30.0	–	66.4	66.0	34.0	–	–	40.6	-4.0	-4.0
Wandsworth, Balham & Tooting	23 July 36	62.9	37.1	–	61.8	53.7	46.3	–	–	49.2	-9.2	-9.6
Sussex, East Grinstead	23 July 36	78.4	21.6	–	61.2	79.6	20.5	–	–	45.5	1.1	1.1
Birmingham, Erdington	20 Oct 36	58.3	37.4	4.3	65.5	56.5	43.5	–	–	64.7	-4.0	-4.4
Derbys., Clay Cross	5 Nov 36	25.4	74.6	–	73.6	24.9	75.1	–	–	72.4	-0.6	-0.6
*Greenock	26 Nov 36	–	44.0	56.0[2]	84.4	–	53.4	–	46.6	83.3	–	–
St Pancras, North	4 Feb 37	53.7	42.3	4.0	68.3	50.6	49.4	–	–	50.9	-5.2	-5.4
Manchester, Gorton	18 Feb 37	44.1	55.9	–	77.7	42.3	57.7	–	–	66.8	-1.8	-1.8
Richmond-upon-Thames	25 Feb 37	73.5	26.5	–	69.8	72.7	27.3	–	–	47.3	-0.8	-0.8
Kent, Tonbridge	23 Mar 37	61.3	24.6	14.1	68.2	56.9	24.7	18.4	–	58.2	-2.2	-1.6
Surrey, Farnham	23 Mar 37	78.5	21.5	–	59.8	66.7	25.3	–	8.0[2]	50.0	-7.8	-6.0
Cheshire, Stalybridge & Hyde	28 Apr 37	55.5	44.5	–	78.7	50.4	49.6	–	–	74.6	-5.1	-5.1
Birmingham, West	29 Apr 37	64.4	35.7	–	63.6	56.6	43.4	–	–	56.0	-7.8	-7.8
*Wandsworth, Central	29 Apr 37	58.6	41.4	–	65.0	49.0	51.0	–	–	63.2	-9.6	-9.6
York	6 May 37	57.0	43.0	–	82.5	55.1	44.9	–	–	74.2	-2.0	-2.0
Glasgow, Hillhead	10 June 37	68.2	31.8	–	73.2	60.1	29.8	–	10.1[2]	56.1	-3.0	-1.3
Bucks, Buckingham	11 June 37	58.0	42.0	–	75.1	52.6	37.6	9.8	–	71.4	-0.5	0.3
Plymouth, Drake	15 June 37	58.3	41.7	–	74.8	58.8	41.2	–	–	54.6	0.6	0.6
*Cheltenham	22 June 37	70.5	29.5	–	70.4	38.8	21.2	–	40.1	69.3	-11.7	-5.8
Herts., Hemel Hempstead	22 June 37	62.5	15.4	22.1	69.4	57.7	14.1	28.3	–	55.0	-1.7	0.2
Lincs., Holland-with-Boston	24 June 37	–	34.5	65.5	63.6	–	40.0	–	60.0	59.4	–	–
Worcs., Bewdley	24 June 37	Unop.	–	–	–	63.9	–	36.1	–	60.6	–	–
Ilford	29 June 37	63.1	36.9	–	64.0	61.2	38.8	–	–	37.3	-2.0	-2.0

By-Election and Date	Previous General Election					By-Election Result					Swing to Con.	
	Con. %	Lab. %	Lib. %	Others %	Turnout %	Con. %	Lab. %	Lib. %	Others %	Turnout %	Butler	Steed
Cornwall, St Ives · 30 June 37	–	–	–	Unop.	–	–	–	49.6	50.4	66.1	–	–
Kingston-upon-Thames · 1 July 37	67.5	20.5	12.0	–	65.5	66.6	33.4	–	–	38.1	-6.9	-10.1
Surrey, Chertsey · 2 July 37	71.4	–	28.6	–	60.2	64.8	–	35.2	–	39.2	–	–
Dorset, North · 13 July 37	50.1	5.2	37.9	6.8	79.7	51.1	–	48.9	–	73.4	–	–
Glasgow, Springburn · 7 Sep 37	36.9	63.1	–	–	71.1	37.4	62.6	–	–	50.9	0.5	0.5
*Islington, North · 13 Oct 37	54.4	45.6	–	–	59.7	47.5	52.5	–	–	40.4	-7.0	-7.0
Hastings · 24 Nov 37	69.0	31.0	–	–	66.5	62.1	37.9	–	–	65.3	-6.9	-6.9
Lancs, Farnworth · 27 Jan 38	39.5	51.7	–	8.8	82.4	40.9	59.1	–	–	77.9	-3.0	-2.4
Glam, Pontypridd · 11 Feb 38	–	Unop.	–	–	–	–	59.9	–	40.1	78.3	–	–
*Ipswich · 16 Feb 38	57.3	42.7	–	–	82.1	47.0	53.0	–	–	82.8	-10.3	-10.3
*Fulham, West · 6 Apr 38	53.4	43.3	3.3	–	69.9	47.8	52.2	–	–	65.5	-7.3	-7.5
*Staffs, Lichfield · 5 May 38	–	46.2	–	54.8	64.2	–	50.9	–	49.1	57.8	–	–
Bucks, Aylesbury · 19 May 38	57.4	11.0	31.6	–	70.2	54.1	19.1	26.8	–	63.1	*-5.8*	*-10.1*
Derbys, West · 2 June 38	Unop.	–	–	–	–	48.6	32.5	18.9	–	79.4	–	–
Staffs, Stafford · 9 June 38	56.4	43.6	–	–	79.0	57.6	42.4	–	–	77.2	1.2	1.2
Barnsley · 16 June 38	–	58.9	–	41.1	82.6	–	64.4	–	35.6	72.7	–	–
Willesden, East · 28 July 38	57.8	35.0	7.3	–	62.0	56.6	43.4	–	–	39.3	-4.8	-5.7
Oxford · 27 Oct 38	62.8	37.2	–	–	67.3	56.1	–	–	43.9	76.3	–	–
*Kent, Dartford · 7 Nov 38	51.8	48.2	–	–	69.6	47.6	52.4	–	–	68.5	-4.2	-4.2
Walsall · 16 Nov 38	–	39.4	–	60.6²	75.2	–	42.9	–	57.1	75.9	–	–
Yorks, Doncaster · 17 Nov 38	42.4	57.7	–	–	76.7	38.7	61.3	–	–	75.4	-3.7	-3.7
*Somerset, Bridgwater · 17 Nov 38	56.9	19.8	23.4	–	72.7	46.8	–	–	53.2	82.3	–	–
Lewisham, West · 24 Nov 38	64.7	35.3	–	–	63.9	57.1	42.9	–	–	58.4	-7.6	-7.6
Lancs, Fylde · 30 Nov 38	70.8	29.2	–	–	72.0	68.4	31.6	–	–	64.8	-2.4	-2.4
Kinross & Perthshire, West · 21 Dec 38	60.2	–	39.8	–	73.3	52.9	–	–	47.1	66.6	–	–
Norfolk, East · 26 Jan 39	–	31.2	–	68.8	66.8	–	37.1	–	62.9	53.1	–	–
Yorks, Holderness · 15 Feb 39	53.6	21.5	24.9	–	72.2	39.4	21.4	25.7	13.5	66.3	*-7.1*	*-6.6*

					Constituency	Date							
77.2	22.8	–	–	68.6	Yorks, Ripon	23 Feb 39	69.5	30.5	–	–	57.3	-7.7	-7.7
46.4	53.6	–	–	79.3	Batley & Morley	9 Mar 39	44.6	55.4	–	–	72.6	-1.8	-1.8
55.9	–	44.1	–	75.6	Aberdeenshire, West	30 Mar 39	52.7	–	47.3	–	71.4	–	–
42.4	57.6	–	–	78.0	Ayrshire, South	20 Apr 39	42.0	58.0	–	–	74.5	-0.4	-0.4
67.3	32.7	–	–	71.7	Sheffield, Hallam	10 May 39	61.7	38.3	–	–	57.9	-5.6	-5.6
68.8	31.2	–	–	64.7	Birmingham, Aston	17 May 39	66.3	33.7	–	–	45.0	-2.6	-2.6
–	49.8	–	50.3	56.1	*Southwark, North	17 May 39	–	57.4	–	42.6	38.9	–	–
77.5	22.5	–	–	49.2	Westminster, Abbey	17 May 39	67.4	–	–	32.6	30.3	–	–
51.1	48.9	–	–	55.7	*Lambeth, Kennington	24 May 39	39.9	60.1	–	–	40.6	-11.2	-11.2
23.8	76.3	–	–	72.3	Glam., Caerphilly	4 July 39	32.0	68.0	–	–	68.4	8.3	8.3
48.7	–	51.3	–	79.9	Cornwall, North	13 July 39	47.8	–	52.2	–	79.3	–	–
63.9	–	36.1	–	68.3	Hythe	20 July 39	54.2	–	43.2	2.6	62.4	–	–
63.4	36.6	–	–	76.8	Mon., Monmouth	25 July 39	60.1	39.9	–	–	58.2	-3.3	-3.3
25.8	39.5	30.6	4.1	76.0	Yorks, Colne Valley	27 July 39	25.4	48.6	26.0	–	63.7	-4.8	-5.2
52.6	47.4	–	–	84.3	*Brecon & Radnor	1 Aug 39	46.6	53.4	–	–	79.9	-6.0	-6.0
39.0	42.2	14.4	4.5	76.3	Stirlingshire, East & Clackmannan	13 Oct 39	–	93.7	–	6.4	35.4	–	–
64.4	35.6	–	–	72.5	Lancs, Stretford	8 Dec 39	79.8	15.1	–	5.2	36.6	17.9	19.7
–	53.3	–	46.7	57.2	Southwark, Central	10 Feb 40	–	64.3	–	35.7[2]	24.7	–	–
19.0	81.0	–	–	53.4	West Ham, Silvertown	22 Feb 40	–	92.8	–	7.2[2]	40.1	–	–
52.1	47.9	–	–	77.3	Northants., Kettering	6 Mar 40	73.0	–	–	27.0	37.8	–	–
64.8	35.2	–	–	66.1	Leeds, North-East	13 Mar 40	97.1	–	–	2.9	35.0	–	–
53.6	–	46.4	–	56.6	Argyll	10 Apr 40	62.8	–	–	37.2	47.9	–	–
41.3	58.7	–	–	63.5	Battersea, North	17 Apr 40	–	92.6	–	7.4	25.1	–	–
72.1	27.9	–	–	70.1	Glasgow, Pollok	30 Apr 40	88.1	11.9	–	–	44.5	16.0	16.0
55.6	34.0	–	10.4	76.0	Renfrewshire, East	9 May 40	80.7	19.3	–	–	43.4	19.9	18.7
61.1	38.9	–	–	74.6	Lancs, Middleton & Prestwich	22 May 40	98.7	–	–	1.3	49.0	–	–
77.0	23.1	–	–	70.3	*Newcastle-upon-Tyne, North	7 June 40	28.8	–	–	71.2	22.0	–	–
23.0	77.0	–	–	59.5	Poplar, Bow & Bromley	12 June 40	–	95.8	–	4.2	32.4	–	–
67.1	32.9	–	–	64.6	Croydon, North	19 June 40	90.7	–	–	9.3	18.3	–	–
51.5	48.5	–	–	79.6	Northampton	6 Dec 40	93.4	–	–	6.6	30.0	–	–
50.3	42.0	–	7.8	80.5	†Dunbartonshire	27 Feb 41	–	85.0	–	15.0	38.7	–	–
56.8	43.2	–	–	74.6	Birmingham, King's Norton	8 May 41	86.9	–	–	13.1[2]	35.0	–	–

| Previous General Election | | | | | By-Election and Date | By-Election Result | | | | | Swing to Con. | |
Con. %	Lab. %	Lib. %	Others %	Turnout %		Con. %	Lab. %	Lib. %	Others %	Turnout %	Butler	Steed
64.9	22.0	13.2	–	67.0	Hornsey, 28 May 41	72.8	–	–	27.2	27.1	–	–
54.8	45.2	–	–	75.3	Dudley, 23 July 41	56.2	–	–	43.9	34.7	–	–
53.9	7.4	38.7	–	74.7	Yorks., Scarborough & Whitby, 24 Sep 41	60.8	–	–	39.2	35.9	–	–
57.9	42.1	–	–	79.1	Shrops., Wrekin, 26 Sep 41	53.2	–	–	46.8[2]	40.5	–	–
53.7	20.0	26.3	–	79.0	Lancs., Lancaster, 15 Oct 41	56.9	19.5	23.6	–	41.9	1.9	1.5
73.2	18.1	8.8	–	59.0	Hampstead, 27 Nov 41	67.4	–	–	32.6[3]	17.3	–	–
62.7	37.3	–	–	64.4	Middx., Harrow, 2 Dec 41	80.9	–	–	19.1	10.7	–	–
54.0	41.4	4.7	–	64.5	Edinburgh, Central, 11 Dec 41	71.0	29.1	–	–	20.0	14.7	14.4
58.1	41.9	–	–	74.2	*Lincs., Grantham, 25 Mar 42	49.2	–	–	50.8	42.6	–	–
53.4	37.8	8.7	–	73.1	Cardiff, East, 13 Apr 42	–	24.8	–	75.2	33.1	–	–
62.1	37.9	–	–	74.3	Glasgow, Cathcart, 28 Apr 42	59.6	13.8	–	26.6[2]	39.1	–	–
67.4	32.6	–	–	66.1	*Wallasey, 29 Apr 42	31.7	–	–	68.3[2]	34.2	10.8	19.1
61.5	38.5	–	–	73.9	*Warwicks., Rugby, 29 Apr 42	48.2	–	–	51.8	38.5	–	–
65.2	31.9	–	3.0	68.5	Wandsworth, Putney, 8 May 42	74.9	–	–	25.1	23.0	–	–
78.3	21.7	–	–	59.5	Sussex, Chichester, 18 May 42	58.1	–	–	41.9[2]	29.2	–	–
51.3	48.8	–	–	77.0	Glam., Llandaff & Barry, 10 June 42	56.9	–	–	43.2[2]	41.5	–	–
53.3	28.9	17.7	–	73.8	*Essex, Maldon, 25 June 42	31.3	–	–	68.8[2]	44.4	–	–
Unop.	–			–	Berks., Windsor, 30 June 42	58.4	–	–	41.6	27.9	–	–
71.5	28.5	–	–	66.2	Wilts., Salisbury, 8 July 42	67.8	–	–	32.2[2]	39.7	–	–
26.8	73.2	–	–	55.3	Poplar, South, 12 Aug 42	–	86.2	–	13.8	9.3	–	–
46.3	53.7	–	–	77.0	Manchester, Clayton, 17 Oct 42	–	93.3	–	6.7	20.8	–	–
34.3	65.7	–	–	74.0	Lanarks., Hamilton, 29 Jan 43	–	81.1	–	18.9	36.8	–	–
59.2	17.6	23.2	–	73.6	Kent, Ashford, 10 Feb 43	69.7	–	–	30.3	27.7	–	–
62.9	37.1	–	–	74.3	Midlothian, North, 11 Feb 43	51.9	–	–	48.1	34.6	–	–
50.0	34.5	15.5	–	71.7	Norfolk, King's Lynn, 12 Feb 43	54.2	–	–	45.8	39.8	–	–
66.6	33.4	–	–	64.9	Portsmouth, North, 16 Feb 43	59.7	–	–	40.3	21.9	–	–
52.5	47.5	–	–	72.8	Bristol, Central, 18 Feb 43	52.1	–	–	47.9[3]	32.9	–	–

Constituency	Date	Prev C	Prev Lab	Prev L	Prev %T	By C	By Lab	By L	By Oth	By %T	Swing	Swing
Herts., Watford	23 Feb 43	65.4	34.6	–	63.6	53.9	–	–	46.1	32.4	–	–
*Cheshire, Eddisbury	7 Apr 43	Unop.	–	–	–	–	–	15.3	84.7[2]	56.1	–	–
Northants., Daventry	20 Apr 43	63.8	36.3	–	76.0	45.8	–	20.8	33.4[2]	48.8	–	–
Hartlepools	1 June 43	47.8	37.1	15.2	83.0	64.0	–	–	36.0[3]	39.5	–	–
Notts., Newark	8 June 43	62.4	37.6	–	69.9	44.8	–	10.8	44.4[2]	44.4	–	–
Birmingham, Aston	9 June 43	68.8	31.2	–	64.7	72.5	–	–	27.5[2]	22.2	–	–
Wilts., Chippenham	24 Aug 43	53.3	12.2	34.5	77.5	50.6	49.4	–	–	41.4	–	–
Northants., Peterborough	15 Oct 43	56.6	43.4	–	80.8	52.4	–	–	47.6	44.2	–	–
Woolwich, West	10 Nov 43	58.7	41.3	–	75.8	65.2	27.2	–	7.6	20.8	10.4	11.9
Middx., Acton	14 Dec 43	58.5	41.5	–	67.8	60.3	28.1	–	11.6[2]	17.1	7.6	9.7
Lancs., Darwen	15 Dec 43	41.1	20.9	38.0	89.9	50.2	–	49.8	–	45.0	–	–
*Yorks., Skipton	7 Jan 44	56.2	43.8	–	79.6	44.0	–	–	56.0[2]	54.9	–	–
Kirkcaldy Burghs	17 Feb 44	43.7	56.3	–	79.9	–	51.6	–	48.4[2]	37.2	–	–
*†Derbys., West	17 Feb 44	Unop.	–	–	–	41.5	–	–	58.5[2]	65.4	–	–
Suffolk, Bury St Edmunds	29 Feb 44	Unop.	–	–	–	56.2	43.8	–	–	50.8	–	–
Camberwell, North	30 Mar 44	32.8	64.7	2.5	55.6	–	79.8	–	20.3	11.2	–	–
†Derbys., Clay Cross	14 Apr 44	25.4	74.6	–	73.6	–	76.3	–	23.7[2]	40.3	–	–
Manchester, Rusholme	8 July 44	62.6	29.4	8.0	69.8	53.2	–	–	46.8[2]	34.7	–	–
Wolverhampton, Bilston	20 Sep 44	51.2	48.8	–	36.3	50.9	–	–	49.1	32.6	–	–
Northumberland, Berwick-on-Tweed	17 Oct 44	49.0	–	51.0	76.0	–	–	87.4	12.6	24.5	–	–
*Lanarks., Motherwell	12 Apr 45	49.3	50.7	–	75.9	–	48.6	–	51.4	54.0	–	–
Carnarvon Boroughs	26 Apr 45	33.4	–	66.6	77.4	–	–	75.2	24.8	58.8	–	–
*Essex, Chelmsford	26 Apr 45	70.8	29.2	–	65.4	42.5	–	–	57.5	54.1	–	–
Glam., Neath	15 May 45	–	Unop.	–	–	–	79.3	–	20.7[2]	58.0	–	–
Newport	17 May 45	51.7	48.3	–	79.4	54.5	45.5	–	–	50.0	2.8	2.8
Smethwick	1 Oct 45	34.1	65.9	–	72.4	31.2	68.9	–	–	65.4	–3.0	–3.0
Ashton-under-Lyne	2 Oct 45	43.6	56.4	–	78.6	35.1	54.0	10.9	–	70.5	–3.1	–4.3
Edinburgh, East	3 Oct 45	37.3	56.4	6.3	69.4	38.4	61.6	–	–	51.0	–2.0	–1.4
Mon., Monmouth	30 Oct 45	51.9	48.1	–	72.0	52.7	47.3	–	–	66.7	0.7	0.7
Bromley	14 Nov 45	44.9	34.1	21.0	71.0	49.6	39.1	11.3	–	60.6	–0.2	–0.9
Bournemouth	15 Nov 45	55.5	21.7	22.9	71.2	46.9	33.7	19.5	–	56.5	–10.3	–13.7

283

Previous General Election					By-Election and Date	By-Election Result					Swing to Con.	
Con. %	Lab. %	Lib. %	Others %	Turnout %		Con. %	Lab. %	Lib. %	Others %	Turnout %	Butler	Steed
69.8	18.9	11.3	—	67.9	Kensington, South — 20 Nov 45	81.7	—	18.3	—	36.8	—	—
28.2	71.8	—	—	70.3	Tottenham, North — 13 Dec 45	36.4	63.6	—	—	39.5	8.2	8.2
38.7	61.3	—	—	75.0	Ayrshire, South — 7 Feb 46	36.4	63.6	—	—	69.0	-2.2	-2.2
58.8	41.2	—	—	67.6	Glasgow, Cathcart — 12 Feb 46	52.5	37.1	—	10.4	55.6	-1.2	-0.3
49.0	51.0	—	—	76.4	Lancs., Heywood & Radcliffe — 21 Feb 46	49.5	50.5	—	—	75.6	0.5	0.5
—	76.4	—	23.6[2]	75.6	Glam., Ogmore — 4 June 46	—	70.6	—	29.4	33.7	—	—
29.8	56.9	13.3	—	76.7	Bexley — 22 July 46	47.5	52.5	—	—	62.6	11.1	13.2
22.7	77.3	—	—	77.0	Mon., Pontypool — 23 July 46	26.8	73.2	—	—	65.8	4.0	4.0
26.1	73.9	—	—	70.9	Battersea, North — 25 July 46	29.6	69.0	—	1.5	57.1	4.2	3.9
33.6	66.4	—	—	58.2	*Glasgow, Bridgeton — 29 Aug 46	21.6	28.0	—	50.4[3]	53.3	*13.2*	*9.9*
20.9	79.1	—	—	68.1	Bermondsey, Rotherhithe — 19 Nov 46	9.7	65.0	22.6	—	50.9	*1.4*	*-7.9*
37.1	61.2	—	1.7	71.0	Paddington North — 20 Nov 46	43.2	55.6	—	1.2	53.9	5.8	6.0
46.7	42.3	11.0	—	71.9	Aberdeen, South — 26 Nov 46	54.8	45.2	—	—	65.6	2.6	2.4
15.7	84.3	—	—	76.1	Merthyr Tydfil, Aberdare — 5 Dec 46	11.7	68.3	—	20.0	65.8	*5.9*	*-1.2*
40.6	59.4	—	—	76.1	Ayrshire, Kilmarnock — 5 Dec 46	32.5	59.7	—	7.8	68.4	-4.2	-5.3
15.7	84.3	—	—	79.9	Yorks., Normanton — 11 Feb 47	17.8	79.8	—	2.4	54.6	3.3	2.5
34.0	66.0	—	—	76.0	Durham, Jarrow — 7 May 47	37.5	59.3	—	3.2	73.4	5.1	4.8
35.1	64.9	—	—	66.1	Liverpool, Edge Hill — 11 Sep 47	42.6	52.0	4.4	1.0[2]	62.7	10.2	10.0
26.2	73.8	—	—	60.1	Islington, West — 25 Sep 47	26.6	57.1	16.0	0.2	51.4	8.5	5.6
35.3	52.5	12.2	—	74.5	Kent, Gravesend — 26 Nov 47	48.2	51.8	—	—	77.3	6.8	8.0
55.9	29.2	14.9	—	71.1	Yorks., Howdenshire — 27 Nov 47	64.0	25.5	10.5	—	67.0	5.9	5.9
37.3	56.4	—	6.3	69.4	†Edinburgh, East — 27 Nov 47	34.3	50.5	10.1	5.0	63.0	1.5	0.6
49.9	37.8	12.2	—	74.6	Surrey, Epsom — 4 Dec 47	61.1	31.5	7.5	—	70.5	8.8	9.1
42.3	57.7	—	—	65.0	*Glasgow, Camlachie — 28 Jan 48	43.7	42.1	1.2	13.0[3]	56.8	8.5	8.6
32.7	55.6	10.0	—	73.9	Paisley — 18 Feb 48	—	56.8	—	43.2	76.0	—	—
31.8	68.2	—	—	80.4	Wigan — 4 Mar 48	35.7	59.1	—	5.3[2]	81.4	6.5	5.8
41.1	40.1	18.8	—	73.2	Croydon, North — 11 Mar 48	54.0	36.6	9.4	—	74.8	8.2	9.0

Constituency	Date												
Lincs., Brigg	24 Mar 48	41.1	58.9	—	—	74.6	45.4	54.6	—	—	77.1	4.3	4.3
Southwark, Central	29 Apr 48	28.1	71.9	—	—	62.6	34.6	65.4	—	—	48.7	6.5	6.5
Glasgow, Gorbals	30 Sep 48	20.0	80.0	—	—	56.8	28.6	54.6	16.9	—	50.0	17.0	14.4
Stirling & Falkirk Burghs	7 Oct 48	43.9	56.1	—	—	71.5	42.8	49.1	8.2	—	72.9	3.0	2.7
Edmonton	13 Nov 48	29.0	68.2	2.8	7.9	69.0	46.6	53.4	—	—	62.7	16.8	16.8
Glasgow, Hillhead	25 Nov 48	58.6	33.6	—	13.5	65.8	68.4	31.6	—	—	56.7	5.9	4.8
Batley & Morley	17 Feb 49	28.4	58.1	—	—	80.8	40.7	59.3	—	—	81.3	5.6	7.8
Hammersmith, South	24 Feb 49	42.0	58.0	—	—	65.7	47.2	52.8	—	—	60.6	5.2	5.2
St Pancras, North	10 Mar 49	34.7	63.8	—	—	71.0	39.5	57.5	3.0	—	65.1	5.5	5.5
Yorks., Sowerby	16 Mar 49	30.9	50.8	—	18.3	81.9	46.9	53.1	—	—	80.7	6.9	9.1
Leeds, West	21 July 49	27.7	59.0	—	13.3	75.2	44.8	55.2	—	—	65.1	10.5	12.9
Bradford, South	8 Dec 49	33.1	52.5	—	14.4	76.7	42.4	51.3	—	6.3	74.4	5.3	6.6
Sheffield, Neepsend	5 Apr 50	27.2	72.8	—	—	83.8	26.8	70.8	2.3	—	62.9	0.8	0.3
Dunbartonshire, West	25 Apr 50	47.8	49.3	2.9	—	85.5	49.6	50.4	—	—	83.9	0.4	0.4
Yorks., Brighouse & Spenborough	4 May 50	47.8	52.2	—	9.5	88.0	49.5	50.5	—	—	85.4	1.7	1.7
Leicester, North-East	28 Sep 50	33.3	56.5	2.6	5.0	85.8	42.1	57.9	1.9	—	63.0	3.7	5.0
Glasgow, Scotstoun	25 Oct 50	46.5	46.0	0.8	11.6	84.6	50.9	47.3	—	—	73.7	1.5	1.5
Oxford	2 Nov 50	46.9	40.6	—	10.3	84.9	57.5	42.5	1.2	—	69.3	4.4	4.0
Birmingham, Handsworth	16 Nov 50	50.6	39.2	—	9.5	83.1	60.7	38.1	—	—	62.2	5.6	5.1
Bristol, South-East	30 Nov 50	26.8	62.6	1.1	—	85.0	35.2	56.7	—	8.1	61.1	7.1	8.3
Mon., Abertillery	30 Nov 50	13.0	87.1	—	11.1	84.6	13.5	86.5	—	—	71.1	0.5	0.5
Bristol, West	15 Feb 51	58.9	30.0	—	—	82.4	81.4	18.6	2.0	—	53.6	16.9	15.1
Lancs., Ormskirk	5 Apr 51	66.3	33.7	—	12.0	83.9	71.5	26.5	—	—	64.7	6.2	6.7
Harrow, West	21 Apr 51	58.5	29.5	2.0²	3.5	86.7	72.0	28.0	—	—	68.0	7.5	5.5
Woolwich, East	14 June 51	33.0	61.6	—	—	83.3	39.3	60.7	—	—	66.8	3.6	4.4
Lancs., Westhoughton	21 June 51	37.7	62.3	—	—	88.2	39.6	60.4	—	—	76.5	1.8	1.8
Bournemouth, East & Christchurch	6 Feb 52	63.3	25.1	—	11.6	80.8	61.9	23.4	4.7	10.1	63.8	0.1	1.0
Southport	6 Feb 52	60.2	24.8	—	15.0	77.7	62.0	28.5	—	9.5	61.0	-0.9	-2.3
Leeds, South-East	7 Feb 52	39.5	60.5	—	—	84.4	36.8	63.2	—	—	55.7	-2.7	-2.7
Dundee, East	17 July 52	46.2	53.8	—	—	87.2	35.6	56.2	8.2²	—	71.5	-6.5	-7.4

	Previous General Election					By-Election and Date		By-Election Result					Swing to Con.	
	Con. %	Lab. %	Lib. %	Others %	Turnout %			Con. %	Lab. %	Lib. %	Others %	Turnout %	Butler	Steed
Yorks., Cleveland	45.2	54.8	–	–	85.1	23 Oct 52		45.9	54.1	–	–	71.4	0.7	0.7
Bucks., Wycombe	51.7	48.3	–	–	86.2	4 Nov 52		52.0	48.0	–	–	83.9	0.4	0.4
Birmingham, Small Heath	30.9	63.4	5.7	–	77.2	27 Nov 52		33.0	67.0	–	–	46.6	-0.7	0.3
Lancs., Farnworth	40.8	59.2	–	–	86.8	27 Nov 52		40.1	59.9	–	–	71.0	-0.7	-0.7
Kent, Canterbury	61.1	31.0	7.9	–	80.1	12 Feb 53		67.1	32.9	–	–	49.2	2.1	0.8
Kent, Isle of Thanet	61.6	38.4	–	–	78.0	12 Mar 53		61.3	38.7	–	–	58.7	-0.3	-0.3
Barnsley	17.3	69.7	13.0	–	77.2	31 Mar 53		27.1	72.9	–	–	58.0	3.4	7.3
Stoke on Trent, North	28.6	71.4	–	–	83.8	31 Mar 53		24.5	75.5	–	–	50.5	-4.1	-4.1
Hayes and Harlington	35.2	64.8	–	–	82.2	1 Apr 53		36.2	63.8	–	–	44.8	1.0	1.0
*Sunderland, South	49.7	50.3	–	–	82.2	13 May 53		48.6	46.1	5.3	–	72.7	1.6	1.6
Berks., Abingdon	55.5	44.5	–	–	80.0	30 June 53		53.2	39.7	7.1	–	75.9	1.3	1.8
Birmingham, Edgbaston	64.3	35.7	–	–	76.1	2 July 53		67.6	32.4	–	–	50.2	3.4	3.4
Notts., Broxtowe	27.3	72.7	–	–	84.1	17 Sep 53		25.9	74.1	–	–	63.5	-1.4	-1.4
Crosby	71.0	29.1	–	–	79.8	12 Nov 53		68.1	26.7	–	4.3	62.5	-0.7	0.2
Lancs., Ormskirk	67.4	32.6	–	–	78.7	12 Nov 53		65.4	34.6	–	–	54.1	-2.0	-2.0
Holborn & St Pancras South	45.8	50.2	4.0	–	73.7	19 Nov 53		45.6	52.1	2.3	–	56.2	-1.1	-1.1
Paddington, North	44.3	55.7	–	–	81.0	3 Dec 53		45.3	53.8	–	0.9	60.3	1.4	1.4
Ilford, North	55.5	38.0	6.5	–	84.8	3 Feb 54		59.8	32.3	7.9	–	45.4	5.0	5.6
Essex, Harwich	58.9	41.1	–	–	78.8	11 Feb 54		59.1	40.9	–	–	58.8	0.2	0.2
Kingston-upon-Hull, Haltemprice	58.1	41.9	–	–	82.8	11 Feb 54		61.8	38.2	–	–	45.7	3.7	3.7
Bournemouth, West	65.5	34.5	–	–	77.7	18 Feb 54		69.7	30.3	–	–	45.1	4.2	4.2
Sussex, Arundel & Shoreham	67.4	32.6	–	–	78.0	9 Mar 54		68.5	31.5	–	–	54.2	1.2	1.2
Yorks., Harrogate	70.6	29.4	–	–	78.7	11 Mar 54		70.8	29.2	–	–	55.3	0.2	0.2
Edinburgh, East	45.9	54.1	–	–	83.8	8 Apr 54		42.4	57.7	–	–	61.8	-3.6	-3.6
Lanarks., Motherwell	42.8	57.3	–	–	84.7	14 Apr 54		39.3	56.4	–	4.3	70.5	-1.3	-1.7
Croydon, East	58.8	41.2	–	–	84.2	30 Sep 54		56.6	35.4	8.0	–	57.5	1.8	2.7
Shoreditch & Finsbury	27.4	72.6	–	–	73.2	21 Oct 54		21.8	78.2	–	–	40.7	-5.6	-5.6

				Constituency	Date							
41.7	58.3	–	85.3	Wakefield	21 Oct 54	41.9	58.1	–	–	68.6	0.2	0.2
60.3	39.7	–	77.8	Hants., Aldershot	28 Oct 54	60.1	39.9	–	–	58.7	-0.3	-0.3
15.4	78.6	6.1	86.1	Aberdare	28 Oct 54	14.5	69.5	–	16.0	69.7	4.1	0.9
62.8	37.2	–	81.7	Sutton & Cheam	4 Nov 54	66.6	33.5	–	–	55.6	3.8	3.8
28.1	71.9	–	85.5	Northumberland, Morpeth	4 Nov 54	28.7	71.3	–	–	73.0	0.6	0.6
51.6	48.4	–	80.3	Liverpool, West Derby	18 Nov 54	53.2	46.9	–	–	58.9	1.6	1.6
64.5	35.5	–	69.3	Inverness	21 Dec 54	41.4	22.6	36.0	–	49.2	-5.2	0.1
54.5	45.5	–	82.4	Norfolk, South	13 Jan 55	51.5	48.5	–	–	66.2	-3.0	-3.0
62.7	37.4	–	82.0	Kent, Orpington	20 Jan 55	65.8	34.2	–	–	55.4	3.2	3.2
62.1	37.9	–	81.3	Twickenham	25 Jan 55	64.0	36.0	–	–	47.3	2.0	2.0
58.8	41.2	–	80.0	Edinburgh, North	27 Jan 55	59.4	40.6	–	–	46.4	0.6	0.6
54.2	45.8	–	84.2	Stockport, South	3 Feb 55	54.3	45.7	–	–	64.6	0.1	0.1
34.9	61.5	3.6	84.8	Denbighs., Wrexham	17 Mar 55	30.8	57.9	–	11.3	62.4	-0.2	-1.4
34.7	65.3	–	72.5	Gateshead, West	7 Dec 55	33.5	66.5	–	–	42.3	-1.2	-1.2
48.6	51.4	14.2	77.9	Greenock	8 Dec 55	46.3	53.7	–	–	75.3	-2.3	-2.3
60.4	25.4	–	75.5	Torquay	15 Dec 55	51.0	25.3	23.8	–	62.6	-4.6	-3.5
33.5	66.5	–	80.7	Durham, Blaydon	2 Feb 56	30.1	69.9	–	–	56.5	-3.5	-3.5
61.5	38.6	–	73.1	Leeds, North-East	9 Feb 56	63.2	36.8	–	–	39.9	1.7	1.7
51.8	23.4	24.8	78.8	Herefs., Hereford	14 Feb 56	44.3	19.3	36.4	–	61.5	-1.7	0.8
55.8	44.2	–	76.8	Lincs., Gainsborough	14 Feb 56	40.8	37.6	21.6	–	62.0	-4.2	-3.7
52.1	39.5	8.4	85.5	Somerset, Taunton	14 Feb 56	50.8	49.2	–	–	75.0	-5.5	-6.0
34.3	65.7	–	72.5	Walthamstow, West	1 Mar 56	20.2	64.7	14.7	0.4	54.0	-6.6	-10.5
60.4	39.6	–	75.5	Kent, Tonbridge	7 June 56	52.0	48.0	–	–	60.6	-8.4	-8.4
46.3	53.7	–	81.6	Newport	6 July 56	39.9	56.3	–	3.8	72.1	-4.5	-4.8
23.7	76.3	–	79.6	Durham, Chester-le-Street	27 Sep 56	19.2	80.8	–	–	65.0	-4.5	-4.5
56.7	31.6	11.7	77.9	Cheshire, City of Chester	15 Nov 56	51.7	36.2	12.1	–	71.5	-4.8	-5.3
60.9	39.1	–	81.0	Leics., Melton	19 Dec 56	53.3	46.7	–	–	56.5	-7.6	-7.6
54.0	46.0	–	77.9	*Lewisham, North	14 Feb 57	46.5	49.5	–	4.0	70.8	-5.4	-5.5
39.6	60.4	–	72.9	Wednesbury	28 Feb 57	28.0	62.2	–	9.9	60.0	-6.8	-8.6
–	42.7	49.5	85.1	*Carms., Carmarthen	28 Feb 57	–	47.3	41.2	11.5	87.5	–	–
75.3	24.7	–	74.6	Bristol, West	7 Mar 57	70.2	29.8	–	–	61.1	-5.0	-5.0

287

APPENDIX A

	Previous General Election					By-Election and Date	By-Election Result					Swing to Con.	
	Con. %	Lab. %	Lib. %	Others %	Turnout %		Con. %	Lab. %	Lib. %	Others %	Turnout %	Butler	Steed
Warwicks., Warwick & Leamington	64.5	35.5	—	—	78.8	7 Mar 57	52.3	47.7	—	—	77.9	−12.2	−12.2
Beckenham	69.0	31.0	—	—	76.5	21 Mar 57	62.9	37.1	—	—	64.7	−6.0	−6.0
Newcastle-upon-Tyne, North	63.8	36.2	—	—	77.6	21 Mar 57	60.2	39.8	—	—	64.1	−3.6	−3.6
Edinburgh, South	67.5	32.5	—	—	77.2	29 May 57	45.6	30.9	23.5	—	65.8	−10.2	−7.9
East Ham, North	40.9	59.1	—	—	74.9	30 May 57	29.5	56.3	—	14.3[2]	57.3	−4.3	−6.5
Hornsey	60.2	37.2	—	2.6	76.3	30 May 57	53.5	46.5	—	—	63.0	−8.0	−8.4
Dorset, North	52.1	15.5	32.4	—	82.2	27 June 57	45.1	18.3	36.1	0.5	75.8	−4.9	−5.9
Gloucester	49.1	50.9	—	—	80.9	12 Sep 57	28.6	51.3	20.1	—	71.0	−10.5	−13.3
Ipswich	47.1	52.9	—	—	80.5	24 Oct 57	32.7	45.9	21.5	—	75.6	−3.7	−5.5
Leicester, South-East	64.2	35.8	—	—	78.5	28 Nov 57	61.0	39.0	—	—	56.4	−3.3	−3.3
Liverpool, Garston	63.5	36.5	—	—	71.0	5 Dec 57	49.2	35.6	15.2	—	49.7	−6.7	−5.5
*Rochdale	51.5	48.5	—	—	82.8	12 Feb 58	19.8	44.7	35.5	—	80.2	−14.0	−20.8
*Glasgow, Kelvingrove	55.4	44.6	—	—	67.6	13 May 58	41.6	48.0	—	10.4[2]	60.5	−8.6	−9.0
*Devon, Torrington	65.1	35.0	—	—	69.2	27 Mar 58	37.4	24.6	38.0	—	80.6	−8.7	−4.8
Islington, North	39.7	60.4	—	—	64.7	15 May 8	29.3	67.7	—	3.0	35.6	−8.9	−9.4
Ealing, South	59.6	30.9	9.6	—	77.9	12 June 58	50.3	32.5	17.2	—	64.5	−5.5	−5.1
St Helens	35.7	64.3	—	—	73.5	12 June 58	35.3	64.7	—	—	54.6	−0.4	−0.4
Wigan	32.2	64.4	—	3.4	80.3	12 June 58	26.5	71.0	—	2.5	70.3	−6.1	−6.1
Somerset, Weston-super-Mare	62.7	37.3	—	—	73.8	12 June 58	49.3	26.2	24.5	—	72.2	−1.1	2.6
Argyll	67.6	32.4	—	—	66.6	12 June 58	46.8	25.7	27.5	—	67.1	−7.1	−3.1
Lancs., Morecambe & Lonsdale	71.2	28.8	—	—	74.4	6 Nov 58	65.3	34.7	—	—	63.9	−5.9	−5.9
Sussex, Chichester	70.8	29.2	—	—	71.8	6 Nov 58	70.9	29.1	—	—	51.8	0.1	0.1
Mon., Pontypool	27.1	72.9	—	—	77.1	10 Nov 58	21.5	68.5	—	10.0	61.7	−0.6	−3.2
Aberdeenshire, East	68.5	31.5	—	—	59.8	20 Nov 58	48.6	27.1	24.3	—	65.9	−7.8	−4.3
Shoreditch & Finsbury	26.6	73.5	—	—	61.6	27 Nov 58	24.0	76.0	—	—	24.9	−2.6	−2.6
Southend, West	64.2	20.8	15.0	—	74.1	29 Jan 59	55.6	20.2	24.2	—	42.9	−4.0	−2.2
Harrow, East	54.4	45.6	—	—	82.6	19 Mar 59	52.8	46.2	—	1.0	69.0	−1.1	−1.1

				Constituency	Date							
49.7	50.3	–	82.6	Norfolk, South-West	25 Mar 59	46.4	51.0	–	2.6	75.2	-2.0	-2.0
66.9	33.1	–	69.1	Galloway	9 Apr 59	50.5	23.9	25.7	–	72.8	-3.6	1.0
37.7	62.3	–	80.0	Yorks., Penistone	11 June 59	35.9	64.1	–	–	65.0	-1.8	-1.8
42.0	58.0	–	63.8	Cumberland, Whitehaven	18 June 59	41.4	58.6	–	–	79.2	-0.6	-0.6
70.9	29.1	–	79.2	Harrow, West	17 Mar 60	55.8	18.2	21.4	4.7	61.6	-2.1	4.5
50.0	50.1	–	85.5	*Yorks., Brighouse & Spenborough	17 Mar 60	50.8	49.3	–	–	82.4	0.8	0.8
64.0	36.0	–	73.9	Edinburgh, North	19 May 60	54.2	30.3	15.5	–	53.8	-2.1	0.1
52.8	47.2	17.8	81.0	Bolton, East	16 Nov 60	37.8	36.2	24.8	1.2	68.2	-2.0	-1.7
46.8	35.4	–	84.5	Mid-Bedfordshire	16 Nov 60	45.4	29.3	24.8	0.6	71.1	2.4	3.9
60.3	39.7	–	76.2	Shrops., Ludlow	16 Nov 60	46.4	26.3	27.4	–	63.6	-0.3	3.5
55.6	25.2	19.2	80.7	Devon, Tiverton	16 Nov 60	45.7	17.6	36.7	–	68.4	-1.2	3.4
54.0	30.5	15.5	82.5	Surrey, Carshalton	16 Nov 60	51.7	20.7	27.6	–	54.2	3.7	7.5
60.9	21.3	17.8	73.6	Hants., Petersfield	16 Nov 60	54.4	16.6	29.0	–	53.6	-0.9	2.5
19.0	81.0	–	85.8	Mon., Ebbw Vale	17 Nov 60	12.7	68.8	11.5	7.0	83.8	3.0	0.0
25.4	74.6	–	82.7	Blyth	24 Nov 60	21.7	68.9	–	9.5	54.1	1.0	-1.5
57.7	42.3	–	79.3	Worcester	16 Mar 61	39.7	30.2	30.1	–	64.2	-2.9	-0.9
51.6	35.9	12.5	82.4	Essex, Colchester	16 Mar 61	47.2	33.1	19.7	–	64.9	-0.8	-0.2
46.0	34.0	20.0	82.7	Derbys., High Peak	16 Mar 61	37.4	32.1	30.6	–	72.5	-3.4	-3.7
57.9	42.1	–	78.0	Cambridgeshire	16 Mar 61	45.9	30.1	24.0	–	62.4	0.0	2.5
42.6	57.4	–	65.7	Birmingham, Small Heath	23 Mar 61	28.8	59.2	12.0	–	42.6	-7.8	-9.9
43.7	52.3	–	76.9	Warrington	20 Apr 61	31.6	55.8	12.5	–	56.7	-5.8	-7.6
42.7	57.3	–	78.9	Paisley	20 Apr 61	13.2	45.4	41.4	–	68.1	-18.8	-20.1
43.8	56.2	–	81.4	Bristol, South-East	4 May 61	30.5	69.5	–	–	56.7	-3.2	-13.2
62.3	37.7	–	69.2	Manchester, Moss Side	7 Nov 61	41.1	25.8	27.8	5.2	48.7	-4.6	-0.8
55.9	28.0	16.1	74.2	Shrops., Oswestry	8 Nov 61	40.8	28.0	28.4	2.8	60.8	-7.6	-7.3
70.0	30.1	–	75.2	Fife, East	8 Nov 61	47.4	26.4	26.1	–	67.3	-9.4	-5.7
36.6	63.4	–	68.5	Glasgow, Bridgeton	16 Nov 61	20.7	57.5	–	21.8[2]	41.9	-5.0	-10.1
44.9	55.1	–	84.2	Lincoln	8 Mar 62	30.2	50.5	18.2	1.2	75.0	-5.0	-7.5
57.9	21.6	20.6	74.9	Blackpool, North	13 Mar 62	38.3	26.4	35.3	–	55.2	-12.2	-13.7
56.6	22.2	21.2	82.8	*Kent, Orpington	14 Mar 62	34.7	12.4	52.9	–	80.3	-6.0	1.9
38.5	61.5	–	76.2	Middlesbrough, East	14 Mar 62	15.0	61.7	23.3	–	51.3	-11.8	-18.9

By-Election and Date	Previous General Election					By-Election Result					Swing to Con.	
	Con. %	Lab. %	Lib. %	Others %	Turnout %	Con. %	Lab. %	Lib. %	Others %	Turnout %	Butler	Steed
Pontefract	23.6	76.4	–	–	84.3	19.4	77.3	–	3.4	63.3	-2.6	-3.6
Stockton-on-Tees	46.3	53.7	–	–	83.9	27.8	45.2	26.9	–	81.5	-5.0	-8.3
Derby, North	47.2	52.8	–	–	76.7	22.5	49.5	25.4	2.7	60.6	-10.7	-15.9
Montgomeryshire	31.3	26.6	42.0	–	83.8	21.9	20.6	51.3	6.2	85.1	-1.7	-2.5
*Middlesbrough, West	54.9	35.5	9.7	–	84.5	33.7	39.7	25.8	0.8[2]	72.2	-12.7	-14.8
Derbys., West	61.3	38.7	–	–	82.0	36.0	27.3	32.5	4.2	79.4	-6.9	-4.4
West Lothian	39.7	60.3	–	–	77.9	11.4	50.8	10.8	26.9[2]	71.1	-9.4	-21.4
Leicester, North-East	48.1	51.9	–	–	78.4	24.2	41.5	34.3	–	60.9	-6.7	-11.2
*Glasgow, Woodside	49.3	43.1	7.7	–	75.2	30.1	36.1	21.7	12.1[3]	54.7	-6.1	-7.8
*Dorset, South	49.8	34.7	15.6	–	78.8	31.8	33.5	21.7	13.0[4]	70.2	-8.4	-10.3
Wilts., Chippenham	52.1	31.0	16.9	–	80.3	36.8	29.1	32.5	1.6[3]	68.0	-6.7	-6.9
Northants., South	57.0	43.0	–	–	82.7	41.2	38.6	19.3	0.9	69.0	-5.7	-5.4
Norfolk, Central	50.4	34.8	14.9	–	79.9	37.7	37.1	22.5	2.8[2]	60.2	-7.5	-8.7
Yorks., Colne Valley	29.9	44.3	25.8	–	84.2	15.4	44.5	39.5	0.7	78.9	-7.4	-14.6
Rotherham	37.2	62.8	–	–	78.9	28.4	69.3	–	2.3	56.3	-7.6	-8.1
Swansea, East	22.0	67.5	–	10.5	80.1	7.4	61.1	15.8	15.7[3]	55.9	-4.2	-13.9
Leeds, South	31.0	58.6	10.4	–	79.0	20.1	62.9	14.7	2.2	60.5	-7.7	-10.5
Deptford	38.1	62.0	–	–	69.3	19.2	58.3	22.6	–	44.1	-7.6	-13.3
West Bromwich	42.6	57.4	–	–	72.6	23.6	58.7	17.6	–	55.2	-10.2	-13.9
Warwicks., Stratford	68.5	31.5	–	–	76.9	43.6	34.1	21.0	1.4[2]	69.4	-13.7	-12.4
†Bristol, South-East	43.8	56.2	–	–	81.4	–	79.7	–	20.3[3]	42.2	–	–
*Luton	55.1	44.9	–	–	82.5	39.5	48.0	11.4	1.1	74.0	-9.4	-10.0
Kinross & Perthshire, West	68.2	16.8	–	15.0	71.0	57.4	15.2	19.5	7.9[4]	76.1	-4.6	-1.2
Dundee, West	48.3	49.6	–	2.1	82.9	39.4	50.6	–	10.0[2]	71.6	-4.9	-5.5
Suffolk, Sudbury & Woodbridge	53.0	33.0	14.0	–	81.1	49.6	37.0	13.4	–	70.5	-3.7	-4.4
Manchester, Openshaw	39.8	60.2	–	–	76.0	29.2	65.9	–	4.9	46.1	-8.2	-9.1
St Marylebone	64.5	23.6	11.9	–	65.5	55.0	31.8	13.3	–	44.2	-8.9	-9.9

58.4	41.6	–	–	77.4	Dumfriesshire	12 Dec 63	40.8	38.5	10.9	9.8	71.7	-7.2	-6.9
58.8	41.3	–	–	78.6	Suffolk, Bury St Edmunds	14 May 64	49.0	43.5	7.5	–	74.6	-6.0	-5.8
51.4	41.9	6.7	–	79.2	Wilts., Devizes	14 May 64	46.9	42.9	10.3	–	75.8	-2.8	-2.9
52.1	47.9	–	–	85.9	*Lanarks., Rutherglen	14 May 64	44.5	55.5	–	–	82.0	-7.6	-7.6
67.3	32.7	–	–	76.7	Hants., Winchester	14 May 64	52.2	34.6	13.2	–	68.7	-8.5	-7.2
49.7	50.3	–	–	83.8	Kent, Faversham	4 June 64	44.1	55.1	–	0.8	74.8	-5.2	-5.3
38.2	61.8	–	–	62.5	Liverpool, Scotland	11 June 64	25.7	74.3	–	–	42.0	-12.5	-12.5
29.1	52.8	18.1	–	80.1	Warwicks., Nuneaton	21 Jan 65	34.9	48.9	16.1	–	60.8	4.9	6.1
33.5	50.4	16.2	–	70.2	*Leyton	21 Jan 65	42.9	42.4	14.0	0.8[2]	57.7	8.7	10.4
46.8	28.0	25.2	–	81.2	Altrincham & Sale	4 Feb 65	50.0	29.1	19.4	1.6	62.0	1.1	0.7
53.2	19.9	27.0	–	78.0	Sussex, East Grinstead	4 Feb 65	55.0	13.5	31.5	–	64.5	*4.1*	*7.5*
48.3	34.4	17.3	–	78.6	Wilts., Salisbury	4 Feb 65	48.2	37.4	12.9	1.5	69.1	-1.5	-2.1
49.3	37.5	13.3	–	82.4	Essex, Saffron Walden	23 Mar 65	48.5	39.6	11.9	–	76.1	-1.4	-1.7
42.8	15.9	38.9	2.5	82.2	*Roxburgh, Selkirk & Peebles	24 Mar 65	38.7	11.3	49.2	0.9	82.2	0.2	4.5
14.1	85.9	–	–	75.5	Mon., Abertillery	1 Apr 65	14.3	79.0	–	6.7	63.2	3.6	1.2
55.5	31.8	15.6	–	75.8	Birmingham, Hall Green	6 May 65	54.9	28.8	16.4	–	52.4	2.7	3.4
68.4	31.6	–	–	69.6	Hove	22 July 65	62.2	20.6	16.9	0.3	58.5	2.4	6.7
58.4	30.6	11.1	–	59.7	Cities of London & Westminster	4 Nov 65	59.5	32.9	6.3	1.3	41.8	-0.6	-1.2
32.5	53.1	14.4	–	79.6	Erith & Crayford	11 Nov 65	37.5	55.4	7.2	–	72.0	1.3	2.4
40.8	43.3	15.9	–	77.2	Kingston-upon-Hull, North	27 Jan 66	40.8	52.2	6.3	0.7[3]	76.3	-4.5	-4.7
11.6	46.2	26.1	16.1	83.0	*Carms., Carmarthen	14 July 66	7.1	33.1	20.8	39.0	74.9	4.3	-2.5
31.6	54.0	14.5	–	79.7	Warwicks., Nuneaton	9 Mar 67	32.7	42.1	17.6	7.6[2]	66.1	6.5	6.9
7.8	76.1	–	16.1[2]	80.3	Rhondda, West	9 Mar 67	4.3	49.0	–	46.7[2]	82.2	*11.8*	*-1.3*
47.6	52.4	–	–	79.0	*Glasgow, Pollok	9 Mar 67	36.9	31.2	1.9	30.0[2]	75.7	5.3	6.6
54.4	26.8	18.9	–	78.6	Devon, Honiton	16 Mar 67	57.0	20.4	22.6	–	72.7	4.5	6.6
51.2	48.8	–	–	79.0	Staffs., Brierley Hill	24 Apr 67	53.8	36.2	7.8	2.2	68.0	7.6	8.6
43.4	45.5	10.2	0.9	80.0	*Cambridge	21 Sep 67	51.6	36.6	11.8	–	65.8	8.6	9.7
24.8	61.2	14.1	–	71.0	*Walthamstow, West	21 Sep 67	37.1	36.7	22.9	3.4[2]	54.0	18.4	21.4
41.4	58.7	–	–	74.0	*Leicester, South-West	2 Nov 67	51.6	35.9	12.5	–	57.5	16.5	17.7
39.9	60.1	–	–	72.6	Manchester, Gorton	2 Nov 67	44.5	45.9	5.9	3.7[2]	72.4	9.4	9.3
28.8	71.2	–	–	73.3	*Lanarks., Hamilton	2 Nov 67	12.5	41.5	–	46.0	73.7	6.7	-5.7

Previous General Election					By-Election and Date	By-Election Result					Swing to Con.	
Con. %	Lab. %	Lib. %	Others %	Turnout %		Con. %	Lab. %	Lib. %	Others %	Turnout %	Butler	Steed
49.6	37.2	13.2	–	83.4	Derbys., West — 23 Nov 67	56.7	18.4	19.8	5.2	64.6	13.0	18.4
65.1	19.9	15.1	–	58.1	Kensington, South — 14 Mar 68	75.5	8.6	12.6	3.4²	40.0	10.8	13.2
41.0	59.1	–	–	73.9	*Dudley — 28 Mar 68	58.1	34.0	7.9	–	63.5	21.2	22.2
51.6	36.1	12.3	–	78.9	Warwicks., Warwick & Leamington — 28 Mar 68	68.3	16.5	15.2	–	58.5	18.1	21.7
46.4	53.6	–	–	85.7	*Warwicks., Meriden — 28 Mar 68	64.8	35.2	–	–	66.0	18.5	18.5
42.3	57.7	–	–	74.0	*Acton — 28 Mar 68	48.7	33.9	11.4	6.0³	59.7	15.1	16.6
38.8	61.2	–	–	70.9	*Oldham, West — 13 June 68	46.5	33.6	6.7	13.2	54.7	17.7	19.3
21.3	75.9	–	2.8	66.2	Sheffield, Brightside — 13 June 68	34.8	55.2	–	10.0³	49.8	17.1	16.7
37.0	49.3	–	13.7	81.0	*Nelson & Colne — 27 June 68	48.9	38.4	9.0	3.7	74.2	11.4	13.1
14.6	74.3	–	11.1	76.7	Glam., Caerphilly — 18 July 68	10.4	45.7	3.6	40.4	75.9	12.2	2.1
38.4	61.6	–	–	73.4	Notts., Bassetlaw — 31 Oct 68	47.9	49.6	–	2.4	68.0	10.8	10.8
51.2	26.8	22.1	–	74.2	Hants, New Forest — 7 Nov 68	66.3	13.8	19.9	–	55.9	14.0	17.1
42.3	47.8	9.8	–	80.1	*Walthamstow, East — 27 Mar 69	63.2	36.9	–	–	51.2	15.9	16.2
58.1	41.9	–	–	70.3	Brighton, Pavilion — 27 Mar 69	70.5	18.6	10.8	–	45.1	17.8	21.0
52.1	28.8	19.1	–	78.5	Somerset, Weston-super-Mare — 27 Mar 69	65.7	14.6	19.7	–	60.8	13.9	17.4
57.2	25.1	17.7	–	73.2	Sussex, Chichester — 27 May 69	74.2	12.2	13.6	–	53.4	15.0	16.4
17.4	58.9	23.7	–	59.7	*Birmingham, Ladywood — 26 June 69	16.8	25.5	54.3	3.4²	51.9	16.5	17.0
32.3	58.5	9.3	–	66.4	Paddington, North — 30 Oct 69	48.3	51.7	–	–	46.3	11.4	12.7
30.7	59.5	9.9	–	54.2	Islington, North — 30 Oct 69	38.9	49.2	10.2	1.7	32.8	9.2	10.1
22.8	73.1	–	4.1	61.7	Glasgow, Gorbals — 30 Oct 69	18.6	53.4	–	28.0³	58.6	7.7	2.1
38.2	61.8	–	–	79.9	Newcastle-under-Lyme — 30 Oct 69	44.4	46.6	6.4	2.6	71.5	10.7	10.6
36.7	61.4	–	2.0	73.5	*Swindon — 30 Oct 69	41.7	40.5	15.3	2.4²	69.8	12.9	13.3
47.6	52.4	–	–	86.5	*Northants, Wellingborough — 4 Dec 69	54.4	39.8	–	5.8	69.7	9.7	10.1
46.4	36.9	16.8	–	75.0	Lincs., Louth — 4 Dec 69	58.0	19.9	17.8	4.4	44.7	14.3	18.8
44.4	38.1	17.5	–	80.2	Somerset, Bridgwater — 12 Mar 70	55.5	31.9	12.6	–	70.3	8.6	9.6
32.8	67.3	–	–	75.1	Ayrshire, South — 19 Mar 70	25.6	54.1	–	20.4	76.3	3.0	–0.6

					Constituency	Date							
62.1	29.3	8.6	–	59.6	St Marylebone	22 Oct 70	63.5	27.0	6.0	3.4	35.3	1.9	2.2
57.9	26.2	12.8	3.1	71.3	Enfield, West	19 Nov 70	57.2	26.1	12.4	4.4	49.9	-0.3	-0.1
25.3	74.8	–	–	50.7	Liverpool, Scotland	1 Apr 71	18.4	71.3		10.3	37.7	-1.7	-4.8
60.8	22.9	16.3	–	72.0	Sussex, Arundel & Shoreham	1 Apr 71	64.1	20.9	14.7	0.4	53.1	2.6	2.8
58.5	41.5	–	–	76.6	*Worcs., Bromsgrove	27 May 71	48.4	51.6	–	–	67.0	-10.1	-10.1
39.8	60.2	–	–	69.5	Yorks., Goole	27 May 71	31.1	68.9	–	–	55.6	-8.7	-8.7
–	67.2	–	32.8²	54.2	Southampton, Itchen	27 May 71	31.6	55.4	5.4	7.6	50.1	–	–
41.2	57.7	–	1.1	67.2	Hayes & Harlington	17 June 71	25.3	74.7	–	–	42.3	-16.5	-16.4
36.3	57.3	6.4	–	64.0	Greenwich	8 July 71	28.0	66.7	–	5.3	39.2	-8.9	-9.3
34.8	50.7	–	14.5	73.1	Stirlingshire, Stirling & Falkirk	16 Sep71	19.0	46.5	–	34.6	60.9	*-5.8*	*-11.7*
42.3	57.7	–	–	68.8	Lancs., Widnes	23 Sep71	30.9	69.1	–	–	46.2	-11.5	-11.5
52.1	33.3	14.6	–	76.4	Cheshire, Macclesfield	30 Sep71	44.7	42.7	10.7	1.9	76.6	-8.4	-9.9
9.9	28.7	–	61.5²	77.9	*Merthyr Tydfil	13 Apr 72	7.4	48.5	2.4	41.7²	77.6	*-11.2*	*-12.4*
28.2	67.3	–	4.5	48.2	Southwark	4 May 72	18.1	79.3	–	2.6	29.4	-11.1	-11.0
56.7	31.7	11.7	–	69.1	Kingston-upon-Thames	4 May 72	52.3	31.0	11.3	5.4	53.3	-1.9	-1.4
28.0	41.6	30.4	–	72.9	*Rochdale	26 Oct 72	17.7	31.1	42.3	8.9	69.0	*0.1*	*-4.1*
49.3	41.7	9.0	–	74.9	Uxbridge	7 Dec 72	39.8	36.8	10.2	13.2⁴	56.2	-2.3	-2.1
58.1	27.3	14.6	–	67.6	*Sutton & Cheam	7 Dec 72	31.9	8.7	53.6	5.9²⁴	56.2	*-3.8*	*10.4*
39.0	51.0	–	10.0	74.5	*Lincoln	1 Mar 73	17.5	23.3	–	59.2⁴	72.6	*3.1*	*-0.3*
42.4	48.3	–	9.3²	76.1	Dundee, East	1 Mar 73	25.2	32.7	8.3	33.8³	70.6	-0.8	-2.8
28.4	71.6	–	–	73.7	Chester-le-Street	1 Mar 73	8.4	53.0	38.6	–	71.4	*-0.8*	*-14.7*
44.8	55.2	–	–	62.2	West Bromwich	24 May 73	25.4	53.2	–	21.4²	43.6	-8.7	-12.6
44.6	55.4	–	–	76.9	Westhoughton	24 May 73	42.3	57.0	–	0.7	63.4	-1.9	-2.6
27.8	68.5	–	3.7	57.0	Manchester Exchange	27 June 73	7.1	55.3	36.5	1.1	43.7	*-3.8*	*-17.6*
59.9	40.1	–	–	71.9	*Isle of Ely	26 July 73	35.0	26.7	38.3	–	65.8	*-5.8*	*-2.4*
60.7	26.2	13.1	–	73.7	*Yorks., Ripon	26 July 73	40.5	13.9	43.5	2.1	64.3	*-4.0*	*4.6*
68.7	31.3	–	–	66.8	Hove	8 Nov 73	47.8	11.6	37.3	3.3	62.4	*-0.1*	*18.9*
50.7	27.4	21.9	–	73.7	*Berwick-upon-Tweed	8 Nov 73	39.7	19.8	39.9	0.6²	75.0	*-1.7*	*1.9*
52.8	37.1	10.1	–	70.1	Edinburgh N.	8 Nov 73	38.7	24.0	18.4	18.9	54.4	-0.5	2.9
28.2	60.0	–	11.8²	63.3	*Glasgow Govan	8 Nov 73	11.7	38.2	8.2	41.9	51.7	*2.7*	*-8.4*

By-Election and Date	Previous General Election					By-Election Result					Swing to Con.	
	Con. %	Lab. %	Lib. %	Others %	Turnout %	Con. %	Lab. %	Lib. %	Others %	Turnout %	Butler	Steed
Newham S. — 23 May 74	12.2	66.1	14.8	6.9	63.2	11.1	62.7	12.5	13.7	25.9	*1.2*	*−0.6*
*Woolwich W. — 26 June 75	38.6	47.1	14.3	–	73.9	48.8	42.1	5.3	3.8[5]	62.3	7.6	8.7
Coventry N.W. — 4 Mar 76	31.6	51.9	15.7	0.8	75.2	37.4	47.7	11.3	3.6[4]	72.9	5.0	6.0
Carshalton — 11 Mar 76	45.4	37.9	16.7	–	74.3	51.7	27.5	15.0	5.8[4]	60.5	8.4	10.8
Cheshire, Wirral — 11 Mar 76	50.8	31.6	17.6	–	75.5	66.8	20.3	11.4	1.5[2]	55.5	13.6	16.4
Rotherham — 24 June 76	22.1	64.6	13.3	–	65.5	34.7	50.7	7.8	6.8[3]	46.8	13.3	15.1
Thurrock — 15 July 76	24.4	55.6	20.0	–	68.6	35.4	45.3	12.2	7.1[3]	54.1	10.6	13.1
Newcastle-upon-Tyne C. — 4 Nov 76	16.5	71.8	11.7	–	58.4	19.7	47.6	29.0	3.7[2]	41.0	*13.7*	*10.6*
*Walsall N. — 4 Nov 76	26.1	59.5	13.4	1.0	66.6	43.4	31.6	3.2	21.8[6]	51.5	22.5	27.3
*Workington — 4 Nov 76	32.3	56.0	11.7	–	75.8	48.2	45.6	6.2	–	74.2	13.2	14.8
Cambridge — 2 Dec 76	41.2	36.0	21.1	1.7	69.6	51.0	26.0	18.3	4.7[3]	49.2	9.9	11.8
Cities of London & Westminster S. — 24 Feb 77	51.7	30.9	14.9	2.5	53.2	59.1	19.7	9.8	11.4[7]	39.6	9.3	12.4
*Birmingham Stechford — 31 Mar 77	27.8	57.6	14.6	–	64.1	43.4	38.0	8.0	10.6[3]	58.8	17.6	7.5
*Ashfield — 28 Apr 77	22.3	63.4	14.3	–	74.7	43.1	42.5	9.6	4.8[2]	59.7	20.8	24.3
Grimsby — 28 Apr 77	31.9	47.1	20.6	0.4	69.4	45.1	46.9	6.7	0.7[3]	70.2	7.0	9.0
Saffron Walden — 7 July 77	43.7	26.0	30.3	–	78.1	55.7	14.6	25.2	4.5	64.8	*11.7*	*17.1*
Birmingham, Ladywood — 18 Aug 77	22.1	64.5	13.4	–	56.9	28.4	53.1	4.9	13.6[2]	42.6	8.8	9.4
Bournemouth E. — 24 Nov 77	51.7	21.0	25.2	2.1	70.5	63.4	15.3	13.4	7.9[3]	42.6	8.7	9.3
*Ilford N. — 2 Mar 78	40.9	42.5	16.6	–	74.5	50.3	38.0	5.0	6.7[5]	69.1	6.9	7.9
Glasgow, Garscadden — 13 Apr 78	12.9	50.9	5.0	31.2	70.8	18.5	45.4	–	36.1[4]	69.1	*5.6*	*8.8*
Lambeth C. — 20 Apr 78	26.2	60.1	12.5	1.2[2]	52.6	34.4	49.4	5.3	10.9[8]	44.5	9.4	10.6
Epsom & Ewell — 27 Apr 78	54.1	19.3	26.6	–	73.7	63.6	16.5	12.8	7.1[2]	54.9	*6.2*	*5.3*
Wycombe — 27 Apr 78	46.3	30.8	19.4	3.5	74.3	60.0	28.5	7.4	4.1	59.0	8.0	7.6
Hamilton — 31 May 78	9.5	47.5	4.0	39.0	77.2	13.0	51.0	2.6	33.4	72.1	*3.5*	*3.7*
Manchester, Moss Side — 13 July 78	34.3	47.1	17.6	1.0	62.9	40.6	46.4	9.2	3.8[2]	51.6	3.5	4.5
Penistone — 13 July 78	24.0	54.2	21.8	–	74.7	32.9	45.5	21.6	–	59.8	8.8	11.3

					Constituency	Date							
37.6	43.3	5.9	13.2	83.0	Berwick & E.Lothian	26 Oct 78	40.2	47.4	3.6	8.8	71.2	*-0.7*	*-0.6*
16.2	70.4	12.3	1.1	71.2	Pontefract & Castleford	26 Oct 78	27.3	65.8	6.9	–	48.9	*7.8*	*10.5*
48.0	31.2	20.8	–	78.6	Clitheroe	1 Mar 79	65.0	28.4	6.6	–	62.8	*9.9*	*9.0*
51.0	22.6	26.4	–	76.8	Knutsford	1 Mar 79	67.1	15.6	15.8	1.5	57.2	*12.1*	*11.9*
20.8	51.9	27.3	–	61.2	*Liverpool, Edge Hill	29 Mar 79	9.4	23.8	64.1	2.7	57.2	*8.4*	*-0.2*
22.1	70.8	5.3	1.8	63.7	Manchester C.	27 Sept 79	12.0	70.7	14.2	3.1[3]	33.6	*-5.0*	*-9.3*
51.7	27.7	16.2	1.4	79.7	Herts. S.W.	13 Dec 79	45.9	16.2	23.6	2.8[3]	48.3	*0.4*	*-4.0*
56.1	28.1	13.1	1.7	70.1	Southend E.	13 Mar 80	36.8	35.6	25.1	2.5[4]	62.5	*-12.9*	*-15.5*
16.4	72.5	–	11.1	59.5	Glasgow C.	26 June 80	8.8	60.8	–	29.4[5]	42.8	*2.1*	*-5.9*
28.8	61.7	9.0	0.5	71.3	Warrington	16 July 81	7.1	48.4	42.4	2.1[8]	67.0	*-3.7*	*-19.1*
49.4	40.1	10.5	–	72.5	*Croydon N.W.	22 Oct 81	30.5	26.0	40.0	3.5[9]	62.8	*-2.5*	*-1.2*
56.9	25.4	15.2	–	75.2	*Crosby	26 Nov 81	39.8	9.5	49.0	1.7[6]	69.3	*-1.9*	*11.5*
41.0	40.4	12.3	1.1	75.7	*Glasgow, Hillhead	25 Mar 82	26.6	27.5	41.2	14.1[5]	76.4	*-0.8*	*-3.7*
61.7	20.2	17.1	–	76.2	Beaconsfield	27 Apr 82	61.8	10.4	26.8	1.0[3]	53.9	*5.0*	*10.2*
43.9	45.2	8.9	–	76.9	*Mitcham & Morden	3 June 82	43.4	24.4	24.4	2.8[6]	48.5	*9.7*	*14.7*
27.5	60.9	–	11.6	75.3	Coatbridge & Airdrie	24 June 82	26.2	55.1	8.2	10.5	56.3	*4.5*	*1.1*
30.5	53.2	9.1	7.2	80.8	Gower	16 Sept 82	22.1	43.5	25.1	9.3[3]	65.4	*0.7*	*-2.7*
28.1	59.8	7.7	4.4	57.7	Peckham	28 Oct 82	12.4	50.3	32.2	4.4	38.0	*-3.1*	*-15.6*
45.4	45.1	8.1	1.4	70.6	*Birmingham, Northfield	28 Oct 82	35.6	36.3	26.1	2.0[4]	55.0	*-0.5*	*-0.7*
24.1	64.5	–	11.6[4]	68.3	Glasgow, Queens' Park	2 Dec 82	12.0	56.0	9.4	22.6[4]	47.0	*-1.8*	*-9.6*
24.9	63.6	6.8	4.7[2]	59.3	*Bermondsey	24 Feb 83	5.5	26.1	57.7	10.7[13]	57.7	*9.0*	*-10.7*
43.4	45.5	10.2	0.9	78.4	Darlington	24 Mar 83	34.9	39.5	24.5	1.1[5]	80.0	*-1.6*	*-2.8*
58.8	13.3	27.9	–	73.0	Penrith & Border	28 June 83	46.0	7.4	44.6	2.0[5]	55.7	*-3.5*	*4.5*
32.4	48.0	18.5	–	72.6	Chesterfield	1 Mar 84	15.2	46.5	34.7	3.6[7]	76.9	*-7.9*	*-15.7*
14.2	56.0	20.6	9.3	73.4	Cynon Valley	3 Apr 84	7.4	58.8	19.9	13.9[4]	65.7	*-2.0*	*-9.0*
59.7	8.1	32.1	–	74.5	Surrey S.W.	3 Apr 84	49.3	6.7	43.4	0.8[3]	61.7	*-4.5*	*0.0*
51.2	23.7	24.7	0.4	76.5	Stafford	3 Apr 84	40.4	27.4	31.8	0.4	65.6	*-7.3*	*-8.8*
50.0	22.6	25.4	2.0[2]	67.3	*Portsmouth S.	14 June 84	34.3	26.5	37.6	1.5[6]	54.5	*-9.8*	*-12.5*
58.1	17.9	23.4	0.7	69.6	Southgate	13 Dec 84	49.6	11.9	35.6	2.9[6]	50.6	*-1.3*	*4.2*

	Previous General Election					By-Election and Date	By-Election Result					Swing to Con.	
	Con. %	Lab. %	Lib. %	Others %	Turnout %		Con. %	Lab. %	Lib. %	Others %	Turnout %	Butler	Steed
*Brecon & Radnor	48.2	25.0	24.4	2.4[2]	80.1	4 July 85	27.7	34.4	35.8	2.1[4]	79.4	−15.0	−21.2
Tyne Bridge	25.2	56.5	18.3	–	61.5	5 Dec 85	11.1	57.8	29.7	1.4[3]	38.1	−7.7	−14.8
*Fulham	46.2	34.0	18.2	1.5[2]	76.1	10 Apr 86	34.9	44.4	18.7	2.0[8]	70.8	−10.9	−13.7
*Ryedale	59.2	10.3	30.5	–	71.8	8 May 86	41.3	8.4	50.3	–	67.3	−8.0	−2.1
Derbyshire W.	55.9	17.1	27.0	–	77.8	8 May 86	39.5	19.8	39.4	1.3[2]	71.9	−9.6	−10.0
Newcastle-under-Lyme	36.4	42.0	21.6	–	77.3	17 June 86	19.0	40.8	38.8	1.4[4]	62.2	−8.1	−15.6
Knowsley N.	20.1	64.5	14.8	0.6	69.5	13 Nov 86	6.3	56.3	34.6	2.8[3]	57.3	−2.8	−16.6
*Greenwich	34.8	38.2	25.1	1.8[3]	67.7	26 Feb 87	11.2	33.8	53.0	2.0[5]	67.3	−9.1	−21.8
Truro	38.1	4.5	57.3	–	79.6	12 Mar 87	31.5	7.1	60.4	0.9[2]	69.9	−4.6	−7.8
Kensington	47.5	33.2	17.2	2.0[3]	64.7	14 July 88	41.6	38.1	15.8[2]	4.4[11]	51.0	−5.4	−6.6
*Glasgow, Govan	11.9	64.8	12.3	11.0[2]	73.4	10 Nov 88	7.3	36.9	4.1	51.6[5]	60.2	11.7	1.1
Epping Forest	60.9	18.4	19.4	1.3	76.3	15 Dec 88	39.5	18.7	38.2[2]	3.6[5]	49.0	−10.8	−9.1
Yorks., Richmond	61.2	11.8	27.0	–	72.1	23 Feb 89	37.2	4.9	54.3[2]	3.6[5]	63.4	−8.5	4.4
Pontypridd	19.5	56.3	18.9	5.3	76.6	23 Feb 89	13.5	53.4	7.0[2]	26.1[3]	62.0	−1.5	0.1
*Vale of Glamorgan	46.8	34.7	16.7	1.8	79.3	4 May 89	36.3	48.9	6.5[2]	8.4[2]	70.7	−12.4	−14.8
Glasgow, Central	13.0	64.5	10.5	12.0[3]	65.6	15 June 89	7.6	54.6	2.5[2]	35.2[5]	52.8	2.3	−4.5
Vauxhall	29.0	50.2	18.2	2.6[3]	64.0	15 June 89	18.8	52.8	17.5	10.8[11]	42.0	−6.4	−9.3
*Staffs., Mid	50.6	24.7	23.2	1.5	79.5	23 Mar 90	32.3	49.1	13.7[2]	5.1[10]	79.1	−21.4	−27.5
Bootle	20.1	66.9	13.0	–	72.9	24 May 90	9.1	75.4	9.4[2]	6.2[4]	50.6	−9.6	−12.4
Knowsley S.	21.6	64.5	13.9	–	74.1	27 Sept 90	15.2	68.8	8.5	7.5[4]	33.4	−5.3	−7.0
*Eastbourne	59.9	8.8	29.7	1.6	75.6	18 Oct 90	40.9	5.0	50.7	3.2[5]	60.7	−7.6	1.8
Bradford N.	39.5	42.8	17.7	–	72.7	8 Nov 90	16.8	51.7	25.3	6.1[7]	53.5	−15.8	−23.5
†Bootle	20.1	66.9	13.0	–	72.9	8 Nov 90	9.2	78.4	7.9	4.6[4]	39.7	−11.2	−12.6
Paisley S.	14.7	56.2	15.1	14.0	75.3	29 Nov 90	13.4	46.1	9.8	30.6[2]	55.5	4.9	1.8

						Date							
15.8	55.5	15.8	12.9	73.5	Paisley N.	29 Nov 90	14.8	44.0	8.3	33.0[2]	53.7	6.3	2.9
60.9	17.7	21.4	–	79.1	*Ribble Valley	7 Mar 91	38.5	9.4	48.5	3.5[6]	71.2	–7.1	–6.8
16.1	63.4	14.1	6.4	78.8	Neath	4 Apr 91	8.6	51.8	11.1[2]	28.6[4]	63.7	2.1	–6.0
47.5	27.7	24.0	0.8	80.8	*Monmouth	16 May 91	34.0	39.3	24.8	2.0[2]	75.8	–12.6	–16.8
14.4	64.4	21.2	–	73.6	Liverpool, Walton	4 July 91	2.9	53.1	36.0	8.1[3]	56.7	–1.4	–13.0
17.2	67.0	15.8	–	75.7	Hemsworth	7 Nov 91	10.5	66.3	20.1	3.2[2]	42.8	–3.0	–6.8
40.7	15.9	36.3	7.1[2]	75.2	*Kincardine & Deeside	7 Nov 91	30.6	7.7	49.0	12.7[2]	67.0	–1.0	8.0
41.7	38.4	19.9	–	78.8	*Langbaurgh	7 Nov 91	39.1	42.9	16.1	2.0[4]	65.4	–3.2	–4.4
55.9	37.3	6.0	0.8	82.8	*Newbury	6 May 93	26.9	2.0	65.6	5.5[16]	71.0	3.2	0.5
63.5	12.1	23.6	0.7[2]	80.7	*Christchurch	29 July 93	31.4	2.7	62.2	3.6[11]	74.0	–11.4	8.1
23.7	63.9	12.3	–	71.7	Rotherham	5 May 94	9.9	55.6	26.7	4.8[2]	43.7	–2.2	–12.0
33.9	51.6	14.5	–	70.0	Barking	9 June 94	10.4	72.1	12.0	5.5[3]	60.0	–22.0	–27.0
36.3	52.3	11.4	–	70.7	Dagenham	9 June 94	9.9	72.0	8.4	9.7[3]	62.1	–23.1	–27.9
30.5	58.3	11.2	–	60.3	Newham N.E.	9 June 94	14.6	74.9	4.2	6.3[4]	60.4	–16.4	–18.1
38.4	47.6	13.7	0.3	75.6	Bradford S.	9 June 94	17.8	55.3	23.9	3.0[2]	44.1	–14.2	–20.3
51.3	20.7	28.0	–	82.9	*Eastleigh	9 June 94	24.8	27.6	44.3	3.4[3]	58.2	–16.7	–23.9
16.0	61.3	4.6	18.0	75.1	Monklands E.	30 June 94	2.3	49.8	2.6	45.3[3]	69.9	–13.6	–16.3
48.8	40.7	10.5	–	82.1	*Dudley W.	15 Dec 94	18.7	68.8	7.6	5.0[7]	47.3	–29.1	–33.2
14.8	74.3	5.7	5.2[2]	81.5	Islwyn	16 Feb 95	3.9	69.2	10.6	16.3[4]	45.6	–8.0	–11.3
40.2	12.5	11.4	36.0	76.9	*Kinross & Perthshire	25 May 95	21.4	22.9	11.8	43.9[6]	62.0	–14.6	–28.0
44.2	19.9	35.9	–	81.6	*Littleborough & Saddleworth	27 July 95	23.6	33.8	38.5	4.1[7]	63.6	–17.3	–27.9
18.6	70.8	10.5	–	75.9	Hemsworth	1 Feb 96	8.8	71.9	6.9	12.4[7]	39.5	–5.5	–10.0
50.7	38.2	9.6	1.6	82.1	*Staffs S.E.	11 Apr 96	28.8	60.7	4.7	5.8[10]	61.4	–22.2	–24.9
14.2	77.2	8.6	–	72.7	Barnsley E.	12 Dec 96	6.9	77.7	7.9	7.5[3]	35.6	–3.9	–8.2
50.8	34.6	13.1	1.6[2]	82.4	*Wirral S.	27 Feb 97	34.4	52.6	10.1	2.9[9]	73.0	–17.2	–20.0

Contests excluded above (see p. 269)

Londonderry, North	(4 Mar 19)
Oxford University	(19 Mar 19)
*Antrim, East	(27 May 19)
Stockport (double by-election)	(27 Mar 20)
Sunderland	(24 Apr 20)
City of London	(19 May 22)
City of London	(1 Feb 24)
Dundee	(22 Dec 24)
Oldham	(24 June 25)
*Stockport	(17 Sep 25)
*Combined English Universities	(8–12 Mar 26)
Combined Scottish Universities	(26–29 Apr 27)
*Preston	(31 Aug 29)
*Sunderland	(26 Mar 31)
Combined Scottish Universities	(7–12 Mar 34)
Fermanagh & Tyrone	(27 June 34)
†Combined Scottish Universities	(17–22 June 35)
Combined Scottish Universities	(27–31 Jan 36)
*Derby	(9 July 36)
Preston	(25 Nov 36)
*Oxford University	(23–27 Feb 37)
*Combined English Universities	(15–19 Mar 37)
†Combined Scottish Universities	(21–25 Feb 38)
*Cambridge University	(19–24 Feb 40)
University of Wales	(25–29 Jan 43)
Belfast, West	(9 Feb 43)
Antrim	(11 Feb 43)
Brighton	(3 Feb 44)
*‡Combined Scottish Universities	(9–13 Apr 45)
City of London	(31 Oct 45)
Preston	(31 Jan 46)
*Combined English Universities	(13–18 Mar 46)
*Down	(6 June 46)
*Combined Scottish Universities	(22–27 Nov 46)
Armagh	(5 Mar 48)
Belfast, West	(29 Nov 50)
Belfast, South	(4 Nov 52)
Mid-Ulster	(12 Aug 55)
†Mid-Ulster	(8 May 56)
Belfast, East	(19 Mar 59)
*Mid-Ulster	(17 Apr 69)
Fermanagh and South Tyrone	(9 Apr 81)
Antrim East	(23 Jan 86)[1]
Antrim North	(23 Jan 86)
Antrim South	(23 Jan 86)
Belfast East	(23 Jan 86)
Belfast North	(23 Jan 86)
Belfast South	(23 Jan 86)
Down North	(23 Jan 86)
Down South	(23 Jan 86)
Fermanagh and South Tyrone	(23 Jan 86)

Lagan Valley	(23 Jan 86)
Londonderry East	(23 Jan 86)
Mid-Ulster	(23 Jan 86)
Newry and Armagh	(23 Jan 86)
Strangford	(23 Jan 86)
Upper Bann	(23 Jan 86)
Upper Bann	(17 May 90)
*Down North	(15 Jun 95)

[1] The 15 by-elections held on 23 January 1986 were the result of the mass resignation of the Unionist MPs in protest at the Anglo-Irish Agreement.

Summary tables

Table 1 Turnout and Swing by Year.

Year	Government	Contests[a]	Mean Turnout	Mean Turnout Change	Mean swing to Conservative Butler	Steed	n[b]
1919	Con/Lib	13	58.3	+2.3	−12.0	−12.7	3
1920	Con/Lib	15	64.0	+7.9	−7.9	−7.1	1
1921	Con/Lib	14	68.1	+14.1	−11.2	−9.9	3
1922	Con/Lib	13	68.8	+11.2	−11.9	−11.6	4
1922–23	Con	16	70.4	−1.3	−3.0	−3.8	4
1924	Lab	7	76.1	+3.2	−0.2	−0.8	5
1925	Con	6	76.3	−1.3	−4.9	−4.9	2
1926	Con	12	77.9	−2.4	−6.9	−7.6	8
1927	Con	8	71.7	−4.0	−5.8	−6.9	2
1928	Con	17	68.9	−5.4	−7.6	−7.9	10
1929[b]	Con	9	73.4	−6.6	−12.9	−13.1	4
1929	Lab	4	51.8	−19.1	−2.5	−2.3	3
1930	Lab	9	63.3	−12.0	+6.9	+8.0	7
1931	Lab	17	62.1	−13.4	+10.1	+10.5	8
1932	Nat/Con	12	58.7	−16.3	−9.8	−9.6	6
1933	Nat/Con	12	68.3	−7.2	−17.6	−18.1	9
1934	Nat/Con	14	62.5	−11.2	−15.3	−15.3	10
1935	Nat/Con	7	57.0	−18.6	−20.8	−20.6	5
1936	Nat/Con	9	56.8	−10.4	−3.4	−3.5	7
1937	Nat/Con	22	56.9	−12.6	−4.0	−3.9	17
1938	Nat/Con	16	69.0	−3.8	−4.7	−4.7	9
1939	Nat/Con	19	57.5	−13.3	−1.2	−1.1	10
1940	Nat	13	34.6	−32.2	+18.0	+17.3	2
1941	Nat	10	29.6	−42.3	+14.7	+14.4	1
1942	Nat	12	33.0	−37.0	—	—	0
1943	Nat	16	34.3	−39.4	+9.4	+10.8	2
1944	Nat	7	33.6	−33.6	—	—	0
1945[b]	Nat	4	54.2	−20.3	+2.8	+2.8	1
1945	Lab	8	55.9	−15.7	+0.1	−0.1	6
1946	Lab	13	59.8	−12.6	+2.3	+2.5	9
1947	Lab	8	65.0	−6.5	+6.3	+5.8	8

Table 1 *Continued*

Year	Government	Contests[a]	Mean Turnout	Mean Turnout Change	Mean swing to Conservative		n[b]
					Butler	Steed	
1948	Lab	10	65.7	−3.6	+8.4	+8.1	9
1949	Lab	6	71.2	−4.0	+6.5	+7.9	6
1950	Lab	9	70.3	−14.7	+2.9	+3.0	9
1951	Lab	5	65.9	−19.0	+7.2	+6.7	5
1952	Con	8	65.6	−17.6	−1.3	−1.4	8
1953	Con	13	58.2	−21.6	+0.1	+0.5	13
1954	Con	17	57.0	−23.8	+0.8	+0.8	15
1955[b]	Con	6	57.1	−25.3	+0.4	+0.2	6
1955	Con	3	60.0	−15.3	−2.7	−2.3	3
1956	Con	11	61.3	−17.1	−4.7	−5.3	10
1957	Con	15	66.7	−11.0	−6.6	−7.0	13
1958	Con	14	61.0	−10.5	−4.3	−3.9	11
1959	Con	6	67.3	−11.4	−1.4	−1.4	4
1960	Con	11	65.0	−15.5	+1.7	+1.3	6
1961	Con	12	58.7	−17.3	−5.4	−5.4	9
1962	Con	17	68.1	−12.3	−6.6	−8.3	8
1963	Con	15	61.1	−16.1	−8.1	−9.0	10
1964	Con	6	69.6	−8.2	−7.1	−6.9	6
1965−66[b]	Lab	13	64.3	−12.8	+1.5	+1.9	11
1966−67	Lab	12	69.4	−8.8	+10.3	+11.4	7
1968	Lab	11	60.6	−13.3	+16.2	+17.4	8
1969−70[b]	Lab	14	58.8	−15.1	+11.3	+12.2	10
1970−71	Con	12	51.2	−15.8	−6.2	−6.6	10
1972	Con	6	56.9	−11.3	−5.1	−4.8	3
1973	Con	12	61.6	−8.4	−3.7	−4.1	3
1974	Lab	1	25.9	−37.3	−1.2	−0.6	1
1975	Lab	1	62.3	−11.6	+7.6	+8.7	1
1976	Lab	9	56.2	−13.7	+12.1	+14.4	8
1977	Lab	7	54.0	−12.7	+11.7	+12.5	5
1978−79[b]	Lab	13	59.8	−11.9	+6.7	+7.6	8
1979−80	Con	4	46.8	−21.5	−12.9	−15.5	1
1981	Con	3	66.4	−6.6	—	—	0
1982−83[b]	Con	10	57.8	−14.1	+3.0	+3.1	4
1983−84	Con	7	61.5	−10.9	—	—	0
1985	Con	2	58.8	−7.0	—	—	0
1986−87	Con	7	66.7	−7.6	−10.9	−13.7	1
1988	Con	3	53.4	−18.1	−5.4	−6.6	1
1989	Con	5	58.2	−13.3	−9.4	−12.1	2
1990	Con	8	53.3	−21.3	−11.9	−14.9	4
1991	Con	7	63.2	−14.2	−7.9	−10.6	2
1993	Con	2	72.5	−9.3	—	—	0
1994	Con	8	55.7	−17.9	−22.5	−26.4	3
1995	Con	3	57.1	−22.9	—	—	0
1996−97[c]	Con	4	52.4	−25.9	−15.0	−18.3	3

Continued

Notes to Table 1

[a] number of contests included in the calculation of turnout figures, all by-elections listed in Appendix A. The '*n*' figure in the final column gives the number of contests on which the swing figures are based, those for which a meaningful Conservative–Labour swing can be calculated; the higher the '*n*' figure, therefore, the more meaningful is the mean swing.
[b] the year divided at the General Election.
[c] up to the 1997 General Election.

Table 2:   Turnout and Swing by Parliament.

Parliament	Government	Contests[a]	Turnout	Turnout Change	Butler Swing	*n*[b]	Butler Swingback	*n*[b]
1918–22	Con/Lib	55	64.7	+9.0	−11.4	11	+4.9	12
1922–23	Con	16	70.4	−1.3	−3.0	4	—	0
1923–24	Lab	7	76.1	+3.2	−0.2	5	−0.8	3
1924–29	Con	52	73.1	−4.2	−7.7	26	+0.9	31
1929–31	Lab	30	61.1	−13.3	+6.7	18	+11.7	17
1931–35	Nat/Con	45	62.2	−12.6	−15.8	30	+4.4	32
1935–39[c]	Nat/Con	64	60.7	−9.5	−3.9	42	−9.9	40
1939–45	Nat	64	34.6	−36.1	+12.8	7	−26.2	8
1945–50	Lab	45	62.9	−8.9	+4.9	38	—	0[d]
1950–51	Lab	14	68.8	−16.2	+4.4	14	−3.1	14
1951–55	Con	44	58.9	−22.2	+0.1	42	+1.1	5[e]
1955–59	Con	49	63.5	−12.5	−4.7	41	+5.4	40
1959–64	Con	61	64.1	−14.4	−5.5	39	+1.7	39
1964–66	Lab	13	64.3	−12.8	+1.5	11	−4.2	11
1966–70	Lab	37	62.4	−12.3	+12.0	25	−6.9	26
1970–74	Con	30	52.7	−15.8	−2.7	30	+3.1	18[e]
1974	Lab	1	25.9	−37.3	*+1.2*	1	*−3.3*	1
1974–79	Lab	30	57.5	−13.1	+6.5	30	−4.7	30
1979–83	Con	17	56.8	−14.5	−0.3	17	+8.2	3[e]
1983–87	Con	16	63.4	−9.6	−7.1	16	+5.8	16
1987–92	Con	23	57.5	−16.9	−4.6	23	+2.8	23
1992–97	Con	17	53.0	−23.6	−13.7	7	+1.2	7[e]

Notes to Table 2

[a] the number of contests is defined as in Table 1.
[b] the '*n*' figure here gives *from 1918 to 1970* the number of contests for which a Con–Lab swing figure is meaningful (as in Table 1). *From 1970*, as the '*n*' figures show, these columns include the total votes in all the seats contested, except where there was a subsequent boundary change.
[c] divided at the outbreak of war.
[d] no swingback figures calculable in view of redistribution of boundaries.
[e] few swing figures available in view of partial redistribution of boundaries.

Bibliography

Where books have been found particularly useful for single chapters, they have been acknowledged in Notes. This list is therefore of a more general nature; it includes only items which are not listed elsewhere in the book and items of general and methodological interest. All books listed were published in London unless stated otherwise.

Reference works

F. W. S. Craig (ed.), *British parliamentary election statistics, 1918–1970*, 2nd edn (Chichester, 1971).

F. W. S. Craig (ed.), *British parliamentary election results, 1918–1970*, 2 vols. (Chichester, 1969, 1971).

F. W. S. Craig (ed.), *British parliamentary constituency boundaries* (Chichester, 1972).

F. W. S. Craig (ed.), *Britain votes, 1974–88*, 2 vols. (Chichester, 1980, 1988).

F. W. S. Craig (ed.), *British electoral facts, 1832–1980* (Chichester, 1981).

F. W. S. Craig (ed.), *Chronology of British parliamentary by-elections, 1833–1987* (Chichester, 1987).

M. Kinnear, *The British voter* (1968).

B. R. Mitchell and K. Boehm, *British parliamentary election results, 1950–1964* (Cambridge, 1966).

Census of 1966: parliamentary constituency tables (1969).

T. Erskine May, *Parliamentary practice*, 18th edn, edited by Sir B. Cocks (1971).

Parker's election agent and returning officer, 6th edn (1959).

A. N. Schofield, *Parliamentary elections*, 3rd edn (1959).

Commentaries

A. J. Allen, *The English voter* (1964).

A. Booth, *British hustings, 1924–1950* (1956).

J. C. Brown, 'Local party efficiency as a factor in the outcome of British elections', *Political Studies* (June 1958).

D. E. Butler, *The electoral system in Britain since 1918*, 2nd edn (Oxford, 1963).

D. E. Butler, *The British general election of 1951* (1952).

D. E. Butler, *The British general election of 1955* (1955).

D. E. Butler and R. Rose, *The British general election of 1959* (1960).

D. E. Butler and A. King, *The British general election of 1964* (1965).

D. E. Butler and A. King, *The British general election of 1966* (1966).

D. E. Butler and M. Pinto-Duschinsky, *The British general election of 1970* (1971).

D. E. Butler and D. Kavanagh, *The British general election of February 1974* (1974).

D. E. Butler and D. Kavanagh, *The British general election of October 1974* (1975).

D. E. Butler and D. Kavanagh, *The British general election of 1979* (1980).

D. E. Butler and D. Kavanagh, *The British general election of 1983* (1985).

D. E. Butler and D. Kavanagh, *The British general election of 1987* (1988).

D. E. Butler and D. Kavanagh, *The British general election of 1992* (1993).

D. E. Butler and D. Stokes, *Political change in Britain* (1969).

H. D. Clarke and G. Zuk, 'Politics, economics and party popularity in Britain, 1979–83', *Electoral Studies* (1986).

H. Drucker, 'Learning to fight multi-party elections: the lessons of Hillhead', *Parliamentary Affairs* (1982).

J. P. Dunbabin, 'British elections: a psephological note', *English Historical Review* (1966).

F. Feigert and P. Norris, 'Do by-elections constitute referenda? A four-country comparison', *Legislative Studies Quarterly* (1990).

M. Franklin, *The Decline of Class Voting in Britain* (Oxford, 1985).

C. A. E. Goodhart and R. J. Bhansali, 'Political economy', *Political Studies* (Mar 1970).

R. T. Holt and J. E. Turner, *Political parties in action* (1968).

T. L. Humberstone, *University representation* (1951).

D. Kavanagh, *Constituency electioneering in Britain* (1970).

A. King, 'Why all governments lose by-elections', *New Society*, 21 Mar 1968.

R. L. Leonard, *Elections in Britain*, 2nd edn (1968).

E. G. Lewis, *British by-elections as a reflection of public opinion* (Berkeley, 1943).

R. B. McCallum and A. Readman, *The British general election of 1945* (1947).

J. P. Mackintosh, *The government and politics of Britain* (1970).

A. Mughan, 'On the by-election vote of governments in Britain', *Contemporary record* (1990).

H. G. Nicholas, *The British general election of 1950* (1951).

P. Norris, *British by-elections: the volatile electorate* (Oxford, 1990).

P. Norris, 'By-elections: their importance in Britain', *Contemporary record* (1990).

P. Norris and F. Feigert, 'Government and third-party performance in mid-term by-elections: the Canadian, British and Australian experience', *Electoral Studies* (1989).

J. K. Pollock, 'British by-elections between the wars', *American Political Science Review* (1941).

P. G. Pulzer, *Political representation and elections in Britain* (1967).

S. F. Rae, 'The Oxford by-election: a study in the straw-vote method', *Political Quarterly* (1939).

J. Rasmussen, 'Women candidates in British by-elections: a rational choice interpretation of electoral behaviour', *Political Studies* (1981).

R. Rose, *Influencing voters* (1967).

R. Rose, 'Money and election law', *Political Studies* (1959).

G. N. Sanderson, 'The swing of the pendulum', *Political Studies* (1966).

B. Sarlvik and I. Crewe, *Decade of dealignment* (Cambridge, 1983).

R. M. Scammon, 'British by-elections, 1950', *American Political Science Review* (1951).

R. M. Scammon, 'British by-elections, 1952', *American Political Science Review* (1953).

R. M. Scammon, 'British by-elections, 1951–5, *Journal of Politics* (1956).

J. S. Stray and M. Silver, 'Do by-elections demonstrate a government's unpopularity?', *Parliamentary Affairs* (1979).

J. S. Stray, 'Government popularity, by-elections and cycles', *Parliamentary Affairs* (1983).

D. Studlar, 'By-elections and the Liberal–SDP alliance', *Teaching Politics* (1984).

G. J. G. Upton, 'The impact of by-elections in general elections: England, 1950–87', *British Journal of Political Science* (1991).

Index of outstanding results

The following list gives the results of all by-elections between February 1919 and the general election of May 1997 where the seat changed hands, where there was an abnormally large swing, or where for other reasons the by-election has been mentioned in the book. Swing figures are quoted as 'conventional swing' (see p. 269) and all swing figures which are quoted as plus figures are swings to the party which retained the seat with an increased majority.

Aberdeen, South: Con. held seat but 17.6 per cent swing to Lab. (21 May 35)
Aberdeenshire, Central & Kincardine: Lib. gain from Con. (16 Apr 19)
Acton: Con. gain from Lab. (28 Mar 68) 189
Anglesey: Lib. gain from Ind. Lab. (7 Apr 23) 38
Antrim, East: Ind. Unionist gain from Unionist (27 May 19)
Ashfield: Con. gain from Lab. (28 Apr 77) 2, 6, 215, 219–21
Ashton-under-Lyne: (1) Lab. gain from Con. (29 Oct 28) 60
                     (2) Con. gain from Lab. (30 Apr 31) 64
Ayrshire, South: Lab. held seat from Con. and SNP (19 Mar 70) 192
Bassetlaw: Lab. held seat but 10.8 per cent swing to Con. (31 Oct 68) 190
Battersea, South: Lab. gain from Con. (7 Feb 29) 61
Belfast, West: Eire Lab. gain from Unionist (9 Feb 43)
Bermondsey: Lib./Alliance gain from Lab. (24 Feb 83) 241, 259
Berwick and East Lothian: Lab. held seat from Con. with + 0.5 per cent swing (26 Oct 78) 215, 226
Berwick-upon-Tweed: (1) Con. gain from Lib.; winning Con. was wife of the Lib. MP unseated on petition (31 May 23) 39
                   (2) Lib. gain from Con. (8 Nov 73) 210
Bexley: Lab. held seat, but 11.1 per cent swing to Con. (22 July 46) 152
Birmingham, Ladywood: Lib. gain from Lab. (26 June 69) 191
Birmingham, Northfield: Lab. gain from Con. (28 Oct 82) 241
Birmingham, Stechford: Con. gain from Lab. (31 Mar 77) 218–19
Blackpool, North: Con. held seat narrowly from Lib. (13 Mar 62) 12, 165
Bodmin: Lib. gain from Coalition Con. (24 Feb 22)
Bolton, East: Con. held seat narrowly from Lab. and Lib. (16 Nov 60) 176
Bosworth: Lib. gain from Con. (31 May 27) 59
Bothwell: Lab. gain from Coalition Con. (16 July 19) 16

Brecon and Radnor: (1) Lab. gain from Con. (1 Aug 39)
           (2) Lib./Alliance gain from Con. (4 July 85) 245, 247, 251–2, 256
Bridgwater: (1) Ind. Progressive gain from Con. (17 Nov 38) 91, 113, 119–21, 123–5
           (2) Con. held seat with +8.6 per cent swing (12 Mar 70) 192
Brighouse and Spenborough: Con. gain from Lab. (17 Mar 60) 156
Brighton: Con. held seat from Ind. (3 Feb 44) 134–5
Brighton, Pavilion: Con. held seat with +17.8 per cent swing (27 Mar 69)
Bristol, Central: Con. held seat from Ind. Lab. (18 Feb 43) 142–3, 147
Bristol, South-East: (1) seat awarded to Con. after Lab. MP disqualified as a peer (4 May 61) 3
           (2) A. Wedgwood Benn re-elected after disclaiming peerage; no Con. candidate (20 Aug 63) 3
Bristol, West: (1) Con. held seat but 13.4 per cent swing to Lab. (2 Feb 28)
           (2) Con. held seat with +16.9 per cent swing (15 Feb 51)
Bromley: (1) Coalition Con. held seat narrowly from Lab. (17 Dec 19) 16
           (2) Con. held seat narrowly from Lib. after intervention by Empire Crusade (2 Sep 30) 62
           (3) H. Macmillan returned to Parliament after defeat at 1945 general election (14 Nov 45) 5
Bromsgrove: Lab. gain from Con. (27 May 71) 198
Burnley: A. Henderson, Home Secretary returned to Parliament after defeat at 1923 general election (28 Feb 24) 5, 41–2
Bury St Edmunds: Con. held seat from Ind. Lib. (29 Feb 44) 145, 147
Caerphilly: (1) Lab. held seat from Con. (4 July 39)
           (2) Lab. held seat narrowly from Plaid Cymru (18 July 68) 190
Camberwell, North: Lab. gain from Coalition Con. (20 Feb 22)
Camberwell, Peckham: Lab. gain from Con. (6 May 36)
Cambridge: (1) Con. held seat but 18.5 per cent swing to Lab. (8 Feb 34)
           (2) Con. gain from Lab. (21 Sep 67) 187
Canterbury: Con. held seat but 13.0 per cent swing to Lib. (24 Nov 27)
Carmarthen: (1) Lib. held seat from Lab. (14 Aug 24) 56
           (2) Lab. gain from Lib. (28 Feb 57) 154
           (3) Plaid Cymru gain from Lab. (14 July 66) 183–4, 262
Chelmsford: Common Wealth gain from Con. (26 Apr 45) 142, 144–5
Cheltenham: Ind. Con. gain from Con. (22 June 37) 92
Chester-le-Street: Lab. held seat but 28.6 per cent swing to Lib. (1 Mar 73) 199, 205
Chichester: Con. held seat from Ind. (18 May 42) 146
Chippenham: (1) Con. held seat narrowly from Ind. Lib. (24 Aug 43)
           (2) Con. held seat narrowly from Lib. and Lab. (22 Nov 62) 176
Christchurch: Lib.Dem gain from Con. (29 July 93) 7, 244, 248, 252, 254, 259
City of London: Con. held seat from Lib. (1 Feb 24) 41
Clay Cross: A. Henderson returned to Parliament after defeat at 1931 general election (1 Sep 33) 103–4
Colne Valley: Lab. held seat narrowly from Lib. (21 Mar 63) 176
Coventry North-West: Lab. held seat but 5.0 per cent swing to Con. (4 Mar 76) 216
Crosby: SDP gain (Shirley Williams) from Con. (26 Nov 81) 11, 228, 238–9
Croydon, North-West: Lib./Alliance gain from Con. (22 Oct 81) 228, 237–8
Darlington: Lab. gain from Con. (17 Feb 26) 59
Dartford: (1) Lab. gain from Coalition Lib. (27 Mar 20) 16
           (2) Lab. gain from Con. (7 Nov 38) 119

Darwen: Con. held seat narrowly from Ind. Lib. (15 Dec 43) 145

Daventry: Con. held seat from Common Wealth (20 Apr 43) 132, 142

Derby: Lab. gain from National Lab. (9 July 36)

Derby, North: Lab. held seat from Lib. and Con. (17 Apr 62) 173

Derbyshire, West: (1) Ind. Lab. gain from Con. (17 Feb 44) 142–4, 146, 148

       (2) Con. held seat narrowly from Lib. (6 June 62) 173, 176

       (3) Con. held seat narrowly from Lib. (8 May 86) 256, 258

Doncaster: Lab. held seat from National Lib. (17 Nov 38) 119

Dorset, North: Con. held seat from Lib. (27 June 57) 154

Dorset, South: Lab. gain from Con. after intervention of Anti-Common Market candidate (22 Nov 62) 11

Dover: (1) Ind. gain from Coalition Con. (12 Jan 21)

   (2) Con. re-elected after being unseated (12 Mar 24) 41

Down: Unionist gain from Ind. Unionist (6 June 46)

Down, North: UK Unionist gain from Ulster Popular Unionist Party (15 June 95)

Dudley: (1) Lab. gain from Coalition Con., Sir A. Griffith-Boscawen, seeking re-election as Minister of Agriculture (3 Mar 21) 10, 18

    (2) Con. gain from Lab. (28 Mar 68) 2, 10, 188–9

Dudley, West: Lab. gain from Con. (15 Dec 94) 7, 247, 251–2, 257, 259

Dunbartonshire: Lab. gain from Con. (18 Mar 36)

Dundee, East: (1) Lab. held seat from Con. (17 July 52)

     (2) Lab. held seat narrowly from SNP (1 Mar 73) 199, 205

Eastbourne: Lib.Dem gain from Con. (18 Oct 90) 244, 248, 257, 261

East Ham, North: Lab. gain from Con. (29 Apr 26) 59

Eastleigh: Lib.Dem. gain from Con. (9 June 94) 248

Eddisbury: (1) Lib. gain from Con. (20 Mar 29) 59

    (2) Common Wealth gain from Con. (7 Apr 43) 132, 144

Edinburgh, South: (1) Coalition Con. held seat but 17.3 per cent swing to Lib. (9 Apr 20)

      (2) Con. held seat but 10.2 per cent swing to Lab. after Lib. intervention (29 May 57) 154

Edmonton: Lab. held seat but 16.2 per cent swing to Con. (13 Nov 48) 152

English Universities: (1) Con. gain from Lib. (8–12 Mar 26) 59

      (2) Ind. Progressive gain from Con. (15–19 Mar 37) 92

      (3) Con. gain from Ind. (13–18 Mar 46) 151

Fulham: Lab. gain from Con. (10 Apr 86) 245, 247, 255–6

Fulham, East: Lab. gain from Con. (25 Oct 33) 11, 66, 89–90, 94–109, 251

Fulham, West: (1) Con. gain from Lab. (6 May 30) 64

     (2) Lab. gain from Con. (6 Apr 38) 128

Gainsborough: Con. held seat narrowly from Lab. (14 Feb 56) 154

Gateshead: Lab. held seat but 13.9 per cent swing to Con. (8 June 31) 63

Glasgow, Camlachie: Con. gain from Lab./ILP (28 Jan 48) 151

Glasgow, Gorbals: (1) Lab. held seat, but with much-reduced majority, after Communist intervention (30 Sep 48) 152

       (2) Lab. held seat from SNP (30 Oct 69) 191

Glasgow, Govan: (1) SNP gain from Lab. (8 Nov 73) 208

      (2) SNP gain seat a second time from Lab. (10 Nov 88) 247, 262–3

Glasgow, Hillhead: SDP (Roy Jenkins) gain from Con. (25 Mar 82) 228, 240–1

Glasgow, Kelvingrove: (1) Con. held seat with +5.8 per cent swing (23 May 24) 51–2

       (2) Lab. gain from Con. (13 Mar 58) 154

Glasgow, Pollok: Con. gain from Lab. after SNP intervention (9 Mar 67) 184–5

Glasgow, Shettleston: Lab. held seat but 9.5 per cent swing to Con. (26 June 30)

Glasgow, Woodside: Lab. gain from Con. (22 Nov 62)

Gloucester: Lab. held seat with +10.5 per cent swing after Lib. intervention (12 Sep 57) 154

Grantham: Ind. gain from Con. (25 Mar 42) 136

Greenock: Lab. gain from Con. (26 Nov 36) 92

Greenwich: SDP/Alliance gain from Lab. (26 Feb 87) 251, 262–4

Grimsby: Lab. held seat but 7.0 per cent swing to Con. (28 Apr 77) 6, 218–21

Hackney, South: Coalition Con. gain after Ind. MP expelled from House of Commons; no Ind. candidate (18 Aug 22) 16, 18

Halifax: Lab. gain from Con. (13 July 28) 60

Hamilton: SNP gain from Lab. (2 Nov 67) 9, 11, 12, 185–6, 208, 262

Hammersmith, North: (1) Lab. gain from Con. (28 May 26) 59

       (2) Lab. gain from Con. (24 Apr 34) 89

Hammersmith South: Lab. held seat but 5.2 per cent swing to Con. (24 Feb 49) 7

Harborough: Con. held seat but 15.4 per cent swing to Lab. (28 Nov 33) 104

Harrow: Con. held seat from Ind. (2 Dec 41) 136

Hereford: Con. held seat narrowly from Lib. (14 Feb 56) 154

Heywood and Radcliffe: Lab. gain from Coalition Lib. (8 June 21) 16

High Peak: Con. held seat narrowly from Lab. and Lib. (16 Mar 61)

Hitchin: Con. held seat but 17.2 per cent swing to Lab. (8 June 33)

Holland-with-Boston: (1) Con. gain from Lab. (31 July 24) 55

       (2) Lib. gain from Con. (21 Mar 29) 59

Hornsey: Con. held seat from Ind. (28 May 41) 130, 133

Hove: Con. held seat but 29.1 per cent swing to Lib. (8 Nov 73) 210–11

Hull, Central: (1) Lib. gain from Coalition Con. (29 Mar 19) 16

     (2) J. Kenworthy, MP, re-elected on transfer from Lib. to Lab. (29 Nov 26) 59

Hull, North: Lab. held seat with +4.5 per cent swing (27 Jan 66) 7, 182, 258

Hythe: Con. held seat from Lib. (20 July 39) 125

Ilford: Con. held seat but 13.6 per cent swing to Lib. (23 Feb 28)

Ilford, North: (1) Con. held seat with +5.0 per cent swing (3 Feb 54) 153

     (2) Con. gain from Lab. (2 Mar 78) 222–4

Ipswich: Lab. gain from Con. (16 Feb 38)

Isle of Ely: Lib. gain from Con. (26 July 73) 208–9

Islington, East: Lab. held seat from Empire Crusade and Con. (19 Feb 31) 62, 69, 71

Islington, North: (1) Lab. gain from Con. (13 Oct 37)

     (2) Lab. held seat but 9.2 per cent swing to Con. (30 Oct 69) 191

Kilmarnock: National Lib. held seat from Lab. (2 Nov 33) 104, 106

Kincardine and Deeside: Lib.Dem gain from Con. (7 Nov 91) 244, 248, 254

King's Lynn: Con. held seat narrowly from Ind. Lab. (12 Feb 43) 142–3

Kinross and Perthshire: SNP gain first-ever seat from Con. at by-election (25 May 95)

Kinross and Perthshire West: (1) Duchess of Atholl, MP, not re-elected on transfer from Con. to Ind. Con.; the official Con. elected (21 Dec 38) 2, 92, 127

       (2) Sir A. Douglas-Home, Prime Minister, elected after disclaiming peerage (7 Nov 63) 9

Kirkcaldy Burghs: (1) Lab. gain from Coalition Lib. (4 Mar 21) 16

      (2) Lab. held seat narrowly from SNP (17 Feb 44)

Lambeth, Kennington: Lab. gain from Con. (24 May 39)

Lambeth, North: Lab. gain from Lib. (23 Oct 34) 89

Lambeth, Norwood: Con. held seat with reduced majority (14 Mar 35)

Lanarkshire, North: Lab. gain from Con. (21 Mar 29) 61

Lancaster: Lib. gain from Con. (9 Feb 28) 59
Langbaurgh: Lab. gain from Con. (7 Nov 91) 248, 254–5
Leeds, North-East: Con. held seat from Lab. (9 Feb 56)
Leeds, West: Lab. held seat but 10.5 per cent swing to Con. (21 July 49)
Leicester, East: Lab. gain from Coalition Lib. (30 Mar 22)
Leicester, North-East: Lab. held seat with increased majority after Lib. intervention (12 July 62) 173
Leicester, South-West: Con. gain from Lab. (2 Nov 67) 187
Leith: Lib. held seat narrowly from Lab. (23 Mar 27)
Lewes: Con. held seat from Lab. (9 July 24) 54–5
Lewisham, North: Lab. gain from Con. (14 Feb 57) 154
Lewisham, West: (1) Con. held seat narrowly from Ind. (13 Sep 21)
           (2) Con. held seat from Lab. (24 Nov 38) 125
Leyton: Con. gain from Lab. (21 Jan 65) 2, 5, 10, 180–1
Leyton, West: Lib. gain from Coalition Con. (1 Mar 19) 10
Lichfield: Lab. gain from Con. (5 May 38)
Lincoln: Dick Taverne, MP, re-elected overwhelmingly after transfer from Lab. to Democratic Labour (1 Mar 73) 2, 4, 11, 195–207, 214
Linlithgowshire: Lab. gain from Con. (4 Apr 28) 60
Littleborough and Saddleworth: Lib.Dem gain from Con. (27 July 95) 248, 251
Liverpool, East Toxteth: (1) Con. held seat but 10.7 per cent swing to Lab. (19 Mar 29)
           (2) Con. held seat with +14.9 per cent swing (5 Feb 31)
Liverpool, Edge Hill: (1) Lab. gain from Con. (6 Mar 23) 38, 51
           (2) Lab. held seat but 10.2 per cent swing to Con. (11 Sep 47) 152
           (3) Lib. gain from Lab. (29 Mar 79) 227
Liverpool, Scotland: (1) election of D. Logan, Lab., after death of T. P. O'Connor, MP, Irish Nationalist (14 Dec 29) 61
           (2) Lab. held seat with +12.5 per cent swing (11 June 64)
Liverpool, Wavertree: (1) Con. held seat with +11.1 per cent swing (23 June 31) 63
           (2) Lab. gain from Con. after Ind. Con. intervention (6 Feb 35) 11, 90
Liverpool, West Derby: Coalition Con. held seat but 10.9 per cent swing to Lab. (26 Feb 19)
Liverpool, West Toxteth: (1) Lab. gain from Con. (22 May 24)
           (2) Lab. gain from Con. (16 July 35) 89
Louth: (1) Lib. gain from Coalition Con. (3 June 20) 16
     (2) Lib. held seat from Con. (22 Sep 21) 16
     (3) Con. held seat with +14.3 per cent swing (4 Dec 69) 192
Lowestoft: Con. held seat but 14.9 per cent swing to Lab. (15 Feb 34)
Luton: Lab. gain from Con. (7 Nov 63)
Macclesfield: Con. held seat narrowly from Lab. (30 Sep 71) 198
Maldon: Ind. Lab. gain from Con. (25 June 42) 138–9
Manchester, Ardwick: Lab. held seat but 9.8 per cent swing to Con. (22 June 31) 63
Manchester, Clayton: Lab. gain from Con. (18 Feb 22)
Manchester, Exchange: Lab. held seat but 24.9 per cent swing to Lib. (27 June 73) 12, 207
Manchester, Gorton: Lab. held seat but 9.4 per cent swing to Con. (2 Nov 67) 185, 187–8
Manchester, Moss Side: Lab. held seat but 3.5 per cent swing to Con. (13 July 78) 225

Manchester, Rusholme: (1) Coalition Con. held seat but 17.5 per cent swing to Lab. (7 Oct 19)
　　　　　　　　　　 (2) Con. held seat but 20.6 per cent swing to Lab. (21 Nov 33) 104

Melton: Con. held seat but 7.6 per cent swing to Lab. (19 Dec 56) 154

Meriden: Con. gain from Lab. (28 Mar 68) 189

Middlesbrough, East: Lab. held seat from Lib. (14 Mar 62)

Middlesbrough, West: (1) Lib. held seat narrowly from Lab. (7 Mar 28)
　　　　　　　　　　　(2) Lab. gain from Con. (6 June 62) 173, 176

Midlothian, North: (1) Lab. gain from Con. (29 Jan 29) 61
　　　　　　　　　　(2) Con. held seat narrowly from Common Wealth (11 Feb 43) 142

Mitcham: Lab. gain from Con. (3 Mar 23) 38

Mitcham and Morden: Con. gain Lab. seat from sitting MP who had defected to SDP and unsuccessfully contested by-election (3 June 82) 2

Monmouth: Lab. gain from Con. (16 May 91) 248, 258, 261

Montgomeryshire: Lib. held seat from Con. (15 May 62) 173, 176

Motherwell: SNP gain from Lab. (12 Apr 45) 141, 147

Nelson and Colne: Con. gain from Lab. (27 June 68) 190

Newbury: Lib.Dem. gain from Con. (6 May 93) 244, 248, 251, 259

Newcastle-under-Lyme: Lab. held seat but 10.7 per cent swing to Con. (30 Oct 69) 191

Newcastle-upon-Tyne, East: A. Henderson returned to Parliament after defeat at 1922 general election (17 Jan 23) 37

Newcastle-upon-Tyne, North: Ind.Con. gain from Con. (7 June 40) 134

Newport: Con. gain; seat previously Coalition Lib. (18 Oct 22) 11, 13–34, 37

Norfolk, South: Lab. gain from Lib. (27 July 20)

Northampton: Lab. gain from Con. (9 Jan 28) 60

Nuneaton: Lab. held seat from Con. (9 Mar 67) 184

Oldham, West: Con. gain from Lab. (13 June 68) 11, 190

Orpington: Lib. gain from Con. (14 Mar 62) 2, 4, 10, 11, 157–78, 229

Oxford: (1) Con. gain from Lib. (5 June 24) 53–4
　　　　(2) Con. held seat from Ind. Progressive (27 Oct 38) 66, 91, 113, 115–18, 121–3

Oxford University: Ind. gain from Con. (23–27 Feb 37)

Paddington, North: Lab. held seat but 11.4 per cent swing to Con. (30 Oct 69) 191

Paddington, South: Empire Crusade gain from Con. (30 Oct 30) 62, 69

Paisley: H. Asquith, Lib. leader, returned to Parliament after defeat at 1918 general election (12 Feb 20)

Penistone: Lab. gain from Lib. (5 Mar 21) 17

Penrith and the Border: Con. almost lost seat to Lib. after elevation of W. Whitelaw to House of Lords (28 June 1983) 247, 249, 254, 256

Perth and Kinross: SNP. gain from Con. (25 May 95) 248, 251, 255

Peterborough: Con. held seat narrowly from Ind. Lab. (15 Oct 43) 142–3

Pontypridd: Lab. gain from Coalition Lib. (25 July 22)17–18

Portsmouth, South: (1) Sir L. Wilson, Con. Chief Whip, returned to Parliament after defeat at 1922 general election (13 Dec 22) 37
　　　　　　　　　　(2) SDP/Alliance gain from Con. (14 June 84) 245, 247, 256

Preston: W. A. Jowitt, MP, re-elected on transfer from Lib. to Lab. (31 July 29) 61

Renfrewshire, East: (1) Con. held seat narrowly from Lab. (29 Jan 26)
　　　　　　　　　　 (2) Con. held seat from ILP (9 May 40) 134

Rhondda, West: Lab. held seat narrowly from Plaid Cymru (9 Mar 67) 184

Ribble Valley: Lib.Dem. gain from Con. (7 Mar 91) 2, 11, 244, 248, 254–5, 258

Richmond: W. Hague just held seat because of split Lib./SDP. vote (23 Feb 89), 247, 254

Ripon: (1) Con. held seat from Lab. (23 Feb 39) 125

      (2) Lib. gain from Con. (26 July 73) 208–9

Rochdale: (1) Lab. gain from Con., Lib. close second (12 Feb 58) 5, 154, 157

        (2) Lib. gain from Lab. (26 Oct 72) 198

Ross and Cromarty: M. J. MacDonald, Colonial Secretary, returned to Parliament after defeat at 1935 general election (10 Feb 36) 91

Rotherham: Lab. gain from Con. (27 Feb 33)

Roxburgh, Selkirk and Peebles: Lib. gain from Con. (24 Mar 65) 12, 181–2

Rugby: Ind. gain from Con. (29 Apr 42) 136–7

Rushcliffe: Con. held seat but 16.7 per cent swing to Lab. (26 July 34)

Rutherglen: (1) Lab. held seat from Con. (21 May 31) 63

       (2) Lab. gain from Con. (14 May 64)

Rutland and Stamford: Con. held seat but 18.7 per cent swing to Lab. (21 Nov 33) 104

Ryedale: Lib./Alliance gain from Con. (8 May 86) 11, 245, 247, 256

St Albans: Coalition Con. held seat narrowly from Lab. (10 Dec 19) 16

St Ives: Lib. gain from Con. (6 Mar 28) 59

St Marylebone: Con. held seat narrowly from Ind. Con. (28 Apr 32)

Scarborough and Whitby: (1) Con. held seat narrowly from Lib. (6 May 31)

       (2) Con. held seat from Ind. (24 Sep 41) 135

Scottish Universities: (1) J. R. MacDonald, Lord President, returned to Parliament after defeat at 1935 general election (27–31 Jan 36) 5

       (2) Ind. gain from National Lib. (9–13 Apr 45) 133

       (3) Con. gain from Ind. (22–27 Nov 46) 151

Sheffield, Brightside: Lab. held seat but 17.1 per cent swing to Con. (13 June 68)

Shipley: Con. gain from Lab. (6 Nov 30) 64

Skipton: (1) Con. held seat but 13.5 per cent swing to Lab. (7 Nov 33) 104, 106

      (2) Common Wealth gain from Con. (7 Jan 44) 142, 144–5, 147

Southgate: M. Portillo held seat for Con. but 9.9 per cent swing to Lib. (13 Dec 84) 252, 256

Southwark, North: (1) Lib. gain from Lab.: L. Haden-Guest, MP, not re-elected on transfer from Lab. to Constitutionalist (28 Mar 27) 59

       (2) Lab. gain from National Lib. (17 May 39)

Southwark, South-East: Lab. gain from Coalition Lib. (14 Dec 21)

Spen Valley: Lab. gain from Coalition Lib. (20 Dec 19) 16

Staffordshire, Mid: Lab. gain from Con. (23 Mar 90) 244, 248, 251–2, 254–5, 259

Staffordshire, South-East: Lab. gain from Con. (11 Apr 96) 244, 247, 251, 257

Stalybridge and Hyde: Con. held seat narrowly from Lab. (28 Apr 37)

Stockport: (1) Coalition Government held both seats in double-member by-election (27 Mar 20) 16

       (2) Lab. gain from Con. (17 Sep 25)

Stockton-on-Tees: Lab. held seat from Con. and Lib. (5 Apr 62) 173

Stourbridge: Lab. gain from Con. (23 Feb 27) 60

Stratford-upon-Avon: Con. held seat, but 13.7 per cent swing to Lab. after resignation of J. Profumo, MP (15 Aug 63)

Stretford: Con. held seat from ILP (8 Dec 39) 134

Stroud: Con. held seat from Lab. (21 May 31) 63

Sunderland: Con. gain from Lab. (26 Mar 31) 64

Sunderland, South: Con. gain from Lab. (13 May 53) 153

Sutton and Cheam: Lib. gain from Con. (7 Dec 72) 2, 198, 202–3
Swansea, East: Coalition Lib. held seat, but 10.5 per cent swing to Lab. (10 July 19)
Swindon: (1) Lab. gain from Con. (25 Oct 34) 89
  (2) Con. gain from Lab. (30 Oct 69) 191
Tamworth: Con. held seat from Lab. (2 Dec 29) 62
Taunton: (1) Coalition Con. held seat but 11.3 per cent swing to Lab. (8 Apr 21)
  (2) Con. held seat narrowly from Lab. (14 Feb 56)
Tiverton: Lib. gain from Con. (21 June 23) 39
Tonbridge: Con. held seat, but 8.4 per cent swing to Lab. (7 June 56) 154
Torrington: Lib. gain from Con. (27 Mar 58) 9, 154, 157–8, 229
Twickenham: (1) Con. held seat narrowly from Lab. (8 Aug 29) 62
  (2) Con. held seat, but 17.8 per cent swing to Lab. (16 Sep 32)
Ulster, Mid: (1) Unionist gain from Sinn Fein, after Sinn Fein MP disqualified (12 Aug 55)
  (2) Ind. Unionist gain from Unionist, after Unionist MP disqualified (8 May 56)
  (3) Ind. gain from Unionist (17 Apr 69)
Uxbridge: Con. held seat but 2.3 per cent swing to Lab. (7 Dec 72) 198
Vale of Glamorgan: Lab. gain from Con. (4 May 89) 248, 262
Wakefield: Lab. gain from Con. (21 Apr 32)
Wallasey: Ind. gain from Con. (29 Apr 42) 132, 137
Walsall: National Lib. held seat from Lab. (16 Nov 38) 119
Walsall North: Con. gain from Lab. (4 Nov 76) 215, 217
Walthamstow, East: Con. gain from Lab. (27 Mar 69)
Walthamstow, West: Con. gain from Lab. (21 Sep 67) 187
Wandsworth, Central: Lab. gain from Con. (29 Apr 37)
Wandsworth, Putney: Con. held seat but 26.9 per cent swing to Lab. (28 Nov 34) 108
Warrington: Lab. hold against SDP challenge from Roy Jenkins (16 July 81) 228, 233–6
Warwick and Leamington: (1) Con. held seat, but 12.2 per cent swing to Lab. after resignation of Sir A. Eden (7 Mar 57) 154
  (2) Con. held seat with +18.1 per cent swing (28 Mar 68) 189
Watford: Con. held seat from Common Wealth (23 Feb 43) 142
Wednesbury: Lab. gain from Con. (26 July 32)
Wellingborough: Con. gain from Lab. (4 Dec 69) 192
West Bromwich: Lab. held seat with +10.2 per cent swing (4 July 63)
West Ham, Upton: Lab. gain from Con. (14 May 34) 89
Westminster, Abbey: (1) Coalition Con. held seat narrowly from Anti-Waste League (25 Aug 21) 44
  (2) Con. held seat narrowly from W. Churchill, standing as Constitutionalist (19 Mar 24) 41
  (3) Con. held seat from Ind. Progressive (17 May 39) 125
Westminster, St George's: (1) Anti-Waste League gain from Coalition Con. (7 June 21) 44, 70
  (2) Con. held seat from Ind. (19 Mar 31) 11, 62, 64–84
Widnes: Lab. gain from Coalition Con. (30 Aug 19) 16
Willesden, East: Lib. gain from Con. (3 Mar 23) 38
Wirral South: Lab. gain from Con. (27 Feb 97) 247, 257
Wolverhampton, West: Coalition Con. held seat from Lab. (7 Mar 22) 16
Woolwich, East: (1) Coalition Con. gain from Lab., J. R. MacDonald (2 Mar 21) 35
  (2) Lab. held seat but 6.5 per cent swing to Con. (15 Apr 31)

Woolwich, West: Con. gain from Lab. (26 June 75) 216
Workington: Con. gain from Lab. (4 Nov 76) 217
Wrekin: (1) Ind. gain from Coalition Lib. (7 Feb 20)
         (2) Ind. held seat from Lab. (20 Nov 20)

Index of Persons

Abrams, Mark 170, 174, 177
Acland, Sir Richard 2, 119, 140–2
Alexander, A.V. 98
Allen of Hurtwood, 1st Lord 106
Allsop, Kay 146
Alton, David 227, 230
Amery, Leo S. 46–8
Angell, Norman 106
Applin, R.V.K. 44
Apsley, Lady 143, 147
Ashby, Corbett 145
Ashdown, Paddy 262
Askey, Arthur 138
Asquith, Herbert 15, 24–5, 41, 46
Astor, Hon. John Jacob 41
Atholl, Duchess of 2
Atkinson, David 222
Attlee, Clement 132, 147, 151–2
Austick, David 209
Austin, J.L. 117

Bader, Douglas 135
Baker, Arthur 107
Baldwin, Stanley 11, 14, 28, 40, 45, 47–9, 59, 62, 65–8, 71–81, 83–4, 88–9, 91, 94–8, 103, 106–9, 113
Balfour, 1st Earl of 46–8
Balfour, Honor 145
Barber, Anthony 5
Barlow, Sir John 144
Barnes, John 97
Barr, James 104
Bartlett, Vernon 101, 119–21, 123, 139
Bassett, Reginald 97
Bayford, see Sanders
Beaverbrook, 1st Viscount 32, 43, 46, 48–9, 66–84, 105, 134
Beckett, Leo 199–200, 214

Beckett, Margaret 214
Beith, Alan 210
Bendall, Vivian 223–4
Benn, Tony 3, 196, 201, 212, 250, 263
Beveridge, Sir William 118, 140, 211
Bevin, Ernest 146
Billing, Pemberton 130–1, 135–6
Birkenhead 1st Earl of 45, 48
Blackburn, Raymond 142
Blair, Robert 221
Blair, Tony 246, 248, 257, 265, 267
Boggis, Jack 139
Bondfield, Margaret 26
Bonham-Carter, Lady Violet 25, 147
Bonham-Carter, Mark 154, 158, 164, 169
Bottomley, Horatio 18
Bottomley, Peter 216
Bottomley, Virginia 263
Bourne, Capt. R.C. 54, 115
Bowden, Herbert 187
Bowen, John 13, 21–6, 28–9, 31–3
Boyne, Harry B. 216
Braddock, Bessie 164
Briant, B. Dutton 134–5
Bridgeman, W.C. 36
Brittan, Leon 249, 254
Brockway, Fenner 45–7, 49
Brown, Ernest 132
Brown, George, Lord George-Brown 164, 181, 190, 202
Brown, W.J. 136–7, 139, 144
Buchanan-Smith, Alick 245
Bull, Sir Arthur 46
Burney, Cdr.C.D. 46
Burnham, 1st Lord 45
Burton, Elaine 142
Butler, David 148, 164, 218, 224, 269
Butler, R.A. 164

Buxton, Ronald 181
Byers, Frank 164

Callaghan, James 183, 197, 201, 215, 217–19, 222, 224–6, 230, 263
Campbell-Bannerman, Sir Henry 99
Campion, W.R. 54
Cartwright, John 232
Cash, William 263
Castle, Barbara 201
Cayzer, H.R. 37
Chamberlain, Austen 13, 15, 20–2, 25–7, 32–3, 45, 48
Chamberlain, Neville 46, 72, 74, 100, 107, 109, 113–14, 118, 120–3, 126–8, 134–5, 137, 161
Channon, Henry 'Chips' 148
Chitnis, Pratap 158, 165
Churchill, Randolph 11, 90–1
Churchill, Sir Winston 41–6, 48–51, 57, 67, 87, 96–7, 118, 130–4, 136–7, 140–1, 145–7, 153, 260
Churchill, Winston 187–8
Chuter Ede, J.C. 38
Clark, George 226
Clark, Percy 220
Clarry, Reginald 13, 20–32, 34, 36
Clynes, J.R. 26, 98
Cook, Sir Thomas 143
Cooper, Brig.R.J. 71
Cooper, Duff 66, 76–83, 114, 118, 122
Cooper, Lady Diana 76–7, 81
Cousins, Frank 5, 184
Cowan, Michael 219
Cowling, Maurice 16, 50, 54
Creasey, John 11
Crewe, Ivor 236, 242
Cripps, Leonard 137–8
Cripps, Sir Stafford 105, 136–7
Critchley, Brig. A.C. 71–2
Crosland, Anthony 174, 197, 201, 218–20
Crossman, Richard 116
Curzon of Kedleston, 1st Marquess 27

Dalkeith, Earl of 12
Dalton, Hugh 55, 97–8, 118, 146–7
Davidson, J.C.C. 47, 68
Davies, Clement 144
Davies, Ivor 115, 117, 122, 138, 145
Davies, Stephen O. 198, 202
Davies, Victor 184
Dawson, Geoffrey 114
Debenham, Sir Piers 11
de Freitas, Sir Geoffrey 199
Devonshire, 10th Duke of 143

Dewar, Donald 224
Dilks, John 204–5
Disraeli, Benjamin 1
Doidge, F.W. 69
Donnelly, Desmond 142
Douglas, Dick 185
Douglas-Mann, Bruce 2, 247
Driberg, Tom 138–9, 147
Duckers, Scott 45–7, 49–50

Eden, Anthony 118, 154
Elkington, Tony 202, 205
Ellis, Geoffrey 71
Ellis-Griffith, E.J. 56
England, Col. A. 46
Erskine, J.M.M. 44, 46, 69–72, 75–6, 82
Erskine, Keith 69, 71
Evans, Gwynfor 183
Ewing, Winifred 186, 208, 225

Fenton, James 221
Ferguson, Aitken 52–3
Ferguson, Sir John 62
Fisher, Doris 191
Fisher, H.A.L. 118
Foot, Michael 96, 196, 232, 234, 259
Forestier-Walker, Leolin 20
Fowler, Sir Norman 259
Fraser, Sir Malcolm 25
Fraser, Tom 185
Freud, Clement 209
Fyfe, Hamilton 96–7

Gaitskell, Hugh 174, 203
Galbraith, Sir Thomas 240
Galloway, Jack 160–1
Gardiner, Sir George 267
Garvin, J.L. 60
Gatti, John 45–6
Gibbs, Raymond 27
Gilbert, John 189
Goldman, Peter 161–7, 173
Good, Alan 142
Goodhart, Philip 170
Gordon Walker, Patrick 5, 115–18, 122, 180–1
Gossop, Don 199
Gott, Richard 182
Gould, Brian 266
Gould, J.C. 44
Graham, Duncan 185
Grattan-Doyle, Henry 134
Gray, Frank 53–4, 117
Greenwood, Arthur 5, 98
Greenwood, Sir Hamar 45

Greenwood, J.H. 99
Gretton, John 28
Grey of Falloden, 1st Viscount 45
Griffith-Boscawen, Sir Arthur 18, 38
Grigg, Sir Edward 45, 53, 71–2, 75
Grimond, Jo 164–5, 194
Guest, Frederick E. 41
Guinness, Jonathan 204–5

Hague, William 263
Hain, Peter 203
Hall, B.W.R. 54
Hamling, William 216
Hampson, Keith 209
Hanley, Jeremy 252
Harmsworth, Esmond 71
Harrisson, Tom 81, 115, 120, 122, 134, 146
Harrod, Roy 116
Hartington, Marquess of 144
Harvey, Oliver 118, 122–3
Haslam, Lewis 13, 19–22
Hattersley, Roy 197
Hazell, A.E.W. 118
Headlam, Sir Cuthbert 134
Healey, Denis 181, 197, 218
Heath, Edward 118, 195, 209, 212, 214, 216,
    223, 226, 260
Heathcoat Amory, Patrick 119–20
Heller, Richard 103–4
Henderson, Arthur 5, 22, 26, 37, 41, 52, 103–5
Henney, Winfred 136
Heseltine, Michael 209, 261
Hinchingbrooke, Viscount 12, 147
Hipwell, Reginald 135–6, 146
Hoare, Sir Samuel 91
Hodge, John 26
Hogg, Quintin 115, 118, 121
Holbrook, Sir Claud 137
Holland, Stuart 266
Hopkinson, Austen 46
Hopkinson, Tom 138
Horabin, T.L. 144
Howe, 5th Earl 71
Hoyle, Douglas 233, 235
Hulton, Edward 141
Hunloke, Henry 143
Hunt, Reuben 139

Iremonger, Tom 222–4

Jacks, L.P. 118
Jackson, Sir. Francis S. 45
Jenkins, Roy 190, 196–7, 200, 203, 206, 209,
    218–19, 231–2, 234–7, 239–40
Jessel, Sir Herbert 44, 70, 71

Jessel, Toby 182
Jinkinson, Alan 161, 164, 173
Johnson, Donald 145
Jones, Alec 184
Jones, J. Emrys 184
Jones, Thomas 13
Jones, Trevor 198, 208
Jordan, Colin 180–1
Joseph, Sir Keith 223
Jowell, Tessa 223
Jowitt, W.A. 61–2

Kavanagh, Dennis 218, 224
Kendall, Denis 136–9, 144
Kennedy, Ludovic 154
Kenworthy, J.M. 59
Kidd, Gerald 146
Kilfedder, Sir James 265
King, Anthony 242
Kinnock, Neil 249, 257
Kipling, Rudyard 79
Kyba, J.P. 104

Lambert, George 154
Lambton, Lord 3, 12, 210
Lamont, Norman 259
Lansbury, George 26, 98
Laski, Harold 80
Law, Andrew Bonar 13–14, 22, 37
Lawler, Wallace 191
Lawson, Hugh 144–5
Lee, Jennie 143
Legge-Bourke, Sir Harry 209
Leslie, George 185
Lever, George 196
Levin, Bernard 197, 203
Lidiard, Sir Herbert 69
Lindsay, A.D. 116–19, 121–3
Lindsay, Kenneth 118
Llewelyn, Leonard 24
Lloyd George, David 11, 14–15, 19, 21–5,
    27–8, 33, 37, 41–3, 46–7, 49, 52, 57,
    59–60, 67, 87, 140
Lloyd George, Lady Megan 154, 183
Lloyd, Selwyn 173
Logan, David 62
Longmore, Sir Arthur 136
Loverseed, John 144
Low, Sir Toby 162, 165
Lubbock, Eric 160–5, 167–9, 173, 175
Lysaght, W.R. 24

Mabon, Dickson 196
MacDonald, Malcolm 5, 91
Macdonald, Margo 208

MacDonald, Ramsay 5, 35, 40, 41, 61–2, 87–8, 92, 94
Mackay, Andrew 219
Mackay, R.W. 141, 145
Maclean, David 249, 263
Macleod, Iain 162, 164, 167, 172
Macmillan, Harold 2, 5, 118, 148, 155–6, 166, 168, 172–3, 181, 187
Major, John 245, 252–3, 258–9, 261
Mandelson, Peter 264
Mander, Geoffrey 80
Manningham-Buller, Reginald 132
Mardy, T.H. 30
Margach, James 163
Margesson, David 137
Marks, Kenneth 187–8, 192
Marquand, David 219–20
Marriott, J.A.R. 53
Martell, Edward 11
Martin, Kingsley 147
Maudling, Reginald 196
McEwen, Robert 181
McGiven, Alec 232
McIntyre, R.D. 147
McKenna, Reginald 25
McKenzie, Robert 164
McLoughlin, Patrick 263
McNally, Tom 222
McNamara, Kevin 182
Middlemas, Keith 97
Mikardo, Ian 200, 209, 218
Millan, Bruce 249
Miller, Millie 222
Millington, Ernest 142, 144–5
Milne, Eddie 195
Mitchell, Austin 219–21
Mond, Sir Alfred 27, 56
Moore, Lynden 13–14, 21, 23–32, 33–4
Moore-Brabazon, John 68, 71–2, 74–5
Moran, Flt.Lt. 141
Morris, Sir Rhys Hopkin 183
Morrison, Herbert 98, 146–7
Mosley, Sir Oswald 49, 79, 137
Mowat, C.L. 97
Muggeridge, Malcolm 32
Mulligan, Pat 199
Murray, Gilbert 32, 107, 116

Newby, Donald 169, 171
Nicholson, J.S. 44
Nicholson, Otho 45–7, 49
Nicholson, W.G. 45
Noel-Baker, Francis 191
Norris, Pippa 235, 266
Norris, Steven 263

Nuffield, 1st Viscount 117–18
Nutting, Anthony 154

O'Connor, T.P. 61
Owen, David 196, 220, 232, 236–7, 240–2, 257, 262

Page Croft, Sir Henry 72
Pakenham, Frank, 7th Earl of Longford 116
Pardoe, John 211
Parkinson, George 44–5
Parr, Sir James 75
Parris, Matthew 265
Peacock, Thomas 144
Pennington, Alderman 137–8
Petter, Sir Ernest 66, 72–82, 84
Pinckard, G.H. 73
Pitt, William 237–8
Plymouth, 1st Earl of 20
Pole, Graham 80
Portillo, Michael 263
Poulson, John 196
Powell, Enoch 164, 196
Pratt, Sir John 52–3
Price, Ward 72, 81
Priestley, J.B. 139, 141
Pryce-Mitchell, Daisy 120

Rankin, J.S. 46
Ray, Sir William 71–2, 75
Raynsford, Nick 255
Reakes, George 132, 137–9, 144
Redmayne, Martin 161
Rees-Mogg, William 197, 199
Rhodes James, Robert 124–5, 217
Rhondda, Lady 25
Robertson, George 225
Robertson, John Home 226
Robinson, Geoffrey 216
Rock, Patrick 258
Rodgers, William 196, 232–3, 237
Rose, Richard 211
Rothermere, 1st Viscount 38, 46, 57, 60, 66–7, 69, 71–4, 77–81, 83, 103
Rowse, A.L. 89, 97, 107, 118
Royce, W.S. 55

Sainsbury, Timothy 210
Salisbury, 4th Marquess of 20, 22, 27, 85
Salvidge, Sir Archibald 51
Samuel, Sir Herbert 60
Sanders, Sir Robert, Lord Bayford 31, 90
Sanderson, 1st Lord 118
Sapru, Sir T.J. 83, 85
Sassoon, Sir Philip 46

Selly, Harry 208
Sever, John 222
Shaw, Ben 52
Simon, Sir John 99, 101, 107
Sinclair, Sir Archibald 132, 144
Smith, Cyril 198, 222
Smith, John 265–6
Snow, Peter 246
Snowden, Philip 29, 51, 60, 87–8, 92
Solomons, Henry 182
Sorensen, Reginald 180–1
Spender, J.A. 50
Stanbrook, Ivor 172
Stannage, Tom 104, 107
Steed, Michael 207, 213, 269
Steel, David 181–2, 203, 210–11, 213, 218–19, 221, 225, 229–32, 235, 237–9, 241
Stevens, John 209
Stockwood, Mervyn 203
Stoddart, Sir Malcolm 209
Stonehouse, John 216–17
Stuart, James 143
Suetter, Read-Adm. 46
Suirdale, Lord 143
Summerskill, Edith 108, 233
Sumner, Donald 159, 161, 168

Tatchell, Peter 259
Taverne, Dick 2, 11, 195–206, 210–11, 214, 231
Taylor, A.J.P. 100, 117
Taylor, Vice-Adm. E.A. 69, 74
Tebbit, Norman 262
Teeling, William 134–5
Tennant, H.J. 80
Thatcher, Margaret 215–16, 218–19, 223, 226, 228, 241, 249, 252, 258–61
Thomas, Sir Garrod 24
Thomas, Miss Goring 27
Thomas, J.H. 21, 26, 87
Thomas, Sir O. 38
Thompson, George 196–7, 201
Thorpe, Jeremy 162, 164, 209–10, 213, 218
Toole, Joe 145
Tope, Graham 198, 210
Topping, Robert 72

Tredegar, 1st Viscount 20
Trimble, David 265

Varley, Eric 265
Vaughan-Morgan, Sir Kenyon 94

Wade, Donald 160, 164
Wadsworth, Ralph 199
Wake, Egerton 52
Walden, Brian 222
Waldron, W.J. 98–100, 102–3
Wallace, William 213
Wargrave, 1st Lord 45–6
Wayland, Sir William 80
Webb, Sir Harry 25
Wedgwood Benn, Antony, see Benn, Tony
Wheeler-Bennett, Sir John 102
White, Charles F. 143
White, Tom 51
Whitelaw, William 249, 254
Wigg, George 142, 188–9
Wilcox, Brian 165
Wilkes, John 1
Williams, Shirley 197, 201, 232–4, 236–9
Williams, Sir Tom 233
Williams, W.R. 29
Wilmot, John 97–100, 102–4, 106–7, 109–10
Wilson, Alex 185
Wilson, Des 210–11
Wilson, Harold 174–5, 182, 188, 192, 196–7, 200, 202–3, 215–17, 225, 258
Wilson, Sir Leslie 39, 70
Winfrey, R.P. 55
Wintringham, Margaret 55
Wintringham, Tom 139, 141, 145
Wise, Fred 143
Wood, Deirdre 263
Worthington Evans, Sir Laming 69–70, 76, 85
Wrigglesworth, Ian 232
Wright, Esmond 185
Wyatt, Woodrow 174

Young, G.M. 97, 107
Younger, Sir George 27

Zilliacus, Konni 187